Families in the
New Testament World

SERIES EDITORS

DON S. BROWNING AND IAN S. EVISON

Families in the New Testament World

Households and House Churches

Carolyn Osiek
David L. Balch

Westminster John Knox Press
Louisville, Kentucky

Scripture quotations are the authors' translations unless otherwise indicated.

Book and cover design by Jennifer K. Cox

First edition

Published by Westminster John Knox Press
Louisville, Kentucky

This book is printed on acid-free paper that meets the American National Standards Institute Z39.48 standard. ♾

PRINTED IN THE UNITED STATES OF AMERICA

97 98 99 00 01 02 03 04 05 06 — 10 9 8 7 6 5 4 3 2 1

Library of Congress Cataloging-in-Publication Data

Osiek, Carolyn.
    Families in the New Testament world : households and house churches / Carolyn Osiek and David L. Balch. — 1st ed.
        p.   cm. — (The family, religion, and culture)
    Includes bibliographical references and index.
    ISBN 0–664–25546–9 (alk. paper)
    1. Family—Biblical teaching. 2. Family—Rome. 3. Sociology, Biblical. 4. Bible. N.T.—Criticism, interpretation, etc. 5. House churches. 6. Rome—Social life and customs. 7. Rome—Religion. I. Balch, David L. II. Title. III. Series.
BS2545.F33085   1997
225.8'30685—dc21   96–37845

Contents

Series Foreword

There is an important debate going on today over the present health and future well-being of families in American society. Although some people on the political right and left use concern about the state of the family primarily to further their respective partisan causes, the debate is real, and it is over genuine issues. The discussion, however, is not well informed and is riddled with historical, theological, and social-scientific ignorance.

This is not unusual as political debates go. The American family debate, however, is especially uninformed and dogmatic. This is understandable, for all people have experienced a family in some way, feel themselves to be experts, and believe that they are entitled to their strong opinions.

The books in this series, The Family, Religion, and Culture, discuss these issues in ways that will place the American debate about the family on more solid ground. The series is the result of the Religion, Culture, and Family project, which was funded by a generous grant from the Division of Religion of the Lilly Endowment, and took place in the Institute for Advanced Study in the University of Chicago Divinity School. Part of the project proceeded while Don Browning, the project director, was in residence at the Center of Theological Inquiry in Princeton, New Jersey.

The series advances no single point of view on the American family debate and gives no one solution to the problems concerning families today. The authors and editors contributing to the volumes represent both genders as well as a variety of religious and ethnic perspectives and denominational backgrounds—liberal and conservative; Protestant, Catholic, and Jewish; evangelical and mainline; and black, white, and Asian. A number of the authors and editors met annually for a seminar and discussed—often with considerable intensity—their outlines, papers, and chapters pertaining to the various books. The careful reader will notice that many of the seminar members did influence one another; but, it is safe to say, each of them in the end took his or her own counsel and spoke out of his or her own convictions.

The series is comprehensive, with studies on the family in ancient Israel and early Christianity; economics and the family; law, feminism, and reproductive technology and the family; the family and American faith traditions; and congregations and families; as well as two summary books—one a handbook and one a critical overview of the American family debate.

Families in the New Testament World provides the reader with the most comprehensive discussion of the family in early Christianity that exists in English or any other language and promises to be a definitive study on the family in the New Testament for years to come. This book is ecumenical, written by Roman Catholic Carolyn Osiek and Protestant David Balch, sets the various New Testament teachings on the family within the social and cultural context of the Greco-Roman world, and creatively synthesizes and adds to the explosion of recent and more specialized studies relevant to the understanding of early Christian families.

In the early days of their research, we heard Professors Osiek and Balch say, "The early Christian family was the Greco-Roman family *with a twist.*" What does this mean? And what was the "twist" or "spin" that early Christianity put on the family of Roman Hellenism? These questions are answered here, and they are well worth studying.

This book shows how the architectural patterns of Roman homes formed and influenced relationships in early Christian house churches and demonstrates how worship in these house churches influenced Christian families. We learn how early Christian women enjoyed wider ranges of freedom and leadership and how early Christian men learned to think of themselves as servants. It explains why early Christianity both valued families and subordinated them to the kingdom of God. We are also shown how conservative reactions to these trends eventually emerged in early Christian communities and how, even afterward, Christian families had changed—the seeds of new understandings had been planted.

We are deeply grateful to Professors Osiek and Balch for this excellent and truly edifying book, for it will have a profound effect on how the New Testament is used in the present and future American family debate.

Don S. Browning
Ian S. Evison

Acknowledgments

I (Carolyn) am grateful to have been invited to take part in a 1991 National Endowment for the Humanities Summer Seminar on the Roman family and household at the American Academy in Rome and especially to the seminar leaders, John Bodell of Rutgers University in New Jersey and Richard Saller of the University of Chicago, from whom I learned more than I ever could have hoped. I am also grateful to the Catholic Theological Union, where I have taught for almost twenty years, for my academic leave in 1993 and 1994, giving me the time I needed to work on this project. We are both deeply thankful to Don Browning for recruiting us for writing this volume.

I (David) was itinerant during 1994 and 1995, which gives me the chance to express here my gratitude to various persons and institutions in Berkeley, California; Rome; and Fort Worth, Texas. I thank Dean Timothy Lull for the opportunity to be a visiting research professor at the Pacific Lutheran Theological Seminary in Berkeley, California, giving me the opportunity to meet fascinating colleagues and to have access to the Graduate Theological Union library and several great libraries of the University of California at Berkeley: Doe (classics), Urban Design (Pompeii), and Science (history of medicine and sexuality). I thank Vice Rector and Professor Robert F. O'Toole, S.J., for inviting me as a guest at the Pontifical Biblical Institute. Rector Klemens Stock and Professor John Kilgallen were more than gracious. Professor Frederick Brenk became a valued friend and was extraordinarily generous with his profound knowledge of classical literature and of Greco-Roman art and archaeology and their connections to the Renaissance. I appreciated the warm welcome from Professer Yann Redalié of the Waldensian Theological Seminary in Rome.

I spent many wonderful weeks at the American Academy in Rome, where Professor Malcolm Bell allowed me to tag along with the fellows on some of their expeditions to archaeological sites. I am deeply indebted to the Academy's librarian, Christina Huemer, who opened the stacks to me, and to Donna Orsuto—an angel in disguise—who invited me to live as an ecumenical guest at the Lay Centre at Foyer Unitas, in the heart of Rome, on Piazza Navona, from where I could walk anywhere in the old city.

I was also able to do considerable research in the German Archaeological Institute library, which is unmatched for resources on Pompeii and Herculaneum. I will always be grateful to the Very Reverend Leonard E. Boyle, Prefect of the Vatican library, for permission to examine Vaticanus, and for his selling (rather, virtually giving) me a copy of (Cardinal) Martini's 1968 edition of the New Testament portion of that manuscript; I left Rome with a priceless treasure. I would also like to thank Professor Roy Bowen Ward, whose critical suggestions, with respect to the roles of women and the art and architecture of Pompeii, are mentioned in chapter 1.

The Soprintendenza Archeologica di Pompei granted me permission to examine a dozen houses, normally locked, so that I might see with my own eyes the domestic spaces we interpret in this book. My spirit was sustained by worship with the extraordinary Catholic community of Sant' Egidio. Their liturgy is indescribably beautiful; their social involvement in feeding the homeless of Rome, their education of gypsy children, their mediation in Mozambique's civil war, and now their involvement in Algeria, as well as their friendship with the Jewish community in Rome helped me "see" the gospel in ways I had never experienced—a house-based lay community as generative as those we researched for this book.[1]

At Texas Christian University I thank Joyce Martindale, the interlibrary loan specialist, for her many efforts, and especially my incomparable secretary and occasional research assistant, Lana Byrd, who did much for me via e-mail, perhaps more than if she had been next door.

Finally, I would like to thank my creative dean, Leo Perdue, whose own scholarship sets a goal for the rest of us and whose support for research and teaching finds endless new means. I offer my portion of this book to my three children, Alison Elaine, Christina Irene, and Justin Jeremiah. The Lilly Endowment grant for the Religion, Culture, and Family project, directed by Don Browning, helped support Alison in her final year at Texas Christian University; Christina in her first year at University of California at Santa Cruz; and Justin in his studies of jazz saxophone at Berkeley High School.

---

[1]See Robert P. Imbelli, "The Community of Sant' Egidio: Vatican II Made Real," *Commonweal* (Nov. 18, 1994): 20–23. Cameron Hume, *Ending Mozambique's War: The Role of Mediation and Good Offices* (Washington D.C.: United States Institute of Peace Press, 1994). Robert Morozzo della Rocca, *Mozambico: Dalla guerra alla pace, Storia di una mediazione insolita* (Milan: San Paolo, 1994). Andrea Riccardi, *Sant' Egidio, Rome et le Monde, Entretiens avec J. D. Durand et R. Ladous* (Paris: Beauchesne, 1996).

Introduction

Contemporary evaluations of early Christian household relationships run the gamut from Mary Daly's *Beyond God the Father*[1] to Lisa Sowle Cahill's *Sex, Gender, and Christian Ethics.*[2] For the one Paul is a misogynist; the other appeals to Jesus' transformative family ethic as normative. Addressing current culture wars, Don Browning argues for a middle way, that contemporary neo-conservatives and neo-liberals have formed a consensus.[3]

As authors we too have commitments; we do not claim to be simply neutral historians. One of us is a female and a Catholic Sister; the other, a male and an ordained Lutheran pastor. Still, we do claim that historical critical research, including social-scientific methods, does lend some objectivity to our subjective commitments and also provides fascinating historical data for further debate among other historians, ethicists, and theologians.

Both of us became deeply involved in the archaeology of early Christian households. Carolyn has investigated these archaeological sites for years, and David spent several months in Rome near Pompeii and Herculaneum, cities that the Vesuvius eruption in 79 C.E. utterly devastated. Although a tragedy for the inhabitants, it is, paradoxically, a treasure for later historians of art and of urban and domestic development. In our first chapter we investigate the radical differences between Greco-Roman and modern households; for example, many ancient urbanites seem to have had little need for their domestic space to be private. The "culture shock" of modern readers may well build as the reader continues on to the second chapter, in which we discuss social patterns—honor, shame, and gender roles—from the perspective of cultural anthropology. Building on this discussion, the focus in the next chapter is on the role of teachers who were employed by wealthy Greco-Roman householders and the gymnasia where students read ancient texts aloud and were taught not to accept all the classics or what their teachers taught about (the) God(s). Next, we show the ways that the institution of slavery in the Greco-Roman world differs from that of eighteenth- and nineteenth-century North America; for example, color was not a distinguishing factor and some slaves were powerful officials. Next, in chapter 4, we examine family religion, picturing elite and slave residents of Corinthian and Roman households worshiping their gods in beautiful, columned gardens and in dark, undecorated kitchens. We also investigate what this environment meant for Christians living and worshiping in such houses—how married partners related to each other (chapter 5), how education occurred (chapter 6), the everyday lives of slaves (chapter 7), and the types of meals and religious celebrations of the Christian family (chapter 8).

Lisa Sowle Cahill, interpreting the New Testament as a "historical 'prototype' of faith in action," the authoritative aspect of which is "a process of social transformation," acknowledges that some of the concrete behavioral models that existed in Roman imperial society are viewed today as morally repugnant. We investigate general values and commitments in our literature as well as concrete behavior through the first and second centuries of the Common Era (c.e.) and beyond. We have found surprising variations through the decades and in different locations; both of us have changed our own perceptions of this material during our research. Neither of us accepts the common Protestant notion that the earliest is best, that subsequent history is a decline—a fall into corruption. We have found, surprisingly "high" and "low" points in the development of early Christian household relationships; sometimes they occur concurrently in different bodies of literature. For instance, the deutero-Pauline epistle 1 Timothy insists, one-sidedly, on slaves' obedience to masters (6:1–2b), which was typical in Greco-Roman culture. In the Gospel of Matthew, however, written at approximately the same time, we are given a parable in which the householder treats workers "equally," a rare word in that culture (20:12). Although the other Synoptic Gospels do not portray Jesus eating with women, Matthew does. The most Jewish Gospel is also, perhaps surprisingly for some readers, the most gender-fair. The deutero-Pauline epistles introduce the Aristotelian household code into early Christian ethics; those in one gender group, wives, are to be subordinate to those in another gender group, husbands. Later authors also emphasize the "obedience" typical of hierarchical Roman society, but surprisingly again, in authors like Ignatius, Polycarp, and Hermas, we failed to find this emphasis on one social group (wives or slaves) in the church being subordinate to another. The author of *1 Clement* is the only one who repeats this emphasis on one social group subordinate to another. There are other surprises. We hope readers experience even half the enjoyment and profit that we have had while doing the research and writing.

PART 1

Material and Social Environment of the Greco-Roman Household

1

Archaeology

A first step toward understanding the ancient Christian family is to take a look at the physical environment in which such families lived, for the arrangement and use of space can be telling indicators of how people behaved and related. We will focus on aspects of that development during the mid–first century C.E. in order to gain as clear a picture as possible of the Pauline setting. Paul's mission was an urban one, and much effort has been expended in recent scholarship in order to understand the Pauline house churches in the context of a Greco-Roman city. Bradley Blue[1] has recently surveyed what we know of houses in cities where Paul actually preached, and Yvon Thébert[2] surveys French work on such houses in North Africa. Those archaeologists work almost exclusively with ground-level remains, with floors that may have mosaics, but without walls, ceilings, windows, stairs, second floors, furniture, paintings, sculpture, or gardens.

In contrast, Pompeii and Herculaneum, the two Roman cities covered by volcanic mud when Vesuvius erupted in 79 C.E., give us a more complete view than do other archaeological sites of Roman houses in such urban centers. Pompeii and Herculaneum still have walls, paintings, silverware, bank records, even a nineteen-hundred-year-old loaf of bread, exhibited at the National Archaeological Museum in Naples![3] Therefore, these two cities offer us the possibility of going beyond merely labeling the rooms, merely labeling an atrium, a peristyle, and so on. Archaeologists and art historians studying these two cities have recently made advances that shed additional light on how people lived in them, on how the houses functioned in their urban contexts.

Of course, we have no houses from the ancient Mediterranean world in the first centuries of the Christian era in which we know for sure that Christians lived, but some of the preserved evidence can be understood, with certain local modifications, to exemplify living arrangements in most of the cities of the empire in the Roman period. Understanding the living situations of various kinds of people is important not only because some of those people were Christians but also because Christians at first worshiped in those same living spaces.

A note on terminology: Neither ancient Greek nor Hebrew nor Latin had words that directly translate what modern Western English means by "family" or "house." The Greek *oikos, oikia,* Hebrew *bayit,* and Latin *domus* can all refer to the physical building but can all just as well, and more often do, mean: household, including material goods and slaves; immediate blood family; or family lineage. Perhaps the more polyvalent English "home" is a more appropriate equivalent for some of the same realities. Nor does the Latin *familia* refer only or even usually to the nuclear family, but rather to all persons and objects under the legal power (*patria potestas*) of the male head of the family.[4]

The mild, brief, rainy Mediterranean winters and long, hot, dry summers create an environment in which, for seven to eight months of the year, the most pleasant place to be is outside, in the shade by day and under the stars by night (see figures 1 and 2). Thus the basic design of the Greco-Roman house of the early imperial period features some kind of central court around which rooms are arranged and to which they give access. The front door and whatever small windows may open onto the street are unprepossessing. The house is turned inward and its life happens inside the walls, yet for the most part out of doors. Even some of the largest and most impressive urban houses preserved have surprisingly small, dark, and airless rooms for sleeping and other indoor functions, with the exception of dining. The early Augustan Latin architect and engineer Vitruvius is describing ideal arrangements not always possible in crowded urban conditions when he suggests that bedrooms should face the rising sun, winter dining rooms should face south, and summer rooms, north, in order to take advantage of the best flow of air (*De architectura* 6.4).

Vitruvius describes the Greek house as giving access from the street through a narrow opening, with stables on one side and porter's room on the other, to a colonnaded peristyle, around which are arranged dining rooms, guest rooms, and space for the male head of the household to receive guests and conduct business affairs (see figure 3). Beyond this grouping of rooms, through a passageway, lay another peristyle and another complex of rooms consisting of the women's rooms, slave quarters, and rooms for domestic activities, called collectively *gynaikonitis,* or women's quarters. The passageway between the two was called by the Greeks, according to Vitruvius, the *mesaulon* (inner hall or between halls) and by Latins, *andron,* a Greek loanword which was the Greeks' name for the front part of the house, or men's quarters—Vitruvius acknowledges the difference in meaning assigned to the same word by the Romans (*De architectura* 6.7.1–5).

This physical division of men's space from women's space in the Greek

Figure 1. Outdoor dining area, Casa dell'Efebo, Pompeii I.7.10-12. Couches are covered in modern glass cases to protect their frescoes from the weather. An aediculated shrine/statue niche stands behind the couches, and serves as the source of water that flows down the series of steps to the platform and fountain in the center of the couches. The columns, now covered in modern netting, would have supported a vine and branch bower to protect the diners from the sun. Photo by P.W. Foss.

Figure 2. Indoor dining area, Casa del Criptoportico, Pompeii 1.6.2+16, couches and benches in loggia. Iron fence in foreground is modern. Benches may have been used by children or slaves based on limited literary evidence, but there is no way to determine this archaeologically. Photo by P.W. Foss.

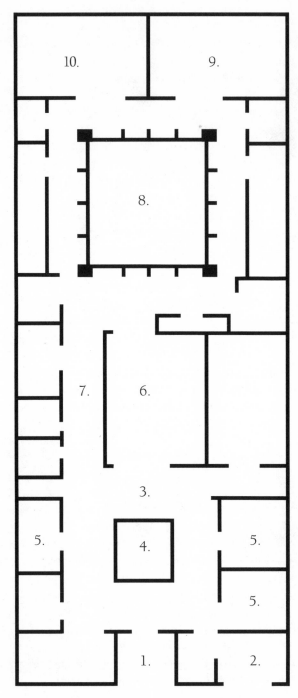

Figure 3. A typical *domus*. Key: 1. fauces; 2. shop; 3. atrium; 4. impluvium; 5. cubiculum; 6. tablinum; 7. andron; 8. peristyle; 9. triclinium; 10. oecus. (For Latin terms, see glossary, pp. 287–89.) Drawing by Deborah Wells.

house would be possible only for those wealthy enough to have a relatively large house. It is also indicative of a particular social construction of gender that will be of significance for later discussion. Though the Greek peristyle began appearing in Italian houses by the second century B.C.E., the eastern ideal of the seclusion of women expressed by the Greek architectural design was never prominent in the West, and Greek houses of the later Roman period do not always exhibit this design, perhaps indicating that social customs were changing in the East as well.

The peristyle design came into fashion in Greek houses in the Hellenistic period and was introduced to the West not long afterward. But the characteristic difference between the Greek and Latin house is the presence in the traditional Latin house of an atrium just inside the front door (*ostium,* mouth) reached by a short entrance hall (*fauces,* jaws). The atrium may have originated with the family hearth, then was adapted by making the roof slope toward the central opening to allow rainwater to fall through the opening, the *compluvium,* into a shallow pool below, the *impluvium.*

The atrium with impluvium became a standard feature of many central Italian houses (though not common outside of Italy), to such an extent that, when a city water supply made it no longer necessary to collect rainwater, as at Pompeii, the impluvium remained as part of house designs, even if a drainpipe now had to be installed to remove the collected rainwater.[5] The atrium of Italian houses provided additional space at the front of the house for public and business purposes, in effect, a reception area. In the houses of very important people with much business to conduct and many clients coming to pay their respects, the atrium of a Roman house could be the scene of constant activity, requiring not only a slave assigned as *ostiarius,* or doorkeeper, but another as *atriensis,* atrium supervisor or majordomo. In later years, as shown at Ostia, the atrium was usually replaced by a peristyle, a garden, or some other kind of open central space that became a site for art, sculpture, and entertainment. But the central open area remained a standard feature of the Latin domus.

Just off the atrium of a traditional Roman house, most often directly opposite the door, was the *tablinum,* originally a master bedroom, then repository of family and personal documents,[6] then the office and study of the head of the household, where as patron he (or she?) most frequently received guests and clients, conducted business, wrote letters, read, and studied. The tablinum was flanked by *alae* (wings), open areas at the rear of the atrium on either side that provided a greater sense of spaciousness and served as space for clerks and secretaries of a busy *paterfamilias,* or could be converted to separate rooms. Other rooms opening off the atrium would include the porter's room, in which the ostiarius virtually spent his life; one or more dining rooms (*triclinia*); and guest rooms or perhaps even the bedrooms (*cubicula*) of members of the household, depending on the size of the house.

Some houses contained another large, usually vaulted room, called an *oecus* by Vitruvius, sometimes with an apse at the far end (as in the House of the Skeleton at Herculaneum), and sometimes peristyled (as in the House of the Labyrinth). The name, though, seems to be an all-purpose term. In his description of the Greek house, the men entertain there (*De architectura* 6.7.5), but the women of the house also do their spinning there (6.7.2), which does not fit his portrayal of the Greek house as having separate quarters for the sexes. The term seems to mean any kind of large room or hall that can be used for receptions, dining, or just everyday living.[7]

Vitruvius also stresses that the design as well as the furnishings of a house must match the social status of its owner, so that those of lower status who are not liable to receive many guests and clients can have more modest dwellings, while those of importance must have imposing atria, peristyles, libraries, and basilicas in their residences (*De architectura* 6.5.1–2).

Through one or more passageways around the tablinum at the back of the atrium (Vitruvius's andrones), one gained access—if invited—to a peristyle courtyard and the more private area of the house, at least of one organized according to what Vitruvius describes as the Greek model. Often though, as in the well-known House of the Vettii at Pompeii, the atrium is dwarfed by the size of the peristyle that opens directly in front of it (see figure 4). In such a case, unless some kind of divider was placed all the way across the wide opening between atrium and peristyle, it would have been impossible visually and auditorially to separate activity in the atrium from that in the peristyle—one indicator among many that the spatial separation of men's and women's lives ideally set up by the design of the Greek house was not as common in the West, and that the ideas of private space are culturally relative. Vitruvius (*De architectura* 6.5.1) remarks that everyone has the right to enter vestibule, atrium, and peristyle, reserving as private space for the family only bedrooms, dining rooms, and baths.

The typical Roman house also included somewhere a *lararium,* a small shrine to the *lares* and *penates,* the household gods, whose worship was traditionally a daily ritual involving the entire household. The location of the lararium varied: at the entrance, in the atrium, in the peristyle, near the kitchen, or elsewhere, but always where the whole familia could assemble. Occasionally, a large house contained two lararia, one in a more public area and one in or near the kitchen. In this case, separate worship according to social status must be presumed.[8]

The basic design of the peristyle house, or atrium-peristyle house in

Figure 4. Peristyle, House of the Vettii, Pompeii VI.15.11. An unusually large peristyle of a luxury house. Fence in foreground is modern. Dining rooms open onto the peristyle at the far end. By contrast, in the same house, the kitchen area and slave quarters are dark and cramped. Photo by C. Osiek.

the West, recurs with surprising regularity but also with surprising variation of size, shape, and arrangement of characteristics.[9] By the Julio-Claudian period (30 B.C.E.–68 C.E.), the Pompeiian evidence indicates greater interest in the possibilities of the peristyle design for creating inner garden space. The peristyle was beginning to replace the atrium, the tablinum was disappearing or evolving into more of a sitting room, and dining rooms were becoming larger and more prominent.[10]

We will now examine some of the detailed evidence for private dwellings, first from several different social strata in the Roman East, then at the major sites of Pompeii and Herculaneum, and finally the evidence for diversification of more moderate housing at Ostia.

Ephesus

The excavations at Ephesus, which have been conducted intermittently since 1869 and are still in progress, have in recent years yielded two complete blocks (*insulae*) of gracious private houses on the north slope of Mount Koressos above and to the south of the main east-west street, called by the excavators Curetes Street. Most of the houses were built in the first century C.E. and inhabited until the seventh.[11]

The houses are built up the hill in terraces. Those of the eastern block rise above a row of shops that open onto a mosaic pavement under the colonnaded portico that ran along the street. Above the shops ran a corridor giving access to a row of rooms, most likely the modest residences of the shopkeepers below, lighted and ventilated by ceiling windows.

Behind them, more affluent houses were constructed up the hill. All had running water and an internal heating system by means of hot air forced through pipes embedded in the walls. Access was gained to the houses from the steep side streets that ascended the hill. Most of these houses rose originally to two or perhaps three stories. In this case, sleeping rooms were probably above the ground level, while daytime activity happened below. One house contained on the first floor an oecus supported by four columns. In the late third century, a fountain faced with colored marble was built into this room.

The eastern block contained at least five houses of similar status, and two of them, houses A and B, were quite extensive on the ground floor. The floors of both were adorned with mosaics in geometric designs and mythological scenes. Walls of many rooms were plastered and frescoed with designs and human figures. Busts, statuettes, a carved ivory frieze, a sixth-century bronze statue of an Egyptian priest, a few pieces of furniture, and table articles were recovered. The tablinum of house B had a floor and walls of inlaid colored marble, and a vaulted, colored mosaic ceiling depicting Dionysus and Ariadne in a rondel surrounded by Dionysiac scenes.

There is evidence of remodeling at various stages of occupation. At one point in their history, house B acquired four rooms from house A, and walls and doors were rearranged accordingly. We know that house A had its own bathhouse, and house B its own kitchen and latrine. None of these are to be taken for granted as household essentials, since the public baths and latrines nearby were frequented by most inhabitants who lacked such private amenities, and, to judge by the evidence of Pompeii, shops on the streets sold prepared food and drink for those who did not have private cooking facilities. What proportion of the population this included is difficult to estimate. One study of one section of Pompeii indicated that every Pompeiian house larger than 80 square meters had its own cooking area.[12] But the frequent presence of food and drink shops argues for a brisk business in these commodities.

Roman Palestine and Syria

The excavations in the Jewish Quarter of Old City Jerusalem beginning in 1969 uncovered the remains of several houses destroyed in the conflagration of 70 C.E., in what was then the affluent upper city in the southwestern quadrant within the walls. One of them, accessible today to visitors as the "Herodian mansion," was a very large house built around a central courtyard with an extensive ground floor of guest and reception rooms, at least a second floor above it for the family residence, and a large area below ground level for service use and bathing.

From the west end of the courtyard a hallway with mosaic floor gives access to the ground-floor reception area. There is a large room with plastered walls frescoed in a style closely resembling that of Pompeii. Another much larger room in this wing was beautifully decorated in white stucco designs imitating ashlar blocks—a style of Greek origin that had already passed out of fashion farther west. This plastered design, both here and in other adjoining rooms, had been superimposed, however, on an earlier painted floral design.

Other houses excavated at the same site seem to have the same basic design of rooms arranged around a central courtyard, though in none of these cases is the courtyard a peristyle.[13] A house built during the late Hasmonean period and deliberately abandoned and destroyed sometime before 70 C.E. was much more modest. It consisted of one ground level of several rooms and cistern, with a central courtyard containing four sunken ovens for baking, and a *mikveh* (ritual bath) to which one descended by a set of stairs. The "Burnt House," so called because it was the first evidence encountered for the burning of the upper city at the time of the destruction of the Temple, was even more modest. It consisted of a small entry courtyard paved with stones, a kitchen, four other rooms of varying sizes, and a mikveh reached by descending steps.

Carved stone tables, several glass vessels made by the same artist in first-century Sidon, and a fine pottery bowl are among the luxury items found in this and similar houses in the area. In addition, a limestone sundial, many ordinary cooking pots, and stone vessels were found. The prevalence of bathing facilities reflects the Jewish concern for ritual purification, as does the use of stone water jars, which were not susceptible to ritual impurity.[14]

The excavations at Sepphoris in central Galilee, a few miles from Nazareth, are still underway. One of the early and spectacular finds was the elaborate mosaic floor of the triclinium of what seems to have been a luxurious private house of the early Byzantine period. The house is located directly across the street from the back of the theater, and has only been partially excavated.[15] The mosaic floor, designed to be seen by banqueters reclining on couches, features aspects of the life of Dionysus, god of wine and revelry, and other themes.[16] The portion of the house that has been excavated has the triclinium at the center of a group of rooms, but the partially excavated portion just to the south is the beginning of a peristyle, so that the triclinium is at the far northern end of a structure with peristyle at the center.

Elaborate mosaic floors in private houses were quite common in the Roman and Byzantine periods. The best evidence of this comes from Antioch, where many villas were excavated in the south suburb of Daphne.[17] Triclinium floors were especially adorned, often with drinking or eating themes. One of the most famous is the "Buffet Supper," a rounded mosaic to be seen from a circular dining couch, or *stibadium,* depicting in the center the mythological motif of Ganymede feeding an eagle of Zeus, but around the border, a series of dishes thought to be presented in the order in which the courses were served. Hors d'oeuvres, fish, ham, and bread can be clearly distinguished.[18] Other dining room floors elsewhere depict items on the menu, and even the fish bones and debris that the guests would throw on the floor.

These gracious urban houses stand in stark contrast to humbler houses like those in a Galilean fishing village exposed by the excavations at the house of Peter in Capernaum, on the northwestern corner of the Lake of Galilee. This chosen center of Jesus' ministry was on a main trade route between Egypt and Syria, and it was certainly not tiny and isolated. Jesus must have selected it as his new home because of its contacts with the wider world which Nazareth lacked. In the fourth century, Capernaum contained an impressive synagogue, probably built at the same site as the one mentioned in the Gospels.

The area just to the south of the synagogue was filled with crowded clusters of simple houses in which, in later years, one was singled out, remodeled, plastered, and eventually destroyed to make way for an octagonal church in the fifth century. At the first-century level, however, small one- and two-room buildings were built into an enclosure wall surrounding a central courtyard. In these kinds of structures, probably extended family groupings lived within the same enclosure.[19]

Pompeii and Herculaneum

Pompeii is an "ordinary Roman town" with an "average urban character."[20] No Roman senatorial families lived there, nor were there the urban slums of Rome. Wealthier families in Rome chose the Palatine, Aventine, or Caelian hills, whereas poorer families lived in valleys like the Subura, Velabrum, and the Transtiberinus.[21] But Pompeii did not have people at the very top or bottom of the economic scale; its people leaned more perhaps to the prosperous end of the spectrum. It was "a mid-sized town with agricultural and market functions, interaction with both hinterland and the coast, and a center both of consumption and production."[22]

The gracious living of the Campanian towns, such as Pompeii and Herculaneum, in south-central Italy came to a crashing end with the eruption of Vesuvius on August 24, 79 C.E. Since their origins probably in the sixth century B.C.E., both cities had been controlled by Oscans, Etruscans, Greeks, Samnites, and finally Romans. While a few structures remain from the Samnite period, such as the second-century B.C.E. "Samnite house" at Herculaneum, most of the construction at the end was Roman.[23] Here the atrium-impluvium design was used from the fourth through third centuries B.C.E., often augmented in later remodeling by a peristyle.[24] Entrances to such houses from the street were through narrow passages (fauces) sometimes adorned with mosaic floors, sometimes with humorous motifs: a skeleton holding a jug, a vicious-looking dog accompanied by the warning cave canem (beware of the dog).[25] (Besides such humorous sightings, there is other evidence of dogs kept as pets or guardians: a wall painting of a faithful animal facing the front door of a house, and at least one dog left behind, still tied, during the panic caused by the eruption of Vesuvius.)

Not all houses are very large: 35 percent are of the smallest size, 100 square meters or less. By contrast, a few houses are larger than 700 square meters, and some could have sheltered quite a large familia.[26] The most modest, a room or two sandwiched into small and irregular spaces, have an average size of only 25 square meters and are usually connected to a shop or double as one. In addition, nearly half of the shops have stairs that led to a second story where shopkeeper, family, or tenant could live.

The next size group consists of modest but somewhat larger houses. Some have an atrium surrounded by a few rooms that could have held only a small group of people. Still larger houses often have an atrium and some, a modest peristyle as well. The largest lead the visitor from atrium to peristyle to another massive peristyle complex, or to a vast garden area. Such houses could have held a large family and household staff. Yet, surprisingly, a few houses with the largest ground space actually have few rooms but a very large garden area.[27] In these cases, the owners seemed to have placed priority on horticulture and outdoor living, being willing to live rather modestly indoors. Perhaps, too, such a house served only as summer residence for a small, modestly prosperous Roman family. At least one of the largest, the Villa dei Misteri, which reverses the usual order by putting the peristyle just inside the entrance with atrium behind,[28] was divided at a later stage of its life into discrete apartments either for related families or for rental.

Lawrence Richardson speaks frequently of a "ladies' dining room" in Pompeiian houses that feature two or more apparent dining rooms side by side. The most interesting architecturally are those of the House of the Labyrinth and the House of the Vettii, where there is actually a connecting passageway between them, so that one would not have to go back out into the peristyle to move from one to the other. (In the case of the House of the Labyrinth the connection is made across a peristyled oecus.)[29] His assumption is that the traditional prohibition of "respectable" women joining men's dinner parties, even wives with their husbands, was still in force, but that women had begun dining together reclining on couches in separate dining rooms. At the end of the meal, they would be invited in to sit on the edges of the couches and enjoy the after-dinner entertainment.[30] Since in the House of Meleager, built during Pompeii's last phase (62–79 C.E.), there is only one "ladies' dining room" in a house seemingly built for summer dinner parties, Richardson concludes "that here ladies sometimes reclined in company with the men, as Valerius Maximus (2.1.2) said was becoming customary in Rome in his day, toward the end of the reign of Tiberius" (d. 37 C.E.).[31] The architectural evidence for multiple dining rooms is fairly clear; that for separate women's dining rooms must await later examination of the literary evidence.

Rather consistently, the different sizes and levels of houses are mixed indiscriminately. There is no identifiably affluent neighborhood where those of more modest means could not live, nor were there parts of town where only the poor lived. While this pattern of integrated economic and social status cannot be taken as a norm for Roman cities, given the lack of sufficient comparable evidence, it is similar to the residential patterns of the commercial, hardworking Ostia of a few centuries later, but different from the regular planned city blocks, house after house of similar size and regular proportions, of the preserved Greek cities, Olynthus of northern Greece in the classical period, and Priene of southwestern Asia Minor in Hellenistic times. The evidence of Pompeii and Herculaneum points to more integrated neighborhood mixtures, but it also therefore "incorporates the expectation of inequality" with its enormous range of different property sizes stacked one next to another. The average property is ten times larger than the smallest, the largest ten times larger than the average.[32]

The most enlightening writer on the function of these houses is Andrew Wallace-Hadrill, the new director of the British School in Rome. Relying on Wallace-Hadrill's work and others, we make two assumptions, not universally shared by writers on the subject: First, the atrium-house is surely not the exclusive but is the primary setting for Pauline *ekklesiai,* which did not meet primarily in apartment buildings. As mentioned above, Vitruvius[33] remarks that *everyone* has the right to enter a vestibule, atrium, and peristyle, reserving as private space for the family only bedrooms, dining rooms, and baths! When Paul writes, "If, therefore, the whole church comes together . . . , and outsiders or unbelievers enter [the house uninvited] . . . " (1 Cor. 14:23), twentieth-century city dwellers might puzzle about how strangers got in the living room, but in the Roman Corinthian setting, Paul feels no need to explain. Similarly, a woman anoints Jesus while he is reclining in a dining room (Mark 14:3–9; Matt. 26:6–13; Luke 7:36–50; John 12:1–8), and the Gospel writers comment only that "she knew he is reclining in the house . . . " (Luke 7:37). Commentators have wondered how she got into the triclinium, and the best answer seems to be that, uninvited, she walked in through the open front door. The English word "house" in North American and English, postindustrial societies easily communicates a mistaken notion of the Greek oikos and Latin domus to us, because we experience public work space as separate from our private homes, and our boundaries are secured by locked front doors.[34] The lack of privacy in Roman houses and society would drive most modern people insane.[35] We must imagine ourselves back in a radically different sociocultural setting in order to gain some perception of an early Christian assembly in one of these houses.

Ostia

A Roman colony at the mouth (ostium) of the Tiber from at least the fourth century B.C.E., Ostia was a thriving and densely populated port city in imperial times. The addition of another port area, Portus, and an inner harbor during the reign of Claudius increased Ostia's prosperity, which was at its height from the late first to early third centuries C.E. While the typical peristyle house is still found here, other variations appear, apparently in response to the need for more creative design to adapt graciously to more crowded conditions.

The discovery in Campania of *opus caementicum,* concrete made from volcanic pozzolana, made it possible to build stronger foundations cheaply, thus increasing the height of buildings. Concrete was used at Rome by the second century B.C.E. The need for more housing at the time of Ostia's greatest prosperity produced a new method of residential design that had already been in use in the East, and can be assumed to have developed in Rome at the same time as in Ostia.

Already at Pompeii, some large private houses were remodeled to add or divide into smaller apartments: the House of Pansa, of Julia Felix, or the Villa of the Mysteries, for example. The same tendency can be seen at Herculaneum in the Samnite House or the House of the Bicentenary. The Casa a Graticio at Herculaneum was built as a series of small apartments, with common cooking facilities and latrine.[36] At Ostia, extensive walk-up apartments above rows of shops at street level can be seen, similar to those on the Via Biberatica in Rome behind Trajan's Market.

Large apartment houses (insulae)[37] to three and four stories begin to appear, not all consisting of small, dark rooms in which a poor family could crowd together (see figure 5). Some contain as many as seven rooms per apartment, with generous windows open to the street and access to a central courtyard. An early version of this kind of building had already appeared at Pompeii in the Sarno Bath Complex at the south edge of the city, where the top three floors were apartments for several living groups who lived above a very extensive bathing establishment. The most famous of these buildings at Ostia, the House of Diana, had what must have been a rather pleasant central courtyard with fountain and mosaics, shops on the ground floor facing the street, large windows on the second-floor facade, and probably a gallery across the front of the building on the third floor (see figure 6). Many such buildings had their own well or cistern and common latrine on the ground floor. At some point, a group of Mithraists took over one of the back rooms on the ground floor of the House of Diana for worship. This case is illustrative of the adaptation of residential or commercial space for religious activities. Some Christian groups may have gathered in very similar circumstances.

The height of the domus with impluvium was limited by the height of the compluvium, but the height of the insula was limited only by architectural ability—not always very efficient, given the high incidence of building collapse and the constant fear thereof in Rome. Augustus limited the height of buildings to seventy feet, Trajan later to sixty. This would allow for four to five stories, quite a precarious situation if the building was defective, which was often the case.[38]

The fear of fire was also ever present, and residents were required by law to keep water at hand for just such a mishap. Juvenal describes the unhappy fate of those on the top floors when a fire breaks out below: They are the last to know.[39] Every town probably had its volunteer fire department of some sort, which might be more or less effective. Claudius sent a cohort of soldiers to defend Ostia from fire (Suetonius, *Claudius* 25.2) and Hadrian sent trained firemen, the *vigili*. Their headquarters include a sanctuary of the imperial cult, a latrine presided over by the goddess Fortuna, and drinking establishments on either side of the main entrance. Not a reassuring sign of their effectiveness![40]

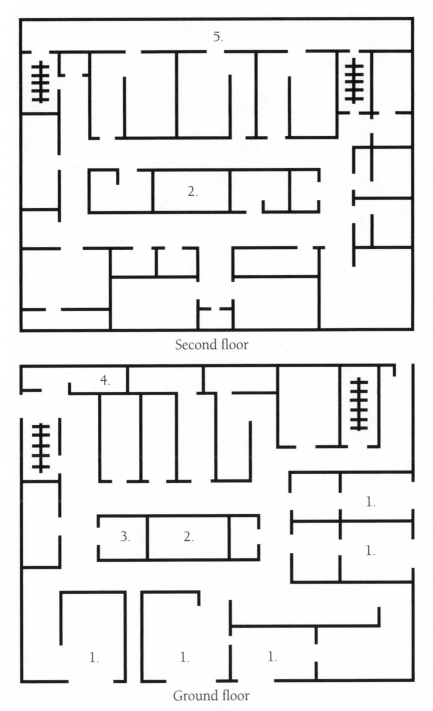

Figure 5. A typical *insula*. Key: 1. shop; 2. lightwell; 3. well; 4. latrine; 5. balcony. Drawing by Deborah Wells.

Figure 6. Insula, so-called House of Diana, Ostia I.28. A multi-storied apartment house with shops at ground level, overhanging balcony on second level. Photo by C. Osiek.

For those who did not want to live in quite such densely populated buildings, there was other multi-unit housing available, some with four living units of four or five rooms and a corridor each on the ground floor, and at least one more floor that probably followed the same design. Some of these, such as those in the Garden House complex in Ostia, have their own built-in latrines, like the larger insulae and domus. Their design is elongated rather than square, with a corridor that gives access to rooms arranged in a row. Thus, there is no central space except for the rather wide corridor, whose light, however, at least on the ground floor, must come through door or windows. The second stories are not preserved, but their presence is attested by stairways.

Increasingly throughout the first to third centuries C.E., the insula and other forms of multiple-unit housing replaced the domus in crowded Ostia, undoubtedly also at Rome, and probably in other cities of the empire as well. Fourth-century Rome listed 46,000 insulae and only 1,790 domus. By the fourth century, however, new domus were being built at Ostia, perhaps in response to lowered population levels that made property costs more affordable. These new or remodeled single-unit residences, like the House of Amor and Psyche, the House of the Nymphaeum, or that of Fortuna Annonaria, emphasized fountains, marble wall facing, and inlaid marble floors.[41] The concept of the inner courtyard revived, this time richly embellished and taking up sometimes inordinate amounts of space relative to the total ground space of the house. Whether this new fashion caught on elsewhere at the same time is not known.

There is no *archaeological* evidence for four- to five-story, low-rent apartment housing (insulae) in pre-Neronian Rome, its port Ostia, or seemingly elsewhere.[42] Rather, many domus are dated to republican and early imperial Ostia, making it similar to Pompeii. Although New Testament scholars often appeal to archaeological remains of apartment housing at Ostia, all of them are Trajanic or later, half a century after Paul, therefore of questionable relevance for understanding the social setting of the earliest Christian churches.[43] Only one or perhaps two such multistory complexes in the Vesuvian cities are earlier than 79 C.E., actually earlier than 62 B.C.—the Sarno Bath complex (VIII.2.17–21), perched on three terraces adjacent to the theater district in Region VIII along the southern cliffs of Pompeii. This huge complex occupies a third of Insula 2, just six doorways south of the triangular forum and just west of the Palaestra complex. The top three floors were private quarters for several families, one of which may have owned the elegant bathing establishment in the lower two floors. A. Koloski-Ostrow[44] describes the complex's more than one hundred rooms, but it was "not lower-class housing"[45]; on the contrary, it was a condominium designed for the rich and run for profit, catering to elite persons' wishes for a personal bath. Koloski-Ostrow argues further against the common idea that Rome was transformed after 64 C.E. into a city of well-built insulae.[46] Rather, "the Sarno complex is convincing evidence that Pompeii may have been close to the forefront of developments"; "the architects in Campania may have been well ahead of Rome in their experiments in well-constructed tenement housing."[47] Jan Bakker in a recent study of Ostia reaches similar conclusions: there were many domus in republican and imperial Ostia, reminiscent of Pompeii,[48] and the later, multistory apartment complexes around a central area (*medianum*) were inhabited by those with "considerable wealth," among the "wealthiest people in second century Ostia."[49] This is not tenement housing in slums, as pictured by some writers. Further, owners and slaves lived together in the earlier republican and imperial houses, with slaves and/or freedmen or freedwomen working for the owner in the shops in the facade of his or her house. But the later medianus-apartment[50] buildings in Ostia changed this: The expensive ground-floor apartments were not connected with workshops, so that the wealthy in their apartments and their clients were more segregated.[51]

A similar picture was sketched by art historians at a 1987 conference at Brown University (papers published in 1991). The organizer of the conference and editor of the essays, Elaine Gazda, and the first and pivotal paper by Eugene Dwyer argue against the tendency to neglect the central role of the atrium house, against the assumption of its decline in the first century C.E. on the way to being replaced by the multifamily apartment complex in the late first and second century C.E.[52] Even the theory they are arguing against makes the widespread building of apartment complexes later than Paul: the older theory understands the multifamily insula as "beginning in Neronian Rome and culminating in second-century C.E. Ostia."[53] But Dwyer attacks even this as "misleading," suggesting that that theory ignores the Pompeian evidence that points in the opposite direction. There was not an evolutionary development, but rather the atrium house continued its function "essentially unaltered" well into the Flavian era.[54]

References that we have to apartment buildings in pre-Neronian Rome are literary. Strabo (born 64–63 B.C.E., died c. 21 C.E.) describes Rome as a city with plenty of food, as well as

> timber and stones for the building of houses which goes on unceasingly in consequence of the collapses and fires and repeated sales (these last, too, going on unceasingly); and indeed the sales are intentional collapses, as it were, since the purchasers keep tearing down the houses and building new ones, one after another to suit their wishes.

Augustus Caesar concerned himself about such impairments of the city, organizing for protection against fires a militia composed of freedmen, whose duty it was to render assistance and also to provide against collapses, and reducing the heights of new buildings and forbidding that any structure on the public streets should rise as high as seventy feet.[55]

Seneca (born between 4 B.C.E. and 1 C.E., compelled by Nero to commit suicide in 65) refers to the contrast between a house with a dining room large enough for a mass meeting, with many slaves shouting, the silver untarnished, marble walls mottled and polished, and pavements more costly than gold, on the one hand, and "tenement walls crumbled and cracked and out of line,"[56] on the other. On the basis of these literary references, apparently, John Clarke concludes that the multistory, multifamily apartment house, or insula, as high as five stories, developed in Rome during the first century C.E..[57] Martial (born c. 40 C.E., died c. 104, published *Epigrams* between 86 and 98 C.E.) refers to living "up three flights of stairs, and high ones"[58] or with some comic exaggeration, "up two hundred stairs."[59] Juvenal (born between 50 and 65 C.E., published his first satires between 100 and 110 C.E.) also refers to living in a third-floor attic under the tiles "where the gentle doves lay their eggs,"[60] where he was "in perpetual dread of fires and falling houses,"[61] again a contrast to houses built of marble, with "nude and glistening statues," books and bookcases, and a "hundredweight of silver-plate."[62] Literary evidence from Strabo and Seneca, not the later archaeological remains of Rome or Ostia, indicates that in pre-Neronian Rome, there were apartment buildings with three or more floors reaching up to seventy feet. Gustav Hermansen points out that the insulae in Rome, like the domus of Herculaneum but unlike the Ostian buildings, were built on very small sites. "[T]his is the explanation for the many houses in Rome which collapse: When one builds high on small lots, the result is spindly, unstable houses."[63] The archaeological remains we have from the mid–first century, in Pompeii and Herculaneum, are for condominiums for the wealthy, while the literary evidence points to the poor living in the third to fifth floors of the tall, narrow Roman apartment buildings.

We need to be cautious about picturing these areas of apartment buildings as if they corresponded to slums in modern cities. The tenement blocks rebuilt by Nero were those around the Palatine hill,[64] hardly the slum section of Rome.[65] Further, observing again that Pompeii and Herculaneum are the best examples we have of mid–first-century C.E. Roman cities, Wallace-Hadrill's survey of larger and smaller houses in those cities becomes important. In Pompeii he studied seven adjacent blocks of 78 houses in Regio I, plus a group of eight blocks of 104 houses in Regio VI, and in addition a group of four blocks of 52 houses in Herculaneum. He does observe a "clustering" of the largest houses, for example along the seawall in Herculaneum, but "there is no hint of the sort of zoning that typifies the post-industrial city."[66] And just as important, he concludes that "the pursuit of 'lower-class' and 'middle-class' housing is misleading, for the poor of Pompeii, as slaves and dependents, were surely to be found in the big houses too, and probably in greater numbers."[67] As a better image of Roman urban society, Wallace-Hadrill suggests the contrasts drawn by the contemporary Naples-born novelist Luciano De Crescenzo, who is defending Naples with its "basement slums" in contrast to sanitized Milan:

> Have you ever reflected that Naples is the only great city in the world that is without exclusively popular quarters? The ghettos of the sub-proletariat, typical of the heavily industrialized cities, like Turin or Chicago, have never existed in our city. In Naples, the working class lived in the basements, the nobles on the so-called "primo piano nobile" and the bourgeoisie on the upper floors. This social stratification of a vertical type has obviously favoured cultural exchanges between the classes, avoiding one of the worst evils of class, that is the ever greater cultural divergence between the poor and the rich."[68]

Still, these apartment houses were just beginning to be built in Roman cities in Paul's decades, and it is likely that most or at least many Pauline ekklesiai occurred in atrium houses, "indiscriminate housefuls" in Wallace- Hadrill's terminology.

Architectural Aspects of Social Life

Atrium houses offered great advantages, as well as disadvantages, for the early Christian mission. Wallace-Hadrill describes one central function of the Roman atrium house that is crucial for understanding the Pauline mission in these settings:

> The Greek house is concerned with creating a world of privacy, of excluding the inquisitive passerby; the Roman house *invites him in* and puts its occupants on conspicuous show. Vitruvius' contrast is not between space for visitors and space for family but between space for *uninvited* and for invited visitors. Much closer in our terms is the contrast between work and leisure. The Romans . . . lacked our distinctions of place of work (office, factory, etc.) from place of leisure (home). Business was regularly conducted at home, whether by an emperor receiving the reports of his secretaries and procurators, by a republican noble giving his legal advice, or by a merchant, craftsman, or shopkeeper operating from the *officina* (workshop) or *taberna* (shop) that were part of his house.[69]

We know how Livius Drusus, the plebeian tribune in 91 B.C.E. wanted his house, built on the Palatine hill overlooking the Roman forum, to function. When his architect promised to make it private so that it could not be overlooked by anyone, Livius responded, "No, you should apply your skills to arranging my house so that whatever I do should be visible to everybody."[70] Cicero, a later owner of the house, also observed, "my house stands in full view of virtually the whole city."[71] Wallace-Hadrill then writes something that, once again, would make modern city dwellers paranoid: "except when closed as a symbol of mourning, *the doors of noble houses stood open to all,* a feature that allowed the entrance of ransacking Gauls in 390 B.C., and of Livius's own assassin in 91 B.C."[72] Cicero tells a relevant story of Verres's escapades as assistant governor: In the Roman province of Asia, he arrived in the town of Lampsacum and manipulated an invitation to Philodamus's house, whom he heard had a beautiful daughter. In the course of the meal, Verres demanded that the daughter be brought in, violating Greek custom. "At the same moment, Rubrius [Verres's assistant] told his slaves to *shut the front door and stand on guard at the entrance*" (Cicero, *Against Verres* II.1.26.66, trans. Greenwood in LCL). Philodamus then told his slaves to save his daughter; somehow a slave went out to tell his son, and the whole town raised an uproar. The story teaches us much about Roman rule and Greek customs, but here, we learn that the Roman guests closed the door to keep the townspeople out of the house. During the meal it had been open, presumably with townspeople entering and leaving the house. Livy narrates another occasion when doors were open:

> [In Rome the Gauls] found the dwellings of the plebeians fastened up,[73] but the halls of the nobles open; and they hesitated almost more to enter the open houses than the shut, so nearly akin to religious awe was their feeling as they beheld seated in the vestibules, beings [sculptures of marble or bronze] who, besides that their ornaments and apparel were more splendid than belonged to man, seemed also, in their majesty of countenance and in the gravity of their expression, most like to gods.[74]

Access was, however, controlled by a doorkeeper.[75] Only wealthy owners could afford this luxury,[76] while poorer persons like Socrates could not.[77] The doorkeeper might be a slave incapable of other work,[78] who in earlier times was chained.[79] He was sometimes assisted by a dog[80] and stayed in a chamber near the entrance to the house.[81] He was resented because he could deny access to the owner of the house, although a bribe for the doorkeeper and food for the dog would sometimes open the house.[82] The doorkeeper might keep the key at night.[83] We conclude that these houses were not simply open, nor were they closed like modern homes. Access was much more fluid than modern persons typically allow, more analogous to modern businesses where customers regularly enter and leave than to modern Western homes. The consequence is that "houses of the wealthy will have been crowded more than poor, cramped properties."[84]

When a passerby looked through the open doors of these houses, he or she could see right through the house![85] Often a visual axis ran from the door through the atrium, then through the tablinum, that is, through the "living room/office" where the owner was displayed as if upon a stage[86] (with the floor actually built a few inches higher than the other rooms), and then into the peristyle, the colonnaded garden.[87] Wallace-Hadrill gives many examples, among them the Casa dell' Atrio a Mosaico in Herculaneum, where the vista from the door passes through the center of the atrium into the tablinum, with a garden opening off to the right of this vista, and the Casa del Mobilio Carbonizzato, also in Herculaneum, where the view from the door is framed by the openings of the tablinum, then focused on the shrine in the garden wall beyond.[88]

> The richly decorated axis of a domus, from the elaborate entrance to the accentuated room behind the courtyard, would inform him

[an Ostian visitor] about the social status of the inhabitants. A room
or area on the axis would be used for his reception, depending on
his relation to the owner. The prominent location of the reception
area would tell him that this relation was much appreciated by the
owner, who awarded a low priority to his private rooms.[89]

For persons living in northern European, left-brained cultures, the
extent of Greco-Roman culture's right-brained, visual orientation is
hard to fathom, difficult to appreciate without seeing some of the
houses in Pompeii or Herculaneum, or the National Archaeological Museum in Naples to which many of the paintings, mosaics, and sculptures
have been transferred. For example, at one villa in Herculaneum an Epicurean library was discovered; a modern book illustrating the wall
paintings, mosaics, and sculpture in this single house has 129 beautiful
plates.[90] The vista into these houses, with their spectacular wall paintings, floor mosaics, and marble or bronze sculptures, functioned to enhance the presence of the owner, and to draw people into the house and
therefore into his or her circle of influence.

The paintings on the walls alluded to a world of buildings outside the
domestic context, and the allusions were to the world of public rather than
private buildings; the constant variations on the column, a symbol of
power, within these paintings already point in that direction.[91] Wallace-
Hadrill observes that the early first style of painting with its two-
dimensional marble panels was used in public buildings like the basilica
at Pompeii. The much more complex second style alludes to stage scenery
or to the Hellenistic palace, "to a world of luxury, grandeur, and public
life, . . . to the palaces of kings and the temples of the gods."[92] Wallace-
Hadrill argues that the third style, which emerged in 30 B.C.E. with the political changes introduced by Augustus,[93] rejects the "chilly public idiom
of the republican aristocracy." The locus of political power had changed
to the informal contacts in the corridors and bedrooms of the imperial
palace, at drinking parties, and contemporary paintings allude to private
dinner parties for chosen *amici* and to family themes.[94] Even third-style
picture galleries, Wallace-Hadrill argues, domesticated art that many felt
belonged in public temples or porticoes: the private display of master-
pieces retained a political value. The fourth style becomes still more flexible. These allusions of the art on the walls mean that householders were
not closing their front doors and withdrawing into their private space, as
in modern houses that try to lock out the confusing, violent, corrupt
world. The opposite was the case: Romans were imagining and projecting
themselves as well as the social, economic, and political activity inside
their homes out into the "public" realm. They wanted the relationships and
activity in their houses to be a microcosm of the city, with influence running from inside the house out into the forum, temple, and comitium.[95]

There was virtually no male/female spatial division within Roman houses, but Ray Laurence argues for a temporal division.[96] He observes that the client traveled to meet a patron at dawn, a greeting that would have lasted until the second hour, after which he says the male patron would typically leave the house until the tenth hour.

> For most of the day, the male members of the household were out-side the house. Although there was no structural division of female and male space in the house . . . , there was a temporal division of this space. If the male member of the household was out from the second to the eighth or ninth hours, for half the day the house was a female space. The space was male-dominated at the *salutatio* and at dinner at the ninth hour. Therefore, the beginning and end of the day were male-dominated, whereas the central portion of the day was female-controlled.[97]

Laurence assumes that the patron was always male, and that only males went to the baths, both incorrect assumptions. On the contrary, Ward observes: "we know that women engaged in business transac-tions, perhaps at the basilica or the building of Eumachia, from the tablets of receipts found at the house of L. Caecilius Iucundus."[98] In-deed, women owned businesses and houses, in Pompeii, for example, Eumachia and Julia Felix.[99] The largest building (c. 60 meters by 40 me-ters, so 2400 square meters) on the Forum (VII.ix.1/67) has the in-scription: "Eumachia, daughter of Lucius, public priestess, in her own name and that of her son, Marcus Numistrius Fronto, built at her own expense the outside porch, the cryptoporticus and the porticoes and dedicated them to Concordia Augusta and Pietas."[100]

Walter Moeller argues that the edifice was built in C.E. 3 when Eu-machia's son Marcus Numistrius Fronto was *duovir*,[101] but Paavo Cas-trén shows rather that his father was *duovir* in C.E. 2/3.[102] She had some connection with fullers, dyers of wool: in the eastern portico of the building the statue of a woman was found with this inscription, "To Eu-machia, daughter of Lucius, public priestess, the fullers [dedicated this statue]."[103] Amphorae, large pottery jars, that she and her family shipped, have been found in Africa, for example, in Carthage.[104] The largest ex-tant tomb of Pompeii, according to Roy Bowen Ward, is outside the Porta Nuceria with the inscription, "Eumachia, daughter of Lucius, [built this] for herself and her household."[105]

Another woman, Julia Felix, owned the largest Pompeian residence so far excavated (Region II. insula iv), on which she placed this ad-vertisement: "In the property of Julia Felix, daughter of Spurius, to lease: the Venus baths, fitted up for the best people, taverns, shops and second story rooms, for the space of five years, from the ides of next August to the ides of the sixth August thereafter."[106] We can

Figure 7. Kitchen, Casa dell'Efebo, Pompeii I.7.10-12. Stove at left, latrine at right, sink in back corner. Amphorae are not in situ, but were taken from the northeast corner of the garden and are now "stored" in the kitchen. The stove is reinforced with a metal I-beam to keep it from collapsing. Photo by P.W. Foss.

imagine *her* on stage in the tablinum of her house advising clients, freedmen, and slaves running shops in her house, at her baths, or managing and enjoying her gardens. Eumachia and Julia Felix are independent women, whose inscriptions do not defer to any male authority figure, running their businesses, exercising their feminine influence within their own households and in the city, in Eumachia's case both on the forum in Pompeii and as far away as Africa. They are specific examples of what is possible for wealthy women in Roman cities,[107] possible for women householders like Prisca with her husband Aquila (1 Cor. 16:19; Rom. 16:3–5), Phoebe (Rom. 16:1–3), and Nympha (Col. 4:15).

Figure 8. Slaves' peristyle, with crude stripe designs. Villa of Oplontis. By contrast, the rooms around the main peristyle are lavishly adorned with frescoes. Photo by Michael Larvey, Austin, Texas.

Most slaves, however, were segregated in the Roman house: The Pauline gospel would have introduced tension into these relationships. "Roman domestic architecture is obsessively concerned with distinctions of social rank, and the distinctions involved are not merely between one house and another . . . but within the social space of the house."[108] Slaves did not, of course, remain in only one area of the house, but served everywhere, day and night.[109] But there were servile areas of the house, places where menial or low-status activity like cooking, washing, and working occurred, and where they slept (see figure 7). They were usually housed in one of the small rooms called cells (*cellae, cellulae*), alternatively used for storage purposes.[110] Some upper-class writers made a few references to slaves as physically and socially "dirty,"[111] picturing them snacking in the kitchen, scavengers for leftovers. The service areas of the house were marginalized, pushed away to the edge of the master's beautiful and often symmetrical quarters, located in dark, ill-decorated rooms sometimes accessible only down long, narrow corridors. Wallace-Hadrill[112] gives an example of the Casa dei Vettii with its opulently decorated atrium, the frescoed rooms that open off it, the elaborate peristyle garden, and one of the most elegant dining rooms in Pompeii, all a striking contrast to the dark, ill-decorated bedrooms and storerooms for the slaves.[113] The beautiful villa at Oplontis just north of Pompeii, probably owned by Nero's wife Poppaea Sabina, sets off the slave area with crude diagonal black-and-white zebra stripes[114] (see figure 8). This renders the low-status areas "invisible" to high-status visitors. Wallace-Hadrill also points to Pliny's descriptions of his own villas, minute accounts of "every corner," which, however, virtually pass over the slave areas.[115] When such a house owner became Christian and the house ekklesia assembled for worship, eating and drinking the Eucharist together, at which there is "neither slave nor free" (Gal. 3:28), how did they reconstruct the relationships?[116]

Wallace-Hadrill notes that there is no archaeological indication of where children may have slept, other than the exceptional child's bed on the second floor of the Casa a Graticcio in Herculaneum; presumably they often slept with slave nursemaids and tutors.[117]

A number of things may be learned by comparing the archaeology of the Mithras cult with the early Christian house church, two groups in intense conflict with each other from the late first to the fourth century C.E., both of which met in houses. Scholars have pointed out enlightening parallels between the two[118]; much can also be learned from possible contrasts. The Mithras cult room symbolizes a (typically quite) small,[119] dark cave with access and any view into the meeting room restricted, a significant contrast to the larger, more visible, public areas of the Christian house that might be seen from the street. The Mithraic cult meal probably involved between six and fifteen diners in each triclinium, that is, three couches with between two and five persons on each one.[120] Assuming the Christian assemblies not only gathered in the triclinia but also spilled over into the peristyle gardens, significantly larger numbers are possible.[121] Mithraic ceremonies were private, Christians ones more public; Mithraic gatherings were small, Christian ekklesiai sometimes larger. Mithraic gatherings were without women, but did include slaves. Early Christian ekklesiai included both groups actively engaged in worship and leadership roles.[122]

These contrasts are all the more significant in light of Wolf Liebeschuetz's argument that Mithraism probably spread from Rome and Ostia, not from Iran.[123] Roman Mithraism "was a new synthesis of Persian, but also of classical . . . , and perhaps even of Judaeo-Christian . . . elements," a new synthesis created by a particular unknown individual who could have been a compatriot of Paul of Tarsus. It may even have been founded in the West, perhaps among Greeks, although it very quickly became Latinized.[124] David Balch has interpreted the deutero-Pauline and deutero-Petrine Christian "household codes" as a conservative reaction against earlier progressive possibilities for women in the Jesus movement and for both women and slaves in the early

Pauline churches.[125] These household codes do regulate and drastically reduce the social and religious roles that women and slaves had played earlier, so are a conservative reaction against freedom in the Jesus movement and the earlier Pauline churches. But the possibility of a Roman center for the missionary spread of Mithraism means that syncretistic Roman religion could take a significantly more reactionary attitude toward women, excluding them from membership and worship.

Everyday Reality

While the best-preserved evidence, especially from Pompeii and Herculaneum, is of the domus, and therefore more attention is given to this form of domestic structure, it must be kept in mind that the vast majority of people, perhaps as many as 90 percent in larger cities, lived in the much more constricted quarters of the insula or in apartments of one or two rooms crowded above or behind shops.[126] Rome at the height of its prosperity is commonly thought to have had nearly a million inhabitants. Other cities were smaller, but were just as crowded. Juvenal remarks that nobody can sleep because of the noise in the poor housing of Rome.[127] The picture of a vast unwashed multitude is not unfounded.

The evidence suggests that some kind of central open space was nearly always desirable in house planning, whether an open courtyard around which small and poor houses were built as at Capernaum, the stone-paved courtyard of moderate houses in Jerusalem, the open courtyard of the multistoried insulae of Ostia, the impluvium of the Roman domus, the peristyle of typically Greek and Eastern design, or the combination of both impluvium and peristyle as found in some of the wealthier houses of Pompeii. Yet the majority of a city's population probably lived in housing that was just too poor to afford such extra space, and common buildings such as the intermediate multi-unit houses of Ostia, which do not exhibit this centralized design, had back rooms on the ground floor that must have been dark indeed.

Except for those houses wealthy enough to have their own hygienic and cooking facilities, or those insulae that provided them for their residents, people used the public latrines and public baths, or chamber pots to be dumped out on the street and no bath at all. Many people often purchased food and drink on the street or in neighborhood shops, as witnessed by the bakeries, eating establishments, and *thermopolia* (a Greek loanword for hot drink shops) of Pompeii and Herculaneum (see figure 9).

Figure 9. Thermopolium, a shop for selling hot drinks from large vats embedded in marble-faced counters. Traces of painted plaster remain on rear wall next to marble-top shelves. Herculaneum IV.15, at intersection of Cardo V and Decumanus Inferior. Photo by C. Osiek.

By modern standards, even the wealthiest inhabitants within a large and comfortable domus lived in crowded and unhygienic conditions, and in a great and confusing mix of social classes that may have included, besides the nuclear family, slaves, other dependents, and lodgers renting a few rooms to provide extra income. The majority of urban dwellers lived in small, dark, poorly ventilated, crowded buildings where privacy was unavailable, adequate sanitation impossible, and the spread of disease inevitable. Hygienic practices were, by modern standards, appalling for everyone,[128] and medical knowledge and practices extremely limited. While the most luxurious houses offered a certain gracious living, the vast majority of residents of an ancient Mediterranean city or town lived lives full of hardship, poor health, and crowding, with high rates of infant mortality and low life expectancy.[129]

From Familia to House Church

In this environment, earliest Christianity was born and developed. All evidence points to domestic buildings as the first sites for Christian gatherings. Even during the life of Jesus, the house seems to have been a favorite site for teaching (Mark 2:1; 3:20; 7:17; 9:28; implied in 4:10). Beyond the households that welcomed Jesus for meals and residence, the first groups of his followers after his death began meeting in private houses. Many Jewish communities and private Greco-Roman cults began in a particular place as small gatherings in private houses, and it was the same with the first circles of Jesus' followers.

The early community in Jerusalem is depicted in Acts as meeting regularly in houses, in addition to their attendance at worship in the Temple (Acts 2:46; 5:42).[130] At the time of Peter's arrest, the Jerusalem community was gathered for prayer in the house of the mother of John Mark (Acts 12:12). In Philippi, Paul and Silas encountered the merchant Lydia, who accepted baptism "with all her household" and prevailed upon Paul to accept her hospitality (Acts 16:14–15). Following their miraculous deliverance from prison, Paul and Silas were taken by the jailer into his house, where the whole household was assembled, preached to, and baptized—in the middle of the night! (Acts 16:31–34.) Before leaving the city, Paul and Silas went back to Lydia's house, where a group of believers was already established (Acts 16:40). In Paul's final journey through Asia Minor, he paused in a Christian group gathered for the breaking of bread in an upper room, a gathering that turned into an all-night discussion with a tragic accident miraculously righted (Acts 20:7–12).

In the Pauline letters, the missionary couple Prisca and Aquila have a Christian assembly (*ekklesia*) in their house (1 Cor. 16:19; Rom. 16:3–5), as does Philemon with Apphia and Archippus (Philemon 2). An otherwise unknown Nympha hosts a church in her house in Laodicea (Col. 4:15), and "those connected with Chloe" (1 Cor. 1:11) may be members of a regular gathering in Chloe's house, apartment, or business that has been in recent contact with Paul. His patron Phoebe, deacon of the church at Cenchrae (one of the seaports of Corinth, about six miles away), undoubtedly provided hospitality for Paul, part of a patron's role, and may have hosted the local gathering as well (Rom. 16:1–3).

Given what we know about the structure of domestic buildings, how are we to envision the physical arrangements in which these gatherings took place? In these earliest years, perhaps for the first century and a half,[131] there were probably no structural adaptations for Christian worship, but rather, the adaptation of the group to the structures available. The size of the meeting space in the largest house available must have determined the size limit of a worship group. When the group became too large, another was founded in another location.

Assemblies of the "whole church" could take place from time to time on important occasions in a place large enough to accommodate it: perhaps a very large domus, or a rented hall (see Acts 19:9, where Paul lectured in such a hall). In Corinth, Gaius seems to have had a large enough house, where Paul also lodged (Rom. 16:23; contrast v. 5; 1 Cor. 1:11; 16:19).

No doubt, early Christians preferred a good-sized domus as the venue for a local church gathering, and the patronage system would impose on wealthy members the expectation that they host the gathering. Such a group would spill out from the triclinium into the atrium and/or peristyle or oecus. The triclinium was designed to hold nine diners reclining on three couches arranged together as three sides of a square, with the open side toward the open inner space of the house. There was also limited space in the dining room for others sitting on chairs alongside the couches. The inner courtyard or open space was the key to flexibility, for there, people could be placed in any kind of arrangement, depending on space available: makeshift dining couches, tables, or seated on the ground. How many people could comfortably fit into a house church gathering under these circumstances is almost impossible to estimate. It would depend entirely on the size of the house and the amount of open space available.[132]

To the extent that separate dining facilities for men and women remained the custom, this separation according to sex, smaller children with the women, may have continued in Christian assemblies as well. But all would presumably have been positioned in such a way as to be able at least to hear the voice of the presider and/or preacher. Another possible scenario, however, is that women were led by a woman presider in a separate section of the dining facilities during the meal, only joining the men for the teaching, or perhaps only when an important visitor presided.

If no members of the community possessed a domus, which was probably often the case, the group would have to gather elsewhere, most likely in one or two rooms of an insula, perhaps in a large ground-floor room as did the devotees of Mithras in one of their fourteen Ostian sanctuaries in the House of Diana. The first church buildings of San Giovanni e Paolo and San Clemente in Rome seem to have been built over original insulae.[133] Although there is no archaeological evidence for Christian habitation in the insulae, one has to ask why these particular locations were later chosen as Christian sites. It is quite possible that these are examples of locations where the earliest Christian meetings took place in a room or apartment of the original insula. "Those with Chloe" (1 Cor. 1:11) may be an example, and Paul's late-night discourse in the third-story room at Troas (Acts 20:7–12) is probably another.

It is also possible but not likely that in the case of meetings held in a domus, the neighbors may not have known what was taking place. But certainly in the case of meetings held in an insula, there could have been no question of secrecy, for everyone in the building must have known everyone else's business. Recall that 1 Corinthians 14:23 seems to suggest that outsiders regularly were invited or perhaps even wandered into Christian meetings. It would be a mistake, therefore, to envision every Christian gathering at this time in a spacious private house, or even operating with full privacy.

This first phase of Christian worship lasted until the middle or end of the second century, by which time numbers had grown considerably and liturgy was evolving beyond the capacity of domestic architecture to support it. No longer was Eucharist celebrated at a common meal, but at a ritual commemoration that retained only the stylized structure of a meal. Participants were no longer reclining or sitting at table, but standing before a common table that functioned as altar. This seems to be the case already in Justin's description of the Christian Eucharist in mid–second-century Rome (*Apology* 1.61–66). Common meals, called *agape* feasts, were still celebrated, but separately.[134]

By this time, houses used as gathering places for Christian assemblies began to be remodeled into buildings better adapted for assembly and worship. The clearest and best-preserved example of this change is the Christian house church at Dura-Europos on the frontier of Roman Syria. Without altering the exterior, a house with eight ground-floor rooms, a staircase to the roof, and a central courtyard was converted before the middle of the third century into a building better suited for group worship and activities. This remodeled *domus ecclesiae*[135] provided a larger rectangular room for worship by the removal of one wall between two rooms. The new room, 5.15 by 12.9 meters, could have accommodated perhaps sixty-five to seventy-five people. A small platform, extending almost a meter from the wall, about 1.5 meters long and .20 meters high, was added to the east, short wall. A built-in baptistery with canopy supported by columns was also added in yet another room. While the wall decoration of the large assembly hall remained traditional, the walls of the baptistery room were adorned with biblical scenes.[136]

Thus what was once a private house became a building devoted to Christian religious use. While archaeological evidence of this stage of development, except for the Dura house church, is very slim due to demolition for later construction of larger edifices, it is to be assumed that the same thing was happening throughout the third, and even perhaps late second, century. The separation of Eucharist from meal and the growing numbers of believers necessitated the removal of worship from the venue of the private dwelling, and thus from the family setting. From then on, Christian worship was conducted according to the profile of public liturgy and no longer took place in a family environment.[137] The growing authority of the bishop concentrated more and more power in the hands, not of local leaders, but of centralized authority figures responsible for larger and larger groups of believers.

2

Cultural Anthropology

Physical space and social structures reflect each other and interact with each other in complicated ways. In this chapter we will discuss some of the findings of cultural anthropology and other social sciences as they relate to what we know of social and family life in the ancient Mediterranean, with a view to better understanding of the worldview of ancient Christian families, and how it differs from our own. The discussion will of necessity trace broad, general lines. It is of the nature of such a portrayal that it does not deal with exceptions or local and regional variations, of which there are many.

The Problem of "Culture"

Anthropologists study living cultures and relate them to one another across various grids in order to see the common elements at a higher level of abstraction. The application of these grids to ancient peoples, to whom we have no access except through those artifacts that they have chosen—for very different purposes—to leave behind, can help create a portrait of ancient peoples who belong to the same cultural groupings. This must be done with caution, but the method is no less objective than the historian's or exegete's reading of the evidence without acknowledgment of his or her own cultural biases.[1] The verb tenses in the descriptive portions of this chapter waver deliberately between present and past in order to affirm this belief. The relationship of these findings to early Christianity will be continued throughout the book.

First, a word about cultural systems. Macrosociologists classify the ancient Mediterranean world as a traditional preindustrial society.[2] In such a system, politics, religion, and economics are subsumed under military and kinship structures, which sustain and support the balance of power. There is a close economic relationship between the city as market center and the agricultural territory that it controls and protects, and which in turn supports it with food production. Most of the land, the most precious commodity, is concentrated in the hands of ruling elites for whom the combination of supervising agricultural work on their rural estates from their country houses and participating in leadership in the urban political system is the idealized life.

This aristocratic group, consisting of no more than 3 percent of the population, consists of both military and religious elites. From their families both army and temple leaders are chosen. This elite class is crowned by a ruler, in the Roman system by the imperial family and its apparatus, which controlled vast amounts of property and power. Unfortunately, most literary, archaeological, and epigraphic remains from the ancient Mediterranean—early Jewish and Christian materials being a notable exception—were produced by or for this small elite population.

The aristocratic elite was supported most directly by a small class of "retainers"[3] who served the needs of the ruler and elite class. They were the governmental and religious functionaries and bureaucrats whose positions depended directly on the elites, but who profited socially and economically by their status. In the Roman Empire, many of these were the slaves and freedmen/women of the emperor and the aristocrats. Others, the class of urban nonelites, were in less direct contact with centers of power through the complex networks of patronage. Some of these constituted a merchant class that tended to benefit from the dependence on them of the city elites, to whose tastes they primarily catered. In no way, however, were any of these groups a middle class, as that term is understood today.

In most areas, probably no more than 7 percent of the population lived in cities, while the vast majority of the rural populations were peasants who worked the land or those who provided support for them through small crafts or trade. This silent majority who worked the land and supported small peasant villages ultimately bore the crushing economic burden of taxation, which forced them to give up the fruit of their labors to support the luxuries, military campaigns, and religious pomp of the urban wealthy.

The theory of a common base to all Mediterranean cultures has been under discussion since the 1960s by field anthropologists studying traditional living cultures of the area. Both diachronic and synchronic cautions must be exercised if this material is to be used for the study of an ancient culture. The diachronic concern raises critical questions about the validity of the assumption of a common culture across the centuries. This is so especially in view of the ethnic and cultural changes that have occurred through the various waves of migration that have swept the Mediterranean in the past two thousand years, particularly the Arab and

Turkish migrations. Here the question must be asked, To what extent did newcomers bring their own cultural variations, and to what extent did they absorb the cultural cues of the residents? The synchronic concern questions the applicability of general categories to the many smaller varieties in custom and thinking from one culture to another. Within the ancient Mediterranean world, there were variations of language, custom, and such from region to region, within the overall structure of Greco-Roman culture. With these cautions in mind, however, proponents of a common Mediterranean culture contend that some common patterns do emerge, even though the ways in which they are practiced will differ somewhat from group to group.

Honor and Shame

All cultures have some kind of symbolic construction of honor, and all cultures have a sense of social shame. The contention of those who would maintain a common cultural heritage in Mediterranean societies is that the fundamental values of these societies revolve around honor and shame especially as a way of structuring social relationships through sex and gender roles.[4] According to this theory, male and female honor and shame systems are distinctly different yet totally involved with each other.

Male honor consists in maintaining the status, power, and reputation of the male members of a kinship group over against the threats that may be thrown against them by outsiders. Each exchange between males of different kinship groups is seen as a contest for honor. Within the kinship group, the absolute loyalty and deference of each male member is expected, according to his proper role in the hierarchy of authority within the family. Aggressiveness, virility, sexual prowess, and the production of sons are important components. The crucial thing, both for individual males and for families, is that one's claim to status and power is matched by others' perception; this is the coherence of ascribed and attributed honor. To claim greater honor than is recognized by others would incur the shame of one who does not know his place in society.[5]

One important element of the demonstration of male honor is the function of patronage and hospitality. It is the duty and expected role of the powerful to protect and support the less powerful. To fulfill this role is honorable; for the powerful to take advantage of the weak is despicable. The patron functions as a kind of surrogate father, and the patronage system is a way of replicating kinship systems. The patron must provide some material benefits to the client, but most important, benefits for social advancement. The complementary role of the client is proper deference toward the patron, the pouring on of attributed honor, and the performance of certain actions that contribute to the support of the patron, especially help in any way that the patron might need. Because male society held all political power and because it was heavily structured along patronage lines, it "resembled a mass of little pyramids of influence, each headed by a major family . . . not the three-decker sandwich of upper, middle and lower classes familiar to us from industrial society."[6]

An important part of the role of patron is the provision of hospitality to those under one's protection. It is part of what the client can expect to receive. But the stranger, too, must come under the hospitality of a patron, for otherwise, the stranger has no identity, no status. Receiving a stranger as guest, especially the invitation to a meal, creates a bond within the patronage system whereby the stranger is welcomed as fictive kin.[7] The host violates the rules of hospitality by allowing the guest to be dishonored or harmed; the guest violates the rules by dishonoring the host or anyone in his household.

The honor of women in the public male world consists in preserving the family's honor by guarding their own sexual purity. Women are, in men's eyes, the mysterious gateway of birth and death. Because they ultimately have the power that provides legitimate offspring, they must be protected from outsider males and therefore controlled. Women are the weak members of the family for whom sexuality is irresistible and sex drive indiscriminate. (Contrary to modern Western stereotypes, women were thought in antiquity to have less ability to control their sex drive than men.[8])

But it is women's very weakness that gives them the fearful power of being able to shame their family through its male members by sexual activity with any male other than a legal husband. Virginity before marriage is a girl's highest duty and greatest value. The surest way for a male to dishonor an individual male or family is to seduce or rape its women, for this demonstrates that the males lack the power to protect their vulnerable members. In many traditional cultures, a raped woman is damaged goods that will not be able to command a good marriage, and a seduced woman is a pollution that must be eliminated by a father or brother in order to restore the honor of the family.

The positive aspect of shame is generally seen as sensitivity to one's honor. The person who lacks this sensitivity, and will therefore act in a dishonorable fashion, is "shameless." But the other aspect of shame is negative. Males incur shame by being bested in a contest for honor, by engaging in dishonorable conduct *that others with whom they are in an antagonistic role know about,* and especially by allowing their women to be violated. Females incur shame in the public male world primarily by compromised sexual purity, or by other public conduct unbecoming the male ideal of feminine modesty. By such conduct, they dishonor not only themselves but their whole family.[9] This kind of shame can be passed on from person to person and even from generation to generation, as if it were contagious.[10]

Some would argue that male thus symbolizes honor, and female shame,[11] the latter meant here as positive sensitivity to the maintenance of sexual honor over against men. Others contend that it is not helpful to look at this close relationship of female with shame as a primary symbolization.[12] In many aspects of public, male society, it seems to work that way, and women can even internalize these attitudes. Yet it has often been found that within the private world of women, the standards of honor and shame can work quite differently. There the code of female honor stresses values of honesty, confidence, friendship, and industriousness.[13] Thus, to see women in these cultures as symbolizing only shame, and that only with regard to their sexual status, is to perpetuate the dominance of the male paradigm as the only one and carry it into contemporary analysis. Further, in peasant societies, where women are necessarily less enclosed, their contribution to the family's economic production is also significant in the social construct of women's public honor, and thus that of the entire family.[14]

Cultural Constructions of Gender

In any society in which male consciousness is the norm, women are perceived as the other. There is no known culture in which this perception has not led to the devaluation and subordination of women to some degree.[15] But because women constitute approximately half of all evenly distributed status groups and classes, and because the intimate interaction of males and females is essential for the continuation of the group, women cannot be seen by males as *totally* other. Women, who almost universally bear the burden of child care, therefore differ from all other social status groups, and it is the structure of the family, however construed, that makes this so.[16]

To the extent, therefore, that a society emphasizes the dangerous liminal power of women to bring shame on the family, and to the extent that the economy allows, women will be controlled, enclosed, and guarded. One way of enforcing this guard is the traditional separation of the worlds of men and women's daily lives as an important part of gender identity. Public space, agricultural tools, and political activities belong to the world of men. Private space, domestic tools, and family activities belong to women. Thus, where possible, the division of the house into men's and women's quarters, the latter the less accessible from the outside (though usually husbands and wives sleep together in the family or women's quarters), and the separation of dining according to sex are cultural indicators of the way the world was ordered. This is one of the most important areas, however, in which ideals seem to have differed considerably between ancient East and West.

With such a cultural construction of gender, the question of equality between the sexes is not at issue. No ancient Mediterranean man would have thought that a woman could be his equal; only a man of similar education and social status could be. Only a man could be equal to a man, a woman to a woman. But social equality is not a meaningful category in this kind of culture. Each sex is assigned a role with regard to the other and to the ordering of tasks, both physical and psychosocial, that must be done to sustain the life of the social group. The central issues are how social subgroups perform their assigned role, and how persons within those subgroups conform to the expectations of the group.

Anthropologists sometimes speak of the "dyadic person," that is, that the social construction of the personality is primarily to meet the expectations of the group rather than to develop as a unique individual. Family and social traditions dictate what men and women are to be in each stage of the life cycle: child, initiand, young adult, husband or wife, father or mother, widow or widower, elder. Persons in this kind of culture generally spend their lives meeting those expectations as communicated through parents, other adults, peers, and religious and political ideology. To go outside the limits of these predetermined social roles is to risk disapproval and rejection by the very people upon whose approval the person depends not only for affirmation but for identity.

Defining the Family

Kinship is a dominant category of social organization in traditional Mediterranean societies.[17] The family in a traditional Mediterranean society can be understood as a diachronic and synchronic association of persons related by blood, marriage, and other social conventions, organized for the dual purpose of enhancement of its social status and legitimate transfer of property. The major means of achieving these ends are marriage and childraising. The family is diachronic, inasmuch as all known generations, often even those deceased, belong. It is synchronic inasmuch as many living units, united by blood, marriage, patronage, or other contractual obligations participate simultaneously. It is also patriarchal, being both patrilineal, that is, organized both diachronically and synchronically according to the male line, and in most cases either patrilocal or neolocal, that is, a newly married couple take up residence either in the husband's family's home or in a newly established one, which will, however, have closer ties to the husband's family than to the bride's. The bride in some sense passes from her family of origin to her husband's family, though the understanding of what this means varies widely.

The traditional preindustrial family was a center of production rather than of consumption. The labor and skill of the members produced most of the items of household consumption: food, clothing, tools, and furniture, though urbanization and trade of course brought many changes in these patterns. Property was kept in the family from generation to generation. The family's most precious possessions were therefore its children, who were socialized to assume their place in the next generation according to established gender roles: Boys to preserve the family property, protect their women, and beget sons; girls to contract good marriages, assure favorable alliances between families, and produce sons. In many situations, therefore, endogamous marriages, that is, with the closest kin allowable by law or custom, are preferred.

Marriage, therefore, is a legal and social contract between two families for the promotion of the status of each, the production of legitimate offspring, and the appropriate preservation and transferal of property to the next generation. How much choice husband and wife are expected to have in the selection of a marriage partner, as well as the degree of marital affection expected, differ considerably by culture and class. Divorce is the severance of the relationship between two families at the initiative of one of the marriage partners, with the consequent severance of property agreements.

Young children of both sexes were raised largely by women in the women's quarters, men having little to do with childrearing, at least in those families where the ideal segregation according to sex was possible. At or soon after puberty, girls left their own families to be married, and boys were suddenly wrenched from the world of women into the world of men, where their emotional ties to their mothers, however, did not cease. One of the closest and most conflicted relationships in Mediterranean culture is that of mother and son, and each will defend the interests of the other against others, especially father and daughter-in-law.[18] Brother and sister also retain extremely close relationships, and a brother is often considered the first-line protection of a sister's interests, even after marriage. One of the most antagonistic relationships is between mother-in-law and daughter-in-law, for the latter finds herself in constant competition with the former for her husband's affection.

Mothers often dote on their male children, giving them more attention than they do the girls, for their sons are the key to their own status in their husband's family. Men, too, can maintain throughout life deeper emotional ties to their mothers than to their wives. In virilocal marriages, the bride enters the realm of her husband's family and must often live under the tyranny of a demanding mother-in-law.

Once thrust into the male world, sons found themselves subject to stern discipline and testing from their fathers in order to prepare them for the anticipated ordeals of adult manhood.[19] The dynamic between demanding father with high expectations of his son, and son who must strive to meet those expectations, a major force in most cultures, is highly charged here. The stereotyped contrast between disciplinarian father and indulgent mother, whatever the lived reality, has made its way even into the familial ethic and religious piety of Western Christianity. It is no accident that Marian devotion is strongest in Mediterranean and Mediterranean-influenced cultures.

Space as Boundary

All cultures allocate space according to social divisions as a major way of ordering their world. The most common classifications for locations and limits of social behavior are gender, power, religion, and social stratification. Because the human body is one of the major cultural symbols, the use of the body to convey symbolic meaning through adornment, behavior, and spatial arrangement is also a primary factor in the cultural symbolism of space. Who is allowed to enter where, for what purpose, with whom, in what condition, and in what attire, are important boundary markers between categories of people.[20]

The architectural design of buildings in which access is limited usually employs some kind of linear or concentric pattern of increasing intimacy, so that the farther one advances, either the more powerful one is or the greater the intimacy one shares with the proprietor. An example is the religious site, at which nearly anyone can be admitted to the outskirts (except in the case of Mecca, in which the entire city is forbidden to non-Muslims), only believers to the next stage, and only priests to the innermost area. Sometimes, further access is classified by gender, as in the case of the Jerusalem Temple, where all male Israelites proceeded to the next stage of access beyond women, but behind the priests. In some churches of the Eastern Christian tradition, male babies but not female are brought for baptism to the inner room behind the altar screen. The relegation of women behind barriers to separate them from men at worship in some forms of orthodox Judaism and Islam is well known.

Concepts of public and private exist in all cultures, but how they are concretely expressed can differ widely. Here the open public spaces of markets, temples, civic buildings, and law courts are male space because public civic life is male activity. When it is necessary for women to be there, they are expected to behave with feminine modesty and cover their heads with a veil to mark clearly the gender distinction and the fact that they are under proper male control.

In the arrangement of domestic space, we have already seen in the previous chapter that the Roman architect Vitruvius characterizes the Greek house as having a front area for the men and their social activities, while the back part of the house is reserved for the women and for family activities. While the male head of the house dominates in the front, the more public space, his wife dominates the domestic activities of the more private women's quarters, subject always to his ultimate authority.

The inner recesses of private homes are female space, where men spend little time and do not feel at ease. But not the whole house would be considered private, for those areas used for the conducting of business, patronage, and political life by an important household head are in fact public space to which anyone has access who has business there. We have already seen that for Vitruvius, both atrium and peristyle of a Roman house are public areas.[21]

This Eastern Mediterranean upper-class male ideal of male public dominance and female isolation from public space is beautifully expressed by Philo in his well-known statement that "Market-places and council-halls and law-courts and gatherings and meetings where a large number of people are assembled, and open-air life with full scope for discussion and action—all these are suitable to men both in war and peace. The women are best suited to the indoor life which never strays from the house, within which the middle door is taken by the maidens as their boundary, and the outer door by those who have reached full womanhood."[22] Philo concedes, possibly under Roman influence, that adult women of the family will have some occasion for social encounter with outsiders, but not unmarried daughters. Obviously, this is a class-specific ideal to which poorer families could not adhere. In such a culture, the confinement of women becomes a symbol of family status and affluence.

However varied the pattern from place to place and time to time, however, the general identification of public space as male, truly private space as female, is widely to be found.[23] Because of the complexity of defining what "private" really means, however, some find public/private not a helpful dichotomy and would prefer public/domestic as the proper opposition, that is, all that pertains to household production and consumption belongs to the sphere of women.

The Symbolic Function of Meals

If the use of space and the significance of spatial boundaries are highly charged symbolically, so are meal customs. Eating is one of the most significant social functions we perform. "Meals, then, are a potential source of information about a group's symbolic universe."[24] What one eats, how, food in what condition, where, when, with whom, in what position, with what utensils (if any), and in what relationship to others are extremely significant cultural issues that communicate codes of identity and social relationships, whether actual or desirable.

Meals can be of two kinds: Ceremonies that celebrate the way things are, and rituals that celebrate status transitions. Most meals are ceremonies in this sense, whether in family, among friends, or a state banquet. They not only symbolize but reinforce the social realities that they celebrate. Ritual meals would include such occasions as initiatory banquets, birthdays, funerary banquets, and the like. They recognize and celebrate the transformation of status that they symbolize. Meals symbolize communication with those present, with those commemorated, and with those believed to be present though unseen. Funerary banquets and those commemorating the anniversary of a death make the deceased symbolically present. Nearly every ancient Mediterranean banquet or formal meal featured some form of religious rite, usually prayer and libation, thus recognizing the presence of divinity. Families, associations, and social groups all had patron deities to which sacrifice was made at the beginning of a meal. And the religious or sacrificial banquet of devotees of a particular cult constitute one of the major types of formal meal.

Generally, the sexual separation prevalent in the idealized social construction of space applied to the space and time of dining as well. For formal dining men and women dined apart, though for informal family dining, the whole family ate together. For formal banquets, the reclining position, which seems to have originated with the Assyrians, came into fashion among the Greeks by the sixth century B.C.E., and was copied by the Romans by about the second century B.C.E.[25] It was at first reserved to men and prostitutes, it being considered improper to female modesty and proper shame for respectable women to recline. The combination of reclining on couches with heavy drinking necessarily rendered the banquet an erotically charged context. During the Hellenistic and early Roman periods, when women and children dined with men, the men usually reclined while women and children sat. In the later Roman period, this separation by sex, under Roman influence, was changing, and wives more frequently joined their husbands on the dining couch, though it is still doubtful that unmarried girls mixed with unrelated males at a dinner party.

Diet is nearly always determined by social status, but also by special convictions and beliefs that concern the difference between clean and unclean food. In the ancient Mediterranean world, certain philosophical and religious groups were known for their dietary laws, of which the most outstanding example were the minimally hellenized, for example, those Jews who were law-observant. The question of food polluted by contact with alien gods also arose in Christianity. But in the general urban population, greater anxiety centered on questions about *who* would share the common table and where in terms of status ranking the guests would be placed.

The traditional Greek symposium emphasized more the camaraderie of male social equals in intellectual repartee and philosophical discourse, in a context of heavy imbibing. The Roman banquet, while continuing this tradition, added a heavier load of status symbolization, since sensitivity to one's social status was everywhere indicated in the mode of issuing invitations, the guest list, seating, and conversation. The formal dinner was one of the most important occasions on which attributed honor might be gained, ascribed honor vindicated, and patronage acquired and exercised.

In ancient Mediterranean culture, the banquet represents prime space and time for the symbolization of social relationships, both hierarchical and vertical, including those with the deceased and with divinity. It is no wonder that it became an important locus for the symbolization of Christian social relationships.

Geographical and Chronological Variation

Everything said above is an attempt to trace broad lines of a common Mediterranean reality. There is good evidence that there were then, as there are today, many regional variations and exceptions. One major distinction has been alluded to, and needs to be further clarified. There is good evidence that the ordering of social life according to separation by sex that has been described as a characteristic of ancient Mediterranean culture was never as marked in the West and in Roman society as it was in the East among Greeks and other easterners such as Syrians and Palestinian Jews.

We saw in the previous chapter that Vitruvius describes the Greek house with its separate quarters for men and women. He does not say the same for the Roman house, and he is aware that the Greek term *andron*, originally referring to the men's quarters, has been adapted by Romans to refer to the corridor between front and back of the house. While undoubtedly present in some small degree, differentiation of domestic space by gender was not a significant Roman classification, while "[i]n the Greek house the most important single contrast was that between male and female space."[26] The allocation of space is indicative of social classification in general, so that other customs of social classification by gender may not have been as pronounced in the Roman West. Correspondingly, the veiling of women's heads in public, while it remained an ideal of feminine modesty, was not as widely practiced in the Roman West as in the Greek East.[27]

With regard to dining, the traditional Roman mores may have been just as strict in the segregation of the sexes as were those of the Eastern Mediterranean. We have seen that the side-by-side dining rooms at Pompeii are interpreted by some archaeologists as indications of sexually segregated dining.[28] Yet there is other evidence, to be taken up elsewhere, that Roman dining customs were changing.

These geographical and chronological differences would also have been affected by social status, since elites are usually much more ready to adopt the new but foreign customs of the dominant power, in this case, to become romanized. While gender distinctions may have been much more important in the East and in more traditional groups, the Roman preoccupation with classification lay more in the realm of social status and rank.[29] House, household, and state reflected this concern.

We have traced some of the larger patterns of social life and worldview pertaining to the family, as they can be reconstructed from comparison with contemporary Mediterranean anthropology. These patterns and differences should give us caution not to assume that ancient Mediterranean people meant the same thing we do by such terms as woman, man, child, marriage, divorce, and household. In chapter 3 these patterns will be discussed with regard to the social and literary data from the ancient Mediterranean world and early Christian sources.

3

Social World

Much has been written on the patronage system, both in cross-cultural perspective and in the ancient Greco-Roman world, so there is no need to give a comprehensive presentation.[1] Here we will simply trace the broad lines, discuss certain aspects relevant to the family, and assess the impact of this social institution on the family and especially on early Christianity.

Patronage, Clients, Freedpersons

Forms of patronage exist in all cultures, but the particular forms it takes and its extensiveness in a given culture depend on many factors, notably the effectiveness, or lack thereof, of governmental systems for distribution of goods and power, and the degree of trust generally placed in those systems. Patronage is a mutual relationship between unequals for the exchange of services and goods. In addition, the client acquires protection and access to power, while the patron acquires political support where applicable, and prestige and stature in the eyes of others, including peers. Patronage systems develop and are necessary to the extent that a government does not provide adequate access to goods and power for the majority of its citizens, that power can be successfully brokered through intermediaries, and that power functions to enhance the powerful rather than to serve the needs of the many.

Patrons and clients enter into long-standing mutual obligations that bind either legally or socially or both. Usually, however, the relationships are social, informal, and unwritten, but highly determined nevertheless. Participants in a patronage culture have little trust in the legal and political structures and little sense that they can change those structures themselves, so they will seek to exploit them for themselves and their kinship group. The patronage relationship is personal, based on informal and friendship ties, but it serves ends that exceed the personal domain, because family, religion, politics, and business are not clearly distinguishable spheres of life. Hence personal, familial, political, and business affairs are not distinct, but fold into one another. The patronage relationship is vertical; it necessarily fosters unequal relationships and undermines horizontal ones. The patronage system is therefore a good way to keep social inferiors dependent on their superiors, unable and unwilling to establish horizontal social solidarity.[2]

In the Roman world, well-established patronage systems were already in place in the early republic. Under the principate, the emperor, beginning with Augustus, used the patronage system to establish himself as primary patron and benefactor, surrounded by the circle of his immediate clients. Emperors capitalized on the system to build tiered patterns of personal loyalty.[3] The principal terms connoting patronage, words like *patronus* and *patrona* and *cliens* are sure indicators of the patronage system in operation, but its action also extends to many other contexts in which the explicit terminology is not used. The semantic field is much wider, because the social system had a far greater extension than the most obvious terminology. In fact, some have thought that because the technical terminology of patronage diminishes in private use in the early empire (though its public use in inscriptions continues), the system was also in decline.[4] On the contrary, the semantic connotations of the terminology seem to have changed, so that by the imperial period, to call a freeborn person a client, for example, was considered derogatory. The continuation of the terminology in inscriptions witnesses to its continued relevance in the public domain.

Another explanation may be even more indicative of the subtleties of the social connotations of terms: looking to who sets up the inscription. Public inscriptions were set up by inferiors in honor of superiors, to extol the generosity and nobility of the patron. For a client to name his or her patron as such publicly promoted the patron's honor. For a patron to name his or her client publicly would dishonor the client by calling attention to social dependence.[5] While this dependence on social superiors was an ever-present reality, when called attention to, it diminished the honor of the dependent one.

The identification of the *patron* was constant in one particular aspect of the patronage structure: The ongoing relationship of former owner to manumitted slave, subsequently a *libertus* or *liberta*. Here a legal relationship pertained, rather than the less formal social ties. Under Roman law, applicable in Roman cities and colonies and elsewhere in the activity of Roman citizens, the freed slave continued to owe to the *patron obsequium* (obedience, compliance) and *operae* (specified rendered services). An example of this relationship is the possibly Christian Ulpia Domnina, a deceased Roman matron of the early third century, four of whose grown and now freed and married *alumni* (foundlings raised as slaves) dedicated her sarcophagus with their wives.[6] (See figure 10.)

Apart from the specific relationship of former owner and former slave, the hard language of patronage was widely replaced in male personal relationships by the time of the early empire with the softer language of friendship, *amicitia* in Latin, *philia* in Greek. The Latin term *amicus* particularly carried a wide semantic field in male society, "sufficiently ambiguous to encompass both social equals and unequals,"[7] companions in the intellectual and social life as well as clients worthy of the personal attention of the magnanimous benefactor. The language of friendship as it was used in the patronage system is an interesting revelation of how the system worked. It does not mean that social differences were leveled and relationships became more egalitarian, for one could speak of "lesser friendships" (*amicitiae inferiores*) that one could treat quite differently than more important ones.[8] Rather, it meant that significant power exchanges were brokered through personal relationships.

The key is reciprocity. The ideology of friendship provides the aura of open exchange and disinterestedness, and the admired social image of the good patron was of one who was conspicuously generous to inferiors out of sheer nobility of character. Yet patronage is a long-standing personal relationship in which mutual fidelity is assured for the benefit of both parties.

Public patronage, whereby a wealthy benefactor endowed a city with public buildings, banquets, and the like for the enjoyment of the citizenry, and in return received praise in the form of statues, inscriptions, and public office, was ubiquitous in the ancient Greco-Roman world, as was the patronage of clubs, trade guilds, and religious associations by persons socially superior to the membership. In both cases, besides inscriptional honors, patrons usually presided at meetings, were explicitly called patrons (in contrast to customs of personal patronage), and received leadership titles that often carried with them the responsibility for special ceremonial duties.

While the vast majority of such known patrons were men, there is sufficient evidence to indicate that wealthy women, too, gave public benefactions and received similar kinds of honors as a result. Class and status took priority over gender determinations, so that high-status women often functioned as patrons to cities, corporations, and private associations. Well-known female examples include Livia, wife of the emperor Augustus, whose patronage extended to cities, social groups, and individuals;[9] Eumachia, early first-century Pompeiian widow, patron of the fullers'

present everywhere at the same time
– ubiquitous

Figure 10. Family funerary monument illustrative of the complexity of Roman households, National Archaeological Museum, Ravenna (*CIL* 11.1.178). It includes at least three generations and a houseborn slave. The older woman at the top, Firmia Prima, and the couple in the second register from the top, Lucius Firmius Principis and Firmia Apollonia, are all freedpersons of one Lucius Firmius. The little girl between them, Lezbia, is probably freeborn. One or other of her parents is undoubtly the child of Firmia Prima, but which is impossible to say. The two young males in the third register, Marcus Latronius Secundus and Salvius Latronius Saturninus, are both freeborn sons of one Salvius Latronius, perhaps brought up as *alumni* or foster children in the household of the couple above them. At the bottom is a young slave born in the *familia* (verna) named Sperato. The main dedicator of the monument is Firmia Apollonia, perhaps joined by Firmia Prima. Photo by C. Osiek.

guild, who provided a prominent building at the forum[10]; Junia Theodora, patron of the city of Corinth in the same years[11]; Plancia Magna of early–second-century Perge in Pamphylia, whose statue and dedicatory inscriptions were erected in exchange for her lavish adornment of the city[12]; Taion, daughter of Straton, who provided funds for a new synagogue in Focea in Asia, and was voted a gold crown and one of the best seats in the synagogue in gratitude[13]; and Iael, synagogue patron of Aphrodisias.[14] Women were also patrons to lesser-status males and females, as evidenced by the patronal role of Phoebe to Paul in Romans 16:1–2, and many inscriptions, for example, that of the freedwoman Manlia Gnome, who boasts of having many clients (*clientes habui multos*).[15]

In a good number of dedicatory inscriptions to women patrons, especially in Asia Minor, the women bear titles related to specific functions in civic administration. Traditional modern scholarship has tended to assume that in the case of women, the titles are merely honorary or derivative of titles held by their husbands. More recently, that assumption has been challenged from several directions.[16] In fact, most civic titles bestowed on patrons, whether male or female, were probably honorary, in the sense that the patrons themselves did not personally carry the tasks of office out, but relied on both public slaves and their own slaves actually to carry out the duties of office.[17] In this sense, there may have been little distinction between how men and women carried out their patronal roles.

In personal patronage, the informal networks of relationships were what counted for personal and political advancement. The duties of clients included the early morning *salutatio* at the patron's residence. The more important clients and the greater number lined up outside the door, the more prestige was attributed to the patron. Clients at the door hoped to receive a gift of food or money (*sportula*) besides the granting of favors requested and, with luck, an invitation to dinner. In return, the loyalty and support of the client was expected. The language of exchange included such terms as *beneficium, officium, meritum,* and *gratia,* and their contextual meanings are so elusive that distinguishing one from another is not totally possible, except that *gratia* carries the meaning of an attitude rather than a specific action, whereas the others refer to particular gifts or favors granted.[18] Together, they create a climate of generosity and at the same time, the expectation of reciprocal but not exact exchange.

The documented evidence of personal patronage is nearly all male, and mostly from the aristocratic classes. Yet even here, in the letters and histories written by male aristocrats, the ability of the women of their families to intercede, initiate alliances, and affect the course of business and politics comes through.[19] Since most marriages were arrangements between families for the furthering of family wealth and power, even marriage negotiations, in which mothers were highly involved, were in fact political negotiations. Both women's influence on the males of their families, especially their sons,[20] and their direct participation in patronage are evident. In keeping with gender concepts of the culture, however, these relationships lack the language or connotations of amicitia, which would not have been possible between men and women. It would be congruent with those gender concepts for women to have had their own informal system of amicitia, in which the same kinds of relationships existed with a view to obtaining access to the kinds of social power available to women, for example, the brokering of marriages or advancement for sons. But most of the surviving evidence comes from the male world and thus does not reveal it.

So much for the aristocrats. But what about the rest of the population, the majority? As with nearly everything that we would like to know about the people of the period, the sources give us little information about the social relations of the underclasses, except inasmuch as we see them in client relationships with more important figures, and sometimes in their own patronal relationships with lesser personages. There is no reason to doubt that the system of informal networks that was so important for the aristocracy was also in operation in the rest of society, though it may have worked very differently according to persons and situations. We see it working in the network of relationships and recommendations embedded in the Pauline letters.[21] The political system worked for the benefit of the powerful. If even for them patronage was necessary, how much more necessary must it have been for those farther from the centers of power.

The important implication of the Greco-Roman patronage system for the family is the realization that the whole social structure operated in this way, with these assumptions about access to power or lack thereof, with vivid awareness of the social inequality of persons, with the presumption that official structures do not work for the good of the whole, that binding reciprocal relationships between unequals are the building blocks of society, and that personal power is more effective than institutional authority. Such a system produces in its members a keen awareness of social status and an inbuilt tendency to treat with greater deference those perceived to be socially powerful.

Every family and household was affected in some way by the patronage system and was an integral part of it. Entire households benefited or suffered from the fortunes of their heads, and those fortunes often depended on success in securing the right patronage. Even within the kinship system itself, in relationships within the household and extended family, we must suspect that a similar set of assumptions was operative.

Patronage is primarily a form of fictive kinship, in which an extension of familiar loyalties is applied to others not related by blood, law, or other traditional ties. It was also an integral part of the social structure of early Christianity. Jesus' relationship with his disciples in an explicitly fictive kinship, the system of financial support that provided for the travel needs of itinerant missionaries like Paul and his companions, the hospitality provided by prominent church members in their houses, the growing concentration of patronal power in the hands of church leaders in the second and third century: All of these were elements and adaptations of the patronage system.

Gender Roles and Concepts

Everything that was said in chapter 2 concerning women's relationship to the use of domestic space and the cultural construction of honor and shame should be taken into account here, and is of crucial importance for understanding the New Testament texts that describe women's activities. The public-domestic dichotomy, in which the public realm is imagined as male and the domestic realm as female, while not absolute and quite diversified from culture to culture, was pervasive in ancient Mediterranean society[22] and continues to be so in its traditional manifestations. Despite the constant presence of women in public spaces in all aspects of public life except the formal political process, their social invisibility as reflected in male language and thinking is not only ubiquitous in the public arena but often carries over into men's reports of private life as well.

This public-domestic distinction, however, is not to be confused with the modern division between work and home or work and leisure. Family residences were usually centers of production and often of business activities. Males were highly involved in the social life of families in homes, and women were active in most aspects of public life. The home was not the place to escape from work, but the place where much of the work was done, even among aristocrats. For upper-class males active in political life, home was not the place to be free of a public role but the place to entertain important people and conduct public business. Recall, too, Vitruvius's list of places within the home of the distinguished to which everyone has access: vestibule, atrium, and peristyle, off which family living quarters were arranged (*De architectura* 6.5.1). In other words, the public-domestic distinction is more a conceptual than social or economic division, and it worked differently than it does in a modern Western society.[23]

Similarly, concepts of basic gender differences, with few exceptions, confirmed the belief in the inherent superiority of male to female in nature (*physis*), strength, and capacity for virtue or courage (*arete*).[24] The well-known thinking of Aristotle on this point seems to have been highly influential: by nature, men command and women, slaves, and children obey. The quality of male rule is different in each case, but decisive.[25] Arete is not the same in men and women, but is apportioned to each on the basis of the work proper to each. However, Plato, and apparently Socrates, affirmed that men and women have the same nature (physis) and therefore the same virtue (arete),[26] and therefore are up to performing the same tasks, still allowing for greater female weakness, and a lesser degree of excellence, however.[27] These two divergent views—and the wavering between them—were to form the basis for male reflection on women for centuries to come.

Plutarch is unusual in his portrayal of the courage (arete) of women in the public sphere in his treatise of the same name. Aretalogies (collected stories about heroic virtue) about women as examples of domestic virtue are not unknown in the ancient world, but the portrayal of women as examples of public political and social virtue is unusual.[28] In *On the Bravery of Women*, Plutarch assembles traditional stories, many previously known and some repetitive, to demonstrate that the arete of men and women is the same.[29] The tales feature women as heroines in military situations, escape from enemies, betraying tyrants, and the like, where the men who should rightly be acting do not. Thus, at least one purpose of the collection is to shame men for not acting themselves. Generally, after accomplishing their patriotic exploits, the women return willingly to their domestic activities as honorable women should. Women should be spoken of in public only in praise after their death.[30] The theme of female sexual shame occurs frequently, as well as the shame brought on men by the courage of women in the face of male cowardice, the worse kind of shame men could experience.[31] And his *Advice to the Married* renders a wife a loyal appendage of her husband, thinking as he thinks and worshiping his gods alone. Here, a man ought to rule his wife, not roughly, but the way the soul rules the body.[32] From the male point of view, female meant soft, undisciplined, and passionate, while male meant all the opposite.

The same gender typology is used by Philo in his exegesis of the Genesis creation narrative, where male is spirit and intellect, female is materiality and sensory perception. Thus, progress in the spiritual life is necessarily movement from symbolic female to symbolic male.[33] It is no wonder, then, that being a man was preferable to being a woman. The Jewish prayer by which a man expressed gratitude to God for being made neither Gentile nor woman nor boor/slave is in fact an echo of a common Hellenistic motif in which the first contrast is Greek and not barbarian.[34] The gnostic Christian *Gospel of Thomas* expresses the same gender prioritization in its famous closing lines (saying 114) with the announcement that every female who makes herself male will enter the kingdom of heaven.

The superior male qualities were summed up in the virtue of *andreia,* which women by definition lacked, and which was the basis for ancient objections to sexual acts between males. The prevailing view of sexual intercourse was that of the active male and passive female. Sex between two males therefore meant that one must be passive, hence compromised because placed in the female role. Philo expresses the common thinking on the subject when he says that same-sex sexual activity robs men of andreia, the necessary quality for war and peace, and instills in their souls the "disease of femaleness" (*theleian noson*), making androgynes of those who should be exemplary for courage.[35]

Even those writers who argued that men and women possessed the same human nature, and therefore the same possibility of exemplifying a virtuous life, showed few signs of translating that philosophical equality into their deepest perceptions of sexual differences or into daily life. A possible exception is the Stoic Musonius Rufus, who argues against the sexual double standard: if a man thinks there is nothing wrong in illicit sexual relations with a woman as long as no man or family is wronged, he should consider how he would feel if his wife did the same. Yet his reason for so arguing is that men as superior rulers must be more virtuous in order to lead by example. If they do not, they will be "thereby revealing the stronger in judgment inferior to the weaker, the rulers to the ruled."[36] Yet lurking behind all the rhetoric of male superiority must have been the fear of female superiority. A satirist could say it: Why am I unwilling to marry a wealthy wife? Because she will dominate instead of being subject. The only way for men and women to be equal is for the woman to submit.[37]

Legal Power
of Men over Women

In the family, the legal and social power of the father over wife, children, slaves, and property was extensive in all the ancient Mediterranean societies known to us. Under Greek law, it was possible for a father to relinquish his paternal authority in favor of a son. In Roman families, this was unheard of except in the rare cases in which children could legally prove their father to be incompetent. In Roman law, the legal term is *patria potestas,* viewed by ancient writers as a unique degree of legal power.[38] Theoretically it included the power of life and death (*vitae necisque potestas*), though that power was always closely hedged in with restrictions, and by the imperial era was essentially inoperative in the case of wife or children, though less strictly controlled in the case of slaves. Those under the legal authority (*in potestate*) of the father (*paterfamilias*) had, strictly speaking, no property of their own during the father's lifetime. Upon his death, sons and those daughters not *in potestate* to their husbands (the vast majority by the imperial era), became financially independent (*sui juris*); the women, however, in earlier years were subject to the male governance of a *tutor.* However, given the low level of life expectancy, most young adults no longer had a living father, and so were in fact independent of this restriction.

In both Greek and Roman systems, theoretically women could not administer their own property without the male guardianship called in Roman law, *tutela.* A woman's dowry was provided by her family of origin and passed with her to her husband in marriage, with the normal expectation that he would administer it. In the case of divorce, it had to be returned with her to her own family.[39] All women were expected to be under the legal guardianship of a male relative, the Greek *kyrios* or Latin *tutor,* whether father, husband, or next of kin. Without his consent, a woman could not make major decisions about her own property, whether that of inheritance or dowry.

However, that this male control was viewed at least by Romans as custom more than necessity is indicated by the fact that in the imperial period, Roman women began to acquire much more independent control of their property. First, Augustus abolished this male guardianship (tutela) as a reward for those freeborn citizen women who had borne three children (the *jus trium liberorum*), and freedwomen who had borne four. Later in the first century C.E., Claudius abolished altogether agnatic tutela, that is, in the male familial line, thus essentially doing away with male control of the property of citizen women. This meant that on the death of her father, every such woman became capable of freely administering her own property.[40]

This custom was a rare exception in ancient Mediterranean societies, and of course, as with all Roman family law, necessarily applied only to Roman citizens.[41] Whether noncitizens in cities under strong Roman influence followed suit with such customs is largely unknown. The evidence from Hellenistic Egypt suggests that Greek women there continued to be subject to male guardianship, while those under the Egyptian law that applied to indigenous inhabitants did not.[42] Moreover, as with so much Roman legislation, the official enactment of a law does not mean that it is henceforth universally observed. Over two hundred years later, for instance, we find a petition by a Roman woman in Egypt, appealing to the jus trium liberorum for freedom from male guardianship.[43]

Social Freedom of Women

Perceptions of degrees of social freedom, and even what constitutes such freedom, are difficult to judge, since they are always relative to what the judger knows. The social freedom of women varied in ancient Mediterranean societies, and what we know of legal restrictions and protections must be compared whenever possible to what the nonlegal sources indicate is really happening. The current literature on this question is vast, and no attempt can be made here to survey or assess all of it. A general principle, however, is that class and status override sex in determinations of social roles; that is, prominent, wealthy, and high-status women had more social power (though not necessarily more freedom as moderns would see it) than poorer and lower-status women.

High-status women appear in epigraphical commemorations in large numbers as benefactors, patrons of cities, temples, and social clubs, and as priestesses of numerous cults, in both Greek and Roman contexts.[44] They owned houses and brick factories.[45] They were heads of households when no appropriate male was present.[46] Women painters,[47] philosophers,[48] and even barristers[49] are known. Lower-status women probably had greater freedom of movement, since the welfare of their families depended on their ability to share in the family work. The relative seclusion of women was an upper-class ideal, accompanied in elite and affluent circles by less labor and a more pampered existence. Thus lower-class women would not have considered the necessity for their greater involvement as "freedom," since it meant heavier work. Women managed small businesses, sold and bought in the marketplace, even fought as gladiators.[50] Slaves and freedwomen especially were secretaries, hairdressers, and doctors,[51] and in general were present everywhere except in public office and representative political assemblies.

Although formally excluded from political decision making, the women of aristocratic ruling families were often in fact quite influential in the informal, behind-the-scenes political maneuvering that represented the real power.[52] There is no doubt from literary and epigraphical evidence that women participated fully and publicly in Greco-Roman society, even as more conservative male voices tried to pretend they did not. They were not invisible, but on the contrary, very visible, even as the language of public male discourse and political structures tried not to acknowledge that visibility, but rather to render women socially invisible.

The development of greater legal and social freedom for women in ancient Mediterranean society can be charted along both a chronological and a geographical axis, though not along perfectly clear lines. Chronologically, changes like the abolishment of agnatic tutela by Claudius in the mid–first century and the noticeable leadership of women in public cults in the Roman period signal expanding acceptance of women in public roles. Geographically, the greater movement of women into public life seems to have been strongest in the more romanized, less hellenized areas of the West and in those eastern locations that were under heavy Roman influence because of colonization, such as Corinth, Philippi, and the province of Asia. The older classical Greek ideals of the strict seclusion of upper-class women are still echoed in some of the eastern Mediterranean voices that sought to preserve something of "the good old days."[53]

One of the best examples of these different tendencies is the evidence for the presence of women at banquets and formal dinners.[54] In the East and in places under Greek influence, women did not ordinarily attend either public or formal domestic dinners with men, but dined apart—not necessarily more poorly, just separately. In the case of intimate family dinners, probably both women and children were present with men. For family celebrations such as weddings, women probably were present, sitting for the meal (*deipnon*), while the men reclined; probably the women left if there was a *symposium* of drinking and philosophical discussion to follow. The exception is the presence of *hetairai,* cultured female companions for upper-class men, who were both present and reclined alongside men for the entire event. Hence the strong association in Greek culture between women reclining with men at a dinner and sexual license.

In addition to the architectural information given by Vitruvius about the differences in space allotment in Greek and Roman houses,[55] Cornelius Nepos, writing at Rome about 35 B.C.E., comments on the social difference: "What Roman would be shamed to take his wife into a dinner party? What matron does not occupy the important places of her house and take part in its celebrations? It is very different in Greece: Neither is she allowed at dinner parties except with relatives, nor does she appear anywhere in the house except in the interior part called the women's quarters, where no one enters except close relatives."[56] So it seems that already in the first century B.C.E. in Rome, at least in some social circles, it was not thought unusual for Roman women to attend formal dinner parties with their husbands, in contrast to what Cornelius Nepos perceives to be the Greek custom still in force.

The other famous example frequently cited is Cicero's attack on Verres for abuse of power (especially in regard to women) during his governership.[57] This example must be used with some caution, since Cicero's strategy is to portray Verres as a rascal. Yet it assumes the Greek custom whereby women do not attend meals with guests from outside the family; for Romans to expect their presence is culturally insensitive but not outrageous. The indignant reaction that Cicero desires hinges

on his audience's sense of honor and shame: In this story, Verres has
brought shame upon a respectable Greek house, upon himself, and
even upon Rome, by his conduct, which affronts local sensitivities.

Even if, however, the custom of women attending dinner parties with
men was established at Rome by the late republican period, separate
dinners for women did not disappear. Dio Cassius reports that Livia reclined with Octavian at their wedding; yet at official banquets celebrat-
ing military triumphs and other public occasions, Octavian presided
with the men, while Livia gave a separate banquet for the women.[58] Nor
is it necessarily to be assumed that when women were present, they reclined alongside men. Sometimes they sat next to the men's couches.
Valerius Maximus (2.1.2), writing in the early first century C.E., notes
that this was the traditional way, now less observed. When in the Greek
East family women were present at dinners, this is more likely how they
dined, as did children. Sometimes, too, women were present in the
same room, but together on a separate couch.[59] While Plutarch sniffs
that respectable women do not belong at a symposium, but only at a
family dinner, he nevertheless depicts one dinner scene in which apparently one woman reclines while another sits. Both, however, are
silent and leave before the symposium proper is over.[60]

The literary evidence indicates that, as Valerius Maximus says, the
older traditional way was for men and women to dine separately, or, in
the case of family meals and celebrations, together, but men reclining
and women sitting next to their couches. Hetairai and prostitutes were
the only women who mixed freely with men at dinners. This custom
seems to have lingered longer in the Greek East, whereas the Roman
custom by the late Republic was changing: Women of the family were
more frequently dining, and even reclining, with men. The Roman custom was slow to replace the older Greek custom in the East. Undoubtedly several different customs existed side by side in one time and place,
since such developments in social custom spread out on a continuum.
As is often the case, change in practice seems to have been moving faster
than social opinion about it,[61] which created clouds of suspicion in traditional circles about the respectability of women who engaged in such
changes. Nevertheless, the relative freedom of Roman women was increasing and spreading into non-Roman areas during the early empire.

Marriage and Divorce

Men's public role of governance and guardianship of women and minors simply replicated in public matters the way it was supposed to
function in the family. Though citizenship did not mean the social

equality of all male citizens, a man's male social peers were expected to be his true friends and companions. In spite of these ideals, however, there is ample literary and epigraphical evidence that many marriages became true friendships between men and women, and that marital affection was considered essential to a true marriage, so much so that its cessation was cause for divorce.[62]

Greek and Roman marriage customs were largely similar with regard to the payment of dowry, family-arranged marriages, and divorce.[63] It was the parents' responsibility to find suitable marriage mates for their children, usually with the child's consent, though girls more easily and more commonly than boys could be made to yield to parental pressure to marry the partner chosen by their family. In earlier Roman practice most marriages had been accompanied by a transfer of *manus,* personal legal authority, of the bride from father to husband. By the imperial period most marriages were *sine manu,* without this provision, so that even a married woman remained under her father's jurisdiction and legally therefore in his familia until his death, when she acquired legal rights sui juris.[64] This arrangement caused a social ambiguity: While the husband as paterfamilias was supposed to have potestas over everyone in his household, in effect, he did not have it over his wife. This ambiguity gave many Roman women of the imperial period with deceased fathers an unusual legal autonomy.[65] The dowry custom remained in force, however, even though the daughter was now a legal person and potential inheritor from her father. Women with large dowries could wield this fact into considerable social power over husbands of lower economic means.[66]

Marriages of freed male slaves and freeborn women were forbidden to the senatorial class and heavily penalized in law to other citizens, yet continued to occur. Manumission of slaves for marriage to their former owners was quite common in the case of women, which must tell us that not all master-slave sexual connections were exploitative. From the early imperial period, there were legal provisions for this situation, but not for the opposite; in fact, there was a definite legal and social prejudice against marriage of male slaves and female owners, for the sake of status impropriety: If both marriage partners were not to be of equal social status, then only the woman should be inferior, not the man, a social principle understandable in light of prevalent gender typology, and still operative today. Such marriages were finally proscribed by law under Septimius Severus in the early third century.[67] The prejudice against freedmen and freedwomen, in favor of the freeborn, was always present. Yet marriages of nonelite women with men of lower social status, and even with their own former slaves, were not infrequent, probably more common in cases when the *patrona* had originally been a slave herself, and so was a freedwoman at the time of the marriage.[68]

According to Roman law, only Roman citizens could contract a legal marriage, *justum matrimonium* or *justae nuptiae*. We simply do not know in most instances outside Rome what legal system was in force for noncitizens. Yet true marriages existed everywhere, governed by local law and custom. Slaves had no legal status to contract any marriage at all, yet monogamous, lasting slave unions certainly existed, and were occasionally even given grudging recognition at law, as for instance, the acknowledgment that slave parents and children owed certain duties to each other.[69] But no inheritance arrangements were possible for slaves, and of course their unions could be broken at an owner's will. Sexual unions and cohabitation of freeborn women with slaves were especially odious to Roman aristocratic sensitivities.

Ages at first marriage were also disparate according to gender. On the basis of literary and epigraphical evidence, estimates of average age at marriage in classical Greece are between fourteen and eighteen for girls, and about thirty for boys;[70] in imperial Rome, from twelve to nineteen for girls, in the late twenties for boys.[71] One trend is that the higher the social class, the younger the age of girls at marriage. A possible explanation for this pattern is that in poorer households, daughters' labor was more needed for a longer time, whereas in more affluent households, securing a politically advantageous marriage was the first priority.

Divorce was commonly practiced in all ancient Mediterranean societies, and usually did not carry with it any noticeable form of social stigma. Though it was more likely to be initiated by the husband, a wife too in most situations could initiate divorce, though sometimes only through the intervention of her father or male relative responsible for protecting her honor and that of her family of origin. Adultery and infertility were the two leading causes of divorce, but there need not be a cause; mutual consent with family approval sufficed. Minor children, being members of the father's *familia*, remained with him, while the wife would return to her own family household, that of her father or a brother. Marriages second and beyond, occurring when both partners were older and more mature, were less likely to feature the age differential between man and woman that characterized first marriages, and were in Roman custom more likely to be by personal choice of the partners.[72] In spite of the prevalence of divorce, however, the *univira* (wife of one husband), and intimate lifelong marital fidelity continued to be idealized, at least in Roman funerary commemorations.[73]

The unusual Christan prohibition of divorce stands out against its context, but with wide attestation (Matt. 5:31–32; 19:1–12; Mark

10:1–12; Luke 16:18; 1 Cor. 7:10–16). Both of these factors, especially the very early attribution to Jesus in 1 Corinthians, argue for
the authenticity of the saying as a teaching of Jesus himself. Already,
however, Paul is dealing with a situation, a believer married to an
unwilling unbeliever, that he thinks was not envisioned by Jesus and
allows of an exception—whether with or without remarriage is
unclear. Similarly, Matthew's version also knows an exception (5:32;
19:9), *porneia,* which can be understood either as fornication or legal
incest.[74]

Musonius Rufus's discussion of marriage may not always have described the reality, but it expresses some of the highest ideals of
personal union for the sake of producing new life. Musonius, a Stoic
philosopher of the equestrian class, reveals his Stoic leanings in his
teaching that women should receive the same education as men, even
in philosophy—provided that such study does not lead them to neglect
household duties and proper chastity.[75] Musonius stands as a lonely
voice in his insistence that sexual fidelity should not operate on a
double standard: If a husband is tempted to have sexual relations with
a female slave, he should consider how he would feel if his wife did the
same with a male slave.[76] The purpose of marriage is union of life and
the begetting and raising of children, for which the intimate union of
marriage is most highly suited. Marriage is no hindrance to the pursuit
of philosophy by both husband and wife.[77]

Probably few marriages attained such heights of mutual love and respect. Obviously, Musonius is describing the ideal. A generation later,
Plutarch's *Advice to Bride and Groom* paints a more traditional picture.
The virtuous wife is to be clothed with modesty rather than expensive
clothes and makeup (10, 29, 31, 48). She should stay indoors, and she
is not to be heard except through her husband and is to communicate
only through him (30–32). She should have no feeling (*pathos*) of her
own, but follow her husband's mood—though he should also spend
time with her, lest she seek pleasure elsewhere (14, 15). She should be
honored, however, that he shares debauchery with another woman
rather than her (16). She should worship only her husband's gods, de-
parting from whatever religious devotion she may have had prior to
marriage (19). With Plutarch, the conservative patriarchal and androcentric ideal of marriage as it was known in the old Greek tradition is
reasserted. Against such a traditional ideal, the reality at the time of
Plutarch's adult life at the turn of the second century must have been
quite different, at least in the romanized West and in the Greek Eastern upper classes most influenced by Rome. One almost senses in him
the nostalgia for the great classical era of Greece that was no more in

his day. The times were changing, and with them women's roles in society. Even the conservative Plutarch begins to talk about a wife as a friend.[78] And so, there are glimpses of a relational ethic beginning even between men and women.

Children's Education and Adults' Learning

Musonius[79] argues that the birth of a child is marvelous, but not enough for a good marriage. Still, many couples in the Greco-Roman world wanted a child as an heir and one to care for them in old age. The state, too, encouraged the procreation of children. In this setting, the children's education oriented them toward becoming adults as quickly as possible.

Adult male citizens might persuade others by memorable speeches in the forum or the courts, and they could make a name for themselves and their families as soldiers on the battlefield. Children could neither think nor fight. Male children could prepare themselves for such public activities; but female children, with increasingly important exceptions in powerful and/or wealthy families, were prepared for domestic life. Contemporary philosophy defined human beings in rational terms, and the gladiatorial games, even more popular among Romans than Greeks, glorified violence in Greco-Roman society. Hopkins[80] argues that the games became a central ritual of civic life, symbolizing unequal relationships. Those who could not be persuaded by reason were beaten: School children's hands were routinely hit by the teacher with rods, a normal part of educational discipline. "The man who has not been beaten is uneducated."[81] Typically, Seneca observed: "He used to be a child: he has become adult. This is a difference of quality. For the child is irrational, the adult rational."[82]

This qualitative gap between adults and children narrowed in the centuries after Christ. As one example from the upper classes, in the Roman republic and early empire, there had been laws prohibiting young men from assuming offices before their twenties. The Lex Villia Annalis of 180 B.C.E. prescribed ten years of military service before a man's first magistracy. Sulla revised the law, 81–79 B.C.E., according to Varro, raising the minimum age to thirty; then Augustus reduced it to twenty-five. This opened a gap between an upper-class young man's physical maturity and his social maturity; he assumed an adult toga about sixteen but had to wait well into his twenties before being taken seriously. Emiel Eyben concludes that from then on we know the prodigal youngster, reveler, lover, and dandy in the Roman world.[83]

However, in later centuries the emperor's children were named to offices as babies: Constantine's son held the highest office in the empire, consul, by the time he was three or four! Furthermore, hot-headed Latin "new poets," such as Catullus (77?–47? B.C.E.), idealized youth as the best age of all, rejecting their elders' values centered on reason and military valor.[84] Christians baptizing babies fits in the context of these social changes (understood by Thomas Wiedemann as expressing equality of adult and child in a novel and unique manner, but by Eyben as corresponding to contemporary cultural developments).

Throughout this whole period the birth rate was low, families had few children, many of those who were born died, and others were subject to infanticide or exposure, which Greeks and Romans used as a method to control family size.[85] These exposed babies were often raised as slaves. The historian Polybius sees human, not divine, responsibility:

> In our own time [mid–second century B.C.E. writing from Rome] the whole of Greece has been subject to a low birth-rate and a general decrease of the population, owing to which cities have become deserted . . . , although there have neither been continuous wars nor epidemics. . . . For as men had fallen into such a state of pretentiousness, avarice, and indolence that they did not wish to marry, or if they married to rear the children born to them, or at most as a rule but one or two of them, so as to leave these in affluence and bring them up to waste their substance, the evil rapidly and insensibly grew. For in cases where of one or two children the one was carried off by war and the other by sickness, it is evident that the houses must have been left unoccupied.[86]

Men blamed women for having abortions, but then themselves exposed their children.[87] "Childbirth hardly ever occurs in a gold-embroidered bed, since abortionists have such skills and so many potions, and can bring about death of children in the womb."[88] In the early second century C.E. Soranus asked, "Who are the best midwives?" One sentence of his answer is the following: "she must not be greedy for money, lest she give an abortive wickedly for payment."[89] In 112 C.E. Pliny inquired of Trajan about the status of infants who were freeborn but had been exposed, an important problem throughout Asia Minor.[90] Pliny refers to an earlier edict of Augustus and to letters of Vespasian, Titus, and Domitian on the question in Greece, all emphasizing the importance of hearing claims of these formerly exposed persons to freedom. Trajan denied the right of the "nurturer" to compensation for expenses in bringing up the child, a decision later altered by Diocletian. A modern visitor to an ancient Roman city such as Herculaneum sees another reason for the low birth rate and early deaths: Pipes bringing water into these luxurious houses were made of lead! Tim Parkin stresses, more than other factors, simply the mentality that bachelorhood and childlessness brought advantages. (For further details, see his *Demography and Roman Society* [Baltimore: Johns Hopkins, 1992], 119–20.)

When a child was born, two decisions were made. A first, "medical" decision concerned whether it was perfect; if not they cut the umbilical cord short and let it hemorrhage to death.[91] Second came the father's decision, not the mother's, whether to raise the child.[92] Pagan writers were surprised and even offended that Jews raised all their children.[93] Therefore, the change from the pagan to the Christian values with respect to children was dramatic, a contrast of far-reaching significance. From Jews,[94] Christians[95] took over the value that infanticide was murder, and on Feb. 7, 374 C.E., the Christian emperor Valentinian made killing an infant a capital crime.[96] Karl Marx wrote: "We can forgive Christians much, for they taught us to love children."[97]

After birth, doctors agreed, a baby ought to be swaddled: Soranus[98] recommended wrapping it on a pillow in the cradle, fingers straightened and bandaged so that they could not be twisted, arms tied tightly at the wrists and elbows, then the legs and head. Its movement should be restricted this way for two months. Each day nurses would also reshape the head, nose, and a boy's penis, which would later be seen at baths and at the gymnasium. Doctors complained that women of the lower classes refused to follow their advice, but bathed newborn bodies too often, would not wrap them in bandages, rocked them when they cried, and nursed to soothe them.[99]

Richard Saller argues persuasively that these babies were born into nuclear families, not often into extended ones. However, Wallace-Hadrill[100] suggests that the majority of the population lived in "big houses," socially promiscuous "housefuls," so that many nuclear families would live with others, slaves, apprentices, workers, freedmen, clients, and so on in a house that did not distinguish architecturally or decoratively between space for males and females, or adults and children, although free and slave quarters were seemingly separate. In what would be to moderns a home without privacy, children spun their tops and played with nuts in the atrium, the same space in which adult males conducted business and women spun wool until after dark, when children often slept with servile nursemaids and tutors.[101]

These nuclear families themselves were generally small, with only one to three children surviving infancy. Cornelia, mother of the infamous Gracchi, bore an unusually large number, twelve, but only three survived.[102] Augustus's daughter Julia bore five children to Agrippa, and one of them (Agrippina senior) bore nine children to Germanicus, of whom six survived.[103] After Nero, the imperial family failed to produce a natural heir for a century, until Marcus Aurelius's son Commodus. By two laws in 18 B.C.E. and 9 C.E. the *lex Julia de maritandis ordinbus* and *lex Papia Poppaea,* Augustus obliged couples to have children or they would forfeit any legacies, which would go instead to relatives who did have children, a penalty that obviously concerned rich, not poor, families. Men who lived with concubines (women of status inferior to their husbands, with whom, therefore, a legal marriage was impossible) lost their rights of inheritance.

Perhaps a third of the babies born died before they reached ten years of age. We may properly compare Rome with other preindustrial societies, in which half the children do not live to see their fifth birthday, and only 40 percent reach age twenty. "In other words, each couple needed to have five children if two of them were to reach the age of having children themselves."[104] It is not impossible to understand why Greco-Roman parents were not as romantic about children as are modern ones.

In the cities in which Paul preached and the Gospels were written, elite culture depended on the peasants tied to the soil and the seasons. Children of the latter began to work when they were strong enough, learning by doing. For girls and boys, slaves and free, this would include reading, writing, and counting,[105] although our sources do not give much information concerning these children.

Mothers were the primary caregivers of young children. Between seven and sixteen or seventeen the father and often a tutor (*paedagogus*) took over education of the children, until the time when the upper-class son would be given the adult toga and might study with a rhetorician or a philosopher. Judith Hallett emphasizes too the emotional relationship between Roman fathers and daughters, which had far-reaching consequences for Roman politics. After 200 B.C.E. Greek influence grew in Rome, which sometimes meant special schools apart from the home. The child learned reading, writing, and arithmetic early, then in the final three or four years of home schooling, he might be taught language and poetry by a grammarian (*grammaticus*). Even in Rome, these subjects were often taught in Greek by Greeks, so that such Romans were bilingual. Only in the time of Augustus did Latin begin to compete with Greek.

Wiedemann[106] points out an important difference between the Latin word for skill, *ars,* and the Greek, *techne;* the Latin word does not denote merely technical or managerial skills like the Greek one. For Romans, acquired moral virtues are also *artes,* as are political skills. The Greek word was not used to refer to aspects of behavior, but for Romans, even military and rhetorical abilities were skills to be learned by practice, not just by theory. In Rome, even war was learned by watching and participating, not by theory from handbooks, which were produced rather by Greeks.

Opinions and practices differed over how to raise these young men, whether discipline should be severe or lax. The normally severe Stoic Cicero defends his young friend Caelius, who had been involved in an affair with the infamous courtesan Claudia. Just as race horses in the circus encounter difficulties negotiating the curve and often stumble, so also do young men before they settle on the straight path. But after his passionate youth, this young man will grow up to be a responsible citizen, father, and orator.[107] Cicero's view in this legal case contrasts with that of the disciple of Plutarch who wrote in "The Education of Children" that everything possible must be done to keep young people in check and to give them guidance (12A–D).

These contrasting ways of bringing up children are reflected also in Terence, *The Brothers*.[108] One brother, Demea, belongs to the older generation, is thrifty to a fault, and works his own farm, but his expansive brother Micio lives as a citizen in Athens. Demea has two sons, Aeschinus and Ctesipho. The rich Micio is a bachelor without an heir, so he invites Aeschinus, his brother Demeas's son, to Athens. Ctesipho remains with his father on the farm, is raised strictly, and becomes accustomed to hard work. On the contrary, Micio allows his young nephew Aeschinus complete freedom, and he soon develops into a fun-loving young Athenian. He seduces an honorable young Athenian woman, but Micio assists him, and they turn the scandal into a happy marriage: the lax upbringing has a good end. On the other hand, Demeas's strict discipline on the farm fails: despite his father's opposition, Ctesipho carries on with a prostitute. The strict Stoic philosopher and lawyer Cicero and the comedian Terence both encourage a very tolerant attitude toward the young.

Greco-Roman Education

One good way to gain insight into the Greco-Roman value system is to examine briefly the four Plutarchian tractates on education,[109] supplemented by Philo's earlier comments in "Preliminary Studies" on the relation between "lower instruction" (grammar, geometry, astronomy, rhetoric, music, etc.) and philosophy or wisdom, the pursuit of virtue.[110] Often only one of Plutarch's treatises, "The Education of Children" (actually written by a disciple) is commonly studied, but the other three also help clarify the similarities and especially the differences between ancient and modern education. This work begins by praising legitimate parentage, advising abstention from courtesans and concubines, giving advice about how best to conceive worthy children.[111] Later, however, the author argues that education is more important than birth, wealth, reputation, beauty, health, or strength (5DE). He insists that foster mothers and nurses must be Greek, so that the children may not be contaminated by barbarians or persons of low character (3E, 4A). He wants mothers themselves to nurse their children, observing that it facilitates bonding (3C).

When they are older, children must not be entrusted to pedagogues who are slaves taken in war or to barbarians (4A). But as was the thought on parentage, this too is modified at the very end of the tractate. The author commends the example of Eurydice, an Illyrian and an utter barbarian, who late in life took up education in the interest of her children's studies: "she gained her soul's desire to learn" (14B, trans. Babbitt in LCL)! The author thus challenges his audience with what they would regard as an extreme example (compare the function of the story of the exemplary mother of seven sons in 4 Maccabees). The author compares moral counsels and precepts to seed, and encourages children with fewer natural gifts (2A–3B). When the children are older and need a paedagogus, the author finds it necessary to give the following exhortation to fathers:

> Men, whither is your course taking you, who give all possible attention to the acquiring of money but give small thought to your sons to whom ye are to leave it? . . . Many fathers, however, go so far in their devotion to money (*philarguria*) as well as in animosity toward their children (*misoteknia*), that in order to avoid paying a larger fee, they select as teachers for their children men who are not worth any wage at all (4EF).

The author regrets that his advice seems to disregard the education of poor children, so that he may be writing only for the rich. Poor parents must make the best efforts they can to provide an education for their children (8E). Eyben[112] notes Lucian's call to young men of humble descent to follow in his—successful—footsteps by studying rhetoric (Lucian, *Somn.* 18). But employing an unworthy, cheap pedagogue results in immoral children, whose many vices are listed (5B, 12A–D). For a modern reader, the uncertainty of this moralist about whether pederasts (older men's relationships with preadolescent children are under discussion, not equal relationships between male adults) ought to be allowed to have sex with the boys (*erontas ton paidon ean toutois suneinai*, 11D) is astounding. Here we see a radical difference between most ancient Greek opinion on the one hand, and most Roman as well as all Jewish, Christian, and modern opinion on the other hand, which judge such unequal relationships to be sexual abuse of a child.

Later the children would receive further education: Plutarch's disciple opposes rhetoric (6A–7C) and opts for philosophy (7C, 8A), which teaches what is honorable and what shameful:

that one ought to reverence the gods, to honor one's parents, to respect one's elders, to be obedient to the laws, to yield to those in
authority, to love one's friends, to be chaste with women, to be affectionate with children, and not to be overbearing with slaves,
and most important of all, not to be overjoyful at success or over-
much distressed at misfortune, nor to be dissolute in pleasures,
nor impulsive and brutish in temper (7E).

The author then gives and explains some enigmatic Pythagorean alle-
gories as moral exhortations (12D–F), and counsels fathers not to be
harsh and austere (13D), but to restrain their anger. Fathers should also
make an effort to "yoke in marriage" those whose desires are inflamed
and who do not otherwise listen to admonitions (13F), but their wives
are not to be women who are far above them in birth or wealth. Fathers
should be an example, a mirror, for their children.

Some of this sounds very modern: The fathers are stereotypically ab-
sorbed in their work and pay little attention to their children. Ancient
Greeks clearly emphasized character formation much more than do our
modern secular schools, although the Greek tolerance of pederasts is
shocking. Clearly, too, the Gospels and Paul are in high tension with
the ethnic and cultural elitism promoted and produced by Greco-
Roman education—this is not a comment about what our churches
have consistently practiced through the centuries but a contrast with
what we read that Jesus and Paul taught. It raises the question about
whether and how much the church succumbed to these elitist values.
Finally, this pseudo-Plutarchian tractate concerns primarily fathers'
education of sons, except for the concluding and climactic example of
Eurydice. We know that Plutarch himself argued that women too
should be educated,[113] although the Plutarchian fragments we have
hardly relate to the title of the work.

A second Plutarchian tractate on education is probably also by a disciple: "On Music" (1131B–1147A). Aline Rousselle[114] emphasizes the
sensory aspects of Greco-Roman education beginning with childhood
and continuing throughout life, another significant contrast with most
modern education. Gym, music, singing, and the visual arts were central to their lives in a way that is foreign to most modern Westerners,
and histories of education, for example, Marrou's, do not usually communicate this difference. Both rhetoric and music involved physical fit-
ness: the Greek doctor Oribassius wrote that if a man is tired, he can
substitute declamation and exercising the voice for the morning walk
or for work![115] In the final three or four years of home schooling, the
children might study with a *grammateus,* who essentially taught epic,
iambic, elegiac, or lyric poetry, which older adults could still declaim

from memory! These were vocal exercises that extended the low and high range of one's voice. In the gymnasium, students did breathing and singing exercises before tackling such texts.

The work is a historical treatise (cf. 1136D) treating the invention and development of various kinds of music. Students first study the sound of letters, then music, which includes hymns to the gods, so such study is an act of piety (1131D). The earliest forms were simple, without any modulation from one harmony or rhythm to another (1133B), but later Sacadas of Argos composed music that modulated between Dorian, Phrygian, and Lydian tunes (1134A). Further developments led to corruption, and the earlier, graver music dear to the gods was abandoned (1136B). The more ancient music molded the minds of the young to a graceful bearing and helped them meet the challenges of war (1140BC; 1145EF). So ancient music focused on honoring the gods and educating the young, not on entertainment in the theater (1140DE). In this skill, too, philosophy is to be one's guide (1142D), a consistent Plutarchian theme, for music produces moral character (1143B, D; 1146B). It helps us give "grateful return of thanks to the gods . . . and composes the soul in purity, in sureness of tone, and in harmony" (1146D). Philo similarly observes that "music will charm away the unrhythmic by its rhythm, and thus reduce discord to concord" ("Preliminary Studies" 16).

The third of Plutarch's tractates, "How to Study Poetry," discussed what the "grammarian" should teach the teenage child. "Poetry" here means primarily Homer, but also Hesiod, Pindar, Theognis, Aeschylus, Sophocles, Euripides, and Menander.[116] Plutarch wants to give his and his friend's sons oversight in such reading and above all, to blend philosophy with this poetry, because "many the lies the poets tell" (16A, trans. Babbitt in LCL). "Whenever, therefore, in the poems of a man of note and repute some strange and disconcerting statement either about gods or lesser deities or about virtue is made by the author, he who accepts the statement as true is carried off his feet, and has his opinions perverted" (16D).

Whenever one reads in the *Iliad* that Zeus weighed the fates of Achilles and Hector and predetermined Hector's death, this is obviously myth fabricated to please the hearer, but we do not need to share the poet's delusion regarding the gods (17AB; cf. 34A). When we read of visits to Hades, of blazing rivers, and of grim punishments, this too is myth and falsehood, even if believed by Homer, Pindar, and Sophocles (17B). Such feelings disturb us, but we should equip the young with the maxim that "poetry is not greatly concerned with the truth" (17E), and that such questions stagger even philosophers such as Socrates in Plato's *Phaedo*.

Poetry is analogous to painting, which may even depict unnatural acts. In such a case, what Plutarch commends is not the action but the art, repudiating such actions (18B, D). Authors create unnatural and mean persons to discredit their actions and words, and sometimes the poet himself hints that these are distasteful (19A). Or it may be clear from the actions themselves. Another method of interpretation is to notice the mutual contradictions among the poets. When Euripides writes that the gods defeat our plans, the interpreter may quote his other line to the contrary: "If gods do aught that's base, they are no gods" (21A; cf. 23DE; 24BC). If Sophocles praises wealth, he also wrote that "to beg (*ptochos*) doth not degrade a noble mind" (21B; cf. 23F–24A, E; 34D). If the poet does not offer a solution himself, we may cite declarations of other well-known writers (21D). When Theognis wrote, "any man that is subject to poverty never is able either to speak or to act," Bion replied, "How is it then, that you, who are poor, can talk much nonsense and weary us with this rubbish?" (22A).

> Poetry is an imitation of character and lives, and of men who are not perfect or spotless or unassailable in all respects [Plutarch against the Stoics], but pervaded by emotions, false opinions, and sundry forms of ignorance, who yet through inborn goodness frequently change their ways for the better [in 26D and 27A Plutarch writes "repent"] (26A).

One must fear shame, not death (30E); it is good to master anger (31A), and so on.

There is not space to continue giving examples, but clearly, the "grammarian" teaches young teenagers about philosophy, that is, theology and ethics, in ancient and contemporary literature. Pythagoras and Plato may possibly agree with what children read in poetry (35F). So from Plato they will learn that "to do wrong is worse than to be wronged" (*Gorgias* 473A ff.) and "to do evil is more injurious than to suffer evil" (*Republic,* end of book I; 36A). So the child will not be "stuffed with what he has heard always from his mother and nurse, and, I dare say, from his father and tutor (*paidagogos*) as well, who all beatify and worship the rich, who shudder at death and pain, who regard virtue without money and repute as quite undesirable and a thing of naught" (36E).

Finally, as in the tractate on educating children, here too there is the characteristic, radical distinction between Greeks and barbarians, for example, "it is a trait of barbarian peoples to make supplication and to fall at the enemy's feet in combat, but of Greeks to conquer or to die fighting" (30C; cf. 29F). Greeks taught their children that they belonged to the elite. This elitism aside (we hope), Plutarch's "grammarians" who teach critical philosophical ethics have some counterparts in modern private religious schools, few in modern American secular ones.

The hellenistic Jew Philo agrees with his middle-Platonist colleague Plutarch about the function of "grammar," the study of literature in the poets and historians ("Preliminary Studies," 15; cf. 74, 142, 148).[117] The goal of the whole of education, with philosophy/wisdom at its apex, is theology ("Prelim.," 49, 105, 133) and ethics ("Prelim.," 65, 79–107), to have the "courage to say, God and God alone must I honour, not aught of what is below God" (133).

Fourth and finally, Plutarch advised young men of sixteen or seventeen who had finished home schooling and begun to wear the *toga virilis*, the garment of the adult male citizen, to learn by listening to philosophers in "On Listening to Lectures" (literally "On Hearing").[118] These teens were no longer subject to the authority of tutors, so Plutarch advises them not to be subject to the harsh master of desire, but to follow God and obey reason, the same thing, and the only way to be "free" (37D). Since the grammarian has already introduced him to philosophy, the new course will feel like an old familiar friend (37F). Still, some remarks are necessary for, as Theophrastus wrote, hearing is the most emotional of all the senses, although this sense is more rational than emotional, for virtue takes hold of the young through the ears (38A). This tract includes Plutarch's own remarks as a teacher of irresponsible students, whom he insists have duties as listeners to lectures (45CDE): The work concludes, "right listening is the beginning of right living" (48D). There are both great possibilities and also dangers in listening: The result may be egotistical, ignorant students who want a great reputation but have not learned (38DE; cf. Philo, "Prelim.," 64–70). Further,

> it is the easiest thing in the world to find fault with one's neighbor, . . . (but) everyone ought to be ready ever to repeat to himself, as he observes the faults of others, the utterance of Plato, "Am I not possibly like them?" (40D; cf. 42AB, 43B, E, 46C–F).

> In praising a speaker we must be generous, but in believing his words cautious; as touching the style and the delivery of the performers, we should observe with a kindly and simple mind; but as for the utility and truth of what they say, we must play the keen and heartless critics, that . . . their words may do no harm (41A; cf. 45A).

Anticipating the next section, we observe that children were also taught their proper role as masters, how they were to relate to slaves. Some other children were exposed by their parents and brought up as slaves. As we will see later, Jews and Christians also owned slaves; therefore, both taught their children how to treat slaves.

Slavery in the
Greco-Roman World

Modern democratic Westerners have great difficulty imagining the human relationships involved in ancient Greco-Roman and in pre–Civil War American slavery, but however surprising to us, persons in ancient society had the opposite difficulty of imagining an economic system without them. Not until after the Industrial Revolution produced machines that could do much of the work formerly done by slaves did moralists raise serious questions about the institution of slavery itself, and only then did French and American abolitionists reject it. It is mistaken to interpret earlier human history with an abolitionist ethic in mind, to project post–Industrial Revolution abolitionist values back onto an earlier age. Neither Greek philosophers nor early Christians advocated abolishing the institution of slavery. There were many slaves in early Christian communities, although their social roles were quite different than those of slaves in eighteenth- and nineteenth-century North America; for example, in Rome slaves were not allowed to marry, they were employed in virtually all the professions, they were individually manumitted, and no one race was enslaved.

Thought and Practice:
Philosophy

In early Greek comedy, slavery was a personal misfortune that could arouse pity in the audience, but it was not understood as a social evil. In the fourth century B.C.E. Alcidamus concluded that God made all free, that nature made no person a slave, an opinion later rejected by Aristotle.[119] We do not know what social consequences Alcidamus might have drawn; later Roman legal writers also assumed slavery to be unnatural, for example, but nevertheless, regulated it in detail. Plato[120] tells Socrates that the slave must suffer injustice and has no one to turn to for aid. But then later in his *Laws*, Plato proposed strict legislation for manumitted slaves: They still owed services to their former masters and should be punished if they would not perform them, a *paramone* kind of manumission.[121]

Aristotle was the first Greek philosopher or social scientist to discuss slavery as a social institution within the political system. The city-state is the most supreme good, and it is composed of households, which in turn are composed of "master and slave, husband and wife, father and children,"[122] the same three pairs that are exhorted by deutero-Pauline writers in Colossians and Ephesians. The manager of the household needs tools, including some living tools such as a slave who is "a live article of property," "by nature a slave."[123] The husband-father-master "by nature" rules the household because he possesses reason, Aristotle affirms, while others are ruled by feelings, although they may participate to some extent in reason.[124]

Seneca is a later Latin Stoic who discussed "the treatment of slaves, towards whom we Romans are excessively haughty, cruel, and insulting,"[125] not whether slavery itself can be justified. To imaginary interlocutors protesting, "but they are slaves," he replied:

> Nay, rather they are men. "Slaves!" No, comrades. "Slaves!" No, they are unpretentious friends. "Slaves!" No, they are our fellow slaves, if one reflects that Fortune has equal rights over slaves and free men alike. (*Ep.* 1)

> . . . he whom you call your slave sprang from the same stock, is smiled upon by the same skies, and on equal terms with yourself breathes, lives, and dies. It is just as possible for you to see in him a free-born man as for him to see in you a slave. (ibid., 10)

However, when he had some influence over the young emperor Nero, Seneca's sentiments did not produce legislation protecting slaves, which has led some to accuse him of hypocrisy. He seems more concerned about the master's ethics than about the abuse of slaves. "The fact is that philosophical disputes were purely abstract, cerebral affairs, utterly divorced from the world of lived reality."[126] Juvenal[127] also exhibits significant concern about the treatment of slaves in the first century C.E.

Both these Greek and Latin philosophers as well as the contemporary scholar K. R. Bradley argue that slavery is primarily "a social institution in which the economic aspect, though important, was subsidiary."[128] Owners gained benefits from their ability to control and coerce their slaves. Bradley argues that "from a legal point of view the Latin words for power (*potestas*) and slave ownership (*dominium*) could be regarded as synonymous, which means that, above all, slave owning was an expression of power."[129] This power was especially visible in Roman triumphs when defeated enemies were paraded as slaves from the Campus Martius to the Capitoline hill, some of them being executed. Bradley also observes that slaves often appear in Roman funeral processions, slaves who had just been set free by their former owners, proof of the slave owners' generosity. The economic factor was not primary for Roman masters and slaves because slaves did not all belong to one class or race.

Sources and
Numbers of Slaves

Beginning about 350 B.C.E. under the Roman republic, wars especially but also piracy sent many slaves westward, which meant that ranches and industry expanded significantly through this form of labor.[130] These victims included Jews: Clashes between Jews in Judea and Samaritans during the reign of Ptolemy Epiphanes (204–181 B.C.E.) resulted in some of the former being enslaved.[131] Antiochus IV Epiphanes, himself needing to pay tribute to the Romans, was prepared to sell thousands of Jews to slave traders when he marched into Judea in 172 B.C.E.,[132] but instead, Judas Maccabeus defeated him. After the war against the Jews won by Vespasian in 70 C.E., nearly one hundred thousand Jews were reduced to slavery.[133] Again after Hadrian suppressed the Jewish revolt in the early second century, another large number were sold; "Hadrian's Market at Gaza remained a vivid memory for centuries."[134] When Augustus established peace with the result that prisoners of war were no longer available, the children of slaves bred within the household and abandoned children became primary sources of slaves.[135] "The height of Western slavery, both in numbers of slaves employed and in the social results of the system is to be placed in the first century B.C.E."[136] Thereafter into the fourth and fifth centuries C.E. there was a decrease in the number of slaves.

The number and percentage of the enslaved population in the Greco-Roman world is debated. In various parts of the Roman world, the percentage of slaves differed significantly. In the first century C.E. in Pergamon in Asia Minor, his home city, Galen estimated that there was a slave for every two adult citizens, so 33 percent; but in the rural villages of Egypt, the number was much lower, below 7 percent.[137] Whereas the earlier Italian slave population had not exceeded 10 percent,[138] Keith Hopkins has estimated that there were about two million slaves in the empire, equal to about 35 percent of the full population.[139] There was significant *downward* mobility in the Roman empire!

The modern prejudice based on skin color seems to have been lacking in the Greek world. And the number of Ethiopian or black slaves even in Egypt was small.[140]

Professions of Slaves

Many slaves were used in agriculture, but in an urban context, their professions were as diverse as those of the free workers. Dale Martin[141] emphasizes that there was inconsistency between some slaves' professions and their legal status; he clarifies our understanding of Roman society by placing slaves *within* the patron-client social system. Some slaves who managed powerful masters' resources (*oikonomoi* or *pragmateutai*) were *patrons* of free, but less wealthy or politically powerful, persons, who became their clients.

Legally slaves owned nothing, but they could control a *peculium,* money or property that the head of a household set apart for sons or slaves. With this *peculium* they could run businesses. There were famous examples of such slave managers in the emperor's household, especially under Claudius and Nero, but analogous relationships existed all over the empire. Quoting both epitaphs on tombs and dedicatory inscriptions, Martin demonstrates[142] that many managerial slaves supported dependents, an economic structure built on the power, influence, and resources of the master, analogous to the master's other clients' businesses. The social status of these few managerial slaves, then, was determined more by the slaves' relation to a powerful master and by their profession than by their legal status. In the city, they sometimes lived independently of the master. Sometimes they managed one of the shops on the street in the front of the master's house.[143] In a tomb used by Augustus's wife Livia's household, inscriptions list fifty different jobs, different in degree but not in kind from other households.[144]

Particularly interesting, as one example, are some wax tablets found in the house of Julius Caecilius Jucundus, a banker in Pompeii.[145] Five of these record a series of loans to C. Novius Eunus, who borrowed 10,000 sesterces from Ti. Iulius Evenus Primianus, an imperial freedman, with Hesychus, his managerial slave, handling the whole affair, making the loan, accepting grain as collateral, and arranging the interest of 1 percent per month. Some days later Hesychus rented a portion of a warehouse to store the grain from C. Novius Cypaerus, not directly but through the warehouse owner's slave manager. The same day Novius borrowed an additional 3,000 sesterces, but this time from the slave Hesychus, not from his master. The next document is dated about a year later in 38 C.E.: Hesychus remains a slave, not of Evenus, but now in the imperial service; he again lends Novius money, 1,130 sesterces, a loan he renews again the following year. Since he has powerful, wealthy owners, Hesychus is able to increase his own social and economic position, in the process becoming the patron of a free businessperson. Hesychus's profession and social position was more important than and inconsistent with his legal status. This slave's position in Pompeii presumably had analogies in other cities in the Roman Empire.

Slaves' clothes did not set them apart; they wore what was appropriate to their job and their master's generosity.[146] Because the toga worn by citizens was reserved for formal occasions and slavery was not identified with any one race in Rome, the difference between slave and free was not immediately obvious from the clothes they wore.

Children of Slaves

Greeks opposed self-sale or the sale of one's children into slavery, which was made illegal by Solon,[147] but in Asia and Egypt it was customary. A man could pledge his wife, children, or himself against a debt; sale into slavery would follow on nonpayment. This continued in Ptolemaic Egypt and in Seleucid lands.[148]

Control of Slaves:
Marriages and Auctions

Cato, in the second century B.C.E. suggested no provisions for family life of slaves, but a century later because of enlightened self-interest, Varro does[149]: A slave with a family life will be bound to the estate and produce slave children, an increase in the owner's property. Slaves lived together, but that did not mean that their relationship was legally recognized as marriage, a possibility only for free citizens. In 52 C.E. the *senatus consultum Claudianum* specified that if a free woman continued to live with a slave when the slave's owner forbade it, she and her children would become the slaves of the owner. Yet the sexual relationship of a free man with his female slave was not regulated by law.

William Westermann notes that promiscuous, sometimes brutal, sexual indulgence with slave women becomes noticeable in Roman historical sources during the last two centuries of the republic.[150] Cato in his old age took a young slave as mistress,[151] and he encouraged paid prostitution of his male slaves with his women slaves in lieu of family ties.[152] C. Antonius, consul in 63 B.C.E., bought a slave girl in the market to serve his desires,[153] and a friend temporarily supplied Marcus Crassus with two slave girls.[154]

Westermann[155] argues that in the first century C.E. there was a new respect for slaves' family relations, exemplified by the Stoic Seneca, by Petronius, and Pliny the Younger, but not caused either by Stoicism or Christianity. Bradley agrees that there is a new emphasis on servile family relations, but more realistically underlines the limited economic motivations.

> The foremen are to be made more zealous by rewards, and care must be taken that they have a bit of property of their own, and mates from among their fellow-slaves to bear them children; for by this means they are made more steady and more attached to the place.[156]

> But be the overseer what he may, he should be given a woman
> companion to keep him within bounds and yet in certain matters
> to be a help to him.[157]

Bradley inquires about the stability of these relationships, about how secure they were. Since slaves were property, they could be sold, transactions over which they had no control. Bradley examines records of these transactions among Egyptian papyri. He notices, first, that the great majority of sales were of individuals, and second, that "the Egyptian evidence offers no example at all of the sale together of a husband and wife, or of a husband, wife and children."[158] Slave owners seem not to have considered preserving family ties when selling their property, and the probability is very high that the slaves' family ties were severed. This possibility would have then been part of the slaves' psychology, open to manipulation by the masters. Further, Bradley examines the ages at which females were sold and finds that the masters sold them during their child-producing years; in fact, there is "no example on record of a female slave being sold who might not have been expected to bear children after sale."[159] So the potential for breeding these women was important for both sellers and buyers. By emphasizing the masters' manipulation of slaves' hopes for a family, Bradley criticizes the position of Westermann among others that Roman slavery was relatively mild. Finally, indeed, in the fourth century C.E. Constantine stipulated that when inherited estates were divided, parent and child, husband and wife, brother and sister, were not to be separated; and those who had been were to be reunited.[160] Nevertheless, slaves were so stigmatized throughout the period that there was no real marital or social improvement for slaves in pagan or in Christian society.[161]

In epitaphs slaves use the same terms of endearment and the same terms for spouse (*coniunx*), wife (*uxor*), husband (*maritus*), mother and father, son and daughter, brother and sister as are used in epitaphs set up by free persons. Bradley[162] concludes that "servile attitudes towards marriage did not differ appreciably from those of the rest of society." Law did not determine their feelings.

The status of the couple's children was determined by the status of the mother at the time of the child's birth. If the mother had her first child while a slave, it too would be a slave; but if she were freed and then had a second child, it would be free. Diocletian finally prohibited the exposure of infant slaves.[163]

Punishment of Slaves

Galen writes of kicking and beating slaves, of knocking out their teeth or gouging out their eyes. He witnessed the wounding of two slaves by a traveling companion, which Westermann rather lightly dismisses as not so-cially countenanced since the slave owner was sorrowful. Jurists discussed whether a slave whose tongue had been cut out was "healthy," a legal con-dition of sale.[164] Slaves were degraded especially through sexual exploita-tion and physical abuse (see Quintillian, *Inst.* 5.11.34–35).[165] Courts regu-larly had slaves tortured for evidence.[166] Many killed themselves rather than be enslaved, or as slaves, they contemplated suicide.[167] Seneca in many passages[168] exhorts masters about the abuse of slaves, and Juvenal[169] worries about the effect on children who see slaves severely punished.

Excavations at Pompeii have produced iron and wooden stocks used to confine and punish slaves used in the wine-growing estates around that city.[170] The elder Cato writes of chaining rural slaves during the winter; Columella approves of healthy, underground jail rooms, *ergas-tula,* for the confinement, often in chains, of those who commit crimes[171]; such jails are not mentioned by Varro. The mistreatment of slaves was one of the major causes of the slave revolts in Sicily, 135–132 B.C.E. and 104–101 B.C.E., as described by Diodorus Siculus,[172] revolts that generated others in Italy, Athens, and Delos.[173] Hadrian passed leg-islation that abolished the ergastula for the punishment of slaves or free persons,[174] and the same emperor stipulated that only the courts, no longer slave owners, had the right to kill slaves.

The harshness of their life among other reasons led many slaves to run away, sometimes in small groups.[175] Owners advertised for help in finding these runaways.[176] It was the owners' responsibility to recover their own property, but they could usually count on support.

Slave owners generally perceived their slaves as criminal and intran-sigent. Columella lists their faults:

> They let out oxen for hire, and keep them and other animals poorly fed; they do not plough the ground carefully, and they charge up the sowing of far more seed than they have actually sown; what they have committed to the earth they do not so foster that it will make the proper growth; and when they have brought it to the threshing-floor, every day during the threshing they lessen the amount, either by trickery or by carelessness. For they themselves steal it and do not guard against the thieving of others, and even when it is stored away they do not enter it honestly in their accounts.[177]

This text and many others represent slaves in negative, moralistic terms.[178] Tacitus's interest in slaves concerns their loyalty and obedi-ence. As is generally true in this period, Romans tend to see lower class socially as also lower morally. Tacitus does praise some slaves: "The pe-riod was not so barren of merit that it failed to teach some good lessons as well. Mothers accompanied their children in flight, wives followed their husbands into exile. There were resolute kinsmen, sons-in-law who showed steadfast fidelity, and slaves whose loyalty scorned the rack."[179]

Manumission

In contrast to the severe treatment of slaves stands the increasingly frequent manumission of their slaves by Roman citizens, whose freedmen would themselves become citizens.[180] This practice stimulated such a backlash that in 177 B.C.E. magistrates required an oath that the motive was not to change the slave to citizen rank.[181] These new citizens joined one of the four country tribes, and later were restricted to membership in a single tribe.[182]

Slaves' Religion within the House

Under the supervision of the male and female head of the domus, the household gods, *Lares Familiares*, were worshiped and expected to protect all inhabitants of the house, including slaves.[183] The statues were placed in a niche that could be in the wall or the floor. Wall niches have an aedicula facade (a miniature temple with columns, perhaps on top of a podium) and often a projecting shelf. Some of these niches were in dining rooms,[184] but most were in courtyards or their porticoes[185] and in other accented rooms.[186] After Augustus many *collegia* of *cultores Larum*, often called *Lares domini* instead of Lares Familiares, are found among imperial slaves and freedmen, organizations free persons rarely joined.[187] Franz Bömer and Peter Herz suggest that slave and free persons were gradually divided in the cult of the Lares, which became as no other a "cult of slaves."[188]

They were worshiped on important occasions, especially Kalendae, Nonae, Idus, and the birthday of the paterfamilias. When Germanicus died in 19 C.E., Romans threw their statuettes of Lares Familiares into the streets, angry that the gods could not prevent his death[189]: Their future depended on the emperor, who would not be Germanicus.

Bömer and Herz argue that in religious practice, there was no boundary between free and slave; in social aspects, there was no visible difference; slaves who were freed continued worshiping divinities of their past.[190] Or the reverse: Some slaves had been free neighbors who fell into debt, or who were defeated in war. There was no closed religious world with particular goals, divinities, or rites of slave against free. However, among slaves the classical divinities are less important than are foreign and/or local divinities.

Slaves had been associated with certain collegia in the civil war leading up to the events of 64 B.C.E., when collegia were forbidden.[191] But
from the beginning of the first century C.E., slaves were ministers in the
household worship of the Lares and wore the *toga praetexta,* so appear
identical to those from great families who had high magistrates. Augustus reformed these household cults in 7 B.C.E., from which time the
year of the ministers was reckoned for the next 230 years.[192] In the middle of the first century B.C.E., free, freed, and slave had worshiped har-
moniously in the cult of the Lares, but according to Bömer and Herz,
this changed, and the domestic cult of the Lares became, as no other, a
cult controlled by slaves, nor did the Augustan reform change this.[193]
After Augustus's reform, organization, titles, and public documentation
became central, so it became more a means of social rather than of religious expression. Under the shelter of these Lares cults, funeral col-
leges formed to provide for the members' graves, thus escaping the prohibition of coalitions.[194] Despite the attack of the church fathers
(Tertulian, *Apology* 13.4), Bömer and Herz conclude that Christianity
had no great opponent here, since real spirituality had turned to other
divinities. It remains striking that many slaves' primary worship was inside the house within the collective family.

In summary, there were many agricultural slaves, but in an urban
context, their professions were about as diverse as those of free persons.
Dale Martin emphasizes a group important for understanding early
Christian ekklesiai, the slave managers, whose professions made them
patrons of some free persons, so that these slaves' social/economic status and their legal status were inconsistent.

Within the household, slaves worshiped and had status. Westermann sees increased respect for slaves' family relations, but this seems
to have had primarily economic motivations: owners could manipulate
slaves by holding out the hope for a family and for manumission, but
when they sold slaves, they did not value or help slaves maintain family connections.

Family Religion

Among the many forms that religion took in the Greco-Roman city,
family religion played an important part. This importance of household
and family religion would translate easily into household assemblies for
Christians. If the principle holds that every social group was also a religious association,[195] then every kinship group was a worshiping
group. The oikos/domus was a center of worship with its male head
(*kyrios/paterfamilias*) as head of the cult, the wife (*kyria/materfamilias*)

also playing an important role. It is probably because of this integral part played by the wife and mother in the family cult that Plutarch advises that, no matter what gods a bride previously worshiped, at marriage she should cease to worship any but those of her husband.[196]

This was an ideal certainly not widely observed, but only the exclusive claims of Judaism and Christianity would have caused a major problem. In all other cases, private devotions were entertained over and above those of family and state, though the paterfamilias in theory always had the authority to prevent anyone in the household from engaging in activities of which he did not approve. Christians seem quite early to have run into this problem, but we hear of it only as a de facto situation in which one spouse is already Christian and the other is not (1 Cor. 7:12–16; 1 Peter 3:1), an indication of the actual religious independence of household members to pursue devotions beyond that of the household.

Everyone in the familia belonged to the family cult, including children and slaves,[197] and in Roman religion, the whole household gathered daily to invoke the protection of its special deities and ancestors. In this way, the present family was connected with its past members. Family festivities included celebrations of special occasions like weddings, births, and funerals and regular yearly festivals like birthdays and commemoration of the dead.

Weddings included a banquet and the processional accompaniment of bride and groom from bride's family house to groom's house, where the bride anointed the doorposts, was lifted over the threshold, and was offered fire and water by the groom as symbols of her domestic authority.[198] Traditional dress for a Roman bride included reddish-yellow shoes and veil of the same color. Once arrived in the new house, husband and wife retired to the marriage bed (*lectus genialis*). The next day, the bride presided as materfamilias over the domestic worship. She assumed responsibility for both the goods and the virtue of the household.[199]

Soon after birth, the Roman child was placed on the ground, perhaps to communicate to it the power of the earth, to make it grow.[200] It is generally understood that the lifting from the earth, usually done by the father, signified the child's acceptance into the family, the alternative being exposure.[201] Births were celebrated in Roman custom on the *dies lustricus*, the eighth (for a boy) or ninth (for a girl) day after birth, when the naming of the child took place and he or she was welcomed into the family.[202] The fact that the first eight days after birth were believed to be full of danger for both mother and child speaks not only of belief in the malevolent aspects of the spirit world but also of the known health risks of childbirth and newborn status, and of the high infant mortality rate.

Funerals in Roman custom included ritual preparation of the body of the deceased, burial, perhaps a ritual banquet at the site immediately after burial, and some kind of purificatory rites afterward because of the contamination caused by contact with a corpse. Then a period of nine or ten days of mourning ensued, ended by a ritual banquet also at the site. The solemn family duty of burying its dead did not end with the actual time of burial, however. On the yearly anniversary of death, family members gathered for a commemorative meal, at the cemetery if possible. Many private mausolea and common burial places had permanent dining couches to accommodate these ceremonies.[203] The custom had roots in the ancient Near East, was common in both Greek and Roman circles, and continued in Christian usage. Its origin was the concern for the continued care and feeding of the deceased by the living, hence its Latin name, *refrigerium,* or refreshment, for the dead were traditionally thought to be in a hot, dry climate not unlike that of the living, but to be able to be present at a meal in their honor with the living. An offering of food to the deceased and a libation of wine were therefore integral to the meaning of the meal.[204]

Either at the burial or at the yearly funerary meal, it was a later Roman custom to use—and perhaps to make for the occasion—special drinking glasses with gold-leaf design in the base. At the conclusion of the meal, the glass was broken and the base sunk into fresh plaster at the grave. This custom was taken over by Jews and Christians, who adapted it to their own religious devotions. Several hundred examples survive.[205]

Among favorite household gods were Hestia/Vesta, represented not in human form but by the presence of the hearth, tended by the women of the family. Janus, too, in Roman families, was venerated at the fauces ("jaws"), the narrow entrance passageway just inside the front door, for the transition point between outside and inside was symbolically important.[206] Favorite divine household patrons were commemorated; several were especially popular and appear with surprising frequency. Vesta, of course, had her primary residence in the House of the Vestals in the Roman Forum, and Janus was the public god of gates, and thus of new beginnings. These two examples illustrate the coherence between household and state: The household was the miniature reflection, the microcosm, of the state, which was the larger version, the macrocosm, of the household. What threatened one threatened the other, for they were both conceptually organized along the same lines.

The particular deities (*numina*) of a specific Roman household included the lares, the penates, and the *genius* of the *paterfamilias*. The origins of the lares are disputed, but they seem to have been originally malicious spirits, perhaps of the dead, that haunted the *compita* (crossroads) and had to be propitiated. At the feast of the *compitalia* at the winter solstice, little woolen effigies of family members, including a woolen ball for each slave, were hung at the crossroads, perhaps originally to distract the lares from harming the real people they represented. But by imperial times, the lares had also moved into houses, shops, and businesses as protective deities, usually depicted as celebratory dancing characters, worshiped in their own shrines, named lararia in their honor, though these shrines represented other deities as well. The *lar familiaris* was a tutelary deity who protected the entire family, and even accompanied the paterfamilias when he journeyed away from home. Other nondomestic lares guarded roads, maritime routes, armies, and the state itself.[207]

The *di penates* were spirits that resided in and protected the family pantry (*penus*), with its cupboards and storage bins, hence their primary responsibility for the food supply. They were worshiped with Vesta and the lares in the household. Their public counterparts, the *penates publici*, were likewise closely associated with the public cult of Vesta.[208] Besides daily veneration, the lares and penates also received on the first day of the month the more significant sacrifice of a piglet in those families wealthy enough to afford it.[209]

The image and role of the genius is obscure and shifting. The genius of a family was its living, guiding spirit, especially resident in the family's paterfamilias, whom it accompanied when he traveled. This genius was part of the family cult, and sacrifices to it were performed not only by the family, but also by guests when they attended dinner in the house.[210] The special feast of the genius was the birthday of the paterfamilias. The genius was perhaps the *numen* represented in serpent form in lararia, especially the imaginary portrayal of the male snake as crested and bearded, which does not occur in nature. Snakes, however, were generally positive, figures that could have many meanings in lararium art, especially that of warding off evil. In later Roman religion every male seems to have had a genius, and every woman the female counterpart, a *Juno,* though the assignment of a genius to a woman is also attested. According to Horace, the genius is mortal, like the person it protects.[211] The Roman people and the emperor also had in later times their particular genius. It was to this guiding spirit of the emperor that public sacrifice was regularly offered—the sacrifice from which Jews were exempt in favor of a daily sacrifice for the emperor's welfare in the Jerusalem Temple, and which Christians refused to perform.

The evidence of Roman houses that has survived, in Delos, Spain, Britain, and northern Europe, but especially in Pompeii, Herculaneum, and Ostia, has yielded abundant archaeological evidence of these family cults in the form of lararia: wall paintings, niches, podia, and aediculae that formed the center of family worship, and in which family gods were depicted and venerated.[212] They were often located in the atrium, peristyle, or kitchen, though they are also found in other places in the house.[213] Not only private houses had such shrines, however, for they are also found in apartment buildings, workshops, inns, bakeries and drinking establishments, as well as wayside shrines at the *compita* (crossroads). Their presence even in modest apartments tells us that family cults were not limited to wealthy inhabitants of a domus.

On special days, the shrines were adorned with garlands and decorated with nuts, fruits, and flowers. Surviving evidence is of serpents (who may represent the genius of the head of the household), heads of ancestors, and dancing lares and penates, usually in Greek dress and carrying a *rhyton* (horn-shaped vessel) filled with wine. They are the abiding proof of the ways in which religion penetrated everyday life, the ancestors of the wayside shrines and family altars of Mediterranean families today.

One of these household shrines in an upper-floor apartment of the so-called House of the Bicentenary[214] at Herculaneum seems to have consisted of a shelf with bottom vertical support attached to the wall above a wooden podium. When the shelf was torn off, either by a fleeing owner or by the force of the mudslide that inundated the city, the impression left on the wall closely resembles a "tau" cross, that is, crossbeams shorter than the vertical lower branch, and no upper branch. This remnant, among other pieces of circumstantial evidence, has given rise to speculation, but no conclusions, about the presence of Christians in the cities of Vesuvius.[215] It is quite possible that there were Christians there, since Acts depicts Christians active in Campania (Acts 28:13–14). But the use of the cross as visual symbol is otherwise wholly unattested for the first several Christian centuries, and is unlikely to be a Christian symbol here.

There is a wider question to raise with regard to Christians, however. Given the ubiquitous practice of household religion, and its pervasive presence in daily family life, did Christians simply live in the midst of it all, despising the whole practice as idolatry? Or did they gradually begin to adapt their own forms of domestic piety, long before we have any evidence of it, using either symbols or images of religious figures in worship? No distinctive Christian art has been identified before the end of the second century. Could Christian families have held out for over a century in the Roman world without creating their own images of faith? That is an intriguing question that can become nothing more unless and until further evidence is discovered.

PART 2

Early Christian Families and House Churches

4

Social Location
of Early Christians

In order better to understand the social experience of early Christian families, we must understand something of their position in the social system. Social location refers not only to class, status, and economic level but also to characteristic attitudes and perspectives born of social identifications. Of course, not all early Christians lived in identical social locations, but much study has been put into ascertaining exactly what we can know of their place in the society of the ancient Greco-Roman Mediterranean world. What follows is a summary of that study as it can illumine our understanding of the ancient Christian family.

The Structures
of Greco-Roman Society

It is not sufficient to ask about social "class," a notoriously elusive concept, much less about vague terms like "upper class" and "lower class," whose meaning is heavily determined by the specific expectations of a culture. Class is a sociological concept that includes persons somehow assimilable to each other beyond distinctions of age, sex, or profession, but as a category, it is not susceptible to exact definition and is often rendered by subjective judgment. In modern Western societies, class is strongly dependent on economic level and ideally gravitates to the great "middle class." Sociologists of ancient societies now readily agree that nothing similar existed in antiquity. Similarly, the use of Marxist analysis would place all who have the same relationship to the means of production in the same "class," which would not work at all in the ancient world.[1]

For ancient Greco-Roman society, within which the first Christians lived, M. I. Finley proposes rather to speak of two other classifications, order (*ordo*) and status. "An order or estate is a juridically defined group within a population, possessing formalized privileges and disabilities in one or more fields of activity, governmental, military, legal, economic, religious, marital, and *standing in a hierarchical relation to other orders.*"[2] In contrast to class, an order is juridically defined and testable by objective norms. In Roman society, the old distinction between patricians and plebeians was obsolete long before the imperial period, and the prominent orders (*ordines*) were the senatorial and equestrian families. Senatorial families were technically those who could count a senator within three generations. Because privilege was generally preserved across generations, in effect, those senatorial families that perpetuated themselves also perpetuated their senatorial rank. But because of low birth rates, high mortality, and the reluctance of many aristocrats to raise many children, thus necessitating the breaking up of inheritance, the ordo itself was in continual need of replenishing from the provincial aristocracy.

Equestrians were formally defined in the late second century B.C.E. as non-senators with a minimum property of 400,000 sesterces—a modest but not extravagant fortune. During the reign of Tiberius, a further requirement was at least two previous generations freeborn—an indication of the growing social aspirations of freedmen. In the provinces, the decurion class and provincial aristocracy were comparably included among the elites. By the definition given, an order of freedmen/women existed, but was rarely significant. Practically, the notion of ordo was confined to the very small upper ranks of society, who constituted the elite in whose hands most power was concentrated. Citizenship too was an identifiable and verifiable classification, but became less significant as time went on. Citizenship conferred certain formal rights, but no guarantee that they could be exercised. It was not seen as a source of privilege, as is evidenced by the numbers of freed slaves of Roman citizens who received citizenship along with manumission. Thus, as Roman citizenship extended and the numbers of Roman citizens multiplied throughout the empire, there was no necessary loss of privilege in numbers, because such privilege in virtue of citizenship had never really existed. By 212 C.E., Roman citizenship had become sufficiently meaningless that it was extended to all free inhabitants of the empire.[3]

A more helpful distinction observable everywhere in the culture was that of "status," that is, importance and honor ascribed to an individual and family, which takes into account aspects such as birth and wealth, but also less tangible elements of character, personal power, and social connections. Status was the great obsession of Romans, which they attempted to demonstrate in social life, relationships, and architecture.[4] It is the key to understanding the real differentiations in Greco-Roman society. The inevitable snobbery produced by this keen sense of status is well documented.[5] Already, for example, within the elite senatorial class, the real access to social power was concentrated in a smaller group of families who could count a consul from their ranks.[6] Thus even the most elite group had become stratified along status lines.

Within every other definable group as well—freedmen and freedwomen, slaves, freeborn traders and craftspeople, for example—status was an ingrained concept that necessitated maintenance of certain appropriate norms of behavior and lifestyle in order to maintain personal and family honor. Freeborn laborers or artisans could and frequently did work alongside slaves for the same owner or manager, with similar relationships to their trade, yet their status was quite different. A responsible slave manager in the imperial service was inferior before the law to a humble freeborn or freed worker, yet superior in status because of whom he or she represented. Women were almost always socially disadvantaged in some way in comparison to men of equal rank, yet women of higher status were socially superior to men of lesser status.

Ancient Mediterranean society was very deliberately static. Ancestral ways were best, elites held tightly to their control of power and economic resources, and the socially privileged and disadvantaged tended to remain so. Yet the possibility for change and advancement was present through acquisition of wealth but, more important, through enhancement of status. As in any society, the two were not unrelated. But still, such possibility for status enhancement operated within limits. No matter how wealthy, a freedman, for example, would gain status vis-à-vis other less wealthy freedmen and perhaps freeborn persons of modest means, but would never attain elite status—though his son or grandson might. Stratification by ordo distinguished elites from nonelites and different legal categories from one another, but status differentiation and stratification worked more pervasively and far more subtly, within groups of equal rank, between families, within families, between friends. It made the patronage system not only possible but necessary, for superior status was access to power.

The other thing that must be stressed is that there was no "middle class" as we know it, a conclusion that can easily be reached by the modern reader who searches for something familiar between the aristocracy and the poorest classes. As has been stated in the discussion of class structure above, there was in this preindustrial agrarian society no middle class: an economically independent majority class of moderate to leisured economic levels, whose social status follows from economic status. This does not mean, however—a conclusion that is sometimes facilely drawn—that there were no economic levels between wealthy and the abjectly poor, nor does it mean that there were not ‿verished elite families[7] and some who rose from abject ‿comfortable means. On the contrary, there seems to have ‿een a good amount of variety in economic status in urban life, though the vast majority must have lived in biting poverty. The point is that neither class nor status was completely connected to economic level. Class was ascribed at birth, and status, a much more elusive concept, was a combination of birth, wealth, and personal and family achievement.

Yet other distinctions were developing during the first and second centuries to divide society more neatly. The language of stratification between the powerful (*potentiores*) and the weak or insignificant in society (*tenuiores*) denoted an informal and fluid distinction between those capable of exerting undue pressure based on prestige and wealth from those capable of being exploited and needing protection. Another growing distinction separated highborn (*honestiores*) from lowborn (*humiliores*), a division that was to have greatest applicability in the ways people were dealt with in courts of law. Roman citizenship, once a legal privilege, was less and less able to protect its humilior holder from severe punishment.[8] The social privilege of the honestiores virtually guaranteed that, if legal punishment fell upon them, it would be with dignity and often mitigated as much as possible: decapitation (*capitis amputatio*), the opportunity to commit suicide with honor and thus avoid the social shame of disgrace, or exile (*deportatio*), instead of crucifixion (*crux*), exposure to wild animals in the amphitheater (*bestiae*), burning alive (*crematio*), or condemnation to the mines (*metalla*)—humiliating and sometimes protractedly painful deaths.[9]

Certain exceptions are known. For example, in the first century, Tiberius condemned an equestrian to the treadmill out of spite for his patron, Livia, and Gaius (Caligula) sent many men of *honesti ordinis* to the mines and an equestrian to the beasts, but these were considered outrages, especially the brutality of Gaius. During the Jewish uprising, the Roman commander Gessius Florus at Jerusalem scourged and crucified Jews of equestrian rank; after reporting without comment the crucifixion of 3,600 men, women, and children, Josephus calls the crucifixion of the equestrians something that had never been done before. At the beginning of the third century, the young Christian matron Perpetua of Carthage was condemned to the beasts, even though she was *honeste nata* (highborn).[10]

The earlier exceptions demonstrate that the distinctions were by custom rather than law. It was the sense of what was fitting to persons because of their rank that dictated appropriate punishment, though magistrates and certainly emperors were free to decide as they wished. By the time of Antoninus Pius (138–161 C.E.), however, the distinction seems to have moved from custom and judicial procedure into law, to disappear only centuries later in the era of romanized barbarian law.[11] The incident of Perpetua's death happened later, and so is more difficult to explain, except that documented exceptions to known Roman laws previously enacted are fairly common. Local magistrates seem to have had wide latitude in their application.

Like most Roman legal concepts, the distinction between honestiores and humiliores was never hard and fast, but constantly fluctuating, depending at the edges on local and even personal sensibilities to the honor system. There can be little doubt that the legal system favored the interests of the privileged, however, based on criteria of honor or *dignitas* derived from power and wealth.[12]

Occupations, too, were classified according to status, at least from the viewpoint of the honestiores. Cicero considers many employments mean or vulgar (*sordidus*), for reasons relative to social ideals: tax collection and money lending, because they incur ill will; unskilled labor, because compensation is given for mere labor instead of skill; retail selling, because it is impossible to make a profit without lying; crafts because they are menial; and services that cater to sensual pleasure, such as that of butchers, cooks, and entertainers. The higher professions are those that require a higher level of intelligence and skill, and which benefit society: medicine, architecture, and advanced teaching. Trade is acceptable only if done in small quantity on the side. But the noblest and most dignified occupation is that of the gentleman farmer in agriculture.[13]

Cicero here reflects the general prejudices of the aristocrats (while he himself did a good deal of money lending, but only as a sideline). It is a common assumption of social historians, however, based on solid research, that aristocratic ideals are internalized by lower social groups to the extent that such groups are able to absorb them. Thus the ranking of occupations according to a perceived hierarchy of prestige was an integral part of the status system.

One way in which poorer people could organize and experience some kind of social support was through the various kinds of clubs or private associations that were widespread in the imperial era and often looked upon with suspicion by the authorities. Usually called a *collegium* in Latin, an *eranos* or *hetaireia* in Greek, these organizations were composed mostly of lower-class freeborn men and freedmen, though both slave and female membership is occasionally found. They were usually religious associations organized around a particular cult and sometimes also around a common occupation. They sometimes held responsibility for certain civic services, such as fire fighting.

Among the most common forms in the Roman West, though apparently not as common in the Greek East, were the burial societies of the poor, *collegia tenuiorum,* which met monthly for a common meal and had regular dues, the proceeds of which went toward the funeral of deceased members.[14] Through the years, there were various attempts to control and contain these associations by legislation and other forms of control. Already by the beginning of the first century C.E., a Julian law required that they be licensed, with the implication that some of them were feared to be hotbeds of political unrest.[15] These associations were apparently powerful enough to make the authorities leery, yet they lacked the ability to organize horizontally precisely because the patronage system encouraged only strong vertical ties.[16] Many of these associations also had wealthy patrons, male or female, who furnished funds and other resources, presided at meetings and banquets, sometimes hosted the association in their house, and whose presence reinforced the vertical differentiation of status. Therefore, while the associations provided one of the few ways for poorer people (mostly men) to experience some kind of parity in a social setting, nevertheless, they did not escape the hierarchical stratification of society at large.

There has long been discussion of the apparent similarity of these religious and social associations to Christian groups, especially in light of Tertullian's description of a church group as a body (*corpus*) united in a common religion and discipline, with a collection once a month that is spent, not on banquets and revelry, but on social services for the needy, including burial for those too poor to afford it.[17] It does seem as if Tertullian deliberately portrays Christian groups in language that will make outsiders understand them in these terms, and it is possible that elsewhere and at earlier periods, Christian groups could have been seen in this light, especially since such associations sometimes met in the house of their patron. The widespread presence of collegia and their Greek counterparts could have provided an element of respectability in the early years of Christianity.

The Social Status
of Christians

Early in this century, large quantities of newly discovered papyrus documents from Egypt were gradually being published, many of them representative of the life of ordinary people rather than the highly educated elites: Legal documents and personal and business letters revealed a variety of educational levels, and a dialect of Greek quite different from the literary Greek of the classics. The discovery of these "nonliterary" papyri by scholars of early Christianity sparked a flurry of interest in their relationship to the New Testament, and thus to the social level of the earliest Christians in the diaspora. Adolf Deissmann, in particular, argued that the similarities of this language to New Testament Greek, previously thought to be a distinctive kind of speech, demonstrated that the early Christians came from very poor and lowly social levels.[18] More recent assessments, however, have reconsidered the evidence and concluded that the written record indicates a higher social level than was previously thought.[19]

But what exactly does this mean? The new attempt to define as precisely as possible the actual social level of the Christians of the first centuries is not an easy task. One possibility can be eliminated without difficulty. They did not belong to the upper orders. With a few possible rare exceptions,[20] there is no solid evidence for persons of senatorial or equestrian rank in the Christian communities of the first century of Christian life. Eusebius's comment, that during the reign of Commodus (180–192 C.E.) many Romans of distinguished wealth and birth entered the church along with their households and families, may be correct, and in fact it may indicate a new trend at the time.[21]

It is in the middle levels (but not as a middle class), between the elites and those of no status at all, that most early Christians are to be located: urban artisans, merchants, traders, slaves, freedmen and freedwomen, most of whom would fall into the categories of inferiores and humiliores, though with some members and families of distinction, and probably also some statusless persons. The status consciousness prevalent in society was in many ways called into question and undermined for Christians by the community ethos of Christianity, inspired by the image of its founder, who was so frequently depicted in story in the act of compromising his status by voluntary association with tax collectors, sinners, and the like.[22] The expectation of welcoming all to the table must have been severely challenging.[23]

The New Testament evidence for social status is available mostly in the Pauline letters and in Acts. Here, a number of people have an oikos in which a Christian group can meet, which presupposes a certain economic and social level: the mother of John Mark in Jerusalem (Acts 12:12), Prisca and Aquila at Rome and/or Ephesus (Rom. 16:5; 1 Cor. 16:19), Nympha (Col. 4:15), Philemon (Philemon 2), and the merchant Lydia (Acts 16:15, 40). In these cases, the host or hostess of the group became patron of the group, with all the social expectations accompanying patronage of groups. The patron provided material subvention, including in this case regular hospitality and social protection and advancement, while clients owed honor and gratitude. Others have an oikos, either as building or family: the Roman centurion Cornelius (Acts 10:2; 11:14); a prison guard at Philippi (Acts 16:31–34); a synagogue official (Acts 18:8); Stephanas at Corinth (1 Cor. 1:16); potential *episkopos* and *diakonoi* (1 Tim. 3:4, 5, 12); Onesiphorus (2 Tim. 1:16; 4:19). The use of this language probably indicates persons of some means and some relative status, but not elites.[24]

The data on social status in 1 Corinthians have been intensively studied by Gerd Theissen among others as indicative of typical Pauline communities.[25] The point of departure for his analysis is 1 Corinthians 1:26, in which Paul reminds the Corinthians that not many of them were wise, powerful (*dunatos,* the Greek equivalent of the Latin *potens* or *potentior*), or of high-status birth (*eugeneis,* corresponding to *honestior*), but that God has chosen all the opposites. In the Corinthian church, most were of lower status, but the few of higher status represented "a dominant minority."[26] Theissen's argument, that the Corinthian Christian community itself was marked by internal social stratification that is at the bottom of the disharmony revealed in 1 Corinthians 11:17–34, fits well with what we know about how stratification and status consciousness worked in the society in general.

By comparison with what is known of others with similar positions and by assuming the reliability of Acts, we can assert that Crispus (1 Cor. 1:14; Acts 18:8) and Sosthenes (1 Cor. 1:1; Acts 18:17), two synagogue officials, were respected, high-status members of the Jewish community. Erastus, the city treasurer (1 Cor. 16:23), was probably at the time a public slave through self-sale, then a freedman with Roman citizenship, who went on to more responsible positions; much depends on whether or not he is to be identified with Erastus the aedile (a sort of superintendent of public works) commemorated on a paving stone near the theater, as is commonly assumed.[27] The Corinth of the imperial period was a Roman freedmen's colony. Eight of the seventeen Christian names known from Corinth are Latin, hence probably Roman citizens and not insignificant citizens of the city.[28]

The amount of travel undertaken by Corinthian Christians may be another indicator of wealth, if not of status. The following Corinthian figures are on the road at some point: Prisca and Aquila (Rom. 16:3; 1 Cor. 16:19; Acts 18:18–19), Phoebe (Rom. 16:1–2), Stephanas, Achaicus, and Fortunatus (1 Cor. 16:15–18), Chloe's people (1 Cor. 1:11), and perhaps Erastus (Acts 19:22) and Sosthenes (Acts 18:17), if these names in Acts refer to the same people. Aquila and Prisca may have moved for business reasons, as apparently did Lydia from Thyatira to Philippi in Acts 16:14. So, too, Phoebe may have been traveling on business as she carried Paul's letter to Rome—or Ephesus, if that was its destination.[29]

Paul, who did not usually baptize, made an exception at Corinth in the case of Gaius, Crispus, and the oikos of Stephanas—perhaps because of their higher status (1 Cor. 1:14).[30] By contrast, the passing reference to "those who belong to Chloe" (1 Cor. 1:11), with no further thanks or greetings directed to them, may indicate a lower-status gathering of people legally connected to Chloe, perhaps her "slaves or dependent workers,"[31] or a church group that meets in an apartment house or rented meeting place, a "tenement church."[32] Similar nonspecific references to those connected with Aristobulus and Narcissus appear in Romans 16:10, 11, and perhaps to other such groups connected with several named people in Romans 16:14, 15. In the case of a church group meeting under such circumstances, leadership was probably very different, not vested automatically in the most prominent members, but perhaps in those—while not the lowest-status members—who showed the spiritual gifts for it.

Personal patronage was also part of the church system of social relationships. Paul probably became patron to those he baptized personally, such as Gaius, Crispus, and Stephanas. His way of dealing with Philemon in the case of his slave Onesimus is through the language of patronage (Philemon 8–19). Yet Paul acknowledges Phoebe as his patron (*prostatis,* Rom 16:1–2), indicating her superior social status besides what she actually did for him (Rom. 16:1–2).[33]

Theissen's conclusion that about half of the Christians mentioned in 1 Corinthians "belong to the upper classes" is not helpful because the category is not specific. His conclusion that most of the people mentioned in 1 Corinthians "probably enjoyed high social status"[34] needs to be qualified, since status is a relational category: High status with regard to whom? And what of all the people in the Corinthian churches who are not mentioned? It can probably be assumed that those about whom we have some social information were prominent figures in the Corinthian churches. Given the way the social system functioned, it can also be assumed that if they were prominent in the churches, it was probably because they were already socially prominent at some level: the most distinguished persons of the city, the Jewish community, the neighborhood, the apartment house, and such, who became Christian. In each social system, each a microcosm of the whole, the most prominent figures would be expected to exercise leadership. With the exception of someone like Erastus, whose civic position is given, prominence in an immediate social circle says little about prominence in the city as a whole. Yet certainly these were not people of no consequence.

The silence of the majority of Christians in Corinth mirrors the silent majority in most early Christian groups, which mirrors the silent majority of the ancient world in general, even of the cities. There were Jews and Gentiles, both of whom were accepted. There were slaves, freed, and freeborn, who were assured that their legal status was not a disadvantage (1 Cor. 7:17–24). Beyond this, we have very few clues.

Most studies agree with Wayne Meeks that the New Testament diaspora urban evidence indicates two missing groups among Christians: the extreme top and the extreme bottom, with good representation of most middle levels.[35] There are some wealthy people, and certainly some considered to have better status than most in the community. There are wealthy widows and others who serve as hosts and patrons to Christian gatherings. If there had been members of the most prominent upper ranks, the ordines, we would know, because they would be mentioned. With regard to those of very lowest status, it must be stressed that the *evidence* is lacking. That does not mean they were not there, for they are less likely to be mentioned except indirectly as objects of charity, and most exhortations to generosity toward the poor in early Christian literature occur in general parenetic material that is difficult to specify in terms of social status.[36]

Post–New Testament evidence confirms the same picture. Both Christian and anti-Christian writers relish the portrait of Christians as ordinary people. In the case of Christian writers, these ordinary people are well instructed in the faith and capable of instructing others. For snobbish hostile writers, they are ignorant and gullible, providing easy targets for leaders who take advantage of them.

Second-century Christian authors Justin and Tatian acknowledge rich and well-educated Christians, but also craftspeople, unskilled laborers, and those of lower social standing. Tatian's term for the last category is *penetes,* often translated "poor," but really meaning not so much an economic as a status designation, those of modest means and capable of being exploited by the powerful. It is significant that he does not use the term *ptochos,* which rather designates the beggar class of those completely without resources.[37]

At the end of the same century, the Christian apologist Minucius Felix wrote a defense of Christianity under the guise of a conversation with an unbeliever friend on the beach at Ostia. The antagonist charges that Christians organize the least desirable segments of the population who are most prone to disgusting immorality. While Minucius Felix is eloquent in his refutation of the charges of immorality, he has not much to say about the social levels of recruitment except that Christians do not belong to the lowest levels of society (*nec de ultima statim plebe consistimus*), which is again consonant with the profile of people of mostly modest status, but not the lowest.[38]

Origen's *Against Celsus* refutes an extensive and apparently quite influential attack on Christianity made some half a century before Origen wrote. That Origen devoted so much energy to refute it when its author was long dead testifies to the work's enduring importance. Among the many charges that Celsus makes is that Christian leaders deliberately seek out the uneducated, the ignorant, children, and those of servile status who will be more gullible, and win them over in the absence of their betters and authority figures, who would know better. Celsus charges that anyone at all is welcome into the church regardless of qualifications. Christians, according to Celsus, are totally indiscriminate in their choice of members. Among those taught by Christian teachers in their own homes and workplaces are working women,[39] wool workers, cobblers, launderers, and the most uneducated, who would not dare to speak before their betters. Like Minucius Felix, Origen energetically refutes charges of exploitation and immorality, but does not claim that Celsus is mistaken about the social level where Christian teachers concentrate.[40]

Even in later years, this popular image of Christianity continued. At the end of the fourth century, the great Antiochene orator Libanius still scornfully asserts that those of high status like himself who become Christians learned the faith from the women of their family or the domestic slaves.[41] And still in the fifth century, the Christian theologian Theodoret claims that the Bible has been translated into many languages, and that those who understand their faith and can instruct others include fishermen, tax collectors, tentmakers, smiths, wool workers, artisans, working women, seamstresses, domestics, herdsmen, and gardeners.[42] By this time, of course, Christianity has penetrated every social level, but the claim to populist appeal is still advantageous.

In contrast to this populist image stand Tertullian's assertions at the end of the second century that Christianity is everywhere, in city and countryside, and among every sex, age, condition, and even social status (*omnen sexum, aetatem, condicionem, etiam dignitatem*).[43] But it is precisely toward the end of the second century that Eusebius also claims that Christianity began to penetrate the higher social levels, even into the aristocracy, so that the two witnesses, Tertullian the contemporary and Eusebius the historian more than a century later, agree. Even in the early fourth century when Eusebius wrote, the senatorial families and the army were still relatively untouched by Christianity.[44] That was to change in the course of the century.

The sources cited above are all literary documents with rhetorical intent, whether hostile to or in support of Christian evangelistic strategies. They do not intend to yield material for social analysis. What they reveal primarily is a literary theme whereby Christianity was presented as accessible to all regardless of social status or education. Yet the very fact that appeal to the popular level was consistent points in a definite direction: Christianity's profile was not that of a highly selective, educated, or high-status group. On the contrary, while there were some higher-status members, probably all of whom functioned as patrons of house churches and later of the organized local church, the church encouraged and welcomed those of modest status and offered them not an esoteric and sophisticated system of beliefs, but one that was freely taught to all and which all could comprehend. Thus most local churches must have included among their members both humiliores and a few potentiores and even honestiores, mingled together in the same kinds of relationships that they had elsewhere. A good many members must have been Roman citizens, especially in such communities as Philippi and Corinth, which were founded as Roman colonies and had considerable enduring Roman character.

Christians were not, of course, immune to their culture, but an integral part of it. The same sensitivity to honor and status that was part of the life of others was part of their life as well. The same patterns of patronage and favor pertained as they were replicated among those of lower status. If there was a difference, it was that all members were asked to embrace an ideology of humility and unity—but not of equality as it is understood today. It is clear that once the church began gaining social power and influence, it replicated the same structures of honor and privilege.

5

Gender Roles,
Marriage, and Celibacy

Gender Roles in the Pauline House Church:
1 Corinthians 5—7 (and 14:33b–36)

The most important extended text for understanding relationships between men and women, including sexual relationships, in Pauline house churches is 1 Corinthians 5—7. After addressing the divisions in the Christian community in Corinth in the first four chapters, Paul refers (5:1) to oral reports that there is sexual immorality[1] among them, a vice that Paul mentions first in both subsequent lists of vices (5:9–11; 6:9–11a), emphasizing it. These two vice lists "speak directly to the epistolary situation of the letter."[2] Paul reminds them of his previous letter, in which he wrote prohibiting their mixing with those engaged in sexual immorality. Emphasizing the contrast between "I wrote" and "but now I am writing" (5:9, 11), Peter Zaas argues that Paul now adds the list of vices, thus extending his prior prohibition. The same is true of the list in chapter 6, which contains the six vices of 5:11 plus four more, so that it is a *quotation* with additions.[3] Both lists connect sexual immorality with idolatry.[4] The same connection is basic in Paul's longest vice list, Romans 1:18–32, where he says that those who "exchanged the glory of God for images" (v. 23a) were given up by God "to degrading passions" (vv. 26–29a; cf. Rom. 2:14; 1 Cor. 10:8; Rev. 2:14, 20).[5]

Paul is still concerned with the same vice at the beginning of 1 Corinthians 7, a central concern of his in all three chapters.[6] The Corinthian slogan that Paul quotes, "it is well for a man not to touch a woman" (7:1b), contains a euphemism for sexual intercourse stated from a male point of view. Paul responds to their slogan, to their ascetic thought and practice, by arguing for marriage because of the eschatological danger of sexual immorality. But as these texts including the two vice lists demonstrate, the concern both of the Corinthian Christians' question and of Paul's response has to do with sex, not primarily with

marriage. Since marriage is in trouble in Western culture, modern
Christians would love to have Paul's advice for our century, but historically, he was not a Stoic philosopher or a Christian theologian writing
generally about marriage in order to shore up Greco-Roman or American urban society. We have instead his pastoral argument against some
particular Corinthian Christian ascetics' rejection of their sexuality.[7]

The connection Paul makes in these vice lists in 1 Corinthians between
idolatry and sexual immorality reflects what John Collins calls "the common ethic" in Hellenistic Jewish tradition: "The characteristic feature of
this ethic was that it emphasized those aspects of Jewish law which were
likely to get a sympathetic hearing from enlightened gentiles—chiefly
monotheism and the prohibition of idolatry, and various sexual laws such
as the prohibition of homosexuality."[8] Collins outlines this common ethic
in three Jewish texts of the first century C.E.[9] In addition to monotheism,
all three place heavy emphasis on sexual matters, forbidding adultery, homosexual acts, rape of a virgin, and abortion.[10] Zaas is correct, then, that
the two vice lists in 1 Corinthians 5 and 6 address the epistolary situation
of the letter; the lists that Paul constructs reflect and even indicate the focus of his concerns in chapters 5—10.

Greco-Roman Medical Handbooks
and Sexuality

Given the Corinthians' question about the legitimate place of sex and
the focus of this book on Greco-Roman households, what can we know
about appropriate and inappropriate, moral and immoral, sex within
the ancient household? Just as modern doctors advise their patients, so
Hellenistic medical doctors gave advice about sexuality and health to
Greek, Roman, Jewish,[11] and Christian families, and this medical science sheds significant light on the exchanges between Paul and the
Corinthians.[12] We do not know on what grounds some Corinthian
Christians rejected sexual intercourse, but the following medical opinions provide the cultural and scientific context for their doing so.

The physician Soranus wrote *Gynecology,* a work "exclusively concerned with women and with intercourse for childbearing"; his "prime
concern is conception."[13] He wrote for midwives and nurses, for male
practitioners, and for "the heads of Roman households, the *paterfamilias,* who may welcome criteria by which to judge potential care-givers
for their infants and their womenfolk."[14] Aline Rouselle is blunter:

> The *Hippocratic Collection* does deal with the problems of sterile
> women. . . . The women of the fifth and fourth centuries B.C. had
> themselves compared their bodies, considering external and inter-

nal details, in order to find out what caused sterility and miscar-
riage. . . . But what began as medical observation aimed at helping
women becomes in Soranus' hands a description of the type of
woman to avoid, or, looked at another way, a study of the general
and genital anatomy of the fertile woman, the future mother. These
anatomical studies were of course drawn up for men. . . .

The doctor, then, helped men to take possession of the female
body. In more general terms, he assisted the domination of the
male, the *dominus,* over the bodies which were in his power.[15]

For Soranus, procreation is the purpose of sexual activity,[16] and the
doctors' knowledge functions toward that end. But how did they regard
the sexual activity that produced children? For a modern person, their
answers are surprising; their science is interwoven with philosophical
values, especially with Epicurean and Sceptical ones.[17]

The physician Galen reports the philosopher Epicurus's (341–270
B.C.E.) conclusion that "sexual intercourse is never good for health."[18]
Similarly, "sexual intercourse, they [Epicureans] say, has never done a
man good, and he is lucky if it has not harmed (*blapto*) him."[19] Writing
in Tiberius's reign during the early first century C.E., Celsus, a layman,
compiled an extensive medical handbook in Latin, giving advice to "a
man in health who is both vigorous and his own master":

> Sexual intercourse neither should be avidly desired, nor should it
> be feared very much. Rarely performed, it revives the body, per-
> formed frequently, it weakens. However, since nature, and not
> number should be considered in frequency, with consideration of
> age and the state of the body, sexual union is recognized as not
> harmful when it is followed by neither apathy nor pain.[20]

> The weak, however, among whom are a large portion of townspeo-
> ple, and almost all those fond of letters, need greater precaution.[21]

Agreeing with Celsus's opinion against Epicurus, the physician Rufus
of Ephesus concedes that intercourse is not absolutely bad (*kakista*).[22]
But many doctors at the end of the first century C.E.[23] agreed rather with
the philosopher. Soranus[24] reports a debate between two medical
schools over sexual abstinence, but both agreed with Epicurus's reported
opinion that abstinence is ideal. Because of its relevance to 1 Corinthians 7, we quote a lengthy extract from Soranus's *Gynecology,* from a
section titled, "whether permanent virginity (*parthenia*[25]) is healthful":

> 30. Some have pronounced permanent virginity healthful, others,
> however, not healthful. The former contend that the body is made
> ill by desire (*epithumia*). . . . Furthermore, all excretion of seed
> [*sperma*] is harmful[26] in females as in males. Virginity, therefore,
> is healthful, since it prevents the excretion of seed. Dumb animals

also bear witness to what has been said; for of mares those not covered excel at running, and of sows those whose uteri have been cut
out are bigger, better nourished, stronger,[27] and firm like males.
And this is evident in humans too: since men who remain chaste
are stronger and bigger than the others and pass their lives in better health, correspondingly it follows that for women too virginity
in general is healthful. For pregnancy and parturition exhaust the
female body and make it waste greatly away, whereas virginity,
safeguarding women from such injuries, may suitably be called
healthful.

31. However, those of the opposite opinion contend that desire
for sexual pleasures appertains not only to [sexually active] women,
but to virgins also. Some virgins, at any rate, they say, have suffered more severe sexual passion than [active] women; for the only
abatement of the craving is found in the use of intercourse not in
its avoidance. . . . And as to the excretion of seed, some people say:
Neither in males nor in females is it harmful (*blabe*) in itself, but
only in excess. . . . Others, however, say that the emission of seed
is injurious (*blaberan*) on the grounds that it brings about atony,
and in this way sometimes actually harms (*lupeo*) people. . . . And
concerning the objection that women who have no intercourse escape the evil resulting from childbearing, they say that by not having intercourse they are harmed (*blaptontai*) in other respects
much worse, the menstrual catharsis being hindered. . . . Permanent virginity, therefore, is harmful.

32. And such are the arguments of the two sides. We, however,
contend that permanent virginity is healthful, because intercourse
is harmful in itself as has been shown in more length in the book
"On Hygiene." Besides, even among dumb animals we see that
those females are stronger which are prevented from having intercourse. And among women we see that those who, on account of
regulations and service to the gods, have renounced intercourse
and those who have been kept in virginity as ordained by law
[Vestal Virgins] are less susceptible to disease. . . . Consequently,
permanent virginity is healthful, in males and females alike; nevertheless, intercourse seems consistent with the general principle
of nature, according to which both sexes, [for the sake] of continuity, [have to ensure] the succession of living beings.[28]

Another aspect of contemporary scientific understanding may have
influenced the Corinthian spiritualists' thought and practice. Early
Hippocratic doctors taught that when men and, some of them thought,
women emit semen during sexual intercourse, they become "weaker"
(*astheneis*).[29] Soranus, as we have just seen, thinks that the emission of
sperm is always harmful. We know little of why ancient doctors reached

this conclusion and are heavily dependent on one second-century C.E. source, Galen's "Concerning Sperm."[30] Galen develops the idea as follows:

> Seed (*sperma*) is spirit (*pneuma*).[31]

> The testicles are even more important than the heart, since . . . they impart to the whole body (*soma*) a power (*dunamis*) [that] . . . causes the male's vigour and virility. . . . When, as a result of continual sexual excess, all sperm has been lost, the testicles draw seminal liquid from veins immediately above them. These veins contain only small quantity of this condensed liquid, so when they are suddenly deprived of it by testicles . . . , they in turn drain veins above them and so on . . . , until it has involved every part of the body. . . . The result will be that all parts of the animal (or the living creature) are drained, not just of seminal fluid but also of their vital spirit (*pneuma zotikou*). . . . Therefore, those . . . who lead a debauched life become weak (*asthenesterous*). . . . People have died from an excess of pleasure. . . . We should therefore not be surprised if those who indulge moderately in the pleasures of love become weak (*asthenesteroi*).[32]

This vivid picture of draining away of vital spirit, surprising for a modern reader, may have been quite real for the "spiritual people" (1 Cor. 3:1) in Corinth, among them heads of households and slave physicians who read medical handbooks like those written by Celsus. Given these contemporary medical theories, it is possible that some Corinthians connected their sexual asceticism with their desire for the spiritual gifts discussed in 1 Corinthians 12 and 14.

Ascetic Practice in the First Century C.E. among Philosophers, Priests, and Charismatics

In this context of such cultural, medical assumptions, we may read Philo's description of ascetic Jewish Therapeutae in Egypt:

> The [Sabbath] feast is shared by women also, most of them aged virgins (*parthenoi*) who have kept their chastity not under compulsion, like some of the Greek priestesses, but of their own free will in their ardent yearning for wisdom. Eager to have her for their life mate they have spurned the pleasures of the body and desire no mortal offspring but those immortal children which only the soul that is dear to God can bring to the birth unaided because the Father has sown in her spiritual rays enabling her to behold the verities of wisdom.[33]

Philo describes married males too as having chosen an ascetic way of life:

11. But it is well that the Therapeutae, a people always taught from the first to use their sight, should desire the vision of the Existent and soar above the sun of our senses and never leave their place in this company which carries them on to perfect happiness.

12. And those who set themselves to this service . . . [are] carried away by a heaven-sent passion of love, remain rapt and possessed (*enthousiazo*) like bacchanals or corybants until they see the object of their yearning.

13. Then such is their longing for the deathless and blessed life that thinking their mortal life already ended they abandon their property to their sons or daughters or to other kinsfolk. . . .

18. So when they have divested themselves of their possessions and have no longer aught to ensnare them they flee without a backward glance and leave their brothers, their children, their *wives,* their parents, the wide circle of their kinsfolk, the groups of friends around them, the fatherlands, in which they were born and reared. . . .

19. Instead of this they pass their days outside the walls pursuing solitude in gardens or lonely bits of country. . . .[34]

The medical opinions of Celsus, Rufus, and Soranus, including Soranus's reference to a widespread debate among doctors on the subject in the late first and early second centuries C.E., contribute to our understanding of sexual asceticism among these Jewish Therapeutae and among the Corinthian Christians. During Philo's lifetime, that is, some decades before Paul wrote, Celsus argues against some who fear sexual intercourse, considering it harmful even for vigorous, healthy persons. Soranus's summary a century later reveals more of the specific arguments in this debate, but it still focuses on the question whether humans should understand sex as "harmful." In fact, the doctors' opinions help us understand why the Jewish author Philo expected his Greek readers to be attracted to the Therapeutai, an attraction to ascetic spiritual practices also felt by some Corinthian Christians who wanted above all else to be "spiritual." Philo expects the reader to understand that both female and male members of this community were sexually ascetic and spiritually "enthusiastic," as were some Corinthian Christian charismatics.

The Stoic philosopher and Egyptian priest Chaeremon similarly describes some Egyptian priests who renounce their income and devote their whole life to contemplation and vision of the divine. The priests practice self control (*enkrateia*), do not drink wine, or only a little, since it causes injury (*blabas*) to nerves and in order to reduce sexual desires. They purify themselves from seven to forty-two days, abstain from animal food, all vegetables, and "above all from sexual intercourse with women," never having intercourse with males.[35] Paul Wendland argues that Philo, when writing his *Apology,* knew and was responding to the slanders of Chaeremon, who about 40 C.E. had polemicized against Jews.[36] Pieter Van der Horst suggests rather a date "between about 30 and 65 C.E." and that both the Stoic and the Jewish philosophers drew on a traditional vocabulary to describe an ideal community of philosophizing saints.[37] In either case both philosophers wrote near the time of 1 Corinthians expecting their readers to admire sexually ascetic men, and in Philo's case women, seeking a vision of the divine.

The *Testament of Job,* dated perhaps about the turn of our era,[38] also describes spiritual women, and although the text is not as clear, the author probably intends the reader to understand them as sexually ascetic. As he is dying, Job with his friends and family enter a house (44.1), where he gives gifts to the poor and to his seven sons, at which the daughters protest that they too are his children (46.3). Job responds that he is giving them "an inheritance better than that of your seven brothers" (46.5). The three daughters receive bands to place around their breasts, so that "the enemy" will not oppose them (47.11). Each then chants hymns, Hemera in the angelic language (48.3),[39] Kassia in the dialect of the archons (49.2), Amaltheias-keras in the dialect of the cherubim (50.2). Hemera no longer thinks about earthly things (48.3),[40] Kassia is no longer anxious about worldly things (*kosmika;* 49.2), and Amaltheias-keras was changed by withdrawing from worldly things (*kosmikon*),[41] phrases which suggest an ascetic lifestyle for these Jewish women. The author places bodily functions, fleshly matters, opposite heavenly matters (38.3–8; cf. 36.4, 6–7). In conclusion, these philosophical, medical, and Jewish texts from the first century C.E. supply the cultural context for male and female Corinthian Christian sexual asceticism.

Having sketched some of the medical and cultural environment Paul is addressing, we continue comment on 1 Corinthians. The "oral report" that "a man is living with his father's wife" (5:1) marks chapter 5 as a new unit, but Paul relates it to his prior criticism of Corinthian theology in chapters 1—4 when he remarks, "Your boast is not good" (5:6; cf. 5:2 and 1:29, 31; 3:21; 4:7). A male Christian had an ongoing sexual relationship with his father's wife, who was probably not his own mother or a Christian, in which case Paul would have included her in the discussion. Such a relationship was forbidden by Torah (e.g., Lev. 18:8) and by Roman law. There was such a case later under Hadrian, who exiled a father who had killed his son, because the latter had committed adultery with the father's second wife. Since divorce was common and children remained with the father and his next (young) wife, this situation would not have been uncommon. Hadrian rebuked the father for exercising his authority with cruelty rather than affection.[42]

In response, however, Paul does not use purity language, but rather, as L. William Countryman persuasively argues,[43] he refers to the Jewish Passover as a new "end time," a festival of liberation during which Christians behave appropriately. Countryman explicates sexual ethics in the Bible, in contrast to modern values, by two basic categories: (1) some actions are "dirty," that is, unclean as outlined in the Levitical code, and (2) others involve "greed," that is, in ancient Jewish and Greco-Roman cultures such sexual actions are basically theft from another male head of household. Paul does not argue for this ethic, but simply assumes it. He assumes that the ethical issue is serious and demands that the community separate from the offender "for the destruction (olethron) of the flesh" (5:5). A. Y. Collins interprets this phrase communally and eschatologically.[44] In 1 Thessalonians 5:2–3 Paul refers to the "sudden [eschatological] destruction (olethros) that will come upon them as travail comes upon a woman with child," a fiery trial of all creation in which the "flesh" hostile to God will be "destroyed." In light of 1 Corinthians 4:4–5, Paul is not judging the eternal fate of the son who is committing incest, but insisting that those who *are* washed, sanctified, and justified (6:11) *must act* that way, a typical "indicative/imperative" style for Paul. Countryman's interpretation enables him to explain the abrupt shift of subject matter, at least as it appears to a modern reader: in chapter 6 Paul moves to Christians suing each other before pagan courts, "acting unjustly," wronging each other also in nonsexual property matters.[45]

Paul does not forget that sexual ethics is his primary topic; moving into the second vice list, he plays on the verb "unjust" that he has just used to describe Christians suing each other (6:7–8 and 9). Defining the unjust, wrongdoers, Paul now adds the words malakoi (literally, "soft ones") and arsenokoitai (6:9), terms of very uncertain meaning[46] that have been translated various ways, but which are often taken by modern authors to condemn homosexual acts. By using the first term Paul assumes an aspect of contemporary Greco-Roman biology, that it is unnatural for a man to be "soft," like a woman, just as five chapters later, he argues that it is "natural" for a female to cover her hair and for a male not to let his grow. Once again, it is helpful to correlate ancient biology with Pauline ethics in order to understand the assumptions behind this term in the vice list. We quote only one text from among many, this one from the philosopher and biologist Aristotle:

> All females are less spirited than the males, except the bear and leopard: in these the female is held to be braver. But in the other

kinds the females are softer (*malakotera*), more vicious, less simple, more impetuous, more attentive to the feeding of the young,
while the males on the contrary are more spirited, wilder, simpler,
less cunning. There are traces of these characters in virtually all animals, but they are all the more evident in those that are more possessed of character and especially in man. For man's nature (*physin*)
is the most complete, so that these dispositions too are more evident in humans. Hence a wife is more compassionate than a husband and more given to tears, but also more jealous and com-
plaining and more apt to scold and fight. The female is also more
dispirited and despondent than the male, more shameless and lying, is readier to deceive and has a longer memory; furthermore
she is more wakeful, more afraid of action, and in general is less
inclined to move than the male, and takes less nourishment. The
male on the other hand, as we have said, is a readier ally and is
braver than the female.[47]

Holt Parker summarizes the difference between Greco-Roman and
modern attitudes, a difference we must note in order to understand
Paul:

Sexuality in our society is constructed on the choice of object, heterosexual versus homosexual. Both Greek and Roman male sexuality was constructed on the division between active and passive.
The active one . . . was "male," and was acting the role of a free
man, whether he used as object a woman, a boy, or a man. The
passive one . . . was "female," and servile, whether woman, boy, or
man. The active role could also be shown not only in mastery over
others but in self-mastery. Thus, paradoxically, the ability to withstand desire, to abstain from sexual pleasure, in classical society is
conceived of as essentially masculine. The opposite is also true: the
inability to withstand desire, indulgence in pleasure, is essentially
feminine, and so equally women's sexuality is feared as unrestrained, uncontrolled, uncontrollable.[48]

Paul refers to these polarities between male and female when he uses
the biological term "soft," but many of these biological and spiritual polarities between males and females are in high tension with the baptismal
confession in his churches: "there is no longer Jew or Greek, there is no
longer slave or free, there is no longer male and female; for all of you are
one in Christ Jesus" (Gal. 3:28). Greeks and Romans discussed sexual
and social relationships on the basis of these biological differences between males and females, considered "natural" by many ancients, intense
discussions that others continue into the twentieth century. We have
seen that Christians living in Greco-Roman households would have assumed current medical knowledge; Paul's term "soft" assumes one of

these male/female polarities. Aristotle, the biologist and philosopher, in his several treatises on ethics wrote that male/female differences also involved further polarities: active/passive, sexual generator/receptacle, spirited/dispirited, civic/domestic, orator/hearer, self-restraint/lack of restraint, endurance/softness (*malakos*), whole/defective, normal/deviant, soul/body, intellect/feeling, ruler/ruled, simple living/luxurious. Which of these male/female polarities did earliest Christians accept as normative? Having been influenced by twentieth-century biology and theology, many modern Christians reject these Greek biological male/female polarities, and the ethical conclusions that depend on them, because they are in tension with the Christian baptismal confession and with modern biology.

Paul then quotes Corinthian Christian slogans, "all things are lawful for me" (6:12a), and "food is meant for the stomach and the stomach for food" (6:13a), which he strongly modifies. In relation to the second slogan, he rejects a parallel between food and sex: He agrees that food is irrelevant to one's relationship to God, but "the body is meant not for fornication (*porneia*, sexual immorality) but for the Lord, and the Lord for the body" (6:13b). "With a nice *double entendre* Paul exhorts the Corinthians to cleave to the Lord (and thus *his* body, the church), instead of cleaving (sexually) with prostitutes."[49] Some Corinthian males who have become Christians have also continued their encounters with prostitutes, which many modern commentators label "libertine." However, this modern label suggests a misunderstanding of the values of Greek males, who typically, whether married or single, had sexual relationships with more than one woman. The most striking example is probably Plutarch, who has been read for centuries for his sober, moral advice; for example, the Loeb translator affirms that Plutarch's suggestions "hold as good today as they did when they were written, nearly two thousand years ago."[50] In "Advice to Bride and Groom," advice for Pollianus and Eurydice soon after they have retired together to the bridal chamber, Plutarch writes as a happily married man (cf. 608A):

> The lawful wives of the Persian kings sit beside them at dinner, and eat with them. But when the kings wish to be merry and get drunk, they send their wives away, and send for their music-girls and concubines. In so far they are right in what they do, because they do not concede any share in their licentiousness and debauchery to their wedded wives. If therefore a man in private life, who is incontinent (*akrates;* cf. 1 Cor. 7:5) and dissolute in regard to his pleasures, commit some peccadillo with a paramour or a maidservant,[51] his wedded wife ought not to be indignant or angry, but she should reason that it is respect for her which leads him to share

his debauchery, licentiousness, and wantonness with another woman. (140B)

Many scholars correctly assume an incipient Gnosticism in Corinth, but that is not necessary to explain Christian males, also married ones, using prostitutes[52]: They were acting like many other males such as Plutarch in their culture, males who considered themselves deeply moral. Given contemporary Greco-Roman male values, it is a modern moral judgment, not a historical description, to label Plutarch's advice "libertine," as if either he or Pollianus (or Eurydice) would have considered male sexual activity with slaves "liberated" behavior. Within the church some males continued their—for them unremarkable—behavior of using prostitutes to take care of their sexual tensions; others, male and female, were rejecting all sexual activity even in marriage, which, as we have seen, has roots in contemporary Greek and Roman medical and philosophical advice. Musonius, in "On Sexual Indulgence" (frag. 12), did voice a minority opinion that a husband should not sleep with the slave woman he owned (especially if she happens to be a widow),[53] but his opinion is clearly a criticism of the predominant moral thought and practice. Plutarch appears to be of a divided mind about his advice, since he uses the terms licentiousness and debauchery, incontinent and dissolute, in speaking of a husband's sexual activity with other women, perhaps in relation to the minority opinion expressed by Musonius. Given this Greek male way of thinking and acting, Rousselle concludes about later Gnostics:

> If we describe this [later gnostic] philosophy as dissolute as some do, we are giving it a moral colour which is entirely modern. . . . The men and women of these sects were not rebelling against sexual repression, they were integrating sexual freedom into worship of the Christian God. . . . The most significant point is the official nature of this integration of sexual behaviour into religion as means of salvation, and the extension of sexual freedom to women. . . . The Gnostics were in effect carrying to the extreme the freedom that was already the rule in their society. We might call this a kind of theoretical sexualism.[54]

Therefore, given the Corinthian Christians' slogan, "all things are lawful" (1 Cor. 6:12), we need only assume Paul's earlier preaching of the gospel that God saves apart from the law, and some male, Plutarchian defensiveness about sexual partners, in order to explain Corinthian male boasting about a son's sexual liaison with his mother-in-law or other male Christians continuing to use prostitutes.

Paul's response, which has both Jewish and Greek sources, rejects the philosophy and practice that assumes sexual encounters are comparable to eating meals,[55] or in Plutarch's analogy, to entertainment after meals. Paul rather admonishes: "Do you not know that whoever is united to a prostitute becomes one body with her? For it is said, 'The two shall be one flesh' [Gen. 2:24]. But anyone united to the Lord becomes one spirit with him" (1 Cor. 6:16–17).

Every sexual act establishes a union of "one body," though Paul does not write that unions with prostitutes are indissoluble.[56] Paul writes that this relationship is of "one body," then quotes Genesis that it is "one flesh." Believers are united with Christ by "one spirit," the power that draws believers toward God (1 Cor. 12:12–13). Sexual union with a prostitute unites two persons in opposing God, the meaning of the term "flesh" in Paul. Their immorality opposes the spiritual union with God and Christ established in baptism. Paul assumes that when people take their clothes off and have sex, the activity is relationally, even eschatologically meaningful, more than entertainment. Paul's Christian ethic insists that bodily actions count. These debates over the meaning of sexuality and the body continue into chapter 7.

The Corinthians have written Paul a letter in which they agree with current Epicurean, medical, Stoic (Chaeremon), and Hellenistic Jewish (Philo) opinions that "it is well for a man not to touch a woman" (7:1). Hans Conzelmann suggests that their question to Paul must have been something like, "Is sexual intercourse allowed (at all)?"[57] Paul responds with the concern about sexual immorality (7:2) that he had voiced throughout chapters 5 and 6. Over against the Corinthian ascetic slogan, Paul argues the polar opposite in gender-fair language: "Each man should have his own wife and each woman her own husband" (7:3), emphasizing exclusivity ("his own," "her own").

In 6:9–10 he had affirmed that wrongdoers, sexually immoral persons, "will not inherit the kingdom of God," a thought he repeats in 7:9, "it is better to marry than to burn." Michael Barré points out that the verb "to burn" in verse 9 may mean to be aflame with passion or desire; however, it is not used absolutely with this meaning, but only in association with a noun that specifies the emotion,[58] which 1 Corinthians 7:9 lacks. Barré shows that Paul uses it here to refer to "the fiery judgment of Yahweh," the eschatological punishment of wickedness.[59] In verse 9, Paul is not proposing marriage as a cure for being "aflame with passion" (as in the NRSV and most modern translations); he is a pastor addressing particular Corinthian males who are using prostitutes (6:15–16a) and who are involved in actual "cases [plural] of sexual immorality" (7:2), including a son living with his father's wife (5:1). Some Christians with ascetic ideals are acting as if they had none. Paul shares their preference for celibacy, but insists that their bodily ethics and actual practice affect their eschatological relationship to God and to Christ's body.

The man and woman *mutually* have each other's body, a Stoic idea opposed to the widespread patriarchal assumption that the man owns the woman, not vice versa. Compare Musonius: "The husband and wife, he used to say, should come together for the purpose of making a life in common and of procreating children, and furthermore, of regarding all things in common between them, and nothing peculiar or private to one or the other, not even their own bodies."[60] Musonius expresses these ideas in a context arguing for marriage as friendship. He and Paul go beyond the discussion of sexuality in terms of "dirt and greed," of purity and property, to play on the title of Countryman's superb book. There was a contemporary debate about the relationship between friendship and sex, seen for example in Plutarch, *Amatorius,* which is different from the earlier erotics. In this work Protogenes praises pederasty because it includes friendship (750D) but denounces the housebound love of women as devoid of it (*aphiloi;* 751B). Daphnaeus argues the contrary, that love between men and women is natural and conducive to friendship (751CD). Plutarch himself (766D–771C, esp. 769A,CD) argues against older views of friendship with boys and men that a wife is a suitable, more graceful, pleasurable, continuous, and constant friend. The middle-Platonist Plutarch illustrates Paul Veyne's thesis[61] that there was a domestication of morals in the early empire.

One conclusive sign that the relationship of women to men was changing dramatically in the first century is architectural: (1) in republican times, men and women went to baths segregated by gender, (2) during the empire, beginning in the first century C.E., these baths were rebuilt so that men and women bathed together nude, and (3) then in the fourth century C.E., men and women were separated again.[62] In contemporary North America it has not been customary for men and women to bathe together nude, whereas it is common in Europe, also among Christians. The culture shock involved in moving from one custom to the other is deep,[63] and in the first century C.E. indicates that women were taking on some cultural roles that had been played exclusively by men. In Plutarch's language, heterosexual marriage was becoming a friendship, no longer just sex to produce children who would carry on the honor and wealth of the family. Friendship was no longer a relationship between males only, and this cultural change was generating debate. Such significant cultural and social changes and the acts that symbolize them (bathing together, friendship in marriage, and women's charismatic speech in worship) would generate conflict, which we see in the Corinthian church.

The Greco-Roman question of pederasty that Plutarch debates, the sexual involvement of an older man with a young schoolboy, is not the same as the modern debate about homosexual or lesbian relationships, two adult men or two adult women loving each other. Greco-Roman marriage also involved an older man having sex with a bride twelve years old, from a modern point of view just as sick as pederasty.[64] Sexual relations between equal partners is a modern ideal, not an ancient one. Few if any modern Christians, heterosexual or homosexual, would want to argue on either side of this Plutarchian debate. Virtually all modern persons would experience intense culture shock over sexual relationships in the Corinthian church.

Hans-Josef Klauck[65] discusses the influence of the Greco-Roman friendship ethic seen above in Plutarch as accepted and modified by Luke, John, and Paul in the New Testament, observing that modern Christians have lost both the Jewish practice of calling each other "brother" or "sister" and the Greek practice of friendship. A modified, critical appreciation of either could contribute depth to relationships in our communities. In 1 Corinthians 7:3–4 Paul applies Stoic friendship themes to marriage, emphasizing mutuality, that each partner shares the other's body sexually. In the rest of the chapter he insists that one is not to be totally identified with the other (v. 29), that the relationship is to reduce anxiety, that each is to make efforts to please the other, that it is for each person's benefit, and that the relationship is to be ordered and not result in distraction (7:32–35).[66] As a Jew Paul also agrees with Musonius's minority opinion that sexual relationships are to be exclusive, with one partner, not also with the male owner's slaves or with prostitutes.

The preference for celibacy may have motivated some Corinthians to separate from their spouses (7:10–16). Paul demands that neither husband nor wife do this, citing the Lord's prohibition (see Mark 10:2–12), but then he permits an exception, "but if she does separate, let her remain unmarried or else be reconciled to her husband" (7:11). This exception is applied only to the case of a woman, who may be seeking religious and/or social freedom. Paul argues that her sanctity would make her spouse holy, as it has her children (v. 14). If the unbelieving spouse wants separation, the believer is to permit it, for the sake of peace to which God has called us (7:15).

Paul's discussion of sexuality contrasts significantly both with the concerns of the state—with Augustus's concern that all citizens marry and have children—and of some Corinthians who wanted to impose celibacy on all. Paul argues for options, for more than one way to live a holy life. If two Christians are married, active, mutual sexual activity is holy (7:3–4, 14), but so is the celibate life (7:34), and Paul himself prefers the latter (7:7, 38). He does observe that some Christians with ascetic ideals are not actually exercising self-control (7:2, 9, 36, 37; cf. chaps. 5 and 6), so they should marry, which is not a sin.[67]

It is crucial for understanding relationships in the early Pauline house churches that 1 Corinthians 14:33b–36 ("as in all the churches of the saints, women should be silent in the churches. For they are not permitted to speak, but should be subordinate, as the law also says") has been shown to be an interpolation.[68] This interpolation projects the massive reinterpretation of Paul in the deutero-Pauline literature—accomplished by importing the Aristotelian household codes into early Christian ethics—back onto Paul himself, and thus it obscures the freedom women experienced in those early communities. Paul himself had written of the "subordination" (*upotassesthai*, v. 32) of the spirits of the prophets to the prophets, the subject of this whole chapter, but some second-generation Christian editor saw a golden opportunity to expand Paul's text by inserting an insistence on domestic "subordination" (using the same key verb)[69] and on the silence of wives (v. 34), both of which post-Pauline Christians assimilating to the Roman Empire considered crucial. Ann Wire, who accepts the authenticity of these verses, is interpreting Paul by the post-Pauline ethic of the household codes; whether this is done by a feminist or a Fundamentalist, the result is disastrous.[70] It is very difficult to assume that Prisca, owner with Aquila of one of the houses where Ephesian congregations met (1 Cor. 16:19), was silent while worshiping in her own house,[71] and Paul himself writes of some women prophets in Corinth who were not (1 Cor. 11:5).

In contrast to these later, interpolated verses in 1 Corinthians 14, the early Pauline churches were sometimes led by women.[72] In Romans 16 Paul calls Prisca a co-worker (v. 3), then commends Mary, Tryphaena, Tryphosa, and Persia for "working" or "laboring" (vv. 6, 12), a verb (*kopian*) Paul uses to characterize his own evangelizing and that of these women. He names Phoebe a *diakonos* (a "minister," v. 1) and Junia an "apostle" (v. 7). In Philemon, Apphia is a "sister" (v. 2). In Philippians, Paul writes that the women Euodia and Syntyche have "struggled beside me in the work of the gospel, together with Clement and the rest of my coworkers" (4:3). Nils Dahl observes that "the two women were outstanding and influential members of the church of Philippi," and concludes that "even the general exhortations in Philippians have been formulated in a way that relates to the conflict between Euodia and Syntyche."[73]

In summary, contemporary medical and philosophical debates about sexual intercourse help clarify the Corinthians' question concerning sexuality and Paul's response. The medical doctors agreed that one had to be cautious, or alternatively, abstain altogether, since sexual activity would make a person "weak" and is potentially "harmful." Sexual abstinence was combined with enthusiasm for spiritual experience in the Jewish Therapeutae, the *Testament of Job,* in the Stoic Chaeremon, and among some Corinthian Christians; in all these cases except for Chaeremon, this ascetic spirituality involved both women and men. In contrast to such opinions, Paul argues in concert with (some, not all) other Jews and with the Stoic Musonius that monogamous sexual activity is holy, but that multiple sexual relationships with prostitutes or slaves threaten one's eschatological relationship to God. In surprising contrast to the predominant political, philosophical, and medical focus on generating legitimate children, Paul never refers to procreation, even when discussing Christian heterosexual couples' relationships. He does use language that reflects the late Stoic (Musonius) and middle Platonic (Plutarch) emphasis on mutuality and friendship in heterosexual marriage. And in the Pauline assemblies, some women were active leaders and evangelists, although a deutero-Pauline interpolation (1 Cor. 14:33b–36) claims Paul for later "orthodox" domestic practice that had assimilated Aristotelian-Augustan household values, insisting on wives' subordination and silence. We should remember, however, that the apocryphal Acts, which emphasize virginity and narrate women preaching, were also popular among the orthodox and were not heretical, although centuries later they were excluded from the canon. Finally, in referring to same-sex relationships, Paul appeals to characterizations ("soft" and "against nature") based on Greco-Roman biology and philosophy that argued for "natural" (primarily active/passive) differences between males and females, polarized characterizations of male and female that are in tension with Pauline churches' baptismal confession (Gal. 3:28) and with modern biology and psychology.

Deutero-Pauline Epistles:
Colossians and Ephesians

Colossians is probably the earliest deutero-Pauline letter written in Paul's name. In great contrast to the leadership of women and their active participation in the worship of early Pauline assemblies, this pseudonymous letter assimilates Pauline household values to Aristotelian politics.[74] The structure of the "household code" in 3:18–4:1 with its (1) three pairs, (2) related reciprocally, (3) emphasizing three domestic groups' (wives, children, slaves) subordination to the paterfamilias in his three roles (husband, father, master—the same male) is ultimately dependent on Aristotle's sociological description and philosophical/

political justification of Greek domestic life. "The primary and smallest parts of the household are *master and slave, husband and wife, father and children.* . . . There is also a department . . . called the art of getting wealth."[75] Aristotle is primarily concerned to order the relationship between each of these three pairs as that between ruler and *subordinate,*[76] the same primary concern reflected centuries later when the deutero-Pauline letters emphasize these three pairs of relationships, a domestic political structure absent from the earlier, authentic Pauline letters. Colossians 3:18–4:1 has the following tripartite structure:

> 1a. Wives, *be subject* to your husbands,
>   1b. Husbands, love your wives.
> 2a. Children, *obey* your parents,
>   2b. Fathers, do not provoke your children.
> 3a. Slaves, *obey* your earthly masters,
>   3b. Masters, treat your slaves justly and fairly.

In each of the three paired and reciprocal exhortations, the first part (1) emphasizes submission, while the second part (2) three times addresses the same, one, male, husband-father-master of the household. The form assumes that there are no women heads of households, over against Colossians 4:15! This pseudonymous, deutero-Pauline author may be opposing women like "Nympha" in his own time who enable Christian assemblies to meet in their houses. Even the name he uses relates her as a "bride" to marriage. The same might be true for 2 Timothy 4:19; this deutero-Pauline author may send closing greetings to the great Prisca in order to claim her memory for Roman "orthodoxy," to associate her name with the later subordinationist ethic of the Pastoral Epistles over against the "old wives tales" (1 Tim. 4:7) he opposes.

This structured domestic code has its origin in Aristotle, but the ethic was reinforced by Emperor Augustus. According to Dio Cassius, Octavian called on his soldiers "to conquer and rule all mankind, to allow no woman to make herself equal to a man."[77] The imperial ideology structured Roman society and households as macrocosm and microcosm. The Stoic philosopher Arius Didymus drew up a summary of Aristotle's politics and household ethics for the emperor; he argues that "a man has the rule of this household by nature, for the deliberative faculty in a woman is inferior, in children it does not yet exist, and in the case of slaves, it is completely absent."[78] Further, Augustus's politics formed the social psychology of the time; the competition, hierarchy, and patriarchy of Roman imperial society were internalized by individual persons and groups. Local elites of the many cities around the empire competed to fit in with the Augustan moral revolution.

The introduction of the Aristotelian/Augustan household code into Pauline and Petrine Christianity brought other dramatic changes, for example in the understanding of baptism. Many scholars think that Galatians 3:27–28 reflects a pre-Pauline baptismal confession: "As many of you as were baptized into Christ have clothed yourselves with Christ. There is no longer Jew or Greek, there is no longer slave or free, there is no longer male and female; for all of you are one in Christ Jesus." This is repeated in Colossians, but the "no longer male and female" pair vanishes: "in that renewal, there is no longer Greek and Jew, circumcised and uncircumcised, barbarian, Scythian, slave and free, but Christ is all and in all" (Col. 3:11). The change is related to the introduction of the household code, which insists that there *still are differences* between male and female, contradicting the earlier baptismal confession. As eschatological urgency wanes and the church acculturates socially, the social reversals that Jesus and Paul's eschatological thought had hoped for disappear, with corresponding changes in both baptism and Christian ethics.[79]

The slave section of the Colossian code is developed most: "slaves, obey your earthly masters in everything, . . . wholeheartedly, fearing the Lord . . . " (Col. 3:22). However surprising it may be to a modern reader, very few texts from the ancient world object to slavery in itself, which had to wait until the industrial age when machines became available to do such work; the Greco-Roman literature we have on household management discusses rather how to treat slaves. Since masters considered slaves their sexual property,[80] an outrage to any modern sensibility, we inevitably wonder that these household codes emphasize obedience "in everything" so one-sidedly. No New Testament text directly addresses the issue of the sexual exploitation of slaves.

The Pauline metaphor of the "body of Christ" (1 Cor. 12:12–31; Rom. 12:4–8) functions in these deutero-Pauline epistles in a way that Paul himself never used it: to reinforce patriarchy. When Paul tries to persuade the Corinthian women prophets to continue wearing veils, to retain this cultural symbol of being women, he does not combine his patriarchal argument (the only one in his authentic letters) with the powerful metaphor that society (church) is a "body" (1 Cor. 11:2–16; contrast his argument in 1 Corinthians 12 and Romans 12).[81]

Both Colossians and Ephesians visually image cosmic order as a "body" of which Christ is the "head" (Col. 1:18; 3:15; Eph. 1:22; 4:4, 16), an image in Roman culture alien to modern democratic egalitarianism. It recalls the legendary story of the conflict in early Rome between patricians and plebeians; when enemies attacked, the plebeians seceded from Rome. The Senate sent out Menenius to address the humble poor, and he persuades them to return and defend Rome, reminding the poor of a symbolic metaphor "quoted in all ancient histories: as the human body has many parts, so society has many classes."[82] Menenius speaks so powerfully that the plebeians grieve: "tears flowed from the eyes of all and they cried out to him with one mind and voice to lead them back to the city" to take their humble station and fight Rome's enemies.[83] Colossians and Ephesians combine Paul's patriarchal argument (from 1 Corinthians 11) with the powerfully persuasive metaphor of society as a body, add that this body has a ruling "head," modify the baptismal confession so that it no longer mentions women (much less their equality), and incorporate the Aristotelian household code, insisting on women's subordination. Theologically and ethically the deutero-Pauline church joined the Augustan moral revolution.

As Colossians expands the slave/master exhortations, so Ephesians emphasizes the wife/husband pair, which the author interprets in light of Christ's relationship to the church, cementing the inferior position of the wife christologically. The Christology/ecclesiology dominates 5:25b–27, so that these exhortations are directed more to the church than to the marital couple. Elizabeth Johnson has noticed several flaws in the metaphorical argument: (1) to use Christ's relationship with the church as a model sets up a divine standard, so builds in difficulties for merely human marriage bonds. (2) Christ died for the church, which husbands do not do for their wives; and whereas Christ *gave* himself, husbands are to *love* themselves (5:25), an alarming shift from altruistic to selfish motivation. (3) Marriage is a "mystery" (5:32), a term he also uses of the inclusion of Gentiles in the ancient people of God (3:4), but the analogy is problematic. Jewish and Gentile Christians become a new humanity (2:11–22) as men and women become "one flesh" (5:31), but in the second union, radical inequalities are strictly maintained.[84]

The Deutero-Pauline
Pastoral Epistles

The Pastoral Epistles (1 and 2 Timothy and Titus) were probably written in the early second century in Asia Minor and are not cited by patristic writers until late in that century. Paul and Timothy serve as apostolic and legitimate ministerial models for the ecclesiology and ethics promoted by the author. One of their major concerns is to limit the role of women in the churches.[85] The author proscribes certain roles and activities for women; most exegetes, therefore, think that women were actually performing these functions in the churches. "Males" (*andras;* 1 Tim. 2:8) are given instructions in public prayer, following which the author orders women to be silent and submissive, forbidding them to teach or have authority over a man (vv. 11–12). First Timothy 2:13–15 then gives one of the only theological arguments in the pastorals, appealing to the creation stories[86] to justify his effort to silence and subordinate women, an argument that shows one of his primary concerns in writing. The deutero-Pauline author opposes women's prophetic speaking in worship, which Paul himself had assumed in 1 Corinthians 11:5–6, 13–15, ministerial roles attested also by Pliny (*Ep. 96 to Trajan*), who writes that he tortured two slave women "whom they call deacons (*ministrae*)." Those whom the author opposes may be Gnostics, but also might be orthodox, like the women mentioned by Pliny and those represented in the apocryphal "Acts of Paul and Thecla,"[87] who preach and baptize. The pastorals and the *Acts of Paul and Thecla* are both second-century narrations of Paul's biography, and both were long considered canonical by many, but Thecla was finally rejected as canonical in the fifth century.[88]

After Paul's death, conflict continued polarizing groups and practices that Paul had tried to hold together in a kind of "unity," for example, in the Corinthian church. Paul had assumed and encouraged women preaching and prophesying in worship (1 Cor. 11:5–6, 13–15; Phil. 4:3; Rom. 16:6–7), on the one hand, but engaged in conflict in Corinth, he removed the clause "there is no longer male and female" (Gal. 3:28c) from the baptismal confession (1 Cor. 12:13b) and made the patriarchal argument that "the husband is the head of his wife" (1 Cor. 11:3b), on the other. In continued polarizing conflict, the *Acts of Paul and Thecla* emphasized the former practice of Paul, while the pastorals rigidly exaggerated the latter.

The pastorals oppose an ascetic forbidding of marriage (1 Tim. 4:3), emphasizing the goodness of creation (4:4–5), just as Paul himself had argued (1 Cor. 7:28; 10:26), but they suppress Paul's preference for celibacy (1 Cor. 7:7–8, 26, 28, 38), insisting against him that young women marry (1 Tim. 5:14, against 1 Cor. 7:25–26). It is theologically and morally outrageous when this "Pauline" author argues that a woman "will be saved through childbearing" (1 Tim. 2:15). The deutero-Pauline author puts into Paul's mouth the words of the emperor Augustus and of the medical doctor Soranus; thus he removes all boundaries between the world and the church, and his theology of salvation for women becomes heretical.

He also opposes and tries to regulate the ministry of communities of widows in the churches, wanting to reduce their numbers, to increase the age of those accepted into the order, to reclaim the younger women for patriarchal marriage, and to deny all of them ministry, reducing the institution to a system of charity for older women (1 Tim. 5:3–16). The contest for patriarchal, ecclesiastical power and control of finances over against these women is clearly visible in Ignatius (*Polycarp* 4.1–3) and Polycarp (*Phil.* 4.1–3; cf. 1 Tim. 6:6–10, 17–19, perhaps also directed against rich widows), letters addressed only to the bishop.[89]

We summarized Paul's own views above (pp. 117–18) and here summarize the discussion of deutero-Pauline epistles. A second-generation Pauline student wrote Colossians, an educated, acculturated Roman. These debates about how humans live together have an especially dense meaning, and are inextricably, directly linked to questions of Christology, ecclesiology, eschatology, ethics, and baptism. The author of Colossians removes any explicit mention of women from the baptismal declaration (Col. 3:11; cf. Gal. 3:28) and then a few verses later introduces Aristotelian household ethics with an exhortation, "wives, be submissive . . ." (3:18). This occurs in Pauline churches that have deemphasized eschatology and modified their Christology, so that Christ no longer dynamically becomes a slave whom God will exalt (Phil. 2:7, 9),[90] but is the cosmocrator, ruler of a hierarchically structured world, who replaces Caesar as the rightful "head" of the "body." The Pastoral Epistles participate in what has become a polarized discussion among Christians. They continue Paul's emphasis on the goodness of creation, but they reject Paul's ascetic distance from this "world." Their this-worldly polarization goes so far that the author suggests a heretical soteriology, that a woman will be saved by childbearing, which Paul himself never mentioned once.

Second-generation, deutero-Pauline Christians acculturating to Roman imperial (tyrannical) society wrote a passive ethic into our canon. Many modern Christians are responding to our recent experiences in social and political history by rejecting passive subjection to domestic and political hierarchical institutions. In the next chapter we will see that Matthew, writing at roughly the same time as the earlier deutero-Pauline epistles, stresses treating others in the household equally; there is diversity within the canon. For Paul himself and Matthew, Christology functions in social settings where some women are leaders, slaves are encouraged toward manumission, and all household members are treated equally; however, in the deutero-Pauline epistles, christological hymns and household codes begin to reassert hierarchical domestic relationships.

Family and Gender
in the Synoptic Gospels and Acts

Paul focuses on ethnic issues, relations between Jews and Gentiles, not on the family as such; the Gospels are concerned with the family in a way that Paul is not. We now take up these issues and briefly refer to three non-Christian stories, in order to sketch a cultural context for discussing family values in the Gospels.

Family Values as Penultimate in Roman, Greek, and Jewish Stories

Three contemporary examples illustrate that ultimate values in Roman, Greek, and Jewish culture were articulated over against family values. Family life in its diverse forms was basic, so that ultimate values and choices were dramatically presented as even more important than one's family relationships.

Dionysius narrates the conflict between Romans and Sabines for military supremacy, a conflict settled in a David-and-Goliath manner. Providence, they thought, had prepared six cousins for the contest: twin daughters of an Alban were married, one to a Roman the other to an Alban, and each sister bore triplets at the same time.[91] These six cousins love each other, but they are asked whether they are willing to give their lives for their country, whether they value their country more highly than their family.[92] Dionysius then narrates the pathetic story of the cousins fighting for their opposing cities, killing each other one by one until the only remaining cousin, a Roman, is victorious.[93] The reader then learns that his sister had been engaged to marry one of her Alban cousins; when she grieves her fiancé's death, her Roman brother kills her, claiming that he "loves his country and punishes those who wish her ill."[94] The father refuses to allow his daughter to be buried, and that night gives a splendid banquet to celebrate Rome's victory, a story of which Romans are proud! This legend both exhibits Romans' highest value, the state, and encourages Romans to maintain that value system by narrating ancient Romans' paradigmatic choices for the state over against their own families.

The Greek Stoic Epictetus writes about the life of a Cynic preacher; he does "not find that marriage, under present conditions, is a matter of prime importance for the Cynic."[95] But according to Epictetus this is the Cynic's choice in light of his or her duty: "Where, pray, is this king [the Cynic], whose duty it is to oversee the rest of men; those who have married; those who have had children; who is treating his wife well, and who ill; who quarrels; what household is stable, and what not; making his rounds like a physician, and feeling pulses?"[96] In this diatribe Epictetus describes the task of an unmarried Cynic as that of a physician of morals who oversees others' marriages. Being single reduces the Cynic's distractions, in order that he be able to focus on proclaiming moral duty, which includes others' domestic responsibilities.

In the Jewish philosophical diatribe 4 Maccabees, love for parents, spouses, children, and friends is also relativized; the Mosaic, divine law may not be broken even for the sake of family (4 Macc. 1:13; 2:9b–14). After narrating the martyrdoms of the old man Eleazar, the seven young brothers, and their mother, a final section reflects on the tension and possible conflict between commitment to God's law and brotherly love:

> You know, surely, the bewitching power of brotherly love. . . . But although nature and companionship and virtuous habits had augmented the bewitching power of brotherly love [in the seven brothers Antiochus martyred], those who were left endured for the sake of piety, while watching their brothers being maltreated and tortured to death. Furthermore, they encouraged them to face the torture. They not only despised their agonies, but also mastered the emotions of brotherly love. (4 Macc. 13:19, 27; 14:1)[97]

The Jewish author reflects back a century and a half earlier on cultural and religious conflict during the Maccabean period and narrates stories of brothers and their mother, each of whom rejected idolatry in spite of wanting to continue living so that they might share life with their family.

These Roman, Greek, and Jewish texts each assume and promote an absolute value, either the Roman state, the duty of a Cynic moralist overseeing humanity, or obedience to Israel's holy God. Each text presents its hearers/readers with a choice, encouraging him or her to share the highest value, recognizing that crises would involve choosing the state, the philosophical call, or the Mosaic way of life over against one's own beloved family.

Family in the Sayings Source Q

The Sayings source Q (texts common to the Gospels Matthew and Luke that have no parallels in Mark) has typically been dated early, around 50 C.E., but Hoffmann has argued that the final redaction reflects the crisis mood of the siege of Jerusalem in the late 60s, so that the source Q would be roughly contemporary with Mark.[98] In Q, Jesus asserts that he "came to" bring conflict within the household between son and father, daughter and mother, daughter-in-law and mother-in-law (Matt. 10:34–36//Luke 12:51–53, alluding to the prophetic lament in Micah 7:6).[99] Matthew 10:37//Luke 14:26 and Mark 10:29 extend this to include a man leaving his children "for my sake and for the gospel." We do not know what family she left, but Mary Magdalene (from Magdala on the sea of Galilee) was among those who left her village and followed Jesus. Response to Jesus divided families, understood

by many to be the foundation of Greco-Roman society. The eschatological crisis meant that persons faced choices about what is most fundamental in life, an ultimate demand more important than family. Parents in a patriarchal society experienced the anarchy of sons, daughters,
and daughters-in-law in the crisis of God's coming rule.

Similarly in Matthew 24:37–39//Luke 17:26–27, 30[100] ancient crises
narrated in the Bible are correlated with the present eschatological crisis: The everyday activities of eating, drinking, marrying, and being
given in marriage (this last a male/female contrast) were interrupted by
the flood in Noah's day, by sulfur from heaven in Lot's, and again in the
present crisis by Jesus' proclamation. Hearing God's will demands in-
terrupting normal activity and living differently. In these eschatological
sayings God's future will not be like the evil present; the coming kingdom disturbs the patriarchal family.

The source Q sets burying one's own father over against following
Jesus: "let the dead bury their own dead; [but as for you, go and proclaim the kingdom of God]" (Matt. 8:22b//Luke 9:60a[b]).[101] In this crisis, one must come to Jesus and "hate his own father and mother and
wife and children and brothers and sisters and indeed his own life"
(Matt. 10:37 [without "wife"]//Luke 14:26). One cannot serve two masters, God and mammon (Matt. 6:24//Luke 16:13).

Like the Roman, Greek, and Jewish texts outlined above, Q rela-
tivizes family without being antifamily.[102] The Q source also contains
marriage law: One may not divorce a wife and marry another, which
would be adultery (Matt. 5:32//Luke 16:18). These Jewish Christian
disciples' primary loyalty is to the Son of Man, who demands love of enemies and mercy,[103] even if such a way of life generates tension with
others in the nation (e.g., Matt. 3:9//Luke 3:8; Matt. 8:10//Luke 7:9;
Matt. 8:11–12// Luke 13:28–29) or in one's own family.

Family in the Gospel of Mark

The roughly contemporary Gospel of Mark expresses similar sentiments more often in the form of stories instead of sayings. At the very
beginning of his ministry Jesus calls Simon and Andrew, James and
John, then Levi, all of whom respond by renouncing father, household,
or occupational ties (Mark 1:16–18, 19–20; 2:13–14).[104] Disciples
leave ordinary ties because the time is extraordinary, eschatological.

Three subsequent passages (3:20–21, 31–35; 6:1–6a) narrate the
relation of Jesus to his own family, stories with negative nuances. After these early stories, Jesus' family disappears, not reappearing even
in the resurrection narratives. In the first two texts, Mark employs the
"sandwich" pattern (3:21–35): Jesus' family charges that he is beside

himself. Second, the Jerusalem scribes say he is possessed by Beelzebul, and third, Jesus' mother and brothers ask for him, stimulating Jesus to characterize his true family. This sandwich pattern brings Jesus' family into dangerous literary proximity to the scribes who are blaspheming. Concluding the pattern, Jesus redefines his family: "Whoever does the will of God is my brother, and sister, and mother" (3:35). Stephen Barton observes that the stories of Jesus and his family in chapters 3 and 6 are bracketed between two passages about the Twelve (3:13–19 and 6:7–13): Jesus' relations with his own family are replaced by relationships with his disciples.[105] Ascribed honor, inherited from one's family by birth, is replaced by honor acquired by doing the will of God.

In 3:19, the crowd of potential disciples is in the house with Jesus, in contrast to his birth family, who are outside (3:31, 32). As Mark's narrative develops, the "house" replaces the synagogue as the place where he teaches (cf. 5:19, 38; 7:17, 30; 8:3, 26; 9:28, 33; 10:10). His "own house" (6:4b) rejects him. In the final section, the Temple itself is set over against a leper's house (14:3–9). The house, the place where the new Markan community gathers, is an architectural symbol of tension between the two orders.[106]

Mark includes a block of material on household-related topics beginning at 10:1: marriage and divorce (10:2–12), children (10:13–16), and possessions (10:17–31).[107] In the last section disciples are amazed when hearing how difficult it is for rich persons to enter the kingdom. In contrast to the rich man who would not renounce his great possessions (10:22) Peter exclaims, "Look, we have left everything and followed you" (v. 28). Jesus responds:

> Truly, I tell you, there is no one who has left house or brothers or sisters or mother or father or children or fields, for my sake and for the sake of the good news, who will not receive a hundredfold now in this age—houses, brothers and sisters, mothers and children, and fields with persecutions—and in the age to come eternal life. (vv. 29–30)

The old family included a patriarchal father (v. 29); the new one does not (v. 30; cf. 3:35), since God is the only Father (11:25; 14:36; explicitly in Matt. 23:9).[108]

In 13:9–13, the longest speech in the Gospel, we learn one social source of this Markan critical evaluation of family. In the eschatological crisis, "brother will betray brother to death, and a father his child, and children will rise against parents and have them put to death; and you will be hated by all because of my name. But the one who endures to the end will be saved" (13:12–13).

Christ's passion is the model for the disciple. Ten times in the passion narrative (chaps. 14—15), Mark writes that Jesus was "betrayed," and three times in 13:9–13 the author uses the same verb of the disciples. Disciples are being betrayed "to death" by their own families. And 13:13a is the only time the verb "hate" occurs in Mark.[109] We begin to understand the commitments and experiences that led to relativizing the old households, replaced by the new eschatological family of Jesus.

Gender Roles in Mark

On a different subject, how are women imaged in the Gospel of Mark? Women are not included in the Twelve, but they are the only faithful followers at the cross and the tomb, which suggests that the Roman Christian community had women leaders.[110] Reading the Gospel through its two long parables, the sower (4:3–9) and the wicked tenants (12:1–12), Mary Ann Tolbert concludes that women exemplify primarily the fourth, the only positive type of response to the word, bearing fruit (4:8, 20). These include the woman who responds to Jesus by ministering (1:31), the hemorrhaging one who takes the initiative in touching him (5:24b–43), a foreign woman and her daughter (7:24–30), the poor widow who gives all (12:41–44), the one who anoints Jesus' head (14:3–9), and the women at the cross and tomb (15:40–16:8). Negative examples are Jesus' mother, Mary, as seen above, as well as Herodias and her daughter (6:14–29).

Two of the most striking are the foreign woman and the one who anoints Jesus. The former is an unclean Gentile, who delivers the only snappy apophthegm spoken by a woman in the Gospel: "Sir, even the dogs under the table eat the children's crumbs" (7:28). Her apophthegm refers to eating customs. Although Jesus and the Gentile woman are not at a symposium, the saying gives Kathleen Corley the occasion to point out how unusual it was for a woman to remain after a dinner for the symposium, where women hardly ever spoke, much less engaged in such witty responses.[111] With this saying the Syrophoenician woman corrects Jesus, changing his mind, the only character in the Gospel to do so, with the result that he heals her daughter; her refusal to be silent produces results. The other woman anoints Jesus in the house of Simon the leper, after which Jesus proclaims that she "has anointed my body beforehand for its burial" (14:8)—not that she has anointed him king/Messiah. Her act of love, pouring out expensive oil, is contrasted to the immediately following one of Judas, who accepts a promise of money to betray his teacher (14:10–11).

Plutarch's story of Eumetis is a rare parallel to both Markan stories:

Engaging in such discourse as this along the way, we arrived at the house. . . . Anacharsis [a Scythian prince][112] was seated in the colonnade, and in front of him stood a girl who was parting his hair with her hands. This girl ran to Thales in a most open-hearted way, whereupon he kissed her and said laughingly, "Go on and make our visitor beautiful, so that we may not find him terrifying and savage in his looks, when he is, in reality, most civilized."

When I inquired about the girl and asked who she was, he replied, "Have you not heard of the wise and far-famed Eumetis? Really, though, that is only her father's name for her, and most people call her Cleobulina after her father" [Cleobulus of Lindos on Rhodos, one of the seven sages].

"I am sure," said Neiloxenus, "that when you speak so highly of the maiden you must have reference to the cleverness and skill that she shows in her riddles; for it is a fact that some of her conundrums have even found their way to Egypt."

"No, indeed," said Thales, "for these she uses like dice as a means of occasional amusement, and possessed of wonderful sense, a statesman's mind, and an amiable character, and she has influence with her father so that his government of the citizens has become milder and more popular (*politikos kai philanthropon ethos*)."

"Yes," said Neiloxenus, "that must be apparent to anybody who observes her simplicity and lack of affectation. But what is the reason for her loving attentions to Anacharsis (*temelei philostorgos*)?"

"Because," replies Thales, "he is a man of sound sense and great learning (*sophron . . . polumathes*), and he has generously and readily imparted to her the system of diet and purging which the Scythians employ in treating their sick. And I venture to think that at this very moment, while she is bestowing this affectionate attention (*philophroneisthai*) on the man, she is gaining some knowledge (*manthanousan*) through further conversation with him (*prosdialegomenen*)."[113]

Eumetis's wit is parallel to that of the Syrophoenician woman's: Her statesman's mind influences her father to milder, more "philanthropic" rule, exactly the subject of the foreign woman's successful debate with Jesus. In Mark, a wise foreign woman plays the role of the wise foreign male, Anacharsis, which is very unusual. "Plutarch, who violates custom by having a woman (non-prostitute) present at a symposion, is nevertheless careful to have her remain silent in spite of his views on the equality of those present at symposia and his notion that all present should participate."[114]

Unlike the wise but silent Eumetis, the Syrophoenician woman raises her voice in the text. Juvenal belittles such women who speak their minds.[115] And as Eumetis strokes Anacharsis's hair and kisses Thales,

another unnamed woman anoints Jesus' head. Plutarch does not narrate Eumetis's actions as erotic (see 154B), but many other symposium
stories and pictures that are erotic mean that the overtones of the
woman's touching Jesus remain a matter of discussion.[116]

At the conclusion of the Gospel, the women at the tomb flee, as the
Twelve had done earlier, for they were afraid (16:8). In its ancient context, this ending was a challenge to the Markan congregations. In the
eschatological crisis and in the current social crisis when Rome was at
war with Judea, would the contemporary readers also flee in fear and
not confess their Lord?[117]

Family in the Gospel of Matthew

Scholars debate whether the radical demands of discipleship—even
over against family—that are voiced in Q and Mark are softened[118] or
further radicalized[119] in Matthew. Matthew was written in Syria after
the Judean-Roman war, and in this setting both of continued social-
religious conflict and of identity formation over against developing rabbinic Judaism, Matthew reflects continued, perhaps even heightened,
tensions between some disciples and their families. Retelling Mark's
story of the call of the first four disciples, Matthew adds that they are
pairs of "two brothers" (4:18, 21), reflecting Matthew's ecclesiastical understanding of the communities as a "brotherhood" (cf. also 23:1, 8;
28:10). The author has made the Q text, Matthew 8:18–22 (including
"follow me, and leave the dead to bury their own dead," discussed
above), an introduction to the story of Jesus stilling the storm, a parable of the church in the end time.

Matthew 10:16–23 in the "missionary discourse," which Ulrich Luz
renames the "disciples discourse," is especially important, the fundamental ecclesiastical text of the Gospel that addresses *all* members of
the Matthean communities, not just an elite group of wandering missionary radicals.[120] This discourse has three parts (10:5b–15, 16–23,
24–42); after verse 16 the sayings have a loose connection to the setting
and are transparent to the church of Matthew's day. Matthew (10:21)
has taken sayings from Mark's eschatological discourse ("and brother
will deliver up brother to death, and the father his child, and children
will rise against parents, and have them put to death," 13:12) and made
them relevant to disciples' present experience as they are flogged in synagogues and dragged before the Gentiles. Other sayings about family
(10:34–36, 37–38) occur in the third section of the discourse, which
concerns relationships. In persecution the disciples are urged not to fear
(vv. 26, 28, 31), for they are related to Jesus and through him to the Father. Jesus' coming provokes violence, one aspect of a chaotic end time,

including tensions in the family (10:34–36, the first Q passage discussed above). Only Matthew includes the final phrase from Micah 7:6, "and one's foes [enemies] will be members of one's own household," emphasizing the more personal "household."[121] Matthew adds another Q passage in 10:37–39, in which the three "against" phrases of verse 35 are followed by three parallel statements in verses 37–38, for example, "whoever loves son or daughter more than me . . . ," all three of which conclude " . . . is not worthy of me." Commitment to Jesus is primary, as seen already in 8:18–22. The passage concludes by emphasizing receiving or giving to one of the "little ones," ordinary members of the community, as one would to Jesus, so stressing solidarity in the new family. The pagan satirist Lucian[122] sketches a somewhat later picture of Christians acting just this way, an ethic that Barton calls "afamilial" or "suprafamilial," verging on an antifamilial stance[123] only in 10:34 ("Do not think that I have come[124] to bring peace on earth; I have not come to bring peace, but a sword"). Even here, the issue is one of ultimate commitment to Jesus during the period when early rabbinic Judaism and Matthean Jewish Christianity were distancing themselves from each other.[125] This is not a social program, for elsewhere Matthew's Jesus regulates divorce (5:27–32; 19:3–12) and emphasizes the Fifth Commandment (19:19).

Matthew 12:46–50 also takes over the Markan passage (3:31–35) on Jesus' true family as well as the story of his rejection by his hometown (Matt. 13:53–58; Mark 6:1–6a). Jesus' family are more polite in Matthew; further, Matthew breaks Mark's ominous connection between the story of Jesus' family and the Beelzebul controversy. Matthew focuses not as Mark does on Christology, but on ecclesiology, on the "disciples," a term the editor adds to the text (12:49). The chapter of parables that follows (13) clarifies the identity of Jesus' new family who do the will of the Father in heaven. Jesus told these stories first to the "crowds," but then in a "house" (13:36, where the Matthean churches would be hearing the Gospel read) he added an explanation and more parables for the "disciples." Afterward Matthew has Jesus going immediately to his "own country" and teaching in "their synagogue," where he is rejected. They can perceive only the honor of his birth family, his mother Mary and his brothers James, Joseph, Simon, and Judas, and his sisters, but not "from where" Jesus has "this wisdom and these mighty works" (13:55–57).

Warren Carter has convincingly argued that Matthew 19—20 is unified by the Greco-Roman cultural concerns that structure contemporary discussions of household management.[126] These two chapters follow the fourth of Matthew's five discourses (chap. 18), one concerned with the right ordering of life within the brotherhood, how to practice community. Carter creatively draws on Victor Turner's model of permanent liminality,[127] and he suggests that Matthew's narrative proposes antistructure, egalitarian relationships that are qualitatively different from the dominant contemporary society. Many modern exegetes want to interpret early Christian relationships as egalitarian, often an anachronistic projection. Within this unit, however, Matthew 20:12 does use the rare adjective "equal" (isos), which means to "put on the same footing," placing the emphasis on "equality of treatment, dignity made manifest and recognized."[128] Whether the adjective "equal" applies to all aspects of household relationships in this unit is doubtful; there are no Greco-Roman parallels for what twentieth-century persons would call egalitarian households. Carter is wise occasionally to use the expression "more egalitarian." He also deals with this by contrasting the implied audience and the real one:

> Matthew's actual audience would be familiar with a call to an alternative household structure [e.g., from the Gospel of Mark], but the reality of that structure was not as evident among the actual first-century audience as the First Evangelist wished it to be, especially now that a new situation vis-à-vis the synagogue has developed. The hierarchical and androcentric pattern of the surrounding society has not been sufficiently abandoned, and the new structure, which the presence of the reign of God required, was not properly visible.[129]

Carter emphasizes Turner's point that liminality occurs when social changes are occurring, so the more egalitarian Gospel stories and sayings would have been one aspect of the churches' agenda.[130] Elaine Mary Wainwright also sees women's active ministry and leadership in some Matthean house churches.[131]

Matthew 19:3–12 deals with divorce, naming it—except for unchastity and remarriage—adultery. The debate is androcentric and patriarchal, focused on what a husband may do (v. 3). Over against common divorces or multiple divorce, the Matthean Jesus opposes the practice if it is followed by remarriage, an interpretation of Genesis 1:27c. There is a similar opposition to the common contemporary practice of divorce in the Damascus Rule (CD) IV, as well as in ancient Roman custom. Spurius Carvilius, the first Roman to divorce his wife (in 231 B.C.E. according to the legend) "was ever afterwards hated by the people," although he swore that he married to have children and that his wife was barren.[132] Analogously, Matthew 19 opposes divorce and remarriage, not hierarchy. Over against Roman, especially Augustan legislation, Matthew legitimates a single lifestyle (19:10–12). Males who have divorced their wives (because of their unchastity) and not remarried are called "eunuchs" (19:12).[133] A clear sign that this group is in tension with developing mainstream synagogues and society is their positive description of themselves by the normally negative terms eunuchs, children (19:14), and slaves (20:26–27). In the next chapter, tax collectors and prostitutes epitomize the new family (21:28–32)!

In Matthew 19:13–15 Jesus blesses children, "for of such is the kingdom of heaven" (19:14). The weak, dependent child is an example or representative of all in the kingdom, which repeats the image that begins the fourth discourse. When the disciples ask who is greatest in the kingdom, Jesus calls a child, places it in the middle of them, and says, "Truly I tell you, unless you change and become like children, you will never enter the kingdom of heaven. Whoever becomes humble like this child is the greatest in the kingdom of heaven. Whoever welcomes one such child in my name welcomes me" (18:3–5, only in Matthew).[134]

Carter rightly emphasizes both the metaphorical and literal meaning of Jesus' saying: Disciples are dependent on God for salvation, and socially, they are to become like children and welcome children into membership in the group.[135] In the infancy narrative (chap. 2), Jesus himself is pictured repeatedly as a child dependent on his mother. In striking contrast to the epistolary literature, Matthew's texts on the household have no reference to the duties of authoritative parents who are to discipline children (cf. Col. 3:21; Eph. 6:4) or to a goal for children of maturing and becoming adult citizens.

Matthew 19:16–30 presents another element of contemporary discussions of the household (according to Carter's thesis) in Jesus' dialogue with the rich young man who has "many possessions" (19:22). In contrast Peter tells Jesus, "look, we have left everything and followed you" (v. 27). Jesus in turn blesses those who have left their houses (20:29, plural in Matthew, singular in the source, Mark 10:29), another critique of the dominant values of contemporary society. Parallels do occur in the Hellenistic Jew Philo,[136] the Essenes,[137] in the Stoic Chaeremon,[138] and among Cynics.[139] Attitudes within the Matthean churches toward owning houses were inconsistent. Peter left "all things" (4:20; 19:27) but later still seems to have family and house (8:14); even Jesus seems to have a house (9:10, 28; 13:1, 36) in Capernaum.[140] The centurion in Capernaum does not give up his property or profession (8:5–13). Still, exhibiting and maintaining status by one's houses and property is being criticized by a prophetic minority in Greco-Roman society, a critique being lived by some in the Matthean church. The Matthean inconsistency may well have resulted from the experience that houses of Christian patrons attracted crowds inside to the resident teacher; they served the missionary and other interests of the group well.[141]

The parable of the householder that follows (20:1–16) raises the question of "what is right" (20:4, *dikaion*) and of not doing "wrong" (v. 13, *adikos*), the central ethical question raised as early as Plato and Aristotle with respect to household relationships. Much more surprising in Greco-Roman society is that workers are treated as "equal" (v. 12, *isos*) to each other.

Then for the third time Jesus prophesies his death (20:17–19), followed by a struggle for precedence among the disciples (vv. 20–28). Carter is correct to connect this section with the treatment in chapter 19 of household relationships.[142] Every Greco-Roman discussion of household management orders the position of slaves; even when the discussion of children drops out, as in 1 Peter, slaves still appear, so that the audience would experience a "gap" if this were omitted. Here the Matthean Jesus clarifies the meaning of his death for his followers: unlike the Gentiles who lord it over their subjects (the Gentiles who will mock, flog, and crucify him, v. 19), those who wish to be great in the Matthean community must be "servant" (*diakonos,* v. 26), and those who wish to be first must become slave (*doulos,* v. 27). Of this, Jesus' death is a model: "just as the Son of Man came not to be served but to serve, and to give his life a ransom for many" (v. 28). Jesus' action as servant and slave is ironic: giving his life as a "ransom" frees all from slavery.[143] Stoics formulated a perhaps analogous paradox: the moral person must make free moral choices but is a slave to God (Epictetus, *Diss.* 4.1.89).

The text in Matthew 20 differs qualitatively from deutero-Pauline[144] and deutero-Petrine epistles. In 1 Peter Christ's passion is also a model, but the language is placed within the *slave* section of a household code (1 Peter 2:18–25). Scholars debate which verses in 1 Peter give moral advice to believers who *legally are slaves* and which verses generalize for all believers,[145] but in Matthew interpreters must decide whether the whole section is directed to the Twelve (vv. 21, 24), to those *who wish to rule,* or rather to all disciples. In 1 Peter, the slaves are to defer to harsh masters; in Matthew the powerful are to serve, somehow to become slaves as Christ did in his death. Whereas 1 Peter drops out any specific instructions to masters, Matthew gives none specifically for slaves. First Peter is open to being misunderstood, not only by slaves but by abused wives, misunderstood to mean that suffering under their powerful masters or husbands is God's will. Whereas 1 Peter adapts more to Roman patriarchal culture, Matthew's household values are countercultural. Strikingly, 1 Peter and Matthew are both "Petrine." Carter has performed an invaluable service in pointing out these qualitative differences between Petrine and deutero-Pauline epistolary ethics on the one hand, and Matthew 19—20 on the other, texts that are virtually contemporary.

In summary, in the context of social/religious conflict in Syria and in the further process of identity formation, Matthew continues Mark's relativizing the family in relation to contemporary discipleship, and this is true for all Jesus' followers, not just for a missionary elite group of prophets. Nevertheless, Carter has shown that Matthew 19—20 makes radical proposals for new family relationships, which oppose divorce followed by remarriage; presents eunuchs, children, and slaves (and in 21:31 prostitutes) as models; and encourages the abandonment of houses, that is, of status based on wealth. The parabolic householder, concerned for "what is right" (20:4) and "wrong" (v. 13), treats all workers "equally" because he is "good" (vv. 12, 15). Carter also suggests that there are significant differences between the implied audience and the real one, which is having difficulty implementing Matthew's more egalitarian narrative ethic.

Gender Roles
in the Gospel of Matthew

In the genealogy of Jesus, the son of David, Matthew lists five women, not matriarchs, but Tamar, Rahab, Ruth, the "wife of Uriah," and Mary (Matt. 1:3, 5, 6, 16). Each is somehow outside the patriarchal household structure[146]; they are presented perhaps as exemplars of "higher righteousness"; for example, Tamar acts when Judah refuses, and Ruth recognizes the power of the Hebrew God.[147] However, Joseph is the model in Matthew's infancy narrative, while Mary is passive and silent.

Chapters 8 and 9 narrate ten miracle stories, which focus on the Messiah's interaction with outcasts or marginal persons. The first group of three concludes with the healing of Peter's mother-in-law (8:14–15// Mark 1:29–31//Luke 4:38–39). Mark concludes the account saying that "the fever left her, and she began to serve (diekonei) them," which Matthew changes to the singular, "to serve him." Scholars debate whether to translate the key verb as "to serve" (food) or "to minister"[148]; the latter is more probable in Matthew (in contrast to Mark or Luke), since this Gospel's point is christological: She ministers to Jesus.

Matthew 9:18–26//Mark 5:21–43 narrates Jesus' raising of Jairus's daughter and the healing of a woman with a hemorrhage; neither is named. This is the first time we hear a woman's point of view in the Gospel, as she speaks to herself (9:21). Doubly marginal because of her bleeding and her gender, the woman approaches Jesus from behind, in contrast to the male ruler who approaches directly. Her daring faith, Jesus says, has made her well (v. 22).

The only parable with a woman as a main character is narrated in 13:33 (//Luke 13:20–21): "he told them another parable: 'the kingdom of heaven is like yeast that a woman took and mixed in with three measures of flour until all of it was leavened.'"[149] Here a woman's work, usually invisible, is paired with that of a man who sowed mustard seed. Her work is transparent for God's; in the hands of a woman baking bread, one can perceive the creative hands of God. Yeast raising the bread symbolizes the eschatological nearness of life.

The first time a woman's voice is heard is in 15:21–28//Mark 7:24–30 (omitted by Luke). The "Caananite" woman is an ethnic and religious outsider in Israel, also outside the patriarchal family structure and associated with harlotry.[150] Three times Jesus opposes her request in behalf of her daughter, but in the struggle, she overcomes his objections. Jesus' third objection is a proverb: "It is not fair to take the children's food [bread] and throw it to the dogs" (15:26). She claims the crumbs under the master's table, and thus receives from Jesus a key messianic gift, bread, again because "great is your faith!" (v. 28).

Herodias (14:1–12, esp. 5, 9) and "the mother of the sons of Zebedee" (20:20) are two negative figures. But in contrast to Mark, Matthew does not present Herodias as having already married Herod, nor does Matthew repeat Mark's (6:19) remark that she was unable to kill John. In this Gospel Herod is the one who resents John and wants him dead (14:3–5), so Herodias is not the primary culprit.[151] The mother of the two sons wants them to rule, but Jesus rejects this and asks them whether they can accept the cup of suffering. They respond, "we are able" (v. 22), and then indeed, she appears at the foot of the cross (27:56)! The two sons are included in the eleven who finally see Jesus on the mountain in Galilee (28:16), "but some doubted" (v. 17).

Jesus' Jerusalem ministry is dominated by males, except for the woman who anoints Jesus in the house of Simon the leper (26:6–13// Mark 14:3–9) and those who "followed" him from Galilee and "ministered" (*diakonousai*) to him (27:55–56//Mark 15:40–41; cf. 8:14–15, Peter's mother-in-law). Further, the first resurrection appearance of Jesus is to Mary Magdalene and the other Mary (28:1, 9–10), striking both because the Christophany to women is not in Mark or Luke and because Matthew *removes* the Christophany to the male leader, Peter, who is named nowhere in the resurrection narrative (28:7; cf. Mark 16:7; 1 Cor. 15:5; Matt. 23:8–12).

Family in the
Gospel of Luke and Acts

This Gospel has the most radical critique of marriage and promotes ascetic values. Luke transforms the call of the first disciples, Simon Peter and the sons of Zebedee, into a story of the growth of the world mission (5:1–11//Mark 1:16–20), for which they leave "everything" (v. 11, Luke only) and follow him. This already anticipates the lists of things and persons a disciple leaves in 14:26 and 18:29. In the latter, the Lukan Jesus says, "truly I tell you, there is no one who has left house or wife or brothers or parents or children for the sake of the kingdom of God, who will not get back very much more in this age and in the age to come eternal life." Unlike the other Synoptics (Mark 10:29–30//Matt. 19:29–30), Luke includes "wife" among those left behind, and then writes only that one will "receive manifold more in this time," dropping the list of new family members that the traditional saying says "he" will receive. Verse 14:26 also includes a "wife" among family members a disciple will "hate" as he bears his cross.[152] These conditions of discipleship follow Luke's parable of the great banquet (14:15–24// Matt. 22:1–14), in which marrying a wife is the third and final excuse that one cannot accept an invitation to the kingdom of God (14:20),[153] an astounding contrast to Matthew, in which the parable is a *marriage* feast.

Editing the story of Levi's call, Luke emphasizes favorite themes: Levi is a "tax collector," an outcast, in whose house Jesus reclines at table with a large company of tax collectors, potentially a new fictive family, one not determined by sexual relationships, whom Jesus has come to call to repentance (5:27, 29, 32//Mark 2:13–17).

Luke repairs Jesus' relations with his own family, omitting Mark 3:19b-21, 33–34a, and 6:2–3, in which they are saying he is crazy and take offense at him, to which Jesus responds by repudiating them; this omission leaves only the nonpolarized redefinition of the new family in 8:21, "my mother and my brothers are those who hear the word of God and do it." This more positive presentation corresponds with the image of Mary presented in the infancy narrative. Mary believes the prophecy of the Lord (1:45) and treasures these words in her heart (2:19, 51). When a woman blesses the womb that bore Jesus, he counters, "Blessed rather are those who hear the word of God and do it" (11:27–28), an evaluation that is basic for both men and women in this Gospel. Turid Seim persuasively argues that this redefinition of motherhood makes Mary a model of women believers whose roles are determined by the Word, not by childbearing,[154] which means that Luke and Acts are radically different from the deutero-Pauline Pastoral Epistles.[155]

Luke also omits the positive instruction on marriage and against divorce in Mark 10:2–12, retaining only Luke 16:18, and Luke separates this one verse from the Markan/Matthean unit on the household. Verse 16:18 primarily prohibits remarriage. Seim argues that Luke "16:18 not only addresses those who want to remarry after divorce but excludes primarily the possibility of remarriage by those disciples who have left their wives behind (without necessarily divorcing them . . .)."[156]

Luke does include other verses from the Markan/Matthean unit on the household, that is, Jesus blessing children (Luke 18:15–17// Mark 10:13–16) and the challenge to the rich man, a "ruler" in Luke (18:18–30//Mark 10:17–31), followed by Jesus' third prediction of his passion (18:31–34//Mark 10:32–34). Luke then significantly delays narrating the dispute over precedence among disciples for four chapters, placing it in the setting of Jesus' last supper (22:24–27//Mark 10:35–45). Luke, therefore, breaks up the earlier unit on the household, showing less interest in relationships within birth families, more interest in ethical behavior in the new fictive families.

The life of the new fictive family is lived both in public and in "houses." The Spirit is poured out on Elizabeth and Mary in the former's home (1:40), so that Mary speaks the Magnificat in a domestic setting. The widow Anna is an exception: she comes to the Temple, praises God, and continually proclaims the child Jesus "to all who were looking for the redemption of Jerusalem" (2:38), therefore publicly.[157] The woman searching for her lost coin, whose action is transparent for God's, searches in her house (15:8), while the male shepherd searching for his lost sheep does so outside. The Spirit comes on "all" at Pentecost (Acts 2:1), both men and women (Joel 3:1–5 [LXX 2:28–32] quoted in Acts 2:17–21), both of whom "prophesy," according to Luke, in a "house" (2:2). In general, the community in Luke-Acts moves from the Jerusalem Temple and from synagogues into houses, although this does not become a sectarian alienation; apologetically, the Lukan Paul claims that "this was not done in a corner" (Acts 26:26).

A qualitatively new element in the household values of Luke-Acts is that groups of ascetic "widows" appear, groups which 1 Timothy 5:3–16 later attempts to regulate.[158] Luke portrays widows who rise above the role of victim, who are positive examples of faith and piety. Two sayings concerning widows have synoptic parallels, the woe on scribes who make a pretense of long prayers while devouring widows' houses (20:47//Mark 12:40) and the parable of a widow who searches for her lost coin (21:1–4//Mark 12:41–44). Four stories of widows belong to Luke's special material: the prophet Anna (2:36–38), Elijah going to the widow at Zarephath in Sidon (4:25–26), Jesus' raising the widow's son at Nain (7:11–17), and the parable of the importunate widow (18:1–8).[159] Acts 6:1–6 narrates a conflict in Jerusalem in which a group of the Hellenists' widows are being neglected. Finally, Tabitha dies, and the disciples call Peter, who finds widows weeping over this woman who had been "devoted to good works and acts of charity" (Acts

9:36, 39). Tabitha may well have been keeping this group of single women in her house. Peter raises her and calls "the saints and widows," showing her to be alive (v. 41).[160]

There are a few married couples in Luke-Acts. Luke 2:41–52 assumes that Joseph and Mary live together as married, and James becomes a leader of the church in Jerusalem (Acts 1:14; 15:13, 19; 21:18; cf. Gal. 1:19; 2:9). Characteristically, however, only Paul, not Acts with its de-emphasis on one's birth family, identifies James as Jesus' "brother." Nevertheless, this may explain why Luke omits Mark 6:3, where James is listed with other family members who have been "offended" by Jesus. Thus Jesus' birth family, Mary and James, are woven into the narrative. Acts mentions only two married Christian women: Sapphira (5:1–11) and Priscilla (18:2, 18, 26); the ruling, pagan couples Felix and Drusilla (Acts 24) and Agrippa and Bernice (Acts 25) also play parts in the narrative.

Many women in Greco-Roman society died in childbirth. Seim observes that Augustus's legislation pressured available single women to remarry, so that the significant numbers of widows in Christian household communities would have been unusual. Lukan stories portray them as models. One poor widow gives her all (21:1–4), in contrast to the rich. The importunate widow is not passive, but takes her own case to the judge (18:1–8).[161] There are both similarities and significant differences between the widows of Luke's narrative and those in 1 Timothy 5:3–16. Anna is a prophet and has been chaste since she was twenty, so she is not a model for deutero-Pauline older widows (contrast Luke 2:37 with 1 Tim. 5:4, 9, 11). Luke does not inform the reader whether Anna had children. She is primarily an ascetic figure, not one oriented toward patriarchal household duties of wife and mother as portrayed by the author of 1 Timothy.

We close this discussion of Luke with a reference to one of its unique stories. Jesus' parable of the prodigal son (Luke 15:11–32) proclaims an eschatological reversal of values. Wolfgang Pöhlmann surveyed the son's place in the household through ancient Greek, Roman, and Jewish literature, including, for example, Aeschines, *Oration* 1, a polemic against a son for wasting his father's property.[162] Another example is Terence's comedy, *The Brothers*, on contrasting ways of bringing up children.[163] Jesus' parable is more open-ended, concerning a "prodigal" father who has compassion on the son who has wasted the household goods as well as the father's challenge to the older son to celebrate the return of his profligate brother. In ancient agrarian society, this challenge would be an alienating, offensive, implausible, potentially transforming metaphor of the kingdom of God clashing with centuries of domestic, didactic wisdom. The goal of the household is to increase property, against which the younger son sins. By its extravagant ending, Jesus' parable collides with this ordered world and evokes the protest of the elder brother. The story is not a parenetic example, but a parabolic metaphor that breaks through and contradicts the order and righteousness of the household. The father accepts the son, so that the hearer encounters the new world of the kingdom of God.

Gender Roles in Luke-Acts

In the narrative of Luke-Acts pairs of men and women occur frequently, so that occasionally there is a complementary gender pattern. A few examples are Jesus' healing of the possessed man as well as of Peter's mother-in-law (Luke 4:31–39), the healing of the centurion's slave and the raising of the widow of Nain's son (7:1–17), the stories of the good Samaritan and of Mary and Martha (10:25–42), the parables of the insistent widow and of the Pharisee and publican (18:1–14), the conversions of Lydia and of the jailer (Acts 16:13–34). And there are numerous other man-woman parallels in these two volumes. Zechariah's disbelief and Mary's belief are contrasted in the infancy narrative (1:20, 45), Simeon and Anna both prophesy (2:25–38), Jairus begs Jesus to heal his daughter, and a woman with hemorrhages touches him herself (8:40–56), Peter heals Aeneas and raises Tabitha (Acts 9:32–42).[164]

Still more important for understanding the composition and structure of Lukan churches, the author refers to groups of men and women separately. The twelve apostles (Acts 1:21, 26) and the seven Hellenists chosen for the daily food "service" (Acts 6:3) are, and—these texts insist—must be, male. On the other hand, Luke gives the following summary of Jesus' Galilean ministry:

> [1]Soon afterwards he went on through cities and villages, proclaiming and bringing the good news of the kingdom of God. The twelve were with him,[2] as well as some women who had been cured of evil spirits and infirmities: Mary, called Magdalene, from whom seven demons had gone out,[3] and Joanna, the wife of Herod's steward Chuza, and Susanna, and many others, who provided for (diekonoun) them out of their resources. (Luke 8:1–3)[165]

Here the male Twelve are juxtaposed to the women, some of whom are named as representative. The women "serve" or "minister" (diakon-). Luke 8:1–3 distinguishes between the women who "serve" and the male function of preaching the kingdom of God. The women "serve" "out of their resources/property" to support the group, two related but not identical themes. Property is more typically "sold," "distributed," "given," or "received" (e.g., Acts 2:45; 4:34, 37; 20:35), not usually associated with "service."[166]

Elisabeth Schüssler Fiorenza claims that "servant" very early had become a title, to be a "deacon" or a "minister," which included preaching and serving the Eucharist, so that Luke has narrowed the meaning of the word and excluded its reference to leadership.[167] The titular or technical use of the noun in the Gospels is not clear; in Matthew, as we saw above, the verb can have the metaphorical meaning "to minister" also in reference to women. In Luke, too, the verb often means "to serve" food.[168] Beginning in chapter 12, the verb "to serve" is transferred from the sphere of women to that of men, and so takes on its metaphorical sense. In Luke, however, gender roles are not abolished or reversed; rather, new ideals for male leadership are established. Unlike Matthew, Luke restricts ecclesiastical leadership to males. In 10:38–42[169] Martha represents a typical woman in Luke who "serves," although even here the contrast is not between one sister who "hears the word" and another who "serves," but rather between hearing and service that is "worried and distracted" (v. 41; cf. 1 Cor. 7:32–35). Nor is this a symbolic fight between two sisters: as in Acts 6:1–6, the word is prioritized. Mary hears but remains silent, as do even the brilliant Prisca (Acts 18:26) and Eumetis,[170] a rare reference in Greco-Roman literature to an honorable woman staying after dinner to learn at a symposium.

The women in Luke 8:1–3 are also models of giving up property to benefit the churches (Luke 14:33; 18:22; 19:8–9; Acts 2:44–45; 4:32–37; 5:1–2), another aspect of their modeling for (male) leaders.[171] This modeling functions in another way as a critique of leadership by the Pharisees—who in Luke have little or nothing to do with the historical Jewish sect in Israel, but are a symbol for the wealthy in his own culture (esp. Luke 16:14).[172] Thus the local whore provides a model for the local wealthy householder (Pharisee) who invited Jesus to dinner (Luke 7:36–50). Modern Christians must deplore that the author chose the Pharisees as a negative model of leadership, a choice that has had utterly disastrous consequences over centuries for how Christians have understood and treated Jews. Historically, the Pharisees represent Christian leaders in Luke's own churches (see, e.g., Acts 15:5), but the literary choice has had lethal consequences for Jews in subsequent centuries.

One other crucial aspect of Luke's portrayal of gender concerns the women at Jesus' cross (23:39), grave (23:55–56), and resurrection (24:1–10).[173] They "see" the crucifixion and the burial (23:49, 55). The two men in dazzling clothes at the grave tell Mary Magdalene, Joanna, Mary the mother of James, and the other women to "remember" how Jesus "told them" the gospel that he would be delivered, crucified, and raised (24:4, 6–7). The women are disciples (cf. the feminine term *ma-thetria* in Acts 9:36) who "hear the word of God" (cf. 8:21) and re-member it, a function not reserved for males, but for all his "mothers and brothers." In Luke the word, not only Christophanies, evokes faith. The women have heard, and they tell everything (24:9), but these words are not believed by the male apostles (24:11, 16, 25, 38, 41). The con-trast between the apostles disbelieving and the women hearing the word in the resurrection story, therefore, forms an inclusion with the infancy narrative, where Zechariah does not believe, but Mary does (1:20, 45). Men's rejection of faith in contrast to women's faith begins and ends the Gospel. Again, women's hearing, remembering, and believing are mod-els for the men. But in Greco-Roman culture despite Luke's narrative af-firmations, women are inappropriate witnesses of the resurrection, not leaders, who in Acts (1:21–22; 6:3) must be male, a necessary mas-culinization that is never theologically justified. "The double message nurtures a dangerous memory."[174]

We have seen that ultimate values in non-Christian Roman and Greek texts, as well as in Jewish and Christian ones, are stated in relation to family. Some Romans' ultimate value was the state; a key legend presents the state as more important than cousins, a sister, or sons. Epictetus teaches that a Cynic gives up family in order to follow moral duty and oversee other human beings. Fourth Maccabees narrates that obeying God is even more important than continuing life with beloved brothers and a mother, more important for a mother than a long life together with her sons. The Sayings source (Q) also presents choices between family and the gospel. Finally edited near the time of the Judean war with Rome, the inaugural discourse in the Sayings source demands love of en-emies, a demand to live God's merciful rule that divided families.

Mark narrates stories in which Jesus calls some disciples to leave their fathers and professions. Honor inherited through one's family is re-placed by honor acquired by doing the will of God. Jesus' "own house" rejects him, and a different "house" becomes the place where the new Markan community gathers, those who have left biological brothers, sis-ters, mother, father, and children. An assertive, witty, vocal Sy-rophoenician woman serves as a paradigm for this community. Matthew continues these radical demands, adding however an emphasis on treat-ing others in the new household equally. Jesus legitimates both married and single lifestyles and blesses children, literally and metaphorically representatives of all in the kingdom. Some in the community are giv-ing up their houses (with their dining rooms), symbols of status in so-ciety. In this section concerning household relationships, Jesus tells the parable of the householder, an image of treating workers equally, and also prophesies his death, teaching leaders in the community to become a servant, a slave. Matthew narrates stories of several striking women, including a parable in which a woman mixing yeast is the main character, her work transparent for God's.

Luke gives the most radical critique of marriage and promotes ascetic values. Jesus' mother Mary becomes a model for all believers whose roles are determined by hearing the word, not emphasizing her as a model for childbearing. Luke also narrates the stories of a number of ascetic widows; for example, Anna—exceptionally for a woman—proclaims the child Jesus to all publicly. Luke omits any mention of her children, a significant contrast to 1 Timothy 5:3–16 that later attempts to direct such widows back in the direction of marriage and childbearing. These women are models of hearing the word and of servant leadership, which establishes new ideals for the male leaders who are actually guiding the community, male leadership that Luke affirms is necessary but never theologically justifies. At the cross, too, the women remember Jesus having told them the gospel, which they believe while the male disciples do not, a story that forms an inclusion with the Mary/Zechariah story in the infancy narrative, contrasts that introduce and conclude this Gospel.

Gender Roles, Marriage, and Celibacy in the Gospel of John and Beyond

Gender Roles and Images

There is not much specific information about family life in the Gospel of John, but the Gospel is an anomaly in many ways, not least of which is its portrayal of gender imagery. The overwhelmingly male images of paternal-filial relationship have been seminal for trinitarian theology from Tertullian through Nicea and into the present era. This has been true to such an extent that some theologians argue, in the face of the obvious need for more balanced gender imagery in contemporary spirituality and worship, that the titles of Father and Son are definitively revealed, and thus normative and inflexible, language for the Trinity. There is a noticeable increase in father-son language as one moves through the canonical Gospels beginning with Mark and ending with John. There is no earthly father, but all response to the paternal image is fixed on God.[175]

But Jesus is known as son of Joseph (John 1:45; 6:42), in contrast to Mark's son of Mary (Mark 6:3), in keeping with the patrilineal custom, a usage that was not seen by the author to stand in contradiction to

Jesus' divine sonship.[176] The Jesus of John's Gospel is preoccupied with "glory" (*doxa;* to be understood as "honor"), that of the Father who sent him, but in which he also shares, for the agent, and especially the son and heir, shares in the status and prestige of the patron. Seen in this light, Jesus invests much energy in the defense of his patron's honor, and his along with it.

Yet the Johannine Jesus, however much he may seem to exemplify *andreia,* is also the incarnate feminine wisdom figure, agent of God's creation, who calls all to a meal and even feeds them with her own flesh like a nursing mother, and gives living water to drink like a well-organized mother of a household.[177] The family of Jesus do appear fleetingly, with as much enthusiasm for his behavior as in the Synoptics (2:12; 7:2, 5, 10). Contrary to the Synoptic tradition, his mother is not only an active participant in his ministry in the scene at Cana but actually seems to inaugurate it (2:3–5). His reluctant compliance with her wishes exemplifies the close mother-son relationship. Also in contrast to the Synoptics, she is present at the cross, and with at least one female relative, which gives a family presence at the execution that is missing elsewhere (19:25–27). Jesus' consignment of mother and beloved disciple to each other in this scene is often seen as the perpetuation of family bonds beyond death. It also provides the means whereby the dying Jesus performs his filial duty of providing for a presumably widowed mother.

The disciples, more clearly delineated in Matthew as the Twelve and in Luke as the Twelve apostles—though in neither case confined to the Twelve—are an indeterminate number in John. Though the tradition of the Twelve is known by the Johannine author (6:67, 71; 20:24), it is only by reading in from the Synoptics that one can conclude they are the only ones in Jesus' inner circle. The two sets of brothers in the circle persist from the Synoptic tradition, Simon and Andrew (1:40–41) and the sons of Zebedee (21:2). The two sisters, Mary and Martha (Luke 10:38–42) are joined by their brother Lazarus (11:1–2 and the rest of the story) to form an unusual set of sibling disciples, all apparently unmarried, thus modeling the priority of discipleship over family.

There are no detailed instructions about discipleship or apostleship in John, nor is the familial language of siblings used for those who place priority on discipleship, in contrast to Mark 3:31–35 and parallels (except at 20:17 by Jesus[178]; 21:23 by the redactor). The major metaphor for the disciples becomes not sisters and brothers but friends (15:15), not members of the immediate household or family but of the extended social circle in a patronage relationship.

If there is no instruction in discipleship and apostleship, there is nevertheless modeling. Instead of one central confession of faith by Peter

augmented by that of the centurion at the cross, as in the Synoptic structure, there are four in John: Nathanael (1:49), Peter (6:68–69), Martha
(11:27), and Thomas (20:28). Two figures in the Gospel exemplify discipleship: the beloved disciple and the mother of Jesus, who is associated with him at the cross, while Martha, Mary, and Lazarus are among
those loved by Jesus (11:5). Two figures exemplify apostleship by com-
municating to others what they have experienced of Jesus: the Samaritan woman and Mary Magdalene.[179]

In short, the Jesus of John's Gospel is a strange blend of masculinity
that reflects many typical traits, and an expression in male form of what
could definitely be considered feminine traits and functions: creating,
feeding, nurturing. The Johannine figure of Jesus defies gender stereotypes and expectations.

The gender images of Revelation and of most of the post–New Testament Christian writings of the period return to much more typical patterns. In Revelation, female images are stereotyped into the familiar categories of public male culture, based on women's sexual and reproductive
status. "Jezebel" is the false name of an apparently very effective Christian
prophet and teacher opposed to the author's policies; she is accused of
false teaching under the familiar prophetic rubric of adultery; her threatened punishment has innuendoes of sexual violence, and her disciples are
called her "children." This woman teacher is forced by the author's rhetoric
into the categories of adulteress and mother.[180] Other female characters
follow suit. The positive ones include the woman who gives birth (chapter 12) and the bride who personifies the city, an old biblical theme (chapters 21—22). The great negative female figure is of course the prostitute
of Babylon, who likewise personifies the anti-city, devourer of the faithful.

As usual, male characters have more flexibility of symbol: the risen
Christ, the lamb, the figure on the throne, the beast, and so on. Some
of them are victims of the prostitute's savagery, but except for the kings
who commit adultery with the prostitute (18:9) and lamb who as anti-
type at the end becomes the spouse of the bride (19:9; 21:2), the male
figures are not defined by their sexuality, but by their symbolic actions,
with the exception of the 144,000 who are defined precisely by their
unpolluted state because they have not been cultically compromised by
sexual contact with women (14:4). The marriage of the lamb and his
bride, full of biblical imagery and power, tells us nothing about early
Christian marriage, however.

As we move into the parenetic material of the post–New Testament
period, the conventionality of ethical teaching is apparent. Polycarp instructs the Philippian males to teach their wives to remain in truth and
to love (though not to submit to) their husbands and everyone else

chastely, teaching their children the fear of God.[181] The direct address to all household groups employed by the author of Colossians and Ephesians has been abandoned here in favor of a return to the literary topos of household management addressed to the male paterfamilias.

Clement of Rome, writing probably toward the end of the first century, praises the male Corinthians for enjoining dutiful submission of wives to husbands and good household management as part of his introduction to the Corinthians' virtuous harmony—until the events that provoke the writing of the letter set him to admonishing them for their unruly behavior in church leadership.[182]

The author of 2 Clement quotes with approval the apocryphal dominical saying that the kingdom will come when "the two are one, and the outside as the inside, and the male with the female neither male nor female."[183] He goes on to exegete the text to mean soul and body for inside and outside, and for the second part of the sentence, an ability of men and women to see each other in terms other than sexuality. A further saying of the Gospel of Thomas sheds light on the ideal behind these sayings: Christ will be revealed on the day that "you take off your clothes and are unashamed, and put your garments under your feet like little children."[184] This idea, more at home in Gnostic circles, is a rare exception to the general treatment of gender issues in this period. There is more at stake here, however, than sociobiology. In a culture like that of the ancient eastern Mediterranean, in which gender is such a deep and pervasive principle of ordering, these sayings speak of a radical reordering of society in light of the gospel, and of a vision of an eschatological era in which not only sexual conflict but cultural divisions can be overcome. This was, unfortunately, a more extreme ideal than most Christians were willing to embrace.

In most situations, rather, early Christians were part of the majority that assumed that careful control of contact between the sexes and the subordination of women were necessary ingredients in the Christian life. The author of 2 Clement goes on in the next chapter to cast ecclesiology in dualistic mode, so that the assertion of creation as male and female (Gen. 1:27) is understood to refer to Christ and the church. The exegesis wavers between affirming the (female) church as spirit (14:2–3) and identifying it as flesh over against the spiritual Christ (v. 4) in order to teach against mistreatment of the flesh. The end result is a positive affirmation of the flesh, but the reader is left in the midst of it with the traditional association of female (church) with flesh over against male (Christ) with spirit.

The Shepherd of Hermas, written at Rome in the first half of the second century, is full of puzzling but rather positive gender imagery. In the opening scene, Hermas sees again after many years a woman named Rhoda bathing in the Tiber,[185] a woman who had once owned him when he was brought up in slavery after having been abandoned as a baby. His admiration of her beauty leads her later, in a vision, to chide him for impropriety. Here, woman is forbidden fruit, and Hermas is, after all, married.[186]

Hermas's marriage is not compromised by this episode, but his own position in it is already in trouble because of his failure to exercise the proper authority of a paterfamilias. Both his children and his wife are offenders. The wife's problem is the female stereotype of the unrestrained tongue. In keeping with Roman familial patriarchal authority, the reproach is delivered to Hermas, who is expected to remedy the situation by ceasing to neglect her, which may not so much mean to give her more affection, as to assert proper authority and thereby keep her under control.[187]

But most of the women in the story are not at all under Hermas's control. Another female figure soon appears, who will be the revelatory agent throughout the remainder of the *The Shepherd of Hermas*, the woman church who shows Hermas the vision of a tower being built, an image of the church, which is herself. She is an old woman who grows progressively younger as the narrative proceeds, as, she explains, the church enters into the process of conversion, which rejuvenates the spirit.[188] It is ironic that allegorical women in the narrative (as opposed to the "real" women of Hermas's life, his former owner and his wife) speak of andreia or exemplify it, not unlike the women of Plutarch's treatise *On the Virtue of Women,* in which women exemplify courage to shame the men who lack it. Meanwhile the andreia of Hermas is sometimes in doubt, due to his inability to control his family and the behavior of others in his community. The woman church challenges him to "be a man" (*andrizou*), a term replete with gender bias not limited to males but expressive of the enthusiasm and courage needed to command and to accomplish.[189] This is what Hermas lacks at the beginning of the story.

The verb reoccurs in a later description of the rejuvenation process: An old man lacks andreia, and simply waits for death, but suddenly, when he learns that he has received an inheritance, he regains his andreia (*andrizetai*), he "gets a new lease on life."[190] While Hermas lacks it, Restraint (*enkrateia*), one of the seven allegorical women who carry names of virtues and support the tower, exemplifies it.[191] Even the twelve maidens, who are some of the builders in the later retelling of the building of the tower, are characterized by the way they could stand with courage (*andreios*), "as if they could carry the whole of the heavens."[192]

The maidens are at the same time "delicate" or "soft and luxurious" (*trupherai*), the exact opposite of andreios! They later come to spend the night with him "not as a husband but as a brother," and eventually to dwell with him. In their presence, Hermas becomes rejuvenated, so that he will be able to fulfill his responsibilities.[193] Thus the irony of the contrast is heightened, for women show andreia, while Hermas struggles to act according to the cultural expectations of gendered behavior placed on him by himself and his revealing agent.

The *Shepherd of Hermas* reflects the organization of patriarchal marriage and traditional gender roles, but at the same time, the function of feminine imagery in the visionary elements goes in a very different direction: women exemplify the characteristic male virtue of andreia while the principal male figure has difficulty expressing it.

Marriage

The presence of wives of unbelieving husbands in the community in 1 Corinthians 7:12–16 and 1 Peter 3:1–2 means that individual members of households were free to make their own choice about religious membership, even though the model of complete Christian households was held up as the ideal. The virtuously submissive conduct of Christian wives in Ephesians 5:22–24, Colossians 3:18, and especially 1 Peter 3:1–6, like that of long-suffering slaves (2:18–25), would be testimony to the truth of the faith and perhaps even convert the other. Thus female submission becomes not only a God-given duty but a missionary strategy, continued in 1 *Clement* 1.3.[194] It is all the more noticeable, therefore, that it is absent in the literature that soon follows: 2 *Clement,* the *Didache,* Ignatius, Polycarp, Barnabas, and Hermas know nothing of it, even in contexts in which the submission of wives is to be expected.[195] The concern for subordination of some to others moves out of the family into the extended family, the church.

Among the contents of the revelation that Hermas receives are regulations about marriage and remarriage. Separation without remarriage is mandated for adultery when the adultery is known by the innocent partner, but so is reunion if the adulterer repents and wishes to be taken back, on the basis that the repentant sinner must be accepted. Remarriage after the death of a partner is permitted but not encouraged, echoing 1 Corinthians 7:39–40.[196]

The Pastoral Epistles had specified a single marriage for those males who would aspire to leadership positions (1 Tim. 3:2, 12). The same is true for an older widow who is to be "enrolled" as recipient of support and as a member of the order of widows (5:9). But the same does not apply to younger widows, who are to remarry and resume their wifely duties (5:14). A contradiction is thus created whereby it would seem that no younger widow will ever be able to become an "enrolled" widow in old age.

However, the development of less-than-positive attitudes toward marriage on the part of Christian writers has already begun at this point by the singling out of church leaders, both male and female. Yet the *Letter to Diognetus,* an apologetic treatise probably written sometime in the second century, says that Christians are in most respects like everyone else, including that they marry and have children, but they differ in that they do not expose unwanted children.[197] Here marriage is assumed to be the normal Christian way.

At the beginning of the third century, the remarkable story of the martyrdom of Perpetua, Felicitas, and their companions at Carthage, though often thought to represent Montanist theology, assumes the normalcy of marriage. Perpetua is a high-status citizen woman (*honeste nata*) in a legal Roman marriage (*matronaliter nupta*),[198] with a new baby. The slave Felicitas, while not in a legal marriage because of her status, is pregnant. In neither case is there any suggestion that they are less than ideal because of their marital and procreative status, even though the *Acts of Perpetua and Felicitas* is often thought to reflect the theology of Montanism, which did idealize celibacy. On the contrary, Perpetua is the true leader of the group.

However, Athenagoras, another second-century apologist, affirms that Christians marry *only* to have children (not for lust), and therefore do not undertake a second marriage after widowhood, which would be "dressed-up adultery."[199] (The assumption that the first marriage bore children must be presumed.) Justin, in the middle of the second century, also writes that Christians marry to raise children, and a second marriage is considered sinful.[200] Minucius Felix, writing toward the end of the second century, also speaks of the Christian custom of marrying only once.[201] Hermas, always the moderate, states that remarriage after the death of a spouse is not sinful—though remaining in widowhood is better.[202]

It is Clement of Alexandria toward the end of the second century who presents the fullest expression of the early Christian ideal of marriage. Like his predecessors, he too affirms that marriage is primarily for the procreation of children.[203] Like them, too, he is quite pessimistic about a second marriage. It is neither the worst, nor the best; yet a few paragraphs later, a second marriage becomes Paul's meaning in 1 Corinthians 6:18: the immorality (porneia) that one is to shun as sin committed against one's own body. What emerges here is in keeping with earlier traditions that considered the only motivation for a second marriage to be lust.[204] Clement also knows the growing tendency to glorify lifelong celibacy, and recognizes it as a special service in the church.[205]

Yet Clement provides a spirited and sustained defense of marriage as the normal Christian way of life, especially against ascetic groups, such as Gnostics, with whom he is in direct contact in the metropolis of Alexandria. Most of book 3 of the *Miscellanies,* as well as other writings, are devoted to biblical and philosophical exegesis of God's will for human marriage. His answer to the question, Is it right to marry? is a resounding yes, for all kinds of philosophical, humane, religious, and even biblical reasons. Peter and Philip were married. At one point, he goes so far as to say that marriage is better because it gives more opportunity for sanctification through the difficulties and complexities of household relationships.[206] *Enkrateia,* which in his day was increasingly being understood as complete continence or celibacy, was understood by Clement in its original sense of self-control, a virtue necessary for everyone with regard to all the passions and appetites: thirst, hunger, and greed, as well as sexual desire.[207] Just as with food, drink, and possessions, self-control does not mean complete abstention, so too with sex, which was to be exercised in moderation in the marriage bed.

His restrained but positive attitude is based on his total affirmation of the good of creation. The goal of marriage is children, its fulfillment a large family, and having children is an action that imitates God, for it is participation in the creation of another human being.[208] Even his detailed but quaintly inexact description of the female reproductive system is followed by the remark that he is not ashamed to speak of the reproductive organs since God was not ashamed to create them.[209] His exegesis of Matthew 18:20, "Where two or three are gathered in my name," with acknowledgment that others have other suggestions, is that it surely means husband, wife, and child. Paul's stated preference for the unmarried state in 1 Corinthians 7:8 refers only to men who do not want the trouble of raising a family.[210] Clement even comes to the surprising conclusion that Paul was married, based on his statement in 1 Corinthians 9:5 that he has a right to take a "sister woman" with him as the other apostles do, combined with the interpretation of the "yoke-fellow" addressed by Paul in Philippians 4:3 as his wife left behind in Philippi![211]

Clement was married himself, and a layperson for most of his life, becoming a presbyter only at a later stage. He was the lay Christian teacher, whose concern was for young Alexandrian Christians, the most vulnerable to the exaggeratedly ascetic teaching of a radical Gnosticism that would totally deny the good of marriage. This is why he takes on directly some of the gnostic schools and teachers, countering biblical exegesis for biblical exegesis. Within orthodox circles, too, he speaks for the married Christian laity in a church that was coming increasingly under the mystique that celibacy was better, especially for church leaders.[212]

Contrary to modern stereotypes, not all Gnostics advocated entire renunciation of marriage. Clement himself tells us that the Valentinians and others married, and this is corroborated by at least one Valentinian text. Several gnostic teachers are also known to have had sons.[213] Family language is often used, and while some marriages probably included procreation, others held to a celibate ideal. But family was a wider social construct than parents and children, and gnostic social groupings must have contained many families of one kind or another, for few gnostic teachers seem to have taught complete abandonment of family social structures.[214]

Tertullian, another married presbyter at the turn of the third century in Carthage, wrote a special treatise, *To His Wife,* to encourage her, if he died first, to refrain from a second marriage, thus giving the Roman univira tradition a Christian literary form.[215] He is aware that the biblical patriarchs married several times, and even simultaneously, but takes this to be an arrangement that was done away with by Christ. Now, a single marriage is good, even though celibacy is better.[216] The regulation against remarriage for bishop and deacons in the Pastoral Epistles has by now become a discipline encouraged for everyone, and the Pastorals' encouragement to younger widows to remarry has been conveniently forgotten.[217]

Tertullian recognizes three ways of sanctification: from birth, the "virginity of happiness"; from second birth (baptism), either within marriage by mutual agreement or by perseverance in widowhood, a "virginity of virtue"; and in monogamy, including a renunciation of sexual contact later in the marriage.[218] Even Tertullian the married presbyter is swayed to value celibacy above marriage.

The dangers of marriage to a nonbeliever husband are taken up in part 2 of *To His Wife,* ready evidence that mixed marriages were still common. His arguments against mixed marriage provide interesting clues to the regular activities of Christian life at the time, and the anticipated difficulties of a Christian wife in a mixed marriage: early morning church attendance (the unbelieving husband will tell her to meet him at the baths); fasting (he will plan a banquet the same day); works of charity (he will find more important family business to attend to); night meetings and an all-night Easter celebration (he will not allow his wife out at night); hospitality to traveling Christians (he will not receive the traveler). She will have to attend to religious rites not her own: memorials on the first day of the year and of the month, and the front door adorned with laurel wreaths and lanterns.[219] He ends by encouraging Christian women to marry Christian men, even if it means marrying below their social status.[220]

This point seems to have been problematic in more than one church of the period. It is one of the things for which the Roman ascetic theologian Hippolytus excoriated his rival Callistus in the early third century. Callistus, he claims, allowed women of high social status to cohabit with lower-status males, including slaves, even though they could not thus contract a legal marriage. Presumably the lower-status males were Christian, and Callistus recognized such unions as true marriages for the sake of finding a Christian partner for Christian women. For Hippolytus, this was outrageous, and he goes on to charge that the practice forced such women, reputedly Christian, to birth control and abortion so as not to bring shame upon their families by bearing children outside legal marriage.[221]

The Growing Custom of Celibacy

The affirmation of marriage given by Clement and even to a certain extent Tertullian was not enough to stem the tide of growing enthusiasm for celibacy among ecclesiastical elites.[222] The false teachers of 1 Timothy 4:3 who forbid marriage would have felt quite at home in the increasing atmosphere of belief in the superiority of virginity, with the turn to celibacy for those who could not embrace virginity from the start running a close second. It is difficult to tell at what point the many general references to enkrateia (self-restraint) in the instructional literature of these centuries take on the technical meaning of celibacy.[223] Sometimes, the reference is quite clearly so.[224]

By the early second century, there seem to be identifiable groups of both men and women who have made a public commitment of virginity: Ignatius greets such a group of "virgins who are called widows" at Smyrna, along with "the houses of the brothers with their wives and children."[225] Justin in mid–second-century Rome refers to both men and women who live virginity into advanced age.[226] Minucius Felix also speaks of perpetual virginity (virginitas perpetua) as a Christian option.[227] By the middle of the third century, such groups were flourishing. Cyprian exhorts the consecrated virgins of Carthage with motives of purity, spiritual fruitfulness, total gift of self, and the eschatological motif of living the angelic life already on earth (based on Matt. 22:30//Mark 12:25). "That which we shall be, you have already begun to be," he tells them. "You already possess the glory of the resurrection. . . . You pass through the world without contagion, like the angels of God." The original command to increase and multiply has now been superseded by the command to continence for those who can.[228]

While some of the enthusiasm for celibacy was motivated by the gnostic denial of matter, there were other factors. The relative freedom especially of the ascetic woman also appealed. In Roman society, where women were both socially and legally fairly liberated by ancient standards, the role of wife and mother was still the only acceptable one. The ascetic life offered an alternative: freedom from the immediate patriarchal control of a husband (though ecclesiastical patriarchal control replaced it), freedom from the real health risks of childbirth and from child-raising responsibilities. The stories of women in the Apocryphal Acts who embrace celibacy instead of marriage are strongly charged with this liberation theme.[229]

Consecrated virgins seemed to live lives of considerable social freedom: Some in Cyprian's church are wealthy, and he complains that they do not share their wealth. He also considers it improper for them to use cosmetics and to attend weddings and the public baths with men.[230] Cyprian repeats an idea already begun at least by Tertullian and echoed many times after: That virginity, widowhood, and marriage are to be ranked in value in that order. He compares them, in reverse order, to the thirty, sixty, and hundredfold harvest of Mark 4:20.[231]

Besides social freedom, the religious ideology for celibate ascetic women included a claim on the traditional andreia of men. Freed from sexual and reproductive roles, such women were no longer to be seen within the structure of socialized gender, that is, no longer as subordinates or objects of male desire, but as potential equals, thus honorary men.[232] Within this context belong the curious references in early Christian literature to females becoming male.[233]

Celibacy, always a choice (but of course the best one) among orthodox Christians, became in the excessive severity of some ascetic circles the only way to be Christian. To Justin's student Tatian the Syrian was attributed this extreme position, though it is doubtful that he and his followers were called by the title Encratites (the Self-Controlled), as some maintained.[234] Marcionites, some Montanists, and some gnostic groups seem to have held the same position.

Encratite theology became the common milieu for many of the Apocryphal Acts of Apostles, such as the *Acts of John,* the *Acts of Paul and Thecla,* and the *Acts of Thomas,* where conversion to Christ necessarily included celibacy, the refusal of marriage, and the breakup of sexual relations within marriage. Here the theme of celibacy as sacred marriage and death as its consummation, a theme that runs through the whole tradition, finds its best audience.[235] A good example is *Acts of Thomas* 124, where the heroine Mygdonia tells her former fiancé that this spiritual marriage with Jesus is one that will last forever and is incorruptible, whose bed is spread with love and faith, and which consists of living words that abide eternally, in contrast to the marriage that she would have made with him.

The Council of Gangra in Paphlagonia (345 C.E.) anathematized those who held that marriage prevented the Christian's entry into the kingdom of God. This condemnation of the extreme did little to check the moderate position, in which marriage was clearly third class, after virginity and widowhood. In the next generation, Jerome's bitter polemical style was aimed at Helvidius (in 383 C.E.) and Jovinian (in 393 C.E.), who tried to argue against the increasingly popular beliefs in the perpetual virginity of Mary because virginity is superior to marriage. Jovinian's defense of the equal status of marriage for salvation was condemned.

The most unusual form taken by the growing enthusiasm for celibacy was that of "spiritual marriage" in the form of *parthenoi syneisaktai* (Greek), *virgines subintroductae* (Latin), a nearly untranslatable expression (perhaps "virgins brought in unofficially"), that refers to the custom of men and women marrying, sharing house and bed, but remaining celibate.[236] The motivation was to have the best of two good things: the eschatological advantages of celibacy, the superior vocation, combined with the obvious advantages of personal companionship, not to say a woman to manage the household. Nearly all the ancient references to the custom are male-oriented.

The first instance may be 1 Corinthians 7:36–38, though none of the Greek fathers understood the text this way—probably because they were largely against the custom. If the text refers to an early form of this practice, Paul is telling the male of such a couple who are trying it but are not sure they can maintain it, that they do no evil simply to marry in the usual way, though they will also do well to remain as they are.

The same custom may be present in the *Shepherd of Hermas*. Because of his new prophetic ministry, Hermas is told by the woman church, his revelatory agent, that his wife must from now on "be to you as a sister."[237] The only plausible interpretation within the context is that they are to cease having sexual relations. Tertullian bids a widower, if he must have female companionship to manage his household, to take a "spiritual wife." The context makes clear what he means, and he feels no need to explain. Elsewhere, he bids a widower instead of remarrying the usual way, to take a widow, and even several, an indication that perhaps the custom was not always confined to two persons.[238]

The official attitude toward the practice was usually suspicious, however, as exemplified by Jerome, who considered it a scandal because, under the guise of seeking "spiritual solace," the real reason is usually lust.[239] Canon 18 of the Council of Ancyra in 314 and Canon 3 of the Council of Nicea in 325 forbid the clergy to take a *subintroducta* other than a mother, sister, aunt, or other person beyond all suspicion. The custom was long in dying, however, for it continued well into the Middle Ages among the idealistic.

One could get the impression from reading the mainstream Christian literature of the third, fourth, and fifth centuries that the majority view rated celibacy as superior to marriage. But it is important to remember that during these centuries, the church increased enormously in population, and that what is preserved in the literature are the voices of an ecclesiastical elite who, through celibacy and clerical orders, were rising to usurp the status of the old Roman elite. We must assume that the vast majority of Christians in these centuries as in every century lived normal married lives.

6

Education
and Learning

Paul seldom alludes to children. Relationships between parents and
children in the Synoptic Gospels have already been treated in chapter 5 in the section on family and gender. Here after quickly summa-
rizing what Paul has to say about children, we will examine teachers
among early Christians. We will see that Jewish and pagan (Philo's and
Plutarch's) discussions of teachers in the household are similar in significant ways to Paul's discussion of teachers and prophets in Christian
households.

Children and Teachers in the
New Testament and Beyond

Paul is concerned about the theology and practice of relationships
between Jews and Gentiles, not nearly as focused on family issues, with
the result that he makes few remarks on the relationships between parents and children.[1] Most of his references are metaphorical; he mentions only two biological children, Rufus and his mother (Rom. 16:13)
and the man living with his "father's wife" (1 Cor. 5:1–5), surprisingly,
for example, not any children of Prisca and Aquila. The only specific
question concerns the children of "mixed" marriages, where he is exclusively concerned with the relationship between the married partners
(1 Cor. 7:12–16). Addressing the ascetics in this chapter, Paul does not
discuss either the advantages or the burdens of having children, which
would have been surprising for Cynic, Stoic, and/or Jewish readers.[2]

In his painful debates with the Corinthians about apostleship and
status, he uses a parental analogy: "Children ought not to lay up for their
parents, but parents for their children" (2 Cor. 12:14b). Already in the
first epistle, he had admonished them as his "beloved children" (1 Cor.
4:14), insisting that they might have many guardians in Christ, but
not many fathers (v. 15). Paul regrets that he could not address the

Corinthians as adults, but only as "babes in Christ" (1 Cor. 3:1–2), a passage O. Larry Yarbrough illuminates by observing that men (usually freedmen) sometimes played significant roles in tending children in the Greco-Roman world.[3] Timothy in a different sense is "my beloved and faithful child in the Lord" (4:17). He also refers to Onesimus, his very own child "begotten" in chains (Philemon 10, 12). Yarbrough concludes from these few references that intimacy is the dominant motif in all Paul's metaphorical applications of parent-child imagery. Paul rarely addresses persons as parents and never admonishes them, a significant contrast to the later deutero-Pauline household codes.[4] It would not be appropriate to try and construct a Pauline ethic of parenthood based on his metaphors.

We turn from these few texts in Paul concerning children to the question of teachers in the Pauline house churches and the Gospels. In chapter 3 we discussed education and learning in the Greco-Roman world, repeatedly citing works by Philo and Plutarch. We find these same tractates very helpful in understanding the activities of prophecy and teaching in the early church, so we will continue to cite them, especially Philo, "Preliminary Studies," and Plutarch, "How to Study Poetry."[5]

Responding to the Corinthians' question about "spiritual things" (1 Cor. 12:1, *pneumatika*), Paul renames them "gifts" (v. 4, *charismata*), listing "first apostles, second prophets, third teachers . . . " (v. 28). Recent scholarship has associated prophets and teachers[6] more closely than had been done earlier. The two are discussed together not only by Paul, but also by Philo,[7] Lucian,[8] and Plutarch.[9] There are similarities between Paul's discussion of teachers and prophets, on the one hand, and Philo's and Plutarch's discussion of teachers in Jewish and Hellenistic schools on the other.

From Paul's point of view, both prophets and teachers are gifted with the Spirit. He discusses prophecy in relation to ecstatic speaking in tongues (1 Corinthians 12 and 14), emphasizing prophecy as the higher gift. He would like "all" to prophesy (12:5), implying that all members might be prophets. But when he asks, "are all prophets?" (v. 29), the Greek construction suggests the answer no. First Corinthians 14:5, 23–24, 31 do not show otherwise. Prophets include women as well as men (11:5; cf. Acts 2:17–18 citing LXX Joel 3:1–2; also Acts 21:9).[10] These prophets had a certain authority in the community (1 Cor. 14:37): Paul demands that they "acknowledge" what he is writing as a command of the Lord. The authority is related to their receiving "revelations" (14:30) from the Lord, to prophetic powers enabling "understanding all mysteries and all knowledge" (13:2; cf. 14:2). First Corinthians 14:15–16 mentions praying, singing praise, and blessing with the mind and the spirit, the former meaning in understandable speech.

Discussing these verses, H. Greeven also cites 1 Corinthians 14:31, translating "for you can all prophesy one by one, so that all may experience[11] and all be encouraged (or exhorted)." The kind of prophetic exhortation meant is clear in 14:24–25; an outsider can be reproved or called to account by all. The same happened in school, and Plutarch gives advice on how to receive such rebukes.[12] Others are to "weigh" (*diakrinetōsan*) what is said (1 Cor. 14:29; cf. 37). "Test everything!" (*dokimazete,* 1 Thess. 5:21). Plutarch also repeatedly emphasizes this "weighing" of what is said to students in schools. He insists on discrimination (*diakrisis*), especially when teaching the young what the poets say about the gods.[13] But with debate there is to be order. Since the spirits of the prophets are subject to the prophets, there is to be no "tumult" (14:32–33, *akatastasia*). Greeven insists that it is incorrect to interpret these verses to say that the divine spirit within a prophet is subject to him or her, but rather, there is to be no competition between various prophets each of whom have the spirit, no tumult: they are to wait for each other. The purpose of prophecy is for upbuilding, encouraging, and consoling the church (14:3).

M. Eugene Boring argues[14] that many or most of these prophets functioned within specific communities, as did those in Corinth; the tensions over speaking in tongues and prophecy in this first epistle do not concern outsiders. Furthermore, we see them involved especially in worship, the context of Paul's discussion. This is also true of the prophetic figures who pronounce the hymns in Luke 1 and 2 and vividly true in the Revelation of John, which is to be read in worship (1:4), and which is permeated with worship materials, songs, hymns, confessions, and scriptural allusions.[15] This means that prophets utilize traditional materials, as had prophets whose oracles are now collected in the Hebrew Bible.

We note again that Philo and Plutarch refer both to teaching and to prophecy when they are discussing education, where traditional texts were studied. The "teacher of righteousness" at Qumran is both a prophet who speaks revelation directly "from the mouth of God"[16] and an exegete of scripture. Lucian presents Peregrinus in his Christian period as a prophet (*prophētēs*) who "interpreted and explained some of their books and even composed many."[17] Philo writes that Moses, founder of the tribe, received both arts of legislation and prophecy; he immediately observes that Moses had the "courage to say, God and God alone must I honour, not aught of what is below God."[18] The first example of Moses' law and prophecy is a monotheistic confession, both related to the Decalogue from scripture and similar to the confessions in 1 Corinthians 8:4 and 8:6a. When discussing education, Plutarch too mentions a "seer," Calchas, whom he disapproves, but Calchas's oracle could have been delivered by Isaiah, John the Baptist, or Anna: He "had no regard to the occasion, and made nothing of accusing the king before the multitude, alleging that he had brought the pestilence upon them."[19] (We note, however, that Plutarach's view of such a "seer" is closer to Paul's view of glossolalia than to his view of prophecy, which does not give up control of the mind.) Both Jesus and Paul were prophets as well as teachers. As Jesus and Paul allude to scripture, so also Philo and Plutarch repeatedly quote Moses and the great classical writers.

Christian prophets' traditional material included words of the Lord. We have space to mention only a few examples. The Matthean churches are to be hospitable to prophets (Matt. 10:41), figures like those sent out on mission in Mark 6:7//Matthew 10:1//Luke 10:1 (cf. the apostles and prophets of *Didache* 11).[20] These figures repeated and elaborated the Beatitudes (Matt. 5:3–12//Luke 6:20b–26),[21] which recalls the prophets in Corinth pronouncing "blessings" (1 Cor. 14:16). The Spirit teaches them what they are to say (Luke 12:11–12//Mark 13:11//Matt. 10:19–20).[22] As Moses the lawgiver and prophet confesses the one God alone, according to Philo, so these prophets confess Jesus, who promises that the Son of Man will acknowledge them before the angels of heaven (Luke 12:8//Matt. 10:32).[23] As the seer Calchas condemned the king for bringing pestilence, according to Plutarch, so Jesus in the Markan apocalypse prophesies earthquakes and famines, prophecies similar to those in the *Apocalypse of John*.[24]

Strikingly, both pagan and Christian prophets spoke for God in the first person. Hundreds of oracles of Apollo at Delphi were spoken in the first person, "I am" or "I have come." The second-century Christian prophet Montanus also spoke with such first-person address.[25] The Christian prophet of the Revelation of John uses this form sixty times, speaking directly for the Son of Man: "Do not be afraid. I am the first and the last" (Rev. 1:17b). To the church in Pergamum,

> "I know where you are living, where Satan's throne is. Yet you are holding fast to my name, and you did not deny your faith in me even in the days of Antipas my witness, my faithful one, who was killed among you, where Satan lives. But I have a few things against you." (Rev. 2:13–14a)[26]

Paul's list of God's gifts in Romans 12:7 also includes the activity of teaching,[27] a participle, not a noun; an activity, not an office.[28] Both teaching and reading were done aloud, not silently.[29] Jesus' oral teaching was powerful, having the same effect as his miracles (Mark 1:21–22; 6:2; 11:18).[30] The whole congregation is encouraged to "teach and admonish one another in all wisdom" in Colossians 3:16 (cf. 1:28; 2:6–7). Paul considers this too a gift of God; when they assemble, "each one has a hymn, a lesson (*didachē*), a revelation (*apocalypse*), a tongue, or an interpretation" (1 Cor. 14:26). But Paul is distancing himself from tongue-speaking in 14:6, "if I come to you speaking in tongues, how will I benefit you unless I speak to you in some revelation or knowledge or prophecy or teaching (*didachē*)?" Teaching has some relation to ethical parenesis in 4:17; Timothy is to remind them of Paul's "ways" in Christ Jesus. But Galatians 1:11b–12 makes it impossible to interpret "teaching" exclusively as ethics: "the gospel that was proclaimed by me is not of human origin; for I did not receive it from a human source, nor was I taught it (*edidachthēn*), but I received (*parelabon*) it through a revelation of Jesus Christ."[31] The verb "receive" and the verb "deliver" (*paradidōmi*) are rabbinic technical terms for passing on tradition, more or less formed confessions, liturgical sentences, prayers, and words of the Lord (1 Cor. 11:2, 23; 15:1, 3; Gal. 1:9, 12, 14; Phil. 4:9; 1 Thess. 2:13; 4:1; 2 Thess. 2:15; 3:6).[32] Paul does "deliver" such traditional confessions, words of the Lord, and ritual sentences (1 Cor. 7:10; 9:14; 11:23; 15:3; 1 Thess. 4:15). Hebrews 6:1–2 refers to what those desiring baptism were taught, including resurrection of the dead, one of the subjects of dispute in the Pastorals (1 Tim. 2:18), a "mystery" according to Paul (1 Cor. 15:51; cf. the Christ hymn in 1 Tim. 3:16).[33] The enigmatic Romans 6:17 may belong here: "you . . . have become obedient from the heart to the form of teaching (*typon didachēs*) to which you were entrusted." So both prophets and teachers pass on words of the Lord. Luke 11:1c presents a disciple's request, "Lord, teach (*didaxon*) us to pray, as John taught his disciples."[34] Paul always uses the verb "to teach" without an object, so as a technical term.[35]

Scholars have been unable to document reference to a "teacher" associated with a (house) synagogue in pre-Christian Judaism, and the Septuagint avoids the term, preferring "wise person" or "scribe." However, the Gospels describe those giving instruction in Torah as "teachers" (Luke 2:46; Matt. 10:24–25//Luke 6:40; Matt. 23:8). Teaching is interpreting scripture in Mark 10:1; 11:17; 12:14, 35, a teaching that has halachic character; scripture is read with questions of lifestyle in mind. Matthew 5:2 at the beginning of the Sermon on the Mount also belongs here.[36] Paul's exegetical excurses in 1 Corinthians 11:7–16, 15:35–49; 2 Corinthians 3:7–18; and Romans 4 are examples. This is probably the context for 2 Timothy 3:14–17 and 1 Timothy 4:13, which refer to what Timothy "learned" from the apostle.[37] In the first century when Jews and Christians were both assembling in houses, not in architecturally separate synagogues and churches, the school activity of teachers may be the best analogy to the scribal study of Torah.[38]

There is some concern for orthodoxy: 1 Timothy 1:3 and 6:3 are concerned with "teaching a different doctrine." Matthew 16:12 warns against the teaching of the Pharisees, but the charges are reversed against Stephen and Paul (Acts 6:11, 13–14 and 21:21). Philo contrasts Abraham with his kinsman Nahor, who has "not accompanied him abroad in his journey from the created to the uncreated," but rather "does not sever himself from the study of astrology; he honours the created before the creator, and the world before God."[39] Plutarch too is concerned that the students not heed "every breath of doctrine," but wants students "to thrust aside a good deal of what is not true or profitable."[40] Plutarch would have students "play keen and heartless critics, that the speakers may feel no hatred, but their words may do no harm. For we unwittingly receive into our minds a great many false and vicious doctrines (*dogmata*) by feeling good will and confidence towards the speakers."[41] In this area of right doctrine lie the greatest contrasts between Paul, Philo, and Plutarch. Paul (e.g., Phil. 2:5, 8) and Philo[42] would have their students learn to be humble, which Plutarch rejects.[43] Second, according to Philo, God banishes the unjust and impious to Hades,[44] but according to Paul, God is the one who justifies precisely the impious and unjust (Rom. 1:18; 4:5; 5:6). We notice that the false teachers opposed by the Pastorals are Pauline (1 Tim. 1:20; 2 Tim. 4:10), not teachers from outside, and they mislead whole houses (Titus 1:11). Acts 20:29–30 point in the same direction.

However, Wolfgang Schrage observes that orthopraxy was often more important than orthodoxy in the early period.[45] This may not be true for Paul (Gal. 1:6–9, although see 5:2). Doing and teaching belong together (Matt. 5:19). Here we might mention the question of who pays the teachers. Galatians 6:6 does refer to a teaching activity that leaves no time for otherwise earning a living. This is a disputed matter in the *Didache* (11.5, 9, 12; 12–13). And in the pastorals, the "elders" are replacing the wandering teachers, a disputed transition (1 Tim. 5:17–18; 6:5).[46]

Orthopraxy in the Pastorals centers on household living (Titus 1:11). The Pastorals absorb much of Greco-Roman culture's ideals about family living, but maintain Jesus' critical attitude toward wealth (1 Tim. 6:17–19).[47] In this orthopraxic household, God is the real *despotēs* (2 Tim. 2:21). The dominant metaphor of Paul and his students is that of father and sons, who have inherited an unchangeable example (*hypotypōsis*, 1 Tim. 1:16; 2 Tim. 1:13). His successors themselves are to become teachers and leaders, examples in works, teaching, and faith (1 Tim. 4:12; Titus 2:7), which will enable salvation (1 Tim. 4:10; 2 Tim. 2:9–10). It is especially around how women are living in Christian households that the polemic of the Pastorals becomes sharpest (1 Tim. 4:1–3; cf. Rev. 2:20–23), with alternative possibilities narrated in the orthodox Apocryphal Acts, especially the *Acts of Paul and Thecla*.[48]

> Blessed are the continent, for to them will God speak. (3.5; cf. 1 Cor. 14:16)

> [Paul teaches] that they should not marry. . . . "Otherwise there is no resurrection for you, unless you remain chaste and do not defile the flesh, but keep it pure." (3.11–12)

> And Thecla said to Paul: "I will cut my hair short and follow you wherever you go." (3.26)

> And she threw herself in, saying: "In the name of Jesus Christ I baptise myself on the last day!" (3.34)

> And Thecla arose and said to Paul: "I am going to Iconium." But Paul said: "Go and teach the Word of God!" (3.41)

All the parties, Paul's orthopraxic sons and their opponents would have agreed with Plutarch, who concludes his advice by suggesting that "right listening is the beginning of right living."[49]

In summary, prophets and teachers are closely associated in Paul, Philo, Plutarch, and Lucian. They have authority in their communities, receive oracles and revelations, but are also associated with tradition. Philo and Plutarch both mention prophets or seers when they are discussing schools, where traditional texts are read aloud and interpreted. Paul, Philo, and Plutarch all write of "testing" these oracles. Christian prophets are involved with worship, including prayer, songs, blessings, and confessions. They repeat, adapt, and generate the living Lord's blessings, warnings, and exhortations to the churches, as well as interpret ancient writings, for example, Homer in Greek schools, Moses in the synagogue and church. Paul, Philo, and Plutarch insist that students be critics of their teachers. Still, in many circles, appropriate lifestyle, especially in the Greco-Roman household, was even more important than right thinking.

The Gospel of John and the Johannine letters reveal little about real, early Christian families and their children, or about family expectations, except inasmuch as the circle of disciples around Jesus functions as a surrogate family, but the specific terminology is that of patronage (friendship, John 15:15) rather than sibling relationships as in the Synoptics, or adoption as coheirs as in the Pauline literature. Yet the parent-child imagery of the Gospel is pervasive, and no other Gospel places so much emphasis on familial language for God and Jesus. One of the guiding metaphors is believing as coming to birth (John 1:12–13; 3:3–8). The relationship between Father and Son is a unique and to a certain extent exclusive one, notwithstanding passages like John 20:17. God is "my Father and your Father," yet the difference is quite clear, for no one but Jesus has seen God (1:18) or has access to God (14:6). Jesus is son, heir, agent, and broker of patronage all in one. The preoccupation with glory (*doxa*) is a preoccupation with the honor of God as Father, augmented but also shared by the Son.

Jesus addresses his disciples as "children" (*teknia*) at the Last Supper (John 13:33; compare Mark 10:24), and the risen Jesus playfully calls the disciples "children" (*paidia*) on the shores of the Lake of Galilee. "Children of God" is a favorite Johannine name for right believers (John 1:12; 11:52; 1 John 3:1–2, 10; 5:2). Community members are often called "children" as an affectionate title by church leaders, an indication of the familial and especially paternal nature of the authority structures being developed (1 John 2:1, 18, 28; 3:7, 18; 4:4; 5:21; 2 John 1, 4, 13; 3 John 4). An ecclesially adapted household code in 1 John 2:12–14 addresses children, fathers, and young men.

None of this tells us anything about real families, but it does tell us that familial relationships continue to be models for church relationships. Later Christian literature contains specific, if brief, mentions of the concerns of parents in their raising of children. Abortion, infanticide, and abandonment were prohibited, as they were in contemporary Jewish moral teaching.[50] The policy of Jews and Christians to raise all children born, thought quite exceptional by others, was clearly taught. Whether it was always practiced is another matter, about which we have no way of knowing.[51]

Clement of Rome sees the instruction of the young in the fear of God as an essential male duty, along with according honor to elders[52] and directing wives toward the good. Children are to learn "the strength of humility, how powerful is pure love before God, and how the fear of God is beautiful, great, and saves all who live in it in holiness with pure intention."[53] The *Didache* and the *Letter of Barnabas* likewise consider teaching children the fear of God as a necessary duty, even with physical discipline to both sexes: "You will not keep your hand from your son or your daughter, but teach them the fear of God from their youth."[54]

The author of the *Shepherd of Hermas*, a Roman Christian householder of the early second century, had much trouble with his (probably adult) children. According to the text, he himself had been an abandoned child raised in slavery in an adoptive family. Now as a freedman, he has his own familia to contend with. Hermas must pray for healing of sin for himself, his household, and all believers. God's anger against him is because his oikos has sinned not only against God, but also against their parents. This sin is seen as blasphemy and betrayal, and Hermas's wife has sinned with an unrestrained tongue. When Hermas is overwhelmed by the high expectations set before him, he is warned that neither he nor his children nor his oikos will be saved without observance of the commandments presented to him.[55]

While Hermas tried to live responsibly, apparently his children did not, though few specifics are given other than the general problems of the community: moral laxity, insensitivity to the needy, and lifestyle compromised by luxury.[56] Roman law held fathers responsible for the actions of their sons of any age and their daughters unmarried or married without manus (transferal of authority to the husband). Hermas's heavenly revealer follows the law by reproaching him for the sins of his children, and follows informal expectation of a husband's control of his wife by including his wife among the transgressors over whom Hermas should have control. His conversion will bring about theirs, and he is to see that they change their ways. Traditional parental authority over adult children is reinforced in this Jewish Christian document. Here we probably have a glimpse of the kind of family solidarity across generations and living units that was typical of most urban people, including Jews and Christians.

Clement of Alexandria's major treatise, *The Pedagogue,* is based on the model of the education of children, though not so much parental training as that of a professional teacher. The parental overtones are nevertheless rich and the details informative. Christ the Logos is the instructor of Christians who are therefore in the position of children with regard to learning, and are often so addressed, though they are not to be children with regard to innocence or childishness.

Just as all kinds of parents take pleasure in their children, whether horses, oxen, lions, or humans, so God delights in us.[57] The education of children involves constant watchfulness, yet parents love their children above all else.[58] The child is the flower of the union of wife and husband, picked by the divine gardener. If the honor of the elderly is their grandchildren, and the honor of children is their father (Prov. 17:6), then the honor of everyone is God the great Father.[59]

Clement's *Pedagogue* is not written about the upbringing of children, but about God's ways with believers, or in contemporary language, spiritual formation, but he organizes this material under the metaphor of the education of children. In doing so, he gives an unusual amount of attention to the phenomenon of childhood, which was seen as a period of life meant to be passed through as quickly as possible so that its participants could become productive members of the family. Clement is certainly not the first to use the metaphor of parent for God; in this regard he represents a long tradition. But by drawing out the metaphor into a sustained meditation, he has taken an important step the other way around: presenting parenting and education as images of God's activity. His treatment draws inspiration from numerous biblical texts that he quotes and comments upon with care.

Christian writers' passing mentions of actual children are for the most part references to the responsibility of parents to bring them up with the proper discipline. These references are in keeping with the usual Greco-Roman and Jewish understanding of children as investments in the family's future, potential adults in need of stern training in order to produce persons worthy of their family's expectations. In much of the ancient Mediterranean literature about children, the genuine affection of parents for children they decide to raise comes through, in spite of legal practices of abandonment and sale into slavery. The distinctive[60] Jewish and Christian prohibition of abortion, infanticide, and abandonment gives a particular theological/moral perspective to children: Each is a precious gift, and a child of God who has first and final parental rights.

The widespread use of the appellation "children" for disciples or believers in some early Christian literature should tell us something that is not automatically clear to the modern reader: most of it refers to adults. One factor that contributes to this is the Semitic use "children of" to associate a particular characteristic to people: children of God, children of darkness, and so on. The other factor is the authority structure of ancient families, reinforced by the Roman law of patria potestas, which made adult children liable to the authority and financial control of their father as long as he was alive, though there were legal procedures that children could initiate in the case of the mental incapacity of a father. Even for those whose actual fathers were dead, the model of paternal authority over adults was a familiar one. It extended early into the church. First Timothy 3:5 sums it up: If one who would be overseer (episkopos) of a community cannot govern his own family well, how can he govern the church? The model is the same, just applied under different circumstances.

If parents had duties toward their children, adult children also had specified duties toward their parents. First was respect and obedience appropriate to time and place. Among vices listed by New Testament writers to symbolize the worst of sinful humanity is disobedience to parents (Rom. 1:30; 2 Tim. 3:2). Contrary to modern assumptions, the Fourth Commandment of the Decalogue, "Honor your father and mother in order to have long days in the land" (Ex. 20:12; Deut. 5:16), is intended for adults, not children. First Timothy 5:1–2 instructs Christians not to be harsh to an old man, but to encourage (*parakalein*) him the way one would an elderly father, to treat young men like brothers, old women like mothers, and young women like sisters. The church is a fictive kinship group in which relationships are to be patterned on familial lines of respect according to age under the leadership of a father figure, the episkopos (1 Tim. 3:5).

Beyond respect and obedience, the foremost duty was to provide for parents in their old age and give them a proper burial. The fact that this seems to have been a constant concern of the elderly suggests that many children were negligent in this area.[61] Beyond occasional banquets given by civic benefactors to citizens and individual patronage arrangements, Greco-Roman society simply had no welfare system on which the indigent could fall back. Family was expected to provide what was needed. Widows and their young children were therefore often in a precarious situation if they had no inherited money or property, or surviving relatives able or willing to provide for them.

The Christian church, along with the synagogue, was one of the few associations that did organize relief services for those in need. The funds came partly from the direct generosity of individual patrons. Hermas teaches that extra wealth should be spent on widows, orphans, and the needy; instead of buying land, Christians should buy "troubled souls."[62] Tensions began to spring up early between the initiative and household authority of wealthy Christian patrons, and the church's desire to control the distribution of funds. The patrons lost, in favor of a more efficient method.[63]

Soon the effort was centralized, with funds provided by regular collections as well as larger bequests. Acts 4:34–37 describes the selling of property to provide common funds, while 11:27–28 tells of a special collection for famine relief.

First Timothy lays down procedures for the acceptance of widows into something that must have looked like a women's service organization that accepted women of proven virtue who qualified by also being in need. It is probably the foundation for the later order of widows. The discussion is both prefaced and concluded by statements to the effect that those who have a needy mother or grandmother should provide for them, so that only those left entirely alone should be candidates for church support (1 Tim. 5:3–16).

The passage has an unpleasant implication: that Christian widows, or at least widows in the families of Christians, were being neglected by their own children who presumed that the church would take care of them. The author declares that those who neglect their own family (oikos) are worse than unbelievers. Readers tend to assume that only Christians are referred to in passages like these, but this is not necessarily true. Given that we know there were individual Christians in non-Christian families already in this period, it is quite possible that a house church would find itself in the position of being expected to care for non-Christian dependents as well. But there is no clear discussion of this eventuality.[64]

Justin describes a collection taken up at the weekly Eucharist to help orphans, widows, the sick, and others in need. Tertullian speaks of a monthly voluntary collection that goes to the relief of those in need, including orphans and old abandoned slaves.[65] By the middle of the third century, the church of Rome was reputed to be supporting fifteen hundred widows and other needy dependents.[66]

Christian concerns about children were not only about the young but also about what those young did as adults to fulfill their familial responsibilities.

Women Teachers of Women

Despite all the recent interest in women's history, one aspect of women's lives that is not frequently spoken of is the intergenerational family activity whereby women in traditional societies convey wisdom and practical knowledge from mother to daughter and surrogate mother to surrogate daughter. This instruction is spread over many years during which daughters are growing up in the household.

In poorer families, children must begin to help with the family work as soon as they are able, and the same was true in antiquity for slave children. For girls, this meant helping their mothers in food preparation, cleaning, and the production of clothing. Girls learned how to do these tasks at the same time that they were learning family wisdom as communicated by the female elders of the family. Sexual initiation and instruction was equally a preparation for girls' future role as wives and mothers.

All of this wisdom constitutes an important legacy of the past and of Christian family life that has been preserved hardly at all. Of its content, we are for the most part ignorant. We can only look at the fleeting references in the mostly male literature and try to imagine how it happened. Three aspects of this female tradition can be discerned: household domestic instruction, instruction of women for baptism and ongoing instruction in the Christian life, and instruction in asceticism in those later ascetic circles in which women were heavily involved. House and family were the primary locus for this tradition.

A possible documented precedent is the remnant of four Neopy-thagorean Hellenistic or Roman women writers, parts of whose advice and instruction to women has been preserved in the Pythagorean texts. Whether the writings attributed to the women were actually written by them is unclear; in any event, the material has been censored and pre-served by men, in the interests of men.[67] Theano, for instance, advises that a wife's place is in obedience to her husband, even to the point of enduring his adultery.[68] She uses the traditional argument that by her fidelity she will win him over, the same rationale used by 1 Peter 3:1–2. Perictione upholds the double standard by granting to men the error of adultery, but not to women.[69] Phintys and Melissa write about feminine virtue and the attractiveness of the virtuous woman without cosmetic adornment. The theme of lack of adornment for virtuous women is an old favorite of Neopythagorean moralists, and the male critique of women's hairdressing, jewelry, and cosmetics was a philosophical and literary commonplace that is later adapted into a Christian context (compare 1 Peter 3:3–5; 1 Tim. 2:9–10).[70] These writers reflect the val-ues and thinking of their patriarchal world, all the while stressing the beauty of virtue and women's responsibility for relationships and fam-ily. A wife is to manage her household wisely and agree with her hus-band about everything. "Otherwise she will be out of tune with her whole universe."[71]

In early Christianity, three brief passages from the Pastoral Epistles illustrate two different aspects of household instruction of women by women. Titus 2:3–5 describes the patriarchal image of what good el-derly women do: Besides being circumspect in their own behavior, they teach younger women to be lovers of husbands and children, examples of domestic virtue, good household managers, and submissive to their own husbands, so as not to give the kind of scandal that would be caused if Christian women were not paragons of conservative feminine behavior. In spite of the prohibition on women teaching in 1 Timothy 2:12, older women (*presbytes*) are here urged to be good teachers (*kalo-didaskaloi*) in order properly to instruct younger women. Obviously the sphere of their envisioned teaching is quite different in the two cases: There it is a question of public teaching in the assembly involving both sexes, while here, it is the private household, where mothers pass on to daughters what male society expects of them. It is ironic that, from the perspective of the modern interpreter, older women are usually the strongest enforcers of that message.

The second reference in the Pastoral Epistles is quite different: It is hostile and denigrating. First Timothy 4:7 exhorts Timothy to reject pro-fane myths of old women (*bebēlous kai graōdeis mythous*), "old wives' tales," in favor of the good (male) teaching that he has received.[72] The contrast between the two passages illustrates well the patriarchal control of women's religious lives. The third reference occurs in the discussion of the role of widows and the church's responsibility toward them in 1 Timothy 5:1–16. The invective against young widows who do not re-marry includes their visiting other women from house to house and, from the author's perspective, talking too much and perhaps becoming caught up in ways of teaching the faith of which the author solidly dis-approves, "for some have already gone off after Satan" (vv. 13, 15).

In most traditional societies, women are the bearers of their own folk subculture of oral tradition through the stories they tell.[73] It has been suggested that many of the collected stories of early Christianity, the Apocryphal Acts, are the product of women's circles, since many of the stories inevitably center on women characters who fulfill the stories' ideals much better than men. Here, the imaginative world of women's storytelling, seen as less than orthodox by the author, is rejected in one quick sweep. But its very mention reminds us of its existence.

Religious instruction of women for baptism and the life of faith was also more directly the responsibility of women teachers than of men, though under the supervision of male authority in most cases. This re-ligious instruction is not to be clearly separated from education for life responsibilities, and in the early years, was probably given largely within a household context, but by specially designated women.

Again, a brief negative comment from the Pastoral Epistles allows us to see the diversity and richness of early church life for women. Second Timothy 3 begins with an attack on deceivers who will be especially ap-parent in the last days, but are active now as false teachers. They seem to have encouraged women to take more initiative in the study of the-ology than the author was willing to grant. One of their strategies was to enter households (oikias) and entrap "little women" (gynaikaria, a pe-jorative diminutive), who are weighed down by sins, easily swayed, gullible, and unable to know the truth (vv. 6–7). Though all reference to these teachers is grammatically masculine plural, this does not mean they were all men (the nearest noun reference in v. 2 is the gender-neutral anthrōpoi rather than the gender-specific andres). Many of those who entered into households and so taught women are likely to have been women.[74] As Dennis MacDonald notes, the viewpoint of the au-thor of the Pastorals won the day in the mainstream churches, yet the continuing popularity of stories like that of Thecla witnesses to a women's subculture that saw the Christian faith very differently.[75]

Another glimpse of such instruction at work, this time sanctioned by the author who mentions it, occurs in the Shepherd of Hermas. Hermas is authorized by his heavenly revealer, a woman who represents the church, to write down the call to conversion that has been revealed to him. He himself is to promulgate it with the elders of the church, but he is also to make two copies, one for Clement[76] to send to other cities, and another for an otherwise unknown woman named Grapte to exhort the widows and orphans. Neither Grapte's title nor her own marital status is given, since she is assumed to be known to the hearers. Her responsibility, however, seems to be the special instruction of those women and their children who are dependent on the church. Her role presumes literacy and a certain amount of autonomy, for she will have the responsibility not only to read the text to the women and children but to interpret it as well.

Clement of Alexandria assumes on the basis of 1 Corinthians 9:5 that the first generation of apostles took their wives with them—not as wives but as sisters—to be ministers to women in households, so that their preaching could reach the women's quarters without scandal. This picture of women living in secluded areas of the house reflects not the Asia Minor and Greece of Paul's day, but Clement's own late second-century Alexandria, and the differences between the Greek and Roman house laid out by Vitruvius.[77]

In the middle of the third century in North Africa, Bishop Cyprian wrote a treatise to the consecrated virgins in his church, exhorting them to greater striving for virtue, and attempting to rein in some of their activities that he considered inappropriate, such as attendance at weddings, wearing jewelry and cosmetics, and attending the baths at the same time as men. At the conclusion, he exhorts older virgins not only to give good example but to teach younger virgins, while the younger are to give good example to their peers.[78] The surprising social freedom apparently enjoyed by Christian virgins in mid–third-century Carthage reflects the earlier practice of such women living in private homes and coming together regularly for prayer and companionship, rather than living together in monasteries as would soon become the custom.

Also in the third century, the Syrian church order, the *Didascalia Apostolorum,* instructs bishops to appoint deaconesses[79] for ministry to women; for pastoral visits in houses where male clergy cannot go, especially to the sick; for the bodily anointing of women during nude immersion baptism, while a bishop or presbyter has anointed the head; and for ongoing religious instruction after baptism, to teach newly baptized women to preserve their commitment "in chastity and holiness."[80] The *Apostolic Constitutions,* which used the *Didascalia* as a basic source, add elsewhere that a deaconess is to accompany a baptized woman who wishes to speak with a deacon or the bishop.[81] This kind of restricted

access of men to women and women to men is typical of the segregation of women into women's quarters and out of public male life that
continued in the east into the Byzantine and Islamic eras. Its preservation also preserved the private world of women in which women's own
culture was able to survive and even thrive.

References to deaconesses occur with some frequency in early Christian literature, usually without information about their role, since that
is already known by the readers. In at least one case, however, the instructional role and fictive kinship are explicit. In the fifth-century Antiochene *Life of Pelagia the Harlot,* the Pelagia in question, repentant of
her sins, throws herself down before Bishop Nonnus in the presence of
other bishops and clergy. When sure of her true repentance, Nonnus
sends a message to the local bishop, who was not present, asking for a
deaconess. Once Romana, head deaconess, arrives, the bishop bids
Pelagia to confess her sins, then baptizes her, with Romana as god-
mother. After the baptism, Romana takes Pelagia away with her to stay
"with the catechumens," probably a group of women catechumens of
whose training the deaconesses are in charge. Not only does a deaconess
here have responsibility for the care and instruction of a woman convert, but the sequence of events suggests that Nonnus does not wish to
act in her regard until the deaconess is present, as indicated in the *Apostolic Constitutions* cited above. Three days later, Pelagia, through the in-
termediation of Romana, makes over all her wealth to the church for the
poor, and eight days after baptism, when it is time to lay aside her white
robe, disappears mysteriously into the ascetic life, leaving a distressed
Romana behind. Nonnus assures Romana that Pelagia has done well.[82]

One more testimony to the tradition of women teachers for women
in the context of church instruction comes from another church order,
the fifth-century Syrian *Testamentum Domini,* where there are identifiable groups of widows, deaconesses, and virgins in the church. Contrary to the church of the *Didascalia* and the *Apostolic Constitutions,* however, here the widows are ordained and seem to be the most authoritative
group of women. Among their duties are to oversee deaconesses, exhort
disobedient women, teach women catechumens, instruct the ignorant,
and organize prayer meetings for women ascetics.[83] They have wider
pastoral responsibility than that given to women in any other early
church order.

The third major way in which we see women teaching women in private contexts is that of the early monastic tradition and women's important role in it from the start. The rich tradition whereby women passed
on to the next generation the accumulated wisdom of the foremothers becomes activated in a new way. A few glimpses will serve as illustration.

When the famous late–fourth-century Western monastic pilgrim Egeria arrived at the sanctuary of Holy Thecla in Seleucia of Isauria (south-central Turkey), she found there not only the shrine itself but also a thriving monastic settlement of both men and women. Egeria's friend Marthana, whom she had previously met on pilgrimage in Jerusalem, welcomed her. Together they prayed and read the whole of the *Acts of Thecla* at the shrine—in itself testimony to the continuing popularity of a story that the male church tried to suppress. Marthana was a deaconess in charge of some of the cells of women ascetics. As both deaconess and superior, her role would have been that of teacher, admonisher, and spiritual guide to these women.[84]

Many of the women ascetics of the fourth century and beyond were teachers and spiritual guides for other women. In the case of two of Jerome's circle in the late fourth century, we have testimony to this effect. The noble Roman widow Marcella was one of the first of senatorial rank to embrace the ascetic life in her own house, which became not only a gathering place for theologians and students but also a training center for women ascetics. After Marcella's death as a result of mistreatment by invading barbarians in 410, Jerome's eulogy of her, written for her disciple Principia, states that Eustochium, daughter of his friend Paula and her successor as superior of the Bethlehem monastery next to Jerome's, was trained in monasticism in Marcella's house, in her "cell," according to the monastic terminology that was developing. Likewise, Principia herself attached herself to Marcella in a substitute mother-daughter relationship, sharing her house first in the city and later in the country near Rome.[85] Later, Paula and her daughter Eustochium moved with Jerome to Bethlehem to set up joint monasteries there. After the death of Paula, Jerome's dear old friend, his eulogy for her, addressed to her daughter Eustochium, gives a detailed description of the order of life in Paula's monastery, and how she trained each of the women, adapting her strategy to the particular character of each.[86]

About a century later, another aristocratic woman of a senatorial family, Olympias of Constantinople, refused marriage and embraced the ascetic life, setting up her own monastery in the city, as was now the custom rather than living in private homes. An ordained deaconess of the episcopal church of Constantinople, she was one of many such women of her day, whose memory was preserved in this case because of an early biography and also because of her staunch friendship with and defense of John Chrysostom in his political woes. Her successor as superior upon her death was one Marina, whom Olympias had "received from baptism" into a close and mutually supportive relationship. Marina was personally trained by Olympias and prepared to be her successor.[87]

Another area that could be fruitfully researched is that of women advocates of women against the male system. A prime example is the *Acts of Paul and Thecla,* where Thecla's mother Theocleia plays the conventional role of trying to get her married off as quickly as possible, but Queen Tryphaena, her surrogate mother at Antioch, protects her from sexual abuse and preserves her virginity for death (a supreme value in the world of the *Acts*), while a lioness that is supposed to kill her in the amphitheater instead dies defending her against a lion.[88] Here we catch a glimpse of an alternative tradition of women's relationships with each other that does not support male interests but rather conspires against them. It has often been suggested that such stories originated in women's storytelling circles.[89]

These glimpses of women's educative relationships with one another are but the tip of the iceberg. Usually located in private houses or, later, monastic communities, this activity remains largely hidden from our eyes, as is the vast majority of the lives of women in antiquity. What we do know of it is replete with familial terminology and social forms. The upbringing of women by their mothers and other female relatives, their socialization into their future roles, and much of their learning were all mediated by the women of the family. Some forms of that learning had male approval, and some of it did not, but it continued nevertheless, much as distinctive female traditions and rituals continue today in traditional societies. Later in early Christianity, when asceticism became popular as a total way of life, formation of women ascetics, while supervised by male authorities to a certain extent, still was mostly in the hands of women spiritual leaders, whose forms of address and treatment of one another created a new fictive kinship of mothers, daughters, and sisters. In quite the same way that women's subculture, rooted in family locus and relationships, had always operated within the dominant male culture, so it continued to do so, taking on new forms in Christian context, all the while preserving much of what had always been.

7

Slaves

For early Jews and Christians, slavery was an ever-present institution of Greco-Roman society. For modern historians, it is difficult to write on this subject. Finley's words are appropriate:

> [M]y immediate concern is with the methodological fallacy that pervades [many accounts of slavery], a common one in the history of ideas, which we may call the "teleological fallacy." It consists in assuming the existence from the beginning of time, so to speak, of the writer's values—in this instance, the moral rejection of slavery as an evil—and in then examining all earlier thought and practice as if they were, or ought to have been, on the road to this realization; as if men in other periods were asking the same questions and facing the same problems as those of the historian and *his* world.[1]

Slaves in Paul
and the Deutero-Pauline Epistles

Given Finley's caution, we observe that Paul claimed to be "Christ's slave" (1 Cor. 3:5; 2 Cor. 2:14; 3:6; 4:5) and so are believers (1 Cor. 7:22; Rom. 12:11; 14:4, 18). Some readers in that culture would have heard this as a metaphor of power, analogous to the slaves of the *familia Caesaris* who administratively ran the empire.[2] Significant too is the usage in the Septuagint, where leaders like Moses, Joshua, David, and Isaiah are "slaves of Yahweh" (e.g., Moses in Deut. 34:5).[3] Brian Dodd argues that the claim in Isaiah 49:1 and Jeremiah 1:5 to such slaves has influenced Paul.[4]

Philemon

Paul refers to slavery four times: in Galatians 3:28, 1 Corinthians 7:21–24, 12:13, and in the letter to Philemon, assuming that Colossians 3:22–24, Ephesians 6:5–9, 1 Timothy 6:1–2, and Titus 2:9–10 are deutero-Pauline.[5] Significant advances have been made in interpreting Philemon in recent years. Sarah Winter expanded John Knox's earlier interpretation and argued that the house church in Colossae *sent* the slave Onesimus to Paul in prison to assist him, opposing the virtually unanimous traditional interpretation that Onesimus was a runaway slave.[6] She argued further that the letter was public, sent to a church whose leaders are named, not a personal letter; that Paul requests that Onesimus might remain with him to work in Christian ministry; and that Onesimus no longer be considered a slave within the Christian community, separately suggesting that he be manumitted. The three church leaders are a coworker, a sister, and a fellow soldier; it is difficult to explain the letter's three addressees if this is a private letter addressed to the head of a household and to his wife (which the hypothesis must assume, although not in the text) concerning a fugitive. Further, the letter is from a church community whose leaders are named (vv. 1b–2, 23), not just from the individual Paul. Winter associates the letter with Philippians, written 53–55, not with the later and probably deutero-Pauline Colossians.

The thanksgiving (vv. 4–7), which introduces the theme of the main body of the letter in other Pauline epistles, fails to do so here on the traditional hypothesis that Onesimus ran away. Verse 7 looks back to what Philemon has already given, not forward to Paul's request that Philemon or Archippus forgive a runaway slave. The main body of the letter (vv. 8–14) is a single complex period. The brief six-word request in verse 10 is preceded by two causal participial clauses and followed by three relative clauses. The request itself is either "I ask you *in behalf of* my child" (a request concerning Onesimus), or "I ask you *for* my child" (in which Paul asks for Onesimus himself). Does Paul subtly hint at what he wants, or is his request explicit? Winter argues for the latter, although the former is the usual meaning of the preposition.

J. Albert Harrill emphasizes Paul's directive in verse 16: Philemon is to receive back his newly converted slave Onesimus "no longer as a slave but more than a slave, a beloved brother—especially to me but how much more to you, both in the flesh and in the Lord."[7] The prepositional phrase "in the flesh" probably suggests manumission, but not certainly.

Why does Paul want Onesimus? Winter argues that Paul wants Onesimus for public church service, for ministry (diakonia, v. 13). She points out that both the verb and the noun always refer to religious service in Paul. Therefore, Paul wants Onesimus's ministerial service. The three other times Paul uses the verb, she observes, he himself is the subject and is indeed giving religious service. Paul lists "varieties of services" or ministries that God activates "in everyone" (1 Cor. 12:5–6) and writes that Onesimus performed them "in your [Philemon's] place" (v. 13).

Winter's arguments have been strengthened by John Collins. Examining 370 instances in texts by ninety authors over eight centuries, he has demonstrated that this word group does not refer primarily to slaves waiting at table.[8] The word can refer to a "go-between": Lucian pictures Hermes as too busily engaged (*diakonēsomenos*) for Zeus to act as a guide for Charon around the world.[9] It can refer to ministry, a medium of the word: Abraham asks Gabriel "to be a medium of my word (*tou diakonē sai moi logon*) . . . unto the most High."[10] Josephus often uses it to stress the deed, acting as someone's agent.[11] Paul writes of Onesimus in Philemon 13 (translating somewhat literally), "whom I was wishing to keep for myself, in order that for you to me he might minister in the bonds of the gospel." The verb "to keep" is very strong; Harrill perceives Paul almost to be saying that he wants to detain the slave for work in bonds of another kind, to "minister for me" in the interests of the gospel, where "for me" has the same force as "for the saints" in Romans 15:25, that is, to designate the person organizing the activity.[12] Paul wants to use Onesimus as a "go-between" in the preaching of the gospel, as Philemon himself as well as Prisca and Aquila have been a "coworkers" in the mission. Onesimus in his new role is to be "more than a slave," a "brother" (16), to take on the role that Philemon had performed, "on your behalf" (13). This slave becomes an active minister.

Peter Lampe added strong evidence that Onesimus was not a runaway slave.[13] Proculus, an important Roman jurist in the early first century C.E., stated that a slave in difficulty with an owner, who suddenly sought out a third party to become the slave's advocate to the angry owner, was not a fugitive,[14] an opinion echoed by later jurists. The legal opinions mean that this was a common event. Lampe notes the irony involved as well as Onesimus's estimate of Paul's character: the non-Christian slave Onesimus slips away to the apostle hoping that Paul would influence his Christian master, Philemon, to have mercy (cf. 1 Cor. 6:7, "why not rather be wronged?"). The pagan requests help from one Christian over against another, showing his trust in Paul! Then Paul wins him for Christ (vv. 10, 16), which Philemon in his own house had not done. A crucial difference between Winter's and Lampe's reconstructions concerns why Onesimus left Philemon's house: did the house church send him to Paul, or did he flee to his master's friend? Given the "wrong" Philemon thinks he has suffered (v. 18), the story Lampe proposes better fits the text.

S. Scott Bartchy argues that slaves were commonly manumitted,[15] that we should ask when, not if, Philemon planned to set Onesimus free, so that verse 16 ("no longer as a slave but . . . as a beloved brother") should be understood as a request that his manumission not be delayed because of any wrongdoing (v. 18). Philemon could continue to be Onesimus's owner, or become his "brother" and "partner" (v. 17), perhaps sending him as a freedman to Paul (v. 13). Freedmen still owed services to their former masters, and in this capacity, he could be of "service" or "minister" to Paul. Both house churches were involved (vv. 2, 23),[16] and the apostle would soon follow his letter with a visit (v. 22).

Onesimus is also mentioned in Colossians 4:9, perhaps an attempt by this deutero-Pauline author to associate the slave's memory with the subordinationist ethic in the later epistle. (Five of the six people who send greetings in Philemon 23 are identical with those in Col. 4:10–17; but the minister Epaphras mentioned in both Philemon 23 and Col. 1:7–8 probably is not the same as the Epaphroditus of Phil. 2:25–30.) All three letters are related by Paul's imprisonment (Philemon 1, 13, 23; Phil. 1:7, 13–14, 17; Col. 4:3, 10, 18), where we do not know, although Onesimus seeking Paul in prison in Ephesus is an attractive hypothesis.[17] We observe that the christological hymn in Philippians 2:6–11 expresses a "liberation symbolism" that would have been attractive to slaves.[18] It narrates/confesses the drama of salvation as follows: "Though he [Christ Jesus] was (hyparchōn) in the form of God (morphē theou; v. 6a), [Christ] did not regard equality with God as something to be exploited, but emptied (ekenōsen) himself, taking the form of a slave (morphē doulou), being born in human likeness, and being found in human form, he humbled himself and became obedient to the point of death—even death on a cross. Therefore God also highly exalted him" (2:6–9a; NRSV).[19] For a slave who himself/herself or whose ancestors had experienced the fall into Roman enslavement,[20] to hear the story of Christ's parallel, although voluntary, experience of descending into slavery may well have been overpowering, especially told by an apostle who also humbled himself (2 Cor. 11:7). Christ's epiphany as a slave is a direct antithesis to the title kyrios (Lord). To hear further that God had "exalted" this slave/redeemer would correspond to Onesimus's own hopes for manumission.[21] However, the christological hymn in the deutero-Pauline epistle Colossians no longer proclaims Christ as a slave, but rather as hierarchical head of the cosmos (Col. 1:15–20; earlier cf., e.g., 1 Cor. 15:24–28), a modified view of Christ—without the humiliation—in the second-generation epistle that also introduces the household code to Christian social ethics. Christology, eschatology, and social ethics are directly connected in these epistles, and all changed significantly after Paul's death. Eschatological hope is intense in Paul's epistles, eschatology that involves present symbolic actions that signal future change. But Colossians and Ephesians trade this temporal eschatology for spatial images that function within present social structures and roles.

Galatians 3:28 and 1 Corinthians 12:13

Galatians 3:28 is a saying that functioned in an early Christian baptismal liturgy,[22] similar to others in 1 Corinthians 12:13 and Colossians 3:11. The line of the saying that is relevant to Paul's argument in Galatians is, "there is neither Jew nor Greek." Paul also quotes "there is neither slave nor free" because it belongs to the tradition, and as just seen above, a slave like Onesimus became a "brother" when baptized into a house church. If Philemon freed him, Onesimus would have attained a slave's most ardent desire, although as a freedman, he would still owe duties to, benefit from, and be attached to Philemon's household as his freedman/client.

Hans Dieter Betz notes that the statements in Galatians 3:28 have "social and political implications of even a revolutionary dimension," because they present "a political alternative to the system which they fight." The old status is abolished and a new status claimed, not as a utopian ideal, but as accomplished fact. "The religious, cultural, and social distinctions between Jews and Greeks are abolished."[23] This is not exaggerated language: Paul insists that Peter and Barnabas practice this eschatological reality at dinner in the present (Gal. 2:11–21), a symbol that this eschatological hope is presently realized.[24] In the letter of Philemon, addressed to a house church, we see Paul suggesting practical, everyday implications of this present eschatological reality for the social, legal, and religious relationship between Philemon, Onesimus, Paul, and other believers in the two households.

Deutero-Pauline Colossians changes this qualitatively by coupling the baptismal formula (Col. 3:11) with a household code, exhorting the slaves to be obedient to their masters (Col. 3:22–25), a reaction against earlier freedom and innovation. In contrast, the earlier Pauline churches, along with the Jewish Essenes and Therapeutae described by Philo, drew practical consequences from their theology by modifying relationships between owners and slaves.

Similarly, the baptismal formula in Colossians drops the phrase in Galatians, "there is no longer male and female"; in fact, women are no longer mentioned explicitly in the baptismal confession (3:11; as already 1 Cor. 12:13), but a few verses later, they are addressed *first* in the household code, "wives, be submissive . . . " (3:18).[25] These dramatic changes in early Christian Christology, ritual, and ethics mean that the secular Greco-Roman household ethic has significantly blunted early Christian theology and ethical practice. Christian assemblies worshiped and members lived in the secular institution of the household, which had both advantages for mission and disadvantages for eschatological ethics.

1 Corinthians 7:21

The key problem of interpreting what Paul writes concerning slaves in 1 Corinthians 7:21 arises because he assumed an object for the verb instead of actually writing it: "But even if you are able to become free, rather you should use ————." Scholars who emphasize the grammar of the sentence often supply "freedom," but those who stress the context of the verse within the whole chapter often supply "slavery," that is, remain a slave.[26] Masters did hold out hopes of freedom to slaves, an incentive for them to please their owners by good work. Furthermore, freed slaves often continued to owe their former masters services, so it could be to the advantage of the owner to free them, receiving continued service but having no obligation to feed and clothe the slave.

There is no indication of problems between Christian masters and slaves in Corinth. There was conflict over male/female roles (1 Corinthians 5—7). As seen above, Paul modified the baptismal formula, dropping out the earlier phrase "there is no longer male and female" (cf. Gal. 3:28 and 1 Cor. 12:13). However, Paul does repeat " . . . slaves or free— and we were all made to drink of one Spirit" (1 Cor. 12:13). In chapter 7 Paul used relationships that were not a problem in Corinth, that is, circumcised/uncircumcised and slave/free (7:17–24), to illustrate his advice for relationships that were problematic, that is, the male/female relationships about which the Corinthians had written him.

Responding to them, Paul introduces his theology of "calling." Just prior to the paragraph we are discussing, Paul is giving advice to Christians whose mates have left or divorced them: "But if the unbelieving partner separates, let it be so; in such a case the brother or sister is not bound [enslaved]. It is to peace that God has called (*keklēken*) you" (7:15). Paul develops this theology of calling in 7:17–24, in which he writes the verb "to call" eight times and the noun "call" (*klēsis*) once. How did Paul and the Corinthians understand the "calling" from God to affect Christian social roles? Must they renounce sexuality and dissolve marriage to follow God's call, as Cynics, many Essenes, and the Theapeutae did, and as some Jesus sayings encourage (e.g., Luke 14:20, 26; 17:27; 18:29–30; 20:34–35)?[27] Must slaves either remain in their slavery or, depending on the exegesis, insist on manumission? Does God's call either encourage or necessitate changing one's social role?[28]

Bartchy highlights[29] the parallels between verses 17, 20, and 24, which repeatedly state Paul's theology of calling:

> 17: Each as the Lord has assigned/as God has called/thus/let him-her walk.
>
> 20: Each in the calling/in which he or she was called/in this/let him-her remain.
>
> 24: Each in the/calling/in this/ let him-her remain with God.

These three are parallel, so that the conclusions of all three, "walking according to God's call" (v. 17) and "remaining in the call" (v. 20), are parallel exhortations. All three are clarified by reference to Paul's other uses of "call" in Philippians 3:14 ("I press on toward the goal for the prize of the upward call of God in Christ Jesus") and Romans 11:29 ("for the gifts and the calling of God are irrevocable"), that is, these verses refer to God's call into relationship with God. Against Luther, "call" in verse 21 does not have a unique meaning, a call to a certain social status in society,[30] but it has the same meaning as in verses 17 and 24. Therefore in 1 Corinthians 7:18–19, Paul is arguing that one's status as Jew (circumcised) or Gentile (uncircumcised) is not the crucial matter with respect to God's call; neither Jew nor Gentile is required to change ethnic/social status. "[Literal] circumcision is nothing, and [literal] uncircumcision is nothing, but obeying the [spiritual not literal] commandments of God is everything" (7:19).[31] "Let each of you remain in the [spiritual] call in which you were called" (v. 20a).

Paul does not proclaim an ideological social ethic that declares the social status quo unchangeable in general. Rather he makes judgments with respect to each issue and "each" person (the pronoun repeated at the beginning of vv. 17, 20, 24). According to Paul, it is eschatologically dangerous for a Gentile Christian to convert to Judaism by being circumcised, for then he takes on responsibility for keeping all the commandments, a change that Paul uses quite violent language to oppose (Gal. 5:1–12).[32] He argues that one of the commandments (Deut. 21:22–23) cursed the crucified Christ hung on a tree (Gal. 3:13); therefore, seeking to obtain God's blessings by keeping the [other] literal commandments was not open to followers of this crucified Christ cursed by Deuteronomy. Paul's problem with the Mosaic commandments is christological.

In a different case, however, Paul demands change. Before his conversion Paul "advanced in Judaism beyond many among my people of the same age, for I was far more zealous for the traditions of my ancestors"

(Gal. 1:14; Phil. 3:6). After the revelation of Christ to him, however, he confronted the apostle Peter for distinguishing between eating with other Jews and eating with Gentiles (Gal. 2:12; cf. Acts 10—11). Peter *must* change his orthopraxic eating habits or face Paul's charge of hypocrisy (Gal. 2:13). The baptismal confession declares that "there is no longer Jew or Greek" (Gal. 3:28a; 1 Cor. 12:13b; Col. 3:11a), and Paul demands that the apostle Peter act out this eschatological declaration by symbolic actions now.[33] "You have stripped off the old self with its practices and have clothed yourselves with the new self. . . . In that renewal there is no longer Greek and Jew" (Col. 3:9b–11a). In conclusion, Paul does not have an ideologically consistent rule about social change. He opposes some social changes but insists on other literal and spiritual changes in social behavior. Harrill points out most interpreters' incorrect assumption that Roman social conservatives opposed manumission, a modern anachronistic assumption.[34] Cicero, Augustus, Seneca, and other "conservatives" supported manumission and often manumitted their own slaves. This resulted in "crowded houses" of clients, which increased the patron's honor, as we have seen in chapter 1.

How does Paul hear the baptismal confession that "Jews or Greeks, slaves or free—we were all made to drink of one Spirit" (1 Cor. 12:13b)? Must Christians remain slaves, analogous to circumcision, a change that Paul violently opposed? Or, on the other hand, must a Christian slave become free, analogous to the change Paul demanded in Peter's eating habits? Bartchy argues that both these questions are wrongheaded, since neither the slave nor their teacher, Paul, had any legal voice in manumission.

Harrill, however, successfully criticizes Bartchy's fundamental thesis: especially in wartime and during political contests, slaves were offered and some chose freedom. He cites a number of instances in which generals offer their opponents' slaves freedom. Aristonicus attracted slaves from the interior of Asia Minor into his army by promising them manumission.[35] And in the late Republic, some senators would offer an opposing senator's slaves manumission.[36] Octavian refused to offer slaves freedom, for he did not want to make them members of the state.[37]

Harrill further analyzes seventeen examples of the Greek construction *mallon* + *chraomai* that Paul employs in 1 Corinthians 7:21, arguing convincingly that

> the *mallon* is adversative not with respect to its protasis (the premise: "if you can *indeed* become free"), but with respect to the previous apodosis (the answering clause: "do not worry about it"). Paul exhorts the slave facing this new situation to be concerned, and to take another option ("use *instead* [freedom]").[38]

His translation is: "You were called as a slave. Do not worry about it. But if you can indeed become free, use instead [freedom]."[39]

In the context, however, it is not necessary to give a unique meaning to "calling," as Harrill proceeds to do: It "refers to the situation and circumstances in which one was called at the time of baptism."[40] Paul, for whom Christ's cross has put distance between him and the world (Gal. 6:14), gives advice about lifestyle in view of the "impending crisis" (v. 26), in a time that has "grown short" (v. 29), advice to which he allows a number of exceptions. He is not presenting an inflexible ideology. Paul commands the married, citing Jesus' word, that they not separate from their mates (v. 10), "but if she does . . . " (v. 11). Again, believers should live with their unbelieving mates, if they consent, "but if the unbelieving partner separates . . . " (v. 15). Still a third time, if a Corinthian male is free from a wife, Paul advises him not to seek a wife, "but if you marry . . . " (v. 28). More strongly, if one is not behaving properly toward a woman, "let him marry! . . . Let them marry!" (*poieito . . . gameitōsan*, v. 36). The latter is not merely an exception to his advice, but rather Paul writes two imperative verbs encouraging them to change their social/marital status. Finally, Paul gives his judgment that a Christian widow is more blessed if she remains single, although he knows that "she is free to marry . . . " (v. 39). Paul is giving wise, but not inflexible, advice in light of Christ's crucifixion and imminent coming, both of which distance Christians from the world. Still, he advises Christian slaves who have the opportunity to accept manumission to "use [freedom]," to accept the change in their social situation, not unique advice in this chapter to change status. Bartchy's case that verses 17, 20, and 24 are parallel remains convincing. Whether single, married, enslaved, or widowed, whether special circumstances stimulate Christians to change their social situation or not, they are to walk in God's calling.

Colossians, Ephesians, the Pastorals: Slaves in Deutero-Pauline Household Codes

The christological hymn of Colossians 1:15–20 praises Christ as the firstborn of all creation, superior to all creation; similarly in Ephesians, Christ is "far above all rule and authority and power and dominion" (1:21). In neither book does the drama of salvation any longer include Christ taking the form of a *slave* who later in the drama is *exalted* by God (contrast Phil. 2:7b, 9a). Instead of being dynamic and dramatic, deutero-Pauline Christology becomes temporal and more intensely hierarchical, and so does the ethic, which is no longer concerned with slaves' possible manumission, but focuses on their suitably submissive role in the hierarchy of the (Roman) cosmos. Tychicus is a "beloved brother, faithful minister (*diakonos*), and a fellow slave (*sundoulos*) in the Lord" with Paul (Col. 4:7), so slave language is used metaphorically of ministers, representatives of the ruler of the cosmos, but no longer of Christ himself. The author opposes his opponents' "philosophy . . . according to human tradition" (Col. 2:8), then introduces the Aristotelian household code against them, a novel philosophical, political structure in Christian ethics. In the fight over Paul's legacy, Pauline house churches polarized, and contestants at both poles appealed to various elements of speculative and practical philosophy. As Eduard Schweizer writes, "just as the house-tables [codes] have been Christianized, so they have also been paganized."[41]

In Colossians the "church" is both a local house-church (4:15), the church of a city, Laodicea (4:16), and the cosmic "body" of Christ (1:18, 24). In Ephesians the localized use of "church(es)" disappears; one can understand the plan of God only against the backdrop of the whole universe. God is enthroned, and Christ is "at his right hand in the heavenly places" (1:20), where God "has put all things under his feet" (Eph. 1:22, citing Ps. 110:1). Mention of Christ's feet stimulates the related metaphor of "head": God "has made him [Christ] the head over all things to the church" (1:22). This first mention of "church" in Ephesians occurs in a context where the author is imaging the cosmic significance of God's action in Christ, and he never refers to "churches" in the plural, to local house-churches.[42]

Christ is not only the "head" of the church, but the source of power that enables its bodily growth (Col. 2:19; Eph. 4:16). In the Greek philosophy and politics of the time, the body must submit to the head,[43] so this philosophical and political Christology generates the ethics, the household codes. Colossians 3:1 makes a transition from the earlier part of the letter into exhortations about life in the earthly realm of Christ. This hortatory section includes instructions about worship, followed by the household code. Not surprisingly for a group meeting in a "house," worship also stimulated reflection on appropriate house-church order, both in Paul (1 Cor. 11:2–16) and in Colossians (3:16–17 and 3:18–4:1). The deutero-Pauline churches are suffering the consequences of the place, Greco-Roman houses, the institution, in which they chose to live, assemble, and worship. Wallace-Hadrill emphasizes that such houses were built to distinguish status, to separate masters' social roles from slaves'.[44] As these churches became more a part of their society, as they lived in the institution of Greco-Roman households, they were tempted to and in varying degrees did accept its social distinctions. As Schweizer observes, the introduction into Christianity of the traditional, cemented, authoritarian, all embracing cosmic order, valid for all time, was dangerous. This order is explicitly Stoic in *1 Clement* 20–21.[45]

"Even more dangerous is the re-interpretation . . . that all service is finally rendered to the Lord himself, because, little by little, the human lords replace the heavenly one."[46] Colossians 3:23 is problematic: "Slaves, obey your earthly masters in everything, not only while being watched and in order to please them, but wholeheartedly, fearing the Lord." Worse is Ephesians 6:5, "slaves, obey your earthly masters with fear and trembling, in singleness of heart, as you obey Christ." Service to the higher class in society comes dangerously close to or is identified with service to God! In *1 Clement* 1:3 and 21:6–8,[47] the exhortations to wives and children are inserted into the address to men; Titus 2:1–10, like its Hellenistic models, deals with the obligations of males toward their inferiors, failing to address either women or slaves directly, thus abandoning what was distinctive about earlier Christian household codes.

Colossians, Ephesians, and 1 Peter, unlike the Pastoral Epistles and the philosophical tradition, address wives and slaves directly in the second person ("you"); that is, these three letters do not only discuss what "they," wives and slaves, must do.[48] Bradley agrees: "Slaves were addressed in a new way, in their own right," but he emphasizes, "though not with the end of breaking down [legal?] barriers between slave and free in mind."[49] The wealthy Therapeutae gave up their families and slaves and retired to the desert; Colossian Christians chose rather to live in Roman cities with their legal limitations and to acculturate. They did integrate slaves into ethical discourse in a new way within the community, but this inclusive, direct address to slaves disappears in the later pastorals, in Ignatius, and in Polycarp. It does have a parallel in earlier Hellenistic Judaism,[50] but not in Greco-Roman "household management" literature. So the Pastorals abandon what had been distinctive of Jewish and Christian household exhortations to slaves in Colossians and 1 Peter.

Second, the wives, slaves, and (adult) children chose their own one God to worship, in high tension with Greco-Roman religious and ethical practice. Some pagan wives did choose gods and goddesses to worship other than those chosen by their husbands, for example, some became Jews, which caused significant tensions; slaves typically did not worship gods other than those of their masters. *Every* household code in early Christian literature occurs in a social context where there is high tension with the Roman state, beginning with these deutero-Pauline "prison epistles." However critical twentieth-century Christians may be of that second generation's ethical choices, we might remember that they were persecuted simply because they chose to worship Christ, and they were living in a tyrannical, hierarchical society, with difficulties and limitations most Westerners living in egalitarian democracies do not face. In this sense, the codes regulated everyday Christian life; they were open to this world and opposed an asceticism that rejected living in society. Opponents of the Colossian author focused on visions (2:18), circumcision (2:11), dietary regulations (2:16a), and laws of purity (2:20–21). Colossians and 1 Peter both insist on "worldliness," while maintaining a critique of tyrannical Roman society, integrating slaves into the house-church, knowing that "Paul" was in a Roman prison (Col. 1:24; 4:10, 18) and/or that their choice for Christ was having the result that others in Roman society were maligning them as "evildoers" (1 Peter 2:12). Nevertheless, it remains true that they drop Paul's interest in manumitting slaves, and they responded to Augustan society's social pressure by marginalizing women. In addition the Pastorals reserve ecclesial office for males, which has had disastrous consequences for two millennia.

Neither masters nor children are ever addressed in the Pastorals, nor are social classes frequently paired. The author gives directions for admonishing slaves (1 Tim. 6:1–2; Titus 2:9–10) with no corresponding admonitions for masters. Where the social classes are paired, the attention of one social group is not always directed toward the other, a contrast to earlier codes. We often read how a wife is to relate to her husband (1 Tim. 2:12–14; 3:4; 6:1–2; Titus 2:4–5), which has close parallels in similar Greco-Roman literature.[51] Onesimus trusted Paul and the gospel of Christ who had himself become a slave, but by the time the deutero-Pauline Pastorals were written, Christians were no longer organized into house-churches with an extraordinary domestic ethic, but lived together in a way that heathen authors would also recommend.

Slavery in the Synoptic Gospels

The following parables involve slave(s) as major characters[52]:

> the unmerciful slave (Matt. 18:23–28 [or –35])
>
> unprofitable slaves (Luke 17:7–10)
>
> slaves watching/guarding the house (Mark 13:34–35; Luke 12:36–38)
>
> the faithful and the unfaithful manager (Matt. 24:45–51//Luke 12:42–46, 47–48)
>
> the unjust manager (Luke 16:1–8)

> the vineyard workers (Matt. 20:1–13)
>
> the talents/pounds entrusted to slaves (Matt. 25:14–30; Luke 19:11–27)[53]

A king settles accounts with his slaves, one of whom owes him ten thousand talents. The slave cannot pay; the lord pities him and forgives the debt![54] But this slave-manager will not forgive a coslave a small debt. The king then hands the first slave over to be tortured (Matt. 18:23–34). Verse 35 is Matthean redaction of this parable, placed at the conclusion of chapter 18, the church order: The slaves become Matthean "brothers" who are to forgive one another.[55]

At the other end of the social spectrum from the social world of the king is Luke 17:7–10, the only parable with an agricultural slave as a main character. This story expresses most radically what being a slave meant. The slave works all day, then fixes dinner for the master, for which he or she is due no thanks.[56] "Thus also you" (v. 10) refers this model too to the disciples' relationship to God (cf. v. 1).

Alfons Weiser groups the remaining slave parables under the category "eschatological." The parable of slaves watching or of the doorkeeper (Mark 13:34–35; Luke 12:36–38)[57] may earlier have symbolized anticipating the kingdom of God, but in the Gospels, it becomes waiting for the Parousia, although Luke removes it from Mark's final eschatological speech, placing it in a diferent setting, warning those who are leaders (12:1, 4, 22, 32). In Mark's eschatological speech the person going on a journey "gives authority to his [other] slaves, to each one his/her work" (13:34b). Paradoxically, as representatives of this master, each slave has his or her own authority.[58] In Luke, Peter asks whether the two earlier parables are for all (Luke 12:41), and Jesus tells the story of a slave "manager" (*oikonomos,* Luke 12:42) who beats the other slaves and gets drunk. For such vicious leadership, the master will punish the slave.[59]

The two parables just discussed (Luke 12:36–38; 42–46) also exhort to preparation and watchfulness for Christ's coming. The parable of slaves watching (vv. 36–38) focuses exclusively on promise, not on warning[60]: When the master returns from the marriage feast to find slaves awake, "he will gird himself and have them sit at table, and he will come and serve them" (v. 37)! Socially, this is upside down, unexpected, suggesting that the masters among the disciples align themselves with the slaves,[61] a contrast to typical everyday reality in 17:9! Matthew's parable of the vineyard workers[62] (20:1–13) is similarly countercultural. We summarized Carter's interpretation above (chap. 5): the master insists on treating the workers "equally" (v. 12).[63]

Luke 16:1–8 recommends quite a different slave manager, an unjust one! Mary Ann Beavis interprets this in light of Aesop's fables, in which the slave outwits his master or mistress, in this case by doing exactly what he is accused of.[64] Plautus, the most popular playwright of the age, who amused Romans by reversing their everyday value system, also narrates masters praising slaves for their roguery.[65] By this behavior Aesop, Plautus's slaves, and Jesus' unjust manager escape punishment and win the respect of their masters, a contrast to the prescriptions for such managers in the ponderous, Greco-Roman philosophical literature on "household management."

A noble inherits a kingdom and instructs slaves to manage affairs while he goes off to be installed in the new kingdom. Later he rewards them with the government of toparchies in the new kingdom, but his subjects rebel and are cruelly punished. The subjects had sent an embassy after the king, according to Luke, declaring that they want a different one (Luke 19:11–27). Somewhere, it is assumed, there is a king of kings, who will replace the unpopular one, again, not the world of Greek cities, but of petty kings, some of whose slaves are powerful and wealthy, although completely dependent on their masters. Some exegetes interpret the Matthean version of the parable (25:14–30) as a polemic against the leaders of Israel, God's slaves.[66] Luke places the parable at the end of his travel narrative, and also after household material from Mark concerning children and the rich (Luke 18:15–43), introducing it with, "as they heard these things" (19:11a), that is, as the disciples heard the story of Zacchaeus (19:1–10). Jesus then tells the parable "because they supposed the kingdom of God was to appear immediately" (19:11b), which refers the parable to Christians' question about the delay of the Parousia.[67] For Luke, God's slaves are not Israel's leaders, but Christians. The story emphasizes the third and final slave, who made no interest on the pound given by the master.[68]

In conclusion, we point to related texts: Mark 10:42b–44//Matthew 20:25b–27//Luke 22:25–27. When James and John want Jesus to place them at his right hand in his glory, in Mark he responds, "You know that among the Gentiles those whom they recognize as their rulers lord it over (*katakurieuousin*)[69] them, and their great ones are tyrants over them. But it is not so among you; but whoever wishes to become great among you must be your servant (*diakonos*), and whoever wishes to be first among you must be slave (*doulos*) of all."[70] This usage opposes the power of petty kings lording it over their inferior subjects and slaves, denying that it is authentic. These secular power structures are not a model for Christ's disciples.

Bultmann suggested that Mark 10:43–44, insisting that the great among Jesus' followers must be a servant, a slave, is "possibly Jewish"[71] and that Mark 10:42, criticizing Gentiles who lord it over others, is the redactor's introductory editing.[72] Troels Engberg-Pedersen gives Stoic parallels,[73] Stanley Stowers suggests that the source of such adaptability as a slave is Cynic,[74] but Weiser suggests rather that the model is from deutero-Isaiah.[75] We observe that according to the Hellenistic Jew Philo,[76] such humiliation and slavery, learning obedience, is a goal of education, of philosophical wisdom, a humiliation that the middle-Platonist Plutarch's educational program repudiates.[77]

Jesus' parables narrated above, however, must be one source of this Markan Christology and discipleship language. The Jesus of Mark's eschatological discourse tells a parable in which a master going on a journey puts slaves in charge, giving them authority, to each one his or her work (13:34).[78] A different version of this parable tells of slaves waiting for a master who, when arriving and finding them awake, will dress as a slave and serve (*diakonēsei*) them (Luke 12:37). Another parable insists that a slave steward not beat the other slaves (Luke 12:42). One source of Mark 10:42–44 then is Jesus' slave parables. During the Jewish war against Rome Mark rejects "lording it over" others, an objection that introduces the passion narrative. Mark's redactional introduction exhorts leaders to be servants, slave managers, which Beavis regards as outlandish for ancient audiences.[79] The communities for whom Mark 10:42–44//Matthew 20:25–27//Luke 22:25–27 were written lived within Roman society, but their christological, parabolic cores reject abusive rule over others.[80]

Slavery in the Gospel of John and Beyond

There is ample evidence that, like Jews,[81] Christians owned slaves and continued to do so well into the Constantinian era, but also that slaves were admitted to baptism and full membership in the Christian community. The human dignity of slaves was recognized by their acceptance into the community, without calling into question the institution of slavery itself.

The uncertain existence of slaves and the hope of every urban slave to attain manumission is reflected in one of the metaphors for discipleship in the Gospel of John. "The slave does not remain in the house forever, but the son remains forever" (8:35). In spite of the evidence for high manumission rates for urban slaves, undoubtedly many did literally remain in the same household for their entire lives. The purpose of the Johannine passage is not social-legal, however. The word *menein* (to abide, remain) is a key Johannine term for discipleship, and its full strength is operative here. Slavery was never a secure existence, and always subordinate, in spite of the possibility of great authority and responsibility over others. The slave had no claim to the house and no rights to be respected in it. But the place of the son and heir was well established.

"But if the son frees you, you will be truly free" from sin that makes you a slave (John 8:36; 13:16; 15:20), that is, by a surrogate legal manumission. The allusion is to a transformation of status from slave to not only freedperson, the usual change brought about by manumission, but freeborn member of the household with full family rights.

During the supper discourse, the Johannine Jesus speaks of the disciples as not slaves but friends. Verses 12–15 of chapter 15 progress by a chain of associations from the love commandment (v. 12), to the greatest love required to lay down one's life for friends (v. 13), to the identification of the disciples as Jesus' friends (v. 14), to the statement that Jesus no longer calls them slaves but friends, that is, those who, unlike slaves, share with Jesus all that is given to him. Discipleship, then, brings about an emancipation, a transformation of status from metaphorical slavery to clientage under the rubric of friendship, all language and social realities with which first-century Christians were familiar.[82] The language of friendship here, therefore, need not presume social equality, a usual characteristic in the wider semantic field of friendship, but a change of metaphor from the social institution of slavery to that of patronage.

The sonship of Jesus was so deeply ingrained in early Christian consciousness, from the Gospels and Paul especially, that it comes as quite a surprise that the author of the *Shepherd of Hermas* cast the Son of God in a parable not as son but as slave. In *Similitude* 5.2, the shepherd tells a story about a vineyard owner who places a faithful slave in charge of the vineyard during his absence and, because of the slave's diligence, grants him freedom and joint inheritance with his son, who rejoices at the prospect. Contrary to expectation, in the explanation, not the son but the slave is the Son of God, not in abjection but in the power of the one responsible for seeing to the upkeep of the vineyard (*Sim.* 5.5, 6). The son in the parable is rather the Holy Spirit (*Sim.* 5.6.6). Here, unexpectedly, servant Christology preempts sonship Christology, in a way somewhat reminiscent of 1 Peter 2:21–25, though here the action is labor in the vineyard, an established biblical image for ministry, rather than the suffering of the slave.

The household codes of Colossians, Ephesians, and 1 Peter testify that slavery as an institution was not questioned, though abusive Christian owners were not acceptable. The slave members, however, are directly addressed in the parenesis.

The passage addressed to slaves in 1 Peter 2:18–25 needs special attention, since it presents so many difficulties for the modern interpreter. The context is an incomplete household code in which only slaves, wives, and (briefly) husbands are addressed, within a larger context of the appropriate submission required as one's duty, whether to God or to legitimate human institutions (2:13–3:7). Slaves are told to submit to their owners, not only to the good ones but also to those who are abusive, after the example of Christ who, though innocent, suffered as if guilty, with the theme of the innocent victim from Isaiah 53 fully alluded to as background. The abused slave therefore becomes not only an imitator of Christ, but an image of the whole community that suffers for the faith (1 Peter 2:25; 4:12–19).

The term for slaves in verse 18 is not the usual *douloi,* but *oiketai,* household servants. This terminology is in keeping with the wide use of household and family images in 1 Peter: The community are the living stones to build the spiritual house (*oikos;* 2:5; 4:17); all believers should use their gifts like good household managers (*oikonomoi;* 4:10). In contrast to the status of resident aliens (*paroikia;* 1:17; 2:11), which is also a prominent metaphor for the believers in 1 Peter, the household image (*oikia*) provides an anchor of identity in a sea of strangerhood.[83]

The primary concern of the letter seems to be to strengthen those who are suffering unjustly as Christians (4:12–19). Some of those are slaves and wives of unbelievers. They are target groups through whom the author develops his point.[84] Even more than wives, slaves are in the vulnerable position of having no recourse when abused. Their conformity to the suffering Christ, therefore, is meant to be comfort and encouragement in suffering that they are powerless to avoid, not a legitimation of the oppression of slavery, as some interpreters later took it, much less a biblical justification for slavery.

For our concerns, the passage is important evidence that slaves of unbelievers were admitted into Christian communities as persons in their own right, a factor that must have caused much confusion and suspicion in many households. Christians were not the only group to allow slaves to belong independently of their owners. There is indication that both Judaism and many of the mystery religions that were popular at the time did the same.

Slavery was a continuing reality in early Christianity. The *Didache* (4.10–11) urges slave owners against abuse but exhorts slaves to be subject to their owners "as representatives of God" (*hōs typō theou*). Like the christologizing of patriarchal marriage in Ephesians 5, the authority structure of slavery, too, was becoming Christianized. Ignatius's *Letter to Polycarp* (4.3) urges that slaves should not be expected to be set free at community expense, suggesting a large number of slave members in Smyrna with high expectations of the benefits of membership.[85] Perhaps the custom of using community funds for this purpose was becoming so widespread that slaves were joining with this motive. The original intent of the use of community funds was to ransom those unjustly imprisoned or enslaved. *First Clement* 55.2 speaks even of a custom of self-substitution in slavery in order to free others.[86]

Pliny the Younger, as Roman governor of Bithynia-Pontus in northern Asia Minor at the beginning of the second century, writes to the emperor Trajan that in his investigation of charges against Christians, he has tortured two Christian slave women (torture was required when questioning slaves) and found nothing but a degenerate superstition. His words are that he inquired by torture "of two maidservants, who are called ministers" *ex duabus ancillis, quae ministrae dicebantur.*[87] The word *ministra* is a feminine form of *minister,* an exact Latin equivalent of Greek *diakonos.* The two slave women are therefore female deacons, a fascinating reference that tells us both that the churches of northern Asia Minor had female ministers in the early second century, and that slaves could be appointed to such church roles.

The apologist Justin in mid–second-century Rome indicates that the slaves of Christians, some of them women and children, have been tortured to extract information about clandestine atrocities committed by their owners.[88] A few years later, another apologist, Athenagoras, argues that Christians cannot be doing secret outrageous things as they are accused because they have slaves, none of whom have reported such things about them.[89] These two statements are mutually contradictory but explainable on the basis of different locations and rhetorical intents. The point here is not historicity of slave reportage, but the fact that both references seem to envision non-Christian slaves owned by Christians, which would indicate the absence of any coercion for dependent members of a household to accept baptism.

In fact, in the early third century, Hippolytus's church order directs that a slave of a believer must have his or her owner's permission to become a catechumen.[90] Yet Aristides had written early in the second century that unbelieving slaves of believers, whether men, women, or children, were persuaded through love to become Christians, after which they were called brothers and sisters without distinction.[91] These seeming contradictions are not significant as such, since there probably was no one unified policy on conversion of slaves. A few years earlier, Tertullian had written that one of the charitable causes for which the monthly collection was taken up was for "old (presumably abandoned) domestic slaves" (*domesticis senibus*), probably not of Christian but of unbelieving owners, but certainly members of the community.[92]

Clement of Alexandria has frequent references to the presence of slaves in Christian households. Having too many slaves and having slaves to pour water over you in the public baths are considered unacceptable luxuries. Husbands and wives should not be intimate at home in the presence of the slaves. Modest women who would not undress in front of free male members of their household are criticized for not hesitating at the baths in front of their male slaves. Slaves, recognizable by their inherently bad disposition, are exhorted to be submissive to their owners (quoting Eph. 6:5, 7 and 1 Peter 2:18), but they are not to be treated like pack animals.[93]

In spite of apparent encouragement of slaves to gain their freedom from unbelieving owners, and in spite of the evidence for independent admission of slaves into the churches without the rest of their household, Christian ownership of slaves does not seem to have been questioned for many centuries. What early Christianity did was to insist on a humanized and nonabusive relationship between owner and slave, but it did not change the structure. Meanwhile, it can be assumed that slaves of Christians, whether themselves Christian or not, were as well integrated into households as in the houses of their unbelieving neighbors. We would like to think that slaves of Christians were better treated, but of this we cannot be sure. Did baptism of slaves bring about a different relationship with a Christian owner? Aristides suggests that it did: slaves were then called brothers and sisters without distinction. But did their roles change? The rest of the evidence suggests that they did not.

Eloquent testimony to the continued practice of Christian slave ownership well beyond the Constantinian era is a bronze slave collar from fifth- or sixth-century Sardinia inscribed: "I am the slave of archdeacon Felix: hold me so that I do not flee."[94]

8

Family Life, Meals, and Hospitality

When sketching the archaeology of Roman atrium-houses in chapter 1, we saw that the paintings on their walls employ public images. Wallace-Hadrill argues that the third style, which emerged in 30 B.C.E. with the political changes introduced by Augustus, pictures informal contacts in domestic settings. Contemporary paintings allude to private dinner parties for chosen friends and to family themes[1] that were simultaneously private and political. Christian worship too occurred in these atrium-houses; eating "the Lord's supper" (1 Cor. 11:20) together as the "assembly (*ekklesia*) of God" (v. 22) symbolized relationships in the eschaton, relationships that were both private and public, actions at home that were symbolic proposals for the way other relationships in the city might be organized.

Peter Lampe and Dennis Smith have made new proposals concerning how everyday meals in these houses structured the way Christians practiced and understood the Lord's Supper. Smith[2] has argued that communal meals in Greco-Roman society all had a common form, a thesis modified by Peter Lampe, who suggests that the Corinthian meal was an *eranos,* a potluck supper to which each individual or family brought food.[3] In what follows, we summarize their conclusions, with the caveat that this is not intended as a complete study of eucharistic traditions, but rather is a brief sketch of the practical, ethical, and religious aspects of Christian families eating together in Roman households.

Community Meals
in Pauline House Churches

The Greek *symposia,* the Roman *convivia,* philosophical banquets, sacrificial meals, communal meals of Greco-Roman clubs and collegia, Jewish meals, and the Christian supper all had a common form in these centuries, although the diverse groups interpreted the meaning of the meal differently. The philosophical literature includes Plato, *Symposium;* Xenophon, *Symposium;* Plutarch, *Table-Talk* and *Dinner of the Seven Wise Men;* Lucian, *The Carousal, or the Lapiths* (his *Symposium*) and *Saturnalia;* Petronius, *Satyricon;* and Philo, *On the Contemplative Life,* the whole of which is a critique of Greco-Roman banquets (40–63), particularly those of Xenophon and Plato (57–62), as well as a eulogy of worship at banquets among the Jewish Therapeutae (24–39, 64–89).

Although Jews, Greeks, and Romans have early traditions of sitting at meals, all later adopted the posture of reclining for formal, evening meals, which meant that they needed slaves to serve the food. It is "womanish and weak to sit on a chair or on a stool," Alcidamus the Cynic remarks. Because no couch is available, he takes his dinner walking about the dining room, and when tired, he lies on the floor leaning on his elbow with his cloak under him (Lucian, *Symp.* 13–14). In the discussion of the archaeology of these houses, we saw that the dining room, the triclinium, was a key area, beautifully painted, and in virtually every case with dining couches placed end-to-end, parallel to three walls, not side-by-side. There were also banquet rooms in some public buildings, including temples, for example in the *Asklepieion* at Corinth, which had three dining rooms; each had eleven couches for as many diners.[4] Typically these dining rooms are small, for fewer than twenty persons, which would have been a problem for citywide gatherings of the church in Corinth.

Famous examples of invitations to meals have been found in Egypt on papyrus dated from the first to the third centuries, for example, "Chaeremon requests you to dine at the banquet of the Lord Sarapis in the Sarapeion tomorrow, the 15th, at the 9th hour" (Oxyrhynchus papyrus 110).[5] Responding to such an invitation by the owner or renter of a house, about sundown in Greek culture but earlier, around mid-afternoon in Roman culture,[6] friends, family, and clients would gather for an evening meal.

The host assigned couches to the guests; in that culture of honor, status was a recurrent problem.[7] Plutarch asks in *Table-Talk* "whether the host should arrange the placing of guests or leave it to the guests themselves?"[8] His younger brother Timon invited (*keklēmenous*) foreigners and citizens, friends and kinsfolk, "all sorts of people," and told them to take whatever place they wished (615D). The father accused him of disorderliness (*ataxia*) for not arranging (*dietassete*)[9] the placing of his guests by age and rank (615E). Plutarch's brother objects that he is not jury and judge of who is better and who worse, that his guests have not come to a contest but to dinner (616C). Guests differ in age, power, intimacy, and kinship; to arrange them by honor would "transfer empty fame from marketplace and theatre to social gatherings" and stimulate vanity, although it would be more fitting for guests to wash vanity from their souls as mud from their shoes (616D). If the host humbles (*tapeinountes*) some and exalts others, hostility and rivalry are set aflame. In other areas Greeks preserve equality (*isoteta*) among men, so why not begin with the understanding that when they enter the door "the dinner is a democratic affair and has no outstanding place like an acropolis where the rich man is to recline and lord it over meaner folk?" (616EF). Plutarch agrees with his brother that this is fine when guests are young; however, when they are learned, foreigners, magistrates, or older men, custom must have its way: Honor must be done as carefully as possible (616F–617A). Lamprias, Plutarch's older brother, objects: not prestige but pleasure determines the placing of guests (618A), although he too agrees that disorder will not do. One does not seat a rich man with a rich man, and so on, but one should seat what suits him to the person who lacks it, one eager to learn with a learned man, the young with the old, athletes and hunters with farmers, that is, the contentious with the gentle, lovers together (whether they love lads, women, or virgins), an honest poor man with one who is rich, "so that an outpouring from a full into an empty goblet may take place" (618E, 619A).

Lucian's *Saturnalia* satirizes the Roman festival of the same name, a slave's holiday during which they played roles of the upper class at the banquet; in other words, this banquet turns normal arrangements upside down.[10] Chronos, king of the feast, observes that "everyone, slave and free man, is held as good as his neighbor" (*Sat.* 7, trans. Kilburn in LCL). One of the "first laws" is: "let every man be treated equal, slave and freeman, poor and rich" (*Sat.* 13). One of the "second laws" is: "rich man shall not send [gifts] to rich man or at Chronus's festival entertain anyone of equal standing" (*Sat.* 15). "Laws for Banquets" include the following:

> Each man shall take the couch where he happens to be. Rank, family, or wealth shall have little influence on privilege. All shall drink the same wine, and neither stomach trouble nor headache shall give the rich man an excuse for being the only one to drink the better quality. All shall have their meat on equal terms. . . . Neither are large portions to be placed before one and tiny ones before another, nor a ham for one and a pig's jaw for another—all must be treated equally. (Sat. 17).
>
> When a rich man gives a banquet to his servants (*oiketas*), his friends shall aid him in waiting (*diakonounton*) on them. (Sat. 18)

Lucian writes Chronos a letter: "Tell them [the rich], moreover, to invite the poor to dinner, taking in four or five at a time, not as they do nowadays, though, but in a more democratic fashion, all having an equal share" (*Sat.* 22, trans. Harmon in LCL). Lucian's *Symposium* also begins with an argument among various philosophers over precedence (6; 9) and ends in a "philosophical" brawl (42–47).

The meal itself would be followed by drinking, entertainment, and discussion. Friendship—both private and political—was celebrated and deepened with good cheer. However, disruptive behavior was a common problem, behavior that sometimes led to court cases (Lucian, *Symp.* 1, 35, which he sums up as "discord").[11] Early in the period women did not attend such banquets, but later they began to attend, and even to recline with the men (Lucian, *Symp.* 8).[12] Several themes are recurrent in the literature on symposia, one of which concerns uninvited or late guests (Plato, *Symp.* 174BC, E; 175C; 213A; 223B; Lucian, *Symp.* 1, 12, 20).[13]

Philo, in *On the Contemplative Life*,[14] describes a symposium as it was adapted by a Jewish mystical group. We will not analyze the whole treatise[15] but will mention some items and then focus on his description of the formal meal. Philo briefly describes a Sabbath, where both men and women sit, separated by a partition, and a senior member gives a wise discourse (30–33). On this seventh day, they also eat bread and water (34–37), not wine (40), nor meat or fish (53–54), so there are no drinking bouts at the "after-dinners" as they call them (54). Therapeutae eat and drink in self-control (34) and simplicity, not vanity (39). These Sabbath meals may not have been symposia.

Philo inserts a digression, about a quarter of the treatise, criticizing Greco-Roman banquets (40–63), particularly those of Xenophon and Plato (57–62). Wine makes them mad (40), and they carry on with license, leaving in enmity calling for advocates and judges (44). Many copy banqueting with Italian luxury (48), eating baked meats (53–54), then have drinking bouts at the "after-dinners." Pleasure is an element in both Xenophon's and Plato's banquet, but the latter talks of love, of the passions of men for young boys, reducing them to the condition of girls (57–63).

With these symposia Philo contrasts a festive meal held every fifty days by those who follow the prophet Moses (64). Those who assemble include aged virgins who have kept their chastity of their own free will, not under compulsion (unlike the Vestal Virgins in Rome; 68). Standing, they pray to God that their feasting may be acceptable; then the seniors recline, men by themselves on the right, the women by themselves on the left (69), and the young men stand (77). At other banquets beautiful young slaves offer service (*diakonia;* 50), but the Therapeutae

> do not have slaves to wait upon them (*diakonountai*) as they consider the ownership of servants is entirely against nature. For nature has borne all men to be free, but the wrongful and covetous acts of some who pursued that source of evil, inequality, have imposed their yoke and invested the stronger with power over the weaker. In this sacred banquet there is as I have said no slave, but the services are rendered by free men who perform their tasks as attendants (*diakonikas*) not under compulsion nor yet waiting for orders, but with deliberate good will anticipating eagerly and zealously the demands that may be made. For it is not just any free men who are appointed for these offices but young members of the association chosen with all care for their special merit who as becomes their good character and nobility are pressing on to reach the summit of virtue. They give their services gladly and proudly like sons to their real fathers and mothers, judging them to be the parents of them all in common. . . . And they come in to do their office ungirt and with tunics hanging down, that in their appearance there may be no shadow of anything to suggest the slave. (*On the Contemplative Life* 70–72, trans. Colson in LCL)

While the attendants (*diakonoi*) stand ready for their ministry and there is silence, the president gives an allegorical exposition of Holy Scriptures (77), and then the president rises and sings a hymn to God, a new or an old one in hexameters and iambics. All the others take their turn, listening in silence except for the closing refrains, when all, men and women, lift their voices (80). After the hymns, the young men bring in portable tables with bread, salt, and water (81–82; cf. 34–37); although some will laugh, there is neither wine nor meat (73; cf. 40, 53–54). While most eat leavened bread seasoned with salt mixed with hyssop, the simplest and purest food is reserved for their superiors, unleavened bread with salt unmixed (81–82). After supper there is an all-night vigil. Standing in the refectory, they form choirs, one of men and one of women, singing hymns to God, sometimes antiphonally, keeping time with hands and feet rapt with enthusiasm (83–84). Then they mix and become a single choir, a copy of the one of old by the Red Sea, where a command of God made the sea a source of salvation to one party, of perdition to the other (86). The ancient choir sang hymns of thanksgiving to God their Savior, the men led by the prophet Moses, the women by the prophetess Miriam (87). They continue till dawn without shame, more wakeful than when they came, then return to their private sanctuaries. The Therapeuteae, who live in the soul alone, are citizens of heaven and the world (*kosmou politōn;* 90). Virtue gains for them God's friendship and the summit of happiness.

Five things are different about this symposium. Some recline while some stand, with no shame attached to the latter. Philo names those who stand young men, but not children. This mixture of postures would allow a greater number of people in the banquet, more than the usual twenty in a triclinium. During the Sabbath meal described earlier, all "sit." Second, the licentiousness of a typical symposium (e.g., Lucian, *Symp.* 46, in which the Cynic Alcidamus tries to ravish the flute girl) is replaced by asceticism, even by perpetual virginity of some women.[16] Philo also stresses the rejection of wine, so essential to the meal that he expects his readers to laugh, but perhaps also ambivalently to admire the Therapeutae's self-control. Third, their insistence on equality, the rejection of slavery, challenges the structure of Roman society. Slaves typically serve and cook food at such banquets, but instead, the Therapeutae choose and honor young men who serve the meal with no hint that they are slaves, a symbol of their different social order.[17] This equality is modified slightly by an infinitesimal difference in diet, which again reverses the usual symbolism: The simplest and purest food is reserved for superiors (81–82). Fourth, family terms of endearment are used, but they are metaphorical (72). The spiritual community has replaced the biological family (cf. 13–18). Fifth, the order of the banquet differs from the form that Smith argues is common to all symposia. The president speaks while the others listen in silence (75–79), and then *after* hymns (80), the young men bring in tables of bread, salt, and water (81–82). This reversal of the standard order of meal followed by conversation is related to the Therapeutae's rejection of wine, the usual accompaniment of after-dinner conversation. Instead, after the meal they become drunk with spiritual enthusiasm (85, 87, 89), attaining God's friendship and the peak of happiness. These significant differences provide a social and spiritual context in which we might better understand the Corinthian Christian symposium.

Do these meal customs shed light on the order and conflicts at the Corinthian Christian Eucharist? Paul and the Corinthians would certainly insist that there be differences, but what were they? First, unlike the Therapeutae, who left their cities, Paul preached exclusively in urban areas. Second, the houses owned by some of the members would have functioned to draw outsiders into the group, also into the gathering for worship, probably through an open front door (1 Cor. 14:16, "if you say a blessing with the spirit, how can anyone in the position of an outsider say the 'Amen' . . . ?").

Positively then, a house functioned to encourage additions to the gathering, but it also presented problems for a group with the baptismal confession affirming that "there is no longer slave or free" (Gal. 3:28b; cf. 1 Cor. 12:13c). The Christian confession and the design of Greco-Roman houses were at odds with each other. As we saw above, "one dominant imperative in a slave-owning society was to contrast adequately the servile and seigniorial areas of the house."[18] Most kitchens, where slaves worked, were poorly lit and never decorated, or they had red vertical stripes in the corners.[19] Owners of larger houses "deliberately segregated" cooking and dining, placing the smells, noises, and persons of the kitchen as many meters as possible from the dining rooms.[20] The kitchens were "nowhere" where "nobodies" worked.[21] At the Greco-Roman symposium, guests and sometimes uninvited guests reclined and were served by these slaves. Plutarch argues, against his two brothers, that typical honors at a symposium must be done as carefully as possible (*Table-Talk* 616F–617A). True, once annually at the Saturnalia, social relationships were turned upside down (Lucian, *Saturnalia* 17–18); without regard to rank, family, or wealth, each took whatever couch he (or she?) wished, drank the same wine as the rich host, ate the same food, and the rich host and his friends served the household slaves. Because they rejected slavery, the Therapeutae described by Philo went further: Slaves never served at their symposia. Instead they appointed the most virtuous young men to serve the others, which surely means that the young aspired to perform this service. How did Pauline ekklesiai resolve these tensions? Unlike the Therapeutae, they seem to have continued their former customs, maintaining distinctions between rich and poor, masters and slaves:

> When you come together, it is not really to eat the Lord's supper.
> For when the time comes to eat, each of you goes ahead with your
> own supper, and one goes hungry and another becomes drunk.
> What! Do you not have homes to eat and drink in? Or do you show
> contempt for the church of God and humiliate those who have
> nothing? (1 Cor. 11:20–22b)

Only the elite had the leisure to go to thermal baths in the early afternoons and to begin their meals in mid-afternoon, a contrast to their poorer clients or slaves who lacked either the time in the afternoon or the resources to bring their own food.[22] Lampe[23] gives an outline of Greco-Roman meals and suggests how they might have structured the Corinthian Eucharist:

Greco-Roman Eranos	Corinthian Eucharistic Potluck
Acclamation to the god(s)	
Dinner at "first tables"	Richer Corinthians eat "early" (v. 21)
Break	
Start of "second tables": sacrifice, invocation of house gods and geniuses of host and emperor	Blessing and breaking of bread, invocation to Christ
Second tables (often with guests who had newly arrived) Toast for good spirit of the house, tables are removed	Sacramental eucharistic meal (some stay hungry)
First wine jug is mixed, libation, singing	Blessing of the cup
Drinking, conversation, music, activities, entertainment in loose sequence	Drinking, perhaps the worship of 1 Corinthians 12, 14 (esp. 14:26–32): singing, teaching, prophesying, glossolalia (with translations), no orderly sequence

"First tables," the afternoon meal, began around 3 P.M., but the poor and some slaves would arrive only in time for "second tables." Two problems result: First, the wealthy would have eaten their food, and the latecomers would have brought little or none. Lampe[24] cites a similar problem in Xenophon, *Memorabilia* 3.14.1: participants in the potluck brought their own meat, fish, and vegetables, but some brought a lot, others little, each keeping their own. Socrates thought this destroyed fellowship at the meal; therefore, he instructed the slaves either to redistribute food baskets to all, or to distribute the food itself, so that sufficient food was placed before everyone. Paul suggests something similar, probably with the slaves still serving. First Corinthians 11:33 shows that Paul wants the Corinthians to eat a meal. Lampe observes that the term Paul uses for "dinner" (*deipnon*, 11:20, 25) never refers only to bread, but also to foods that were eaten with the bread, and he suggests then that verse 34 ("if anyone is hungry, let this one eat at home") must be interpreted in light of verse 33 ("when you come together to eat, wait for one another"). If a wealthy person had visited the baths and was hungry, let him or her eat something at home before going to the congregational potluck.[25]

Second, all the dining couches in the triclinium would be in use; there would not be enough space for the whole congregation to recline. Jerome Murphy-O'Conner calculates the amount of space in typical dining rooms and in atria; he arrives at an average-size atrium of 55 square meters, an average size triclinium of 36 square meters, enough combined for perhaps fifty persons, but with decorative urns, and so on, more probably for thirty to forty.[26] However, both Smith and Lampe think in addition of the courtyard, the peristyle,[27] which could be large. Although Greek houses are typically of a standard size, Roman houses and their peristylia are of quite uneven sizes. Wallace-Hadrill analyzed three different blocks of houses in Pompeii and Herculaneum (a total of 234 houses) and then described four different types of houses that vary from 100 to 1,000 square meters or larger.[28] No architectural format is standard: Type 1 is a shop and back room; type 2 has three rooms, one of which may be an atrium; type 3 has an atrium and a rear garden; type 4 has both an atrium and a peristyle, and in addition may have a horticultural plot, a second atrium, and/or a second peristyle. Fifty-seven of the houses in the sample are type 3, the "average" size in these two cities, between 175 and 345 total square meters; 58 houses are type 4, with between 350 and 3,000 total square meters.

Pedar Foss observes that about 10 percent of a residential building's area, whether small or large, is given to dining areas,[29] which means that an "average" house had 17.5 to 34.5 square meters for dining rooms, not counting the peristyle gardens. Besides triclinia, some houses had much larger "dining halls." In his section on Pompeii, Foss observes that the House of the Citharist (1.4.5 + 25) had two such halls, the first of 75.5 square meters, the second of 65.8 sq. m.[30] Jay Dozier, a student at Brite Divinity School, observes that this house has three large peristyles, measuring approximately 300, 250, and 220 square meters.[31] Six significant rooms (c. 55, 70, 25, 25, 10, and 20 sq. m.) open onto the largest garden. Figuring one-half square meter per person and an equal half square meter for furniture, vegetation, statues, and other artwork, 505 people could be served in this peristyle and adjacent rooms. Three rooms (c. 50, 8, 20 sq. m.) open onto the second largest garden, which could then serve 330 people. The smallest of the gardens has six adjacent rooms (c. 6, 9, 12, 6, 12, 45 sq. m.), so could serve 300 people. The three gardens with adjacent rooms could serve 1,135 people simultaneously.[32] The house of Menander (1.10.4/14–17) is 1,800 square meters including two gardens (c. 150, 115 sq. m.) with a dining hall of 93.8 square meters.[33] Similarly calculating a half square meter per person and another half for statues, and so on, 360 people could be served. The houses of the Citharist and of Menander are, of course, grand houses.

Studying Wilhelmina Jashemski's, *The Gardens of Pompeii*, Dozier surveyed all the gardens in regions I and VI, excluding triclinia and dining halls. He divided houses with their gardens into quarters: (1) 41 gardens measuring between 1 and 15 square meters, (2) 111 gardens between 20 and 100 square meters, (3) 60 gardens between 105 and 250 square meters, (4) 24 gardens between 255 and 2,000 square meters. The "whole church" in Jerusalem (Acts 15:22) or in Corinth might come together (1 Cor. 14:23; cf. 11:18, 22) in houses in the third and fourth quartiles. Noneucharistic assemblies (see Pliny the Younger, *Letters* 10.96.7) might have occurred in large open gardens, only a few of which were adjacent to triclinia. Examples include the Casa di D. Octavius Quartio (formerly incorrectly named Loreius Tiburtinus; 2.2.2), an enormous area related to a priest of Isis.[34] The house is 2,770 square meters, almost two-thirds of which is the open garden. The open garden has a water canal through its center more than 50 meters long, at the head of which is a biclinium for eating in the open. Another is the Casa della Nave Europa (1.15.3). The relatively small house has another huge garden of 1,800 square meters, a fruit orchard in the upper section, a vineyard in the lower, according to a sign the archaeologists have posted.[35] The fruit orchard included citrons, which Jews introduced from Persia into the West, where they were otherwise rare.[36] Finally, there is the Praedia di Julia Felix (2.4) adjacent to the ampitheater, which covers the *entire* insula, one of the largest in the city.[37] It has three separate gardens, including the peristyle in the house with sixteen slender, rectangular, marble columns on the west (c. 35 x 20 m.). There is an *S*-shaped garden (c. 30 m. long) in the north corner of the insula with an outdoor swimming pool, and the rest of the insula (c. 70 × 70 m.) was planted, perhaps with the famous Pompeian cabbage.[38] Cicero might have been able to feed his two thousand (see n. 32) in these spaces.

We do not know the size of the houses of Tabitha (Acts 9:37, 39, 41), Cornelius (Acts 10:2, 48; 11:12), Simon (Acts 10:32; 11:11), Mary (Acts 12:12), Gaius (Rom. 16:23; 1 Cor. 1:14), Crispus or Stephanus (1 Cor. 1:14, 16), Prisca and Aquila (1 Cor. 16:19; Rom. 16:5), and Philemon, Apphia, and Archippus (Philemon 2).[39] The numbers 1,135 for the House of the Citharist and 360 for the House of Menander are shocking, since many have accepted upper limits of 30 to 50 in a house worship service, and indeed, these grand houses would have been quite crowded by so many. But if we calculate a half or a quarter of those numbers, gatherings of the whole church in a city theoretically could still have been of considerable size. It is unwise to set a hard upper limit of 30 to 40 for the number of Christians who might celebrate the Lord's Supper in a Roman triclinium plus peristyle or in open gardens. Many Christian assemblies were certainly much smaller than 40; others could have been significantly larger. In these few paragraphs we have focused on the larger spaces because many writers have assumed that they did not exist. Gaius, head of a synagogue in Corinth; Erastus, perhaps an aedile in the same city; Prisca and Aquila, who owned a house in Asia and another in Rome; and Phoebe, Paul's patron, theoretically might have owned houses like some of those discussed above, although since we cannot visit them, we will never know. The need for all early Christian assemblies to have been small and private is a modern projection, not justified by Roman domestic culture or architecture.

The Corinthian Christians *sat* during worship (1 Cor. 14:30), although those eating meals in the temple reclined (1 Cor. 8:10). Both Smith and Lampe observe that when a latecomer arrives at Lucian's *Symposium* (13), he is offered a place to sit (which he declines). As observed above, the Therapeutae also sat during their Sabbath service. The larger numbers must have meant that Christians did not have enough space (for all) to recline during the meal.

Discussing "religion in the domus," Bakker gives evidence that household gods were actively worshiped in the first century C.E.: In Pompeii and Herculaneum, archaeologists discovered 555 cult rooms, aediculae, pseudo-aediculae, and niches with paintings, many with provisions for sacrifice.[40] In these two cities niches were found in kitchens (37), in atria (front rooms [39]), in peristylia (26), and viridaria (gardens [29]).[41] In Ostia and in North Africa, private religion was observed most often in the courtyard.[42] The gods were worshiped in various rooms or open spaces in these houses; we may conclude that Christians also would have gathered for worship in the same rooms and open areas as did their pagan counterparts. These numbers could easily have been larger than the consistently small groups who worshiped Mithras.

Both Smith and Lampe argue that the worship activities of 1 Corinthians 12 and 14 (acts of prophecy, teaching, healing, tongues) chronologically *followed* the Eucharist discussed in chapter 11, which involves the assumption that they belong to the same service.[43] Paul writes of them in the same order they would have in a symposium: First the meal, then after the cup of wine was mixed, conversation (teaching). As we saw above, the order of the Therapeutae's symposium was more complex: The sermon came before the meal, although indeed, after the meal they sang hymns until they experienced spiritual ecstasy—without wine.

At the symposium Plato narrates, Socrates discusses love (*eros*), a discussion the Jewish author Philo criticizes at length when he writes of the Therapeutae's symposium (*On the Contemplative Life* 57–62). Both Smith and Lampe suggest that Paul's chapter (13) on love may then be a Christian proposal in conscious tension with Plato and contemporary symposia, although neither notices the explicit parallel in Philo.[44]

Community Meals
in the Synoptic Gospels

The amount of material in the Synoptic Gospels related to this subject is so extensive and complex that we will only point to some texts and intriguing practices. Luke 14 has fascinated many readers with its teaching on humility, the question of the place of honor at a feast, and the following parable of the great supper. Recently Willi Braun has shed new light on this text. The chapter begins with Jesus healing a man with dropsy, while Pharisees object since the healing occurs on the Sabbath (Luke 14:1–6). Braun observes that Luke knows little of and is not interested in the historical sect of the Jewish Pharisees in Israel, that they serve rather as useful literary figures.[45] Dropsy, an unquenchable craving for drink even though the body is inflated with fluid, was a Cynic metaphor for consuming passion.[46] Braun argues that the whole section is a *chreia,* a narrative argument developed as the contemporary rhetoricians Theon and/or Hermogenes suggest.[47] Jesus curing the man of dropsy is a chreia in the form of an act, one which is followed by several gnomic sentences, then by a story of the great banquet, all of which is an inductive argument, a kind of persuasive composition. Luke argues in a conventional rhetorical manner for unconventional behavior![48] The story of the great banquet is, then, not formally a symposium, but part of the argumentation.[49] Braun asks what the issue is and notes that meals like the "great supper" typically have a conservative function, but that Jesus' story argues for status transformation, that this ritual meal crosses boundaries.[50] The closest parallel is Lucian parodying Plato in his anti-symposium.[51] Jesus' story concerns the conversion of a rich, dishonored householder, who first invites his upper-class peers, then invites a new social grouping, the "indigent, filthy and such."[52] The poor are reluctant and have to be encouraged.[53] A century later, Hippolytus also made significant efforts to make it easier for the poor to participate in Christian communal meals.[54] Braun suggests that the story may reflect rich Lukan Christians inviting their poor brothers and sisters to dinner, which generated ostracism from wealthy peers.[55]

Luke 22:24–30 is another fascinating text concerning greatness at a meal, a dispute that Luke places in the context of the Lord's Supper, part of the only farewell discourse in the Synoptic Gospels.[56] Neither Luke 14 nor Luke 22 belongs to the literary genre of symposia, although both are informed by that literature.[57] Luke 22:24–30 has close ties to Mark 10:41–45 but is probably not literarily dependent on it.[58] Jesus makes several contrasts:

Position A	Position B
kings ruling/benefactors	Gentile subjects (14:25bc)
the greatest	the youngest (v. 26c)
the leader	the servant (*diakonōn*, v. 26c)
the diner (*anakeimenos*)	the table servant (*diakonōn*, v. 27a)
the diner (*anakeimenos*)	Jesus, table servant (*diakonōn*, v. 27bc)[59]

Position A is negative, and position B is positive. In the final contrast, Jesus makes himself a model of the one serving. Verse 26b contains an imperative: "Let the greatest among you become (*genesthō*) as the youngest, and the leader as one who serves." The apostles remain leaders[60]; there are "great ones among you" (v. 26b). But the leaders are somehow to become "as" (*hōs*) those held in low esteem, as the young, as one serving. The ordinary pattern of kings ruling, of their being benefactors, has something negative about it, so that Jesus is recommending something extraordinary.[61] A benefactor, a patron, places a client in an inferior position by the benefaction, so that the latter is indebted to the patron, which Jesus is criticizing. Some interpreters see a close relationship to John 13, where Jesus washes the disciples' feet, although the term "serve" does not appear in the Johannine account.[62] Luke 12:35–38 and Mark 13:33–37[63] are closer: Slaves (*douloi*) wait for the master (*kurios*) to come home, who when he finds them awake, "will gird himself and have them sit at table, and he will come and serve (*diakonēsei*) them" (Luke 12:37, not in Mark). The Lukan parable of the doorkeeper astoundingly has the master serving the slaves, quite as remarkable as Jesus modeling servant leadership. Reading both Luke 12 and 22, some interpreters understandably suggest that Jesus was serving others reclining at the meal.[64] Such a symbolic action would have been astounding in a Greco-Roman house. We have seen Foss's observations that the wealthier the Greco-Roman house, the farther they "segregated" the kitchen and its slave staff from the dining rooms and their elite

company. For these "nobodies" to be served regularly at Christian ritual meals by the "leader" (Luke 22:26) would indeed have stimulated
other elite citizens to refuse invitations to such dinners.[65]

A number of texts that concern women in relation to meals have
been touched on in chapter 5 and are not repeated here. Mark has little concern for what is improper or scandalous.[66] Jesus does (Mark
2:14–17) what he is accused of in Q (Luke 7:34//Matt. 11:19), "be-
hold, a glutton and a drunkard, a friend of tax collectors and sinners," that is, one who eats with them. Luke is, however, concerned
to portray respectable women. In Luke Jesus does not dine with
women; the "sinner" who anoints his feet is an uninvited guest
(Luke 7:36–50).

Matthew is, however, different. The five women in the genealogy
(1:1–17) foreshadow Jesus' gospel for sinners and foreigners.[67]
Matthew alone explicitly allows for the presence of women at public
meals both in the time of Jesus and in the church. Matthew adds women
to both of Mark's feeding stories (Matt. 14:21, not Mark 6:44; Matt.
15:38, not Mark 8:9). Only Matthew has women reclining for meals; all
recline (14:19), which then includes the women (v. 21), as among
Philo's Therapeutae. Further, only Matthew is not reluctant to refer to
prostitutes (*pornai*) in Jesus' company (Matt. 21:31–32). Strikingly, the
most Jewish of the Gospels is also the most egalitarian.

Thus several significant stories in the Gospel tradition participate in
an anti-symposium tradition best reflected in the satirist Lucian. Luke
14 is a chreia in which the story of the great banquet persuasively argues for the nontraditional practice of inviting poor brothers and sisters
to eat, which may well have generated social ostracism from the host's
wealthy peers. In Mark 10:41–45 Jesus is a table servant, a model for
church leaders. Matthew alone allows for women's presence at public
meals in the time of Jesus, and they recline with the men. Matthew alone
includes prostitutes among Jesus' company; the most Jewish of the
Gospels is also the most inclusive.

Hospitality, Meals, and Family Life
in the Johannine Literature and Beyond

The Importance of Hospitality
and Its Effect on Families

We have already seen from the Pauline letters and Acts the significance for house churches of common meals and the granting of hospitality to traveling Christians, and their effect on families. Through these

activities, Christian families received news of other churches, their horizons were broadened, they built up intercity networks of communication and concern, became a base for mission, and formed a sense of community larger than their urban area.[68] As we shall see, by these means, households were also drawn into inter-church conflicts.

The theme of hospitality and common meal in the Johannine literature is dominated by the image of Jesus' behavior at the Last Supper in John 13. The foot-washing scene and the giving of the love commandment model conviviality and the blurring if not reversal of the social distinctions that were so much a part of the Greco-Roman banquet culture.[69] Within that meal context, those who receive the disciples receive Jesus and the one who sent him (13:20), an echo of the symbolic importance of hospitality in the Johannine churches. Even though his own did not receive him, those who do are empowered (1:11–12; 5:43). The beloved disciple models this hospitality by taking the mother of Jesus, who is in this Gospel a model disciple, into his own home (19:27). What these lines actually meant in terms of church practice is revealed in the Johannine letters.

The Third Letter of John speaks of a crisis of hospitality. The Presbyter, author of the letter, has sent around a previous letter, on what topic we do not know, but a difficult person named Diotrephes refuses not only to receive or accept him and those he represents, but even tries to stop the whole network of hospitality by refusing communion with those who do (3 John 9–10). The situation is obscure because this is a genuine letter sent to real people who knew the whole story and could fill in the details.

We will never know the real issues involved, which for most interpreters are theological, assuming an association with a similiar saying in 2 John 10.[70] There, anyone who comes seeking hospitality but brings a different teaching than that held as normative by the author is not to be received into the house or even given an ordinary greeting. The implication is that such persons would be known by their potential hosts and have to be turned away at the door, a very painful situation. Turned away on the basis of what? A reputation that has gone before them? An interrogation given on the spot? By whom? We wish we knew the answers to these questions.

Besides the theological differences, which according to 2 John 7 have to do with Christology,[71] one suspects that there is also a crisis of authority.[72] We are in the beginnings of early Christian schism, in which house churches are splitting off from one another because of theological differences. The effect on families who have been accustomed to communication with one another can only be imagined. Whatever the issues involved, this glimpse into early house church organization makes clear how crucial hospitality was for evangelization and ongoing religious education.

The sharing of the common meal is a motif utilized even by the author of Revelation. The false teachers satirized as "Jezebel" and "Balaam" profane Christian eating by encouraging the eating of defiled food (Rev. 2:14, 20). By contrast, the risen Christ promises to be a surprise dinner guest of honor to those who are faithful to the author's point of view (Rev. 3:20)—another way of expressing early Christian belief that in their common meal, Christ is symbolically present as preparation for the great marriage feast to be celebrated one day (Rev. 19:9, 17).

Hospitality was an important virtue generally (Heb. 3:2; 1 Peter 4:9). As can already be seen in the Johannine letters, once there is a central authority, that figure holds primary responsibility for hospitality among a group of churches. This practice is reinforced in the job description of a presbyter-bishop in 1 Timothy 3:2 and Titus 1:8, where, among other things, a church leader must be *philoxenon,* a lover of hospitality. Likewise, Hermas describes presbyter-bishops as hospitable because they willingly receive believers into their houses, especially the needy and widows.[73]

But the real work involved may have been done by the women, for widows who are to be officially "enrolled" in the church of the Pastorals must have brought up their children, practiced hospitality, washed the feet of the holy ones, and done other deeds of charity (1 Tim. 5:10). This simple line gives us a glimpse of the role of women as providers of services in the church, especially widows with room in their houses. They were the ones best prepared to receive visiting missionaries, teachers, and other Christian travelers. They too along with their households may have been drawn into the theological conflicts that were beginning to surface at this time.

This kind of situation is illustrated by Ignatius of Antioch, who was a frequent guest along the way to his martyrdom in Rome. After stopping at Smyrna, a community that must have been particularly dear to him because of his friendship with its bishop, Polycarp, he writes back to them, in male style sending special greetings to households of "my brothers" with their wives and children. But one household he treasures is headed by a woman, Tavia, and to them he sends special greetings. If Ignatius, who was traveling under guard, was allowed to visit or stay in a private home in Smyrna, it must have been in hers. She may have been not a widow but a Christian wife with an unbelieving but tolerant husband, if she is to be identified with the only householder wife to whom Ignatius sends greetings in his letter to Polycarp. In this case, her husband must not have been a Christian, since he is not addressed. This is the kind of situation in mixed marriages against which Tertullian warns: A Christian wife whose non-Christian husband will thwart her duties, like giving hospitality to traveling Christians. Here, however, he seems not to have posed an obstacle.[74] The other group whom Ignatius greets with special warmth in the same verse are "the virgins called widows," an identifiable group of celibate women who probably also provided particular attention to the visiting dignitary and were his eager listeners.

The Smyrnaeans were apparently lavish in their welcome of Ignatius, yet they are warned about false teachers, especially those who teach that the suffering of Christ was only an appearance. Ignatius is very firm in his instructions that these people are not to be received and if possible, those in communion with him are not even to meet with them, but only to pray for them—from a distance.[75] The crisis of hospitality, present in the world of the Johannine epistles, is also present in the world of Ignatius and Polycarp.

The same problem is present in the *Didache*, a church order document that probably arose in the East at the turn from the first to the second century C.E. Here, though, there are three categories of travelers seeking hospitality. After giving a suggested text for a eucharistic prayer, chapter 11 instructs readers to receive itinerant teachers whose teaching matches what they have just been given; they are to be received just as the Lord would be, with all the comforts of full hospitality. But if their teaching is otherwise, they are not to be received. In this church, itinerant teachers seem to be called both apostles and prophets, and besides teaching, they may speak prophetic oracles. This presents the problem that always accompanies prophecy: How to discern true prophecy from that which is not of God. Hence the third category of visitors: those about whom one is not sure, whose teaching seems to be all right, but perhaps they are charlatans who freeload on gullible households and families.

The criteria for finding out are very practical: The prophet is to stay a very short time and when leaving, expect to be given nothing more than food for a one-day journey. No one who tries to stay more than two nights or who asks for money is a true prophet.[76] Moreover, while a guest in a Christian household, the prophet's behavior will indicate whether he is a true or false prophet. Some warning signs are the following: In ecstasy, he orders a meal prepared, then sits down to enjoy it; again, he asks for money. The third criterion given here is that he is reluctantly allowed to do "a cosmic mystery of the church" (*mysterion kosmikon tēs ekklesias*), as long as he does not teach anyone else to do it. A prophet who does this is not to be judged for it "because the old-time prophets did it."[77]

Of course, hospitality involved not only receiving travelers but the regular meetings of the house church, at least weekly. Those groups that met in a patron's house could only be as large as fit into that house.[78] The host and most important guests, including visiting missionaries or a founding apostle on his or her return visit, would recline in the triclinium, either men alone, or men and women, depending on the group's degree of romanization. If the leading women were not reclining there, they were either sitting next to the couches or reclining together in an adjoining triclinium.

The rest of the gathering spilled out into the peristyle and/or atrium, either sitting at temporary tables and chairs, or reclining on movable couches, but within hearing of those in the triclinium. Thus, in spite of a certain ethos of shared intimacy, some social distinctions were inevitable. In less romanized areas, men probably ate together, women and children separately, but within hearing of each other. The ordinary dinner conversation during the meal would be with those in the immediate vicinity. For the blessing prayers, reading, and comment led from within the triclinium, all would listen from where they were.

Those church groups not fortunate enough to have a patron capable of hosting the whole gathering, and who therefore met in other surroundings such as an apartment house or the back room of a shop, must have had a very different experience of common worship. It was necessarily less formal, less gracious, and characterized by a different kind of social structure in which leadership did not belong automatically to a socially dominant figure. Given the way the social structure worked, however, it is still probable that anyone with a distinctive status was expected to assume leadership. But it is also possible that such groups were quite a bit more flexible in their leadership structures and necessarily in the style of their dining and assembly.

Meals as Center
of Christian Life

As Christianity developed, at least three kinds of communal meals are known, but how they differed from one another at different times and places is not at all clear. However, for Christian families, family participation in all of them was important. The first is the Eucharist, or Lord's Supper, celebrated weekly on the first day of the week in continuity with the meals of Jesus with his disciples, especially the last one before his arrest. Already Ignatius attempts to exert control over its celebration from a source of authority outside the household, namely, the bishop. For Ignatius, there is to be no genuine Eucharist (*bebaia eucharistia*) without the bishop or someone delegated by him.[79] This does not mean that episcopal structure and supervision were normative by his day, but that the practice was there at least in his church in Antioch, from where he tried to spread central organization as the answer to the confusion of theological heterodoxy.

The special blessing prayers over the bread and cup had become somewhat standardized by the time of Justin, who describes the celebration in detail with the explicit name of Eucharist.[80] It is not certain that what Justin describes was still being celebrated in a household context. The degree of formalization in his description makes it possible that in mid–second-century Rome, the shift has already happened away from the household dinner to the domus ecclesiae, the private residence architecturally adapted to make room for a larger group of people who stand rather than recline and who no longer partake of an entire meal. The one known exception to this standardization of formula is the *Didache,* whose eucharistic prayer is quite different; it also allows prophets to lead eucharist with whatever form they wish.[81]

One of the most interesting testimonies, though still not completely clear, comes from the *Apostolic Tradition* (27–29) of Hippolytus, thought to have originated in Rome toward the beginning of the third century.[82] Here, invitations to dinner are the concern, and the individual patronage of wealthy members is still an important factor, even though we can see in the text itself the process whereby they are being replaced by church authority. Roman dining customs are in force, whereby clients hope for a dinner invitation from their patron, who may instead send portions of food as gifts. Here, however, the meal seems also to be the Eucharist, for it is called the *cena dominica,* or Lord's Supper, and the oblation (*oblatio*), two expressions that usually designate the Eucharist.

While the invitation must come from the host, and thus we are still in the realm of private dinners in houses, the host is deprived of the key leadership role at the meal, pronouncing the blessing, or distributing the blessed food—whichever is meant by "do the blessing" (*benedictionem facere*). This function is reserved to the bishop or, in his absence, a presbyter or deacon, who alone can "do the blessing." In spite of being dated well after Justin, who speaks of the blessing of bread and wine with specific consecratory words ("This is my body . . . this is my blood"),[83] it is not all that clear what the "blessing" is all about in this section of Hippolytus. Perhaps the bishop's eucharistic prayer given in chapter 4 of the *Apostolic Tradition* is what is meant.

The description of this meal reflects a momentous stage of development, however, in which the local patron is losing control of the celebration in favor of a centralized authority. The author emphasizes the gratitude and respect due the patron who has issued the invitation, yet this emphasis inversely reflects the degree to which the patron still has the

complete leadership of the meal.[84] Even though the meal is held in someone else's house, the decisive action is now taken by a bishop, presbyter,
or deacon, "for a lay person (*laicus*) cannot do the blessing." Nor are the
order of widows allowed to perform the blessing. They are constituted for
prayer only, are not among the clergy, and cannot offer the offering.[85]

The second kind of Christian meal is the *refrigerium,* or funereal meal
for the deceased, celebrated in Roman custom at the cemetery at the
time of death, but also annually on the anniversary of the death of a family member (see figure 11). Christians continued this custom in their
own way, adapting it to their own faith by extending the celebration not
only to the immediate family on the death of a member, but by the third
century to the whole church on the anniversary of important figures,
especially martyrs.

The third type of early Christian meal is that known as the *agape* or
"love feast," which may originate from the custom called the "breaking of
the bread" in Acts (2:42–47; 20:7–12), which may or may not be the same
as Eucharist. There may be a reference to it in Jude 12: Inappropriate
deeds are "spots on your agapes," but the textual variants make it unclear.[86] When Ignatius stipulates that he thinks every genuine Eucharist
should be sanctioned by the bishop, he goes on to add two other events
to the same category: baptism and "doing agape" (*agapein poiein*).[87] Many
scholars think that in the early years, Eucharist and agape were the same
event, but that they became distinct later.[88] If so, they were already different, by the early second century, in Antioch and in some parts of the
province of Asia, where Ignatius was writing, as shown by this text in
which they are both mentioned but quite separately.

The *Acts of Perpetua and Felicitas* (17) relate that on the eve of their
martyrdom, those in prison celebrated their last meal as an agape
(*agapem cenarent*). Tertullian describes the agape meal by name as what
we later know it has become: a meal held out of familial duty (*pietas*) to
help those in need, that is, to feed the hungry of the community.[89] In
contrast to what we know is the later order of the Eucharist, reading and
teaching, then the meal, Tertullian's description of the agape meal follows the order of the classical symposium: first the meal, then drinking
and conversation or entertainment. In Tertullian's description, first
there is prayer, then the meal with drinking, then the washing of hands,
lights brought in, then recitation of scripture and singing, ending again
with prayer. There is no indication that what he is describing is also the
Eucharist. Rather, it is a true meal held in a private house, into which
the less fortunate are brought to be nourished both physically and
spiritually. As such, it probably took the form of an extended
family festival.

Figure 11. Funerary stele illustrating traditional banquet customs, Church of St. Peter, Antakya, Turkey. A Greek funerary monument depicts the men reclining on a dining couch, with woman and child seated alongside the couch. Photo by C. Osiek.

Clement of Alexandria also speaks briefly of the agape meal, but without the helpful details given by Tertullian.[90] Clement's context is table manners, the correct behavior of the well-moderated Christian. Moreover, unlike Tertullian, Clement is writing for believers, and so has no need to describe what everyone already knows. He excoriates those who revel in luxurious and sumptuous dinners and want to associate them with the agape meal, which is in reality "feasting on the word." The celebration must be based on love, not gluttony. While some have interpreted Clement's description to refer to both agape and Eucharist as one celebration, there is really no reason to think so, for there is no specifically eucharistic language in the description.

One aspect of the agape meal as a charitable exercise can still be seen in Hippolytus's *Apostolic Tradition,* and it reveals that charitable patronal activity is still practiced. Just after the treatment of the Lord's Supper (*cena dominica*), in chapters 27–29, discussed above, there is a brief treatment of meals held for widows, in chapter 30. It is legislative and deals only with two specific points. First, anyone who wishes to hold a meal for widows should observe propriety by sending them home before the evening is too advanced. Second, one who would like to feed them but cannot because of other responsibilities should give them a portion to take home and eat there, a *sportula,* or small basket of food that was regularly given by patrons to clients who were not lucky enough to be invited to the dinner itself. The text seems to indicate that more widows than could be fed in the house would arrive, perhaps un-invited, like clients expecting a handout.

In chapter 28, this gift of food had been called by its Greek name, *apoferetum* or *apophoretum*. Thus widows in Hippolytus's church who are in need of support or extra nourishment are still invited to private houses for dinner and gifts of food. The patron, though losing author-ity to the centralized power of the bishop, still holds charitable meals to feed widows.

A further stage in the loss of patronal power of individual patrons and its aggregation to the bishop can be seen in the mid–third-century Carthage of Cyprian, where the bishop has successfully usurped most of the social power of individual patrons and functions himself as cen-tral patronage figure. By this time, it is becoming customary for rich Christians to give directly to the church for centralized distribution by the bishop and deacons. Here the transition is virtually complete.[91]

The loss of the practice of individual patronage in the church had to have meant a decline in the place of the household as center of Chris-tian acitivity. Simultaneously, the private house was being replaced by the remodeled house, the domus ecclesiae, which, while resembling a residence on the outside, was no longer a center of private family life. It is not that house and family were devalued in the process, for they re-mained the location in which faith was first nurtured and people lived out their Christian lives. The scattered evidence suggests that families became increasingly centers of private prayer, reading of the scriptures and other religious books, and places in which religious faith found new and more overt means of expression.

Hippolytus, for instance, instructs people living at home to pray upon rising, at the third, sixth, and ninth hours, before going to bed, and even at midnight. On days when there is no common meeting for religious in-struction, the faithful are to read a "holy book" at home.[92] With the rise of Christian art, new domestic forms arose for expressing faith: amulets, religious symbols, and clothing with illustrated Gospel stories began to develop; "They appear like painted walls. . . . In doing this they consider themselves to be religious and to be wearing clothes that are agreeable to God."[93] But by the third century, the household was no longer the heart and center of Christian activity in the way it was in the earlier years.

There is much more to be said on this topic. Some second- and third-century texts, especially those by Clement of Alexandria, are rich with details about such topics as religious education and prayer in the fam-ily. But that is another book.

Conclusion

The study of the early Christian family yields a surprising result: Few Christian writers were interested in the family as such, but rather in family and household as image and proving ground for the church. Yet the sources allow us to glean some information about family life.

Christians lived and worshiped in Greco-Roman culture, which raises the question of the relationship between faith and culture, even between faith and architecture. Many early Christians lived their everyday lives in Roman atrium houses. During our research we became excited about what historians of art and of urban design have taught us about how people in Pompeii, Herculaneum, and Ostia lived in these houses. Wallace-Hadrill has taught us that one key function of such houses was to reinforce social status and difference, and Foss has clarified how this architecture separated owners from slaves, dining rooms from kitchens. Owners of the domus, whether male or—as Eumachia and Julia Felix demonstrate is possible—female, had enormous power over those who lived and worshiped in their domestic setting. These social dichotomies between elite owners and others, patrons and clients, challenged urban persons who converted to Christ and were baptized confessing that "there is no longer Jew or Greek, there is no longer slave or free, there is no longer male and female." Was this only an ideology that did not disturb the ethic of the owners, or did becoming Christian make an actual social difference? The social construction of the person is oriented much more strongly to embeddedness in the group in which the individual belongs by birth and circumstances than to a sense of individuality. Awareness of the effect of one's behavior on one's social group is therefore a major concern. Honor and shame emerge as gendered values in the dominant male culture. Honor for men consists in defending their perceived status level and the sexual virtue of their family's women, while shame as a negative experience is the loss of either. For women, honor according to the public male perspective consists in virginity before marriage and sexual exclusiveness afterward, though among women in the domestic sphere other honor systems are operative. Women possess the dangerous ability to bring shame on their family, especially their male relatives, by their sexual conduct.

The family was a rich social concept that vertically included ancestors and horizontally included the extended family, even though not living together; unrelated persons such as slaves and freedpersons attached by legal bonds; and even the property and assets of a household. Marriage was primarily understood as a social contract between two families for the production of legitimate offspring and the legal transfer of property, though certainly deep and intimate personal relationships did often exist between husbands and wives. If such relationships existed, however, they were more likely to develop after marriage than before.

Public space and public functions such as commerce and politics were traditionally male, while domestic space and household functions were considered female. In spite of this stereotyped dichotomy, women in the Greco-Roman era participated widely in business, public patronage, and public religion, though not formally in politics, and less commonly in the arts. Patronage was the backbone of the social system, operating at all official and unofficial levels: in politics, commerce, education, and personal relationships. It was the principal way of obtaining and using status and power. High-status women participated, especially in economic and informal political aspects, as patrons of trade guilds, religious and social organizations, synagogues and house churches, and as mediators of the power of the males of their families. But there was a marked tendency not to use the raw language of patronage, which would emphasize social inequalities. Rather, the language of friendship was generally used for patronage relationships—which should make the modern reader very cautious about an understanding of this semantic field in the ancient literature. Between the Greek East and the Roman West there were some noticeable differences in customs that are especially evident with regard to the social freedom of women. While the traditional legal power of the Roman paterfamilias was in fact more extreme than that of his Greek counterpart, in practice Roman familial inferiors had by the first century C.E. gained more autonomy. While women were nominally under the control of a male guardian with regard to financial and marital affairs, it was in some circumstances relatively easy to gain their legal freedom, for instance under Augustan legislation by producing three children in the case of a freeborn woman or four in the case of a freedwoman.

In Paul's letters there is a striking absence of such domestic issues. His interest was not directly in family life but in the quality of life in the assembly, first of all in the relationship between Jewish and Gentile Christians symbolized by their eating together. The brief discussions of marriage and women's conduct are less about family life than about how eschatology is to enter Christian living and what kind of public appearance Christians are to present. The ascetic Jewish Therapeutae and the Corinthian Christians' preference for celibacy would have been reinforced by current medical opinions, which generally emphasized the harmfulness of sex, advising that it be engaged in rarely or not at all. Paul was influenced by current medical judgments about sexual activity when he describes the "soft" behavior of a male as a vice: with contemporary doctors and philosophers he apparently assumed that a man should be active sexually, not passive, and therefore should not play the role of a woman. Modern Christian egalitarian value judgments often differ from Paul's acceptance of this hierarchical male/female, active/passive polarity.

On the other hand, with the Stoic Musonius Paul voiced a minority opinion that husbands do not own their wives, but that the relationship should be mutual: Wives also have influence/power over their husbands. Each partner in the relationship has influence over the other. Against the contemporary majority opinion, Paul uses the language of mutuality and friendship of heterosexual couples. And he rejects the common assumption that only the wife need be faithful to the relationship. With Musonius again, Paul argues that husbands should be as moral as their wives, not having multiple sexual relationships with prostitutes or perhaps with their slaves.

Women were active evangelists, coworkers, patrons, even apostles in the early Pauline churches, that is, in assemblies meeting in Roman atrium houses where women had more freedom to speak and act than they did in Greco-Roman town squares. Gender roles were under discussion and debate in Roman society, and we see this conflict reflected in the Gospels and epistles. Women were beginning to recline with the men during the afternoon or evening dinner. Further, as Juvenal's vicious objections demonstrate, some were beginning to raise their voice at dinner; the Corinthian Christian women prophets were among the new voices beginning to make themselves heard. Two of the women in the Philippian church were such key leaders that Paul seems to have structured the whole epistle to deal with their power struggle. Gender roles were undergoing significant change in the first centuries of the common era, one symbol of which, as Ward has demonstrated, is architectural: Instead of males and females bathing in segregated facilities as had been the custom earlier, in the first century C.E. the bath houses were integrated. We see some of the results of this cultural conflict in early Christian texts. Plutarch has left us debates about whether friendship occurs only between males or whether a heterosexual marriage might include friendship between the couple. In 1 Corinthians Paul employs the current gender-fair language of friendship and mutuality between heterosexual Christian couples. Paul's own preference, however, was for the single life devoted to the Lord, a preference that contrasts both with the Roman state's support of marriages that produce children and with some Corinthian Christians' demand that all live sexually ascetic lives. For the married, Paul encourages sexually active relationships, although surprisingly, he never once argues that this is in order to produce children, and for the ascetics who endanger their eschatological future by sexual incontinence, he prescribes marriage.

The Synoptic Gospels yield a pattern of deep suspicion about families and blood ties: They can be inimical to the demands of discipleship, which must clearly take precedence. Beginning with the example of Jesus, the first three Gospels demonstrate that family ties are only as good as their potential to support discipleship. Some early sayings of Jesus recorded in the source Q demand leaving family "for my sake and for the gospel." Similarly, Jesus compares the present eschatological crisis to the flood in Noah's day and to the destruction of Sodom in Lot's, so that ordinary activities like patriarchal marriage should not continue as usual; instead, as Luise Schottroff's eschatological interpretation emphasizes, followers should hope for God's future. Mark too presents the disciples leaving everything and following Jesus under the promise that they will acquire both a new family now—which does not include a patriarchal father—and in the coming age eternal life. In a literary culture that enforced a taboo on honorable women speaking in public, Mark records a foreign woman debating with and correcting Jesus.

Matthew's "disciples discourse" continues to reflect that "one's enemies will be members of one's own household." This is written in a period of high social and religious conflict, so that it is not a social program: The Synoptic Gospels all address family concerns by condemning separation and remarriage and by emphasizing the Fifth Commandment, to honor parents. Despite this contemporary familial conflict and in the midst of it, Matthew makes countercultural proposals for relationships within the new, acquired Christian family, as Carter has recently argued. Matthew 19—20 is united by Greco-Roman concerns about household management. In a parable within this unit, a householder raises the question of "what is right" and insists on treating the "workers" as "equal" to each other. Matthew addresses this parable to leaders in the community and follows it by condemning the ordinary way rulers of Gentiles lord it over them. Rather, for all the Synoptic

Gospels, leaders of house churches must be servants, somehow like slaves. This last proposal must have one of its sources in Jesus' parables. Jesus' poetic images of the kingdom often involved shocking reversals, for example that of a householder who arrives home late at night who would then serve the slaves! The Lukan churches may have challenged their culture by symbolically acting out this reversal at their eucharistic celebrations in the triclinia and peristyle gardens of Roman houses, which, because they were open and public, would have generated resistance in their cities.

The Gospel of John, which has very little to say about human families, sets up a paradigm of familial language in "Father" and "Son" which reinforces intimacy within the patriarchal framework and extends the family model not only to the church but to the life of God. Slaves, unlike our images from eighteenth- and nineteenth-century North American slaves, were not of one race, color, or geographical region, were not all uneducated, not all poor, and individually might be manumitted. On the street one could not always tell the difference between free and slave. A slave might have been one's neighbor who fell into debt, and therefore into bondage. Rome enslaved whole regions, and all the ethnic groups in those regions. But then some slaves who had the skills functioned as bankers for powerful owners and so had free persons as their clients. Some slaves like Epictetus were highly educated, more educated than many free persons. Bradley has demonstrated that slaves of whatever ethnic origin, education, or economic level hoped for freedom and a family and that their masters had absolute control over both. Although owners sometimes allowed slaves a family in order to stimulate productivity, they consistently sold women of childbearing age without their spouse or their children.

In the New Testament we catch only a few glimpses of persons who legally were slaves. We have followed Harrill's argument that Paul advises Corinthian Christian slaves to "use [the] freedom" offered them by their masters. And Lampe and Bartchy have demonstrated that Onesimus was not a runaway slave, but one who trusted Paul and sought him out to intercede with his master Philemon. Subtly, Paul seems to have asked this owner to manumit his gifted slave so that he might "minister" in his owner's stead.

One of the most dramatic shifts in early Christian ethics occurred when Paul died and his students introduced the Aristotelian household code to describe the way Christians ought to relate within these atrium houses. The distance between the dining room(s) and the kitchen was reinforced philosophically, even christologically. Paul confesses in Philippians that Christ took on the form of a slave, but the deutero-Pauline author of

Colossians does not, asserting rather that he is "head" of the cosmos as Caesar was head of the Roman Empire. This christological change is reflected in the ritual and ethics of the deutero-Pauline churches. Colossians, following 1 Corinthians 12, modified the early Christian ethic by removing "there is no longer male and female" from the baptismal confession and adding the Aristotelian imperative that wives, children, and slaves must be subordinate to the male head of the household. Women and slaves are not to be treated "equally," a contrast to the householder's treatment of "workers" in Jesus' Matthean parable. The relationship between faith and domestic Roman culture had shifted.

The literature typified by the household codes seems to take a very different approach from Matthew: Patriarchal household relationships are glorified and even theologized into images of Christ and the church. Yet in one way the message is similar. The church is still the real family, which the domestic living unit reflects. Thus the church came more and more to resemble an extended household, characterized by patriarchal leadership, high expectations of cohesiveness, and exclusive claims to honor by some over other members.

Gradually this patriarchal leadership tried to construct an integrated welfare system for its members. Birth, education, marriage, assistance to the sick and needy, and burial were all provided for by agents of the church. The church had the potential through Jesus' disturbing parables and its baptismal ecclesiology for creating a true equality of discipleship under the unique and sole fatherhood of God. Ironically, it did not do so, but chose instead to multiply the human symbols of patriarchal authority in the name of God.

The heads of such households often employed teachers, and Christian households similarly included teachers. Pagan, Jewish, and Christian authors simultaneously discuss prophetic and didactic activity. Discussing education, the contemporary Platonist Plutarch also mentions the "seer" Calchas who critiqued the king, not beyond comparison to Jesus' and Paul's prophetic activities. Pagan, Jewish, and Christian teachers insisted on critical hearing, in not believing everything that might be taught about God or gods in classical written texts or in oral speech. Teachers themselves did not merely pass on material they had memorized, although Plutarch's quotation of Homer demonstrated his astounding oral memory; they (re)interpreted it, as Paul does all the confessional, baptismal, and eucharistic formulas, as well as the Jesus sayings he passes on. And these reinterpretations of Jesus' parables, of women's roles, and of eating customs were disputed, a disputation that Plutarch and Paul both encourage. Some of the disputes were about orthodoxy; more concerned orthopraxy, especially how to live in Greco-

Roman households, more specifically, how women, slaves, heads of households, teachers, and students were to behave in such households. But as *episkopoi* and presbyters took power in the churches, the role of independent teachers, especially women teachers in mixed groups, declined, as may be seen in Mark, Luke-Acts, and the deutero-Pauline Pastoral Epistles. The continuous tradition of women teachers of women in domestic contexts remained, and the legendary stories of heroic women apostles and disciples such as Thecla that we now know as the Apocryphal Acts may have originated in just such circles.

In later decades and generations, the submission of subordinate persons in the household was diverted to the submission of church members to church leaders as the church increasingly replaced the family as center of allegiance, a conceptual switch already begun in the Synoptic Gospels. But many of the same patterns of life continued: The institution of slavery was not questioned, and Christians continued to marry nonbelievers.

Use of the family as model for the church had both advantages and disadvantages. On the positive side, it provided an open house atmosphere in which appropriate human relationships could be learned, and in which opportunity for mission could proceed along recognized channels. On the negative side, the Greek house was built to segregate by gender, the Roman house by status. The richer the house, the more possibility for segregation according to status. Discrimination was therefore built into the basic model, in spite of Christian baptismal ethics. A social problem expressed in architecture became an ethical problem, to the disadvantage of women, slaves, and social inferiors. Though these dynamics worked slightly differently depending on the degree of Greek, Jewish, or Roman cultural influence in a given situation, the overall effect was to reinforce the social limits and inequality of society, now in the name of God and Christ.

These developments did not happen all at once or even simultaneously. A great variety of approaches can be seen at approximately the same time even in a given geographical area, such as the Gospel of Matthew, the letters of Ignatius, and the *Didache* show for Syria in the late first and early second century. Perhaps, though, some sort of progression can also be seen, from Paul's lack of direct interest in families, to the household as model of church in the deutero-Pauline letters, to the usurping of household subordinationist terminology and values by Ignatius and later writers.

This projection of family onto church takes the focus off the real family in terms of authority and structure in early Christian thought. Yet this very projection emphasized the broader horizon that the family must face and provided an opening to something greater than itself. The political philosophy that leadership and the ordering of the whole are only as good as the leadership and ordering of the parts, that as goes the family, so goes the state, meant in its Christian application that the family continued to be the important testing ground for the strength of the church—never, however, as an end in itself.

Abbreviations

AB	The Anchor Bible
ABD	D.N. Freedman (ed.), *Anchor Bible Dictionary*
ANF	*The Ante-Nicene Fathers*
ANRW	*Aufstieg und Niedergang der römischen Welt*
BA	*Biblical Archaeologist*
BAR	*Biblical Archaeology Review*
BBB	Bonner Biblische Beiträge
BETL	Bibliotheca ephemeridum theologicarum lovaniensium
BJRL	*Bulletin of the John Rylands University Library of Manchester*
BJS	Brown Judaic Studies
BR	*Biblical Research*
BTB	*Biblical Theology Bulletin*
BZNW	*Beihefte zur Zeitschrift für die neutestamentliche Wissenschaft*
CBQ	*Catholic Biblical Quarterly*
CBQMS	Catholic Biblical Quarterly—Monograph Series
CIL	*Corpus inscriptionum latinarum*
DACL	*Dictionnaire d'archéologie chrétienne et de liturgie*
EPRO	Etudes préliminaires aux religions orientales dans l'empire Romain
EvT	*Evangelische Theologie*
FGrH	Fragmente der griechischen Historiker
HTR	*Harvard Theological Review*
HTS	Harvard Theological Studies
HUT	Hermeneutische Untersuchungen zur Theologie
Int	*Interpretation*
JAC	Jahrbuch für Antike und Christentum
JBL	*Journal of Biblical Literature*
JECS	*Journal of Early Christian Studies*
JEH	*Journal of Ecclesiastical History*

JRS	*Journal of Roman Studies*
JSNTSup	Journal for the Study of the New Testament—Supplemental Series
JTS	*Journal of Theological Studies*
KP	*Der Kleine Pauly*
LCL	Loeb Classical Library
New Docs	*New Documents Illustrating Early Christianity*
NovT	*Novum Testamentum*
NT	New Testament
NTAbh	Neutestamentliche Abhandlungen
NTOA	Novum Testamentum et Orbis Antiquus
NTS	*New Testament Studies*
OCD	*Oxford Classical Dictionary*
PG	J. Migne, Patrologia graeca
PW	Pauly-Wissowa, *Real-Encyclopädie der classischen Altertumswissenschaft*
RAC	*Reallexikon für Antike and Christentum*
SANT	Studien zum Alten und Neuen Testament
SBLDS	SBL Dissertation Series
SBLMS	SBL Monograph Series
SBLSBS	SBL Sources for Biblical Studies
SBLTT	SBL Texts and Translations
SCHNT	Studia ad corpus hellenisticum novi testamenti
SNTS	Society for New Testament Studies
SNTSMS	Society for New Testament Studies—Monograph Series
SuppNT	Supplements to Novum Testamentum
SVF	*Stoicorum Veterum Fragmenta*
TDNT	G. Kittel and G. Friedrich (eds.), *Theological Dictionary of the New Testament*
TF	*Theologische Forschung*
VC	*Vigiliae christianae*
WdF	Wege der Forschung
WUNT	Wissenschaftliche Untersuchungen zum Neuen Testament
ZNW	*Zeitschrift für die neutestamentliche Wissenschaft*

Notes

Notes to Introduction

1. Mary Daly, *Beyond God the Father: Toward a philosophy of women's liberation* (Boston: Beacon Press, 1973).
2. Lisa Sowle Cahill, *Sex, Gender, and Christian Ethics* (New York: Cambridge University Press, 1996). She summarizes this in "Sex and Gender Ethics as New Testament Social Ethics," in *The Bible in Ethics,* ed. J. Rogerson (Sheffield: Sheffield Academic Press, 1996). Intriguingly, both Daly and Cahill teach at Boston College.
3. See Don Browning, "Christian Ethics and the Family Debate: An Overview," *The Annual of the Society of Christian Ethics* (1995): 251–62. Don Browning and Ian Evison, "The Family Debate: A Middle Way," *The Christian Century* (July 14–21, 1993): 712–16.

Part 1:
Material and Social Environment of the Greco-Roman World

Notes to Chapter 1. Archaeology

1. Blue, "Acts and the House Church," 119–222: " . . . the 'house' gave the early believers an inconspicuous place for assembly. It was private" (p. 121).
2. Thébert, "Private Life and Domestic Architecture," 315–409.
3. A loaf of bread found in the shop of Modestus the baker in Pompeii is pictured in Marcel Brion and Edwin Smith, *Pompeii and Herculaneum: The Glory and the Grief,* trans. John Rosenberg (New York: Crown Publishers, 1960), 213, fig. 129. Figure 126 shows bowls of eggs, nuts, and lentils found in the Temple of Isis, the priests' meal when Vesuvius erupted. Deiss, *Herculaneum,* 118, and Betty Jo Mayeske, "A Pompeian Bakery on the Via dell'Abbondanza," in *Studia Pompeiana and Classica in Honor of Wilhelmina F. Jashemski,* ed. Robert I. Curtis (New Rochelle, N.Y.: Orpheus, 1988), 1.149–65, fig. 11.

4. Richard P. Saller, "*Familia, Domus,* and the Roman Conception of the Family," *Phoenix* 38 (1984): 336–55; idem, "*Familia* and *Domus:* Defining and Representing the Roman Family and Household," in *Patriarchy, Property, and Death in the Roman Family* (Cambridge: Cambridge University Press, 1994), 74–101. Compare the following for three different meanings of the Greek term: 1 Cor. 1:16, in which Paul has baptized the household (*oikos*) of Stephanas; 16:19, in which Aquila and Prisca hold an assembly in their house or household (*he kat'oikon ekklesia*); and 1 Cor. 14:35, in which women are told to ask their husbands at home (*en oiko*). But see the sharp critique of Saller and Shaw's position by Dale B. Martin, "The Construction of the Ancient Family: Methodological Considerations," *Journal of Roman Studies* 86 (1996): 40–60.

5. Vitruvius, *De architectura* 6.3.1–2, describes five central courtyard designs, one of which is the "displuviate," in which the roof above slopes outward rather than inward, and rain collects in gutters around the outside, but this design is not common in the evidence preserved.

6. McKay, *Houses, Villas and Palaces of the Roman World,* 33–34.

7. Further discussion by Vitruvius in *De architectura* 6.3.8–10. Foss ("Kitchens and Dining Rooms," 95–98, 112–15) argues for use of this space for dining. His detailed investigations found that approximately 10 percent of living space, regardless of size of the house, was used for dining purposes (p. 145).

8. This is the case with the Casa del Citarista and the Casa del Menandro at Pompeii; discussion in Foss, "Kitchens and Dining Rooms," 163–65.

9. That the popularity of the same basic design persists can be seen even at the palatial fourth-century country villa at Piazza Armerina in eastern Sicily, where entry was through a polygonal colonnaded open space into an intervening room or passageway, which gave way to a magnificent peristyle, from which all other rooms and room complexes of the villa were accessed, with the exception of the bath complex, accessible either from the peristyle or the entryway. Many large public Mediterranean buildings still use the same design, which provides a large surface area from which heat can radiate, and to which the cooling night air has access. Both privacy and open space are provided, and exterior walls, being windowless, can be shared with adjoining buildings, reducing cost and fostering population density (Warren and Aaron Johnson, "Keeping Cool," *Aramco World* 46:3 [1995]: 10–17).

10. Richardson, *Pompeii,* 240–41.

11. S. Erdemgil et al., *The Terrace Houses in Ephesus,* trans. Stella Paçal (Istanbul: Hitit Color, n.d.); Ekrem Akurgal, *Ancient Civilizations and Ruins of Turkey from Prehistoric Times until the End of the Roman Empire,* 6th ed., trans. John Whybrow and Mollie Emre (Istanbul: Haset Kitabevi, 1985), 378–82; McKay, *Houses, Villas and Palaces,* 212–17.

12. Foss, "Kitchens and Dining Rooms," 165, 169–70.

13. Just to the north of the mansion, one small portion of a large peristyle building was excavated; the rest was inaccessible for excavation. This structure does not seem to be part of a domestic building.

14. Nahman Avigad, *Discovering Jerusalem* (Nashville: Thomas Nelson Publishers, 1980), 83–139; Nitza Rosovsky, "A Thousand Years of History in Jerusalem's Jewish Quarter," *BAR* 18:3 (1992): 22–40, 78 [28–40].

15. Ehud Netzer, Ephraim Stern, et al., eds., *New Encyclopedia of Archaeological Excavations in the Holy Land* (New York: Simon & Schuster, 1993), 4: 1324–28; Richard A. Batey, "Sepphoris: An Urban Portrait of Jesus," *BAR* 18:3 (1992): 50–62; Ehud Netzer and Zeev Weiss, "New Mosaic Art from Sepphoris," *BAR* 18:6 (1992): 36–43.

16. On the border of the mosaic is the beautiful head of a woman, quickly dubbed the "Mona Lisa of Galilee": "Prize Find: Mosaic Masterpiece Dazzles Sepphoris Volunteers," *BAR* 14:1 (1988): 30–33.

17. Sheila Campbell, *The Mosaics of Antioch*, 2 vols., Subsidia Mediaevalis 15 (Toronto: Pontifical Institute of Mediaeval Studies, 1988); Glanville Downey, *Ancient Antioch* (Princeton, N.J.: Princeton University Press, 1963).

18. Downey, *Ancient Antioch,* figs. 37–40.

19. Virgilio Corbo, *The House of St. Peter at Capharnaum, Publications of the Studium Biblicum Franciscanum,* Collectio minor 5 (Jerusalem: Franciscan Printing, 1969); isometric drawings in Graydon F. Snyder, *Ante Pacem: Archaeological Evidence of Church Life before Constantine* (Macon, Ga.: Mercer University Press, 1985), 72–73; Stanislao Loffreda, *A Visit to Capernaum* (Jerusalem: Franciscan Printing, 1978), 21, 29; Blue, "Acts and the House Church," 138–40; White, *Domus Ecclesiae,* 1.165–69.

20. Foss, "Kitchens and Dining Rooms," 58.

21. Ibid., 37, with n. 155 citing A. Scobie, "Slums, Sanitation, and Mortality in the Roman World," *Klio* 68 (1986): 399–433. Foss observes that Nero's enormous *Domus Aurea* made the neighborhood too exclusive, so that it became a source of jokes (Tacitus, *Ann.* 15.42; Suetonius, *Nero* 31, 38–39; Pliny the Elder, *Nat. Hist.* 36.111). Cf. nn. 53–65 below.

22. Foss, "Kitchens and Dining Rooms," 58.

23. Amedeo Maiuri, *Herculaneum,* 7th English ed. (Rome: Istituto Poligrafico, 1977), 5–8; *Pompeii,* 15th English ed. (Rome: Istituto Poligrafico, 1978), 3–5; Richardson, *Pompeii,* 3–27.

24. By the time of the destruction, 64 percent of the domus of Pompeii and Herculaneum had both atrium and peristyle (Wallace-Hadrill, "Houses and Households," 191–227 [212]).

25. See Overbeck, *Pompeii,* 254–55, for a mosaic image of such a dog with an inscription.

26. Wallace-Hadrill, *Houses and Society,* 205. Of course, such statistics cannot include the floor space of now nonexistent second or even third stories. Zanker, *Pompeji,* 50, fig. 11; 202–4 with figs. 111–13.

27. Examples at Pompeii would include the Houses of Diomedes and Epidius Rufus, the House of the Faun, of which the rear one-third of the property is taken by a huge peristyle garden, and the House of D. Octavius Quarto or Loreius Tiburtinus, of which fully two-thirds of the property is occupied by garden. See Richardson, *Pompeii,* 329–43. The recent attempts to replant the gardens as closely as possible according to their original layout greatly enhances visitors' experience.

28. Vitruvius says this arrangement is more typical of country houses (*De architectura* 6.5.3). The Villa dei Misteri is a ten-minute walk outside the gate of Pompeii and must have been one of many villas in the countryside with convenient access to the town.

29. Richardson, *Pompeii,* 165–67, 327. He draws similar conclusions for the House of the Cryptoporticus and the Faun (pp. 167–70), the House of Giuseppe II (p. 237), and even the succession of rooms on the southwest side of the Villa of the Mysteries, identified by Richardson as dining rooms (pp. 174–75).

30. Richardson, *Pompeii,* 398. Literary support given for this custom, besides Valerius Maximus 2.1.2, is Petronius, *Satyricon* 67. But the latter text does not support the point: Trimalchio's wife Fortunata is called for during the dinner, but the reason given for her delay is not propriety but managerial tasks. Moreover, when she enters, she reclines on the couch where Scintilla, wife of the guest Habinnas, is already reclining (*discumbebat*).

31. Richardson, *Pompeii,* 322. Valerius Maximus remarks that the different dining positions for men and women are now observed more in civic religious banquets than in private, so that it seems goddesses care more for discipline than women do (*diligentius in Capitolio quam in suis domibus servat, videlicet quia magis ad rem pertinet dearum quam mulierum disciplinam contineri*)! Another earlier witness for Roman wives dining with their husbands is Cornelius Nepos, *On Illustrious Men,* preface: "What Roman would be ashamed to take his wife to a dinner party?" (As contrasted with the Greek custom to the contrary.) Andrew Wallace-Hadrill, "The Social Structure of the Roman House," Papers of the British School at Rome, n.s. 43 (1988): 43–97 (93n147), expressly disagrees with Richardson on this point.

32. Wallace-Hadrill, "Houses and Households," 213–14. For the domus in North Africa, see Thébert, "Private Life and Domestic Architecture, 353–405.

33. Vitruvius, *De architectura* 6.5.1. Cf. Bakker, *Living and Working with the Gods,* 31 (cf. pp. 23–25, 170, 173) on Cicero, *De off.* 1.39.138–40; idem, Dio Chrysostom *Or.* 69.6.4.

34. Wallace-Hadrill, *Houses and Society,* chaps. 1 and 3, esp. pp. 5, 10–11, 44, interpreting Vitruvius, *De architectura* 6.5. Thébert, "Domestic Architecture," 321. For Galilean houses, Peskowitz, "Family/ies in Antiquity: Evidence from Tannaitic Literature and Roman Galilean Architecture," 9–36, at pp. 30–34.

35. Clarke, *Houses of Roman Italy,* 1–2: "Unlike our modern house, conceived as a refuge for the nuclear family, located far from the factory or office, the Roman house was in no way private. It was the locus of the owner's social, political, and business activities, open both to invited and uninvited visitors." Contrast Blue (n. 1 above).

36. McKay, *Houses, Villas and Palaces,* 81–83. The house is named for its construction in *opus craticium,* consisting of wooden frames filled in with inexpensive concrete and plastered over.

37. *Insula* (island) came to mean in a derivative sense a large apartment building occupying an entire city block, or a single unit within such a building

(Charlton T. Lewis and Charles Short, *A Latin Dictionary* [Oxford: Claren-don Press, 1969] *s.v.* "insula"). The term was in use in Cicero's day (*Pro Caelio* 17), and Suetonius distinguishes *domus* from *insula* (*Nero* 38.2; 44.2) (Meiggs, *Roman Ostia* 236–37). The same term is often used by mod-ern scholars to refer to an ancient city block, no matter what kind of build-ings were constructed on it.

38. A fear expressed by Strabo, *Geography* 5.3.7; Juvenal, *Satires* 3.190–98. Cf. pp. 22–23 below.

39. Juvenal, *Satires* 3.199–202.

40. Meiggs, *Roman Ostia* 235–36, 241, 304–8.

41. Ibid., 238, 256–61.

42. Contrast Robert Jewett, *Paul, the Apostle to America: Cultural Trends and Pauline Scholarship* (Louisville, Ky.: Westminster John Knox Press, 1994), 77–80; also his "Tenement Churches and Communal Meals in the Early Church," 23–43, and Lampe, *Die städtrömischen Christen.*

43. Koloski-Ostrow, *Sarno Bath Complex,* 104, and Bakker, *Living and Work-ing with the Gods,* 168, 173–77, 181. Cf. Wallace-Hadrill, *Houses and Soci-ety,* 75 with n. 25 and p. 117 referring to the Palaestra block at Hercula-neum, presumably the property of the municipality, put up to offset the costs of the *palaestra* development. Cf. Marion Elizabeth Blake, edited and completed by Doris Taylor Bishop, "Ostia," in *Roman Construction in Italy from Nerva through the Antonines* (Philadelphia: American Philosophical Society, 1973), 139–235, at pp. 152, 154–55, 164, 175, 181–84, 216, 218 with plates 19, 22–26, 28, 30. Now see R. Chevallier, "Dix années de travaux récents sur Ostie antique," *Latomus* 53 (1994): 543–63.

44. Koloski-Ostrow, *Sarno Bath Complex,* xxvii–xxviii, 15–16.

45. Ibid., 85.

46. Ibid., 83n5; 103n99; 104n102, citing Seneca, *De Beneficiis* 4.6, 2; 6.15, 7; *De Ira* 3.35, 5; Aulus Gellius, *Noctes Atticae* 15.1, 2–3 (mid–second cen-tury C.E.); Tacitus, *Annals* 15.43; Suetonius, *Nero* 16.1; Martial, *Epigrams* 1.108, 117; 3.30; 4.37; 5.22; 6.27, 2; 7.20; 8.14; Juvenal, *Satires* 3.6ff. 166, 190–202, 223–25, 235–48, 268–312; 3.12–14; Strabo, *Geography* 235. At the time Martial and Juvenal satirized, Trajan imposed a building limit of sixty feet high.

47. Koloski-Ostrow, *Sarno Bath Complex,* 103–4.

48. Bakker, *Living and Working with the Gods,* 168.

49. Ibid., 174, 175.

50. On this terminology, see Hermansen, "Domus and Insula in the City of Rome," 333–41, who however is able to define legal terms from the time of Hadrian to the time of Justinian (p. 336), so beginning in the second century C.E. Hermansen observes that "during the years from the end of the first century A.D. to the end of the third century A.D., it was fashion-able to live in apartments. From that period we have fine apartments with many rooms and prestigious appearance, like the insula di Giove e Ganimede" (pp. 339–40). Cf. also Hermansen, "The Medianum and the Roman Apartment," *Phoenix* 24 (1970): 342–47: the medianum func-tioned as kitchen and dining room, as well as a hall giving access to all

other rooms of the apartment. Also Hermansen, "The Roman Inns and the Law: The Inns of Ostia," in *Polis and Imperium: Studies in Honour of Edward Togo Salmon,* ed. J. A. S. Evans (Toronto: Hakkert, 1974), 167–81, esp. 171–73, on where Romans ate: not, he argues, in the inns but at home in the medianum cooking on a portable charcoal brazier, especially in the New Rome built by Nero. Hermansen distinguishes pre- and post-Neronian housing, a difference that corresponds to the Pauline, post-Pauline distinction. See his *Ostia: Aspects of Roman City Life* (Alberta: University of Alberta, 1981).

51. Bakker, *Living and Working with the Gods,* 176–77. But see the caution of Wallace-Hadrill, *Houses and Society,* 51–52.

52. Gazda, "Introduction," *Roman Art in the Private Sphere,* 1–24 at p. 7, and Dwyer, "Pompeian Atrium House in Theory and in Practice," 25–48.

53. Gazda and Dwyer in *Roman Art,* 8, 25, 30. On recent Roman excavations, cf. Patterson, "Survey Article, The City of Rome: From Republic to Empire," 186–215, esp. "III. Aristocratic Housing," 200–4 and 214. Patterson observes:

> The impermanence of the houses of the Roman poor, and the numerous fires which ravaged the city in antiquity, have made it hard to identify much in the way of popular housing; however, the late first and second centuries A.D. saw the development of new areas of non-elite housing in the capital, many of which have been identified recently. One interesting example is the complex of insula blocks discovered in the excavations in Piazza Celimontana below the Temple of Claudius on the Caelian hill, created after the Great Fire. . . . [I]n some cases traditional-style *domus* had been transformed into *insulae* by the early third century A.D., perhaps housing several family groups in the subdivided atrium." (204)

54. Dwyer in Gazda, *Roman Art,* 9.

55. Strabo, *Geography* 5.3.7 C235, trans. Jones in LCL.

56. Seneca, *De ira* 3.35.5, trans. Basore in LCL.

57. Clarke, *Houses of Roman Italy,* 26, with bibliography (nn. 75–76) on their disputed origin.

58. Martial, *Epigrams* 1.117, trans. Ker in LCL.

59. Ibid., 7.20.

60. Juvenal, *Satires* 3.198–202, trans. Ramsay in LCL.

61. Ibid., 3.6–7.

62. Ibid., 3.215–220.

63. Hermansen, "Domus and Insula," 340.

64. Tacitus, *Annals* 15.43; Suetonius, *Nero* 16.1.

65. Cf. Marion E. Blake, *Roman Construction in Italy from Tiberius through the Flavians* (Washington, D.C.: Carnegie Institution of Washington, 1959), 42–46, 54–58, 125–31, esp. 55n9, and p. 125: "The Regionary Catalogues prove that the *domus* or house of a single proprietor existed side by side with the *insula* type of multiple dwelling in Rome until the late Empire." Cf. n. 21 above.

66. Wallace-Hadrill, *Houses and Society,* 78, and Laurence, *Roman Pompeii,* 68, 113, 140–41. Bakker, *Living and Working with the Gods,* 175, sees a change toward greater zoning in second-century C.E. Ostia.

67. Wallace-Hadrill, *Houses and Society,* 103, criticizing James E. Packer, "Middle and Lower Class Housing in Pompeii and Herculaneum: A Preliminary Survey," in *Neue Forschungen in Pompeji und den anderen vom Vesuvausbruch 79 n. Chr. verschütteten Städten,* ed. B. Andreae and H. Kyrieleis (Recklinghausen: Aurel Bongers, 1975), 133–46.

68. Wallace-Hadrill, *Houses and Society,* 141–42, quoting De Crescenzo. Bakker, *Living and Working with the Gods,* 175–76, assumes this kind of vertical stratification in second-century C.E. Ostia.

69. Wallace-Hadrill, *Houses and Society,* 45, 47 (our emphases); he discusses Vitruvius, *De architectura* 6.5 on pp. 10–11 and 38–39. See Laurence, *Roman Pompeii,* chap. 6: "Street Activity and Public Interaction," esp. p. 88.

70. Velleius Paterculus 1.14.3. Plutarch, *Precepts of Statecraft* 800F.

71. Cicero, *De domo* 100, trans. Watts in LCL.

72. Wallace-Hadrill, *Houses and Society,* 5 (our emphasis; cf. 58), also the source of the two quotations above. He thanks Richard Saller for the following list of texts mentioning the closure of doors as an exceptional gesture of mourning: Valerius Maximus 5.7.ext. 1; Seneca, *Cons. ad Liv.* 183, *Vit. Beat.* 28.1, *Brev. Vit.* 20.3, *Cons. ad Polyb.* 14.2; Lucan *Bell. Civ.* 2.22; Tacitus, *Ann.* 2.82, *Hist.* 1.62. Wallace-Hadrill, *Augustan Rome* (London: Bristol Classical, 1993), 25, adds Ovid, *Metamorphoses* 1.172. See also Plato, *Symp.* 174E; *Testament of Job* 9.6–9; 10.1–4, but for eating behind locked doors, Lucian, *Sat.* 32, 37, and perhaps Acts 12:13–14, 16. Cf. Trimalchio's door and porter: Petronius, *Sat.* 28–29, 64–65, 78. See Laurence, *Roman Pompeii,* chap. 6: "Street Activity and Public Interaction."

73. On the extraordinary number of lock parts found in houses in Pompeii and their use, see Dwyer in *Roman Art,* 28–29.

74. Livy 5.41.2–8, trans. Foster in LCL.

75. K. Schneider, "Ianitor," Pauly-Wissowa, *Realencyclopaedie* 9 (1916): 692–93, and Walter Hatto, "Ianitor," *Der Kleine Pauly: Lexikon der Antike* 2 (1975): 1310. For Pompeii, see Overbeck, *Pompeji,* 233, 254, 335.

76. Plato, *Protag.* 314C, and *Phileb.* 62c; Xenophon, *Mem.* 1.11.

77. Plato, *Protag.* 310AB; Theocritus 15.43.

78. Aristotle, *Oecon.* 1.6.8 1345a 33.

79. Columella I, *De Re Rustica* praef. 10; Ovid, *Odes* 1.6,1; Suetonius, *Rhet.* 3.

80. Apollodorus in Athenaeus, *Deip.* 1.3c; Seneca, *Dial.* 5.37, 2; Petronius, *Sat.* 29, 2.

81. Petronius, *Sat.* 29, 1; Suetonius, *Vitell.* 16; Varro, *De re rustica* 1.13, 2.

82. Cicero, *Verr.* 3.8; Horace, *Odes* 3.14, 20; Martial, *Epigrams* 5.22, 9; Seneca, *Dial.* I.14, 2 (on bribery); 37, 1–2 (on trying to enter a rich man's house). Cf. Plautus, *Menechmi* 669–73.

83. Apuleius, *Met.* I.15; IV.18; IX.20.

84. Varro, *Vita Populi Romani,* frag. 28 (in Nonius, p. 55M), cited by Foss, "Kitchens and Dining Rooms," 71.

85. Church meetings in these houses would then be significantly different from gatherings of the devotees of Mithras, all of whose shrines are in secluded,

hidden, dark "caves," where the interior of the shrine is shielded from the eyes of outsiders by the position of the entrance; see Bakker, *Living and Working with the Gods*, 113–14. However, contrast Liebeschuetz, "Expansion of Mithraism," 195–216, at pp. 196–97. Cf. chap. 8, nn. 31–38, below.

86. Gazda and Dwyer, *Roman Art*, 13, 26, 27.

87. Clarke, *Houses of Roman Italy*, 2–3, 12, 14, 25.

88. Cf. Wallace-Hadrill, *Houses and Society*, figs. 2.1 and 3:13; also 2.2, 3, 17, 19; 3.9, 10, 12, 24; 4.12, 15.

89. Bakker, *Living and Working with the Gods*, 170.

90. Maria Rita Wojcik, *La Villa dei Papiri ad Ercolano: Contributo alla Ricon-struzione dell' Ideologia della Nobilitas Tardorepubblicana* (Roma: L'Erma di Bretschneider, 1986). Cf. P. Gregory Warden and David Gilman Romano, "The Course of Glory: Greek Art in a Roman Context at the Villa of the Pa-pyri at Herculaneum," *Art History* 17, no. 2 (1994): 228–54, and Deiss, *Herculaneum*, chap. 7. The architecture, frescoes, and sculpture of the Villa dei Papiri were reconstructed in California by J. Paul Getty; see *The J. Paul Getty Museum Guide to the Villa and its Gardens*, ed. Andrea P. A. Belloni (Malibu, Calif.: J. Paul Getty Museum, 1988, 1989).

91. Wallace-Hadrill, *Houses and Society*, 25.

92. Ibid., 27.

93. On the symbolism of Augustus's own house, where he inserted himself into the amalgam of history and legend that was the origins of Rome, see T. P. Wiseman, "Conspicui Postes Tectaque Digna Deo: The Public Image of Aristocratic and Imperial Houses in the Late Republic and Early Em-pire," in *L'Urbs: espace urbain et histoire (1er siècle av. J.-C.- IIIe siècle ap. J.-C.)*, Actes du colloque international organisé par le Centre national de la recherche scientifique et l'École francaise de Rome (Rome, May 8–12, 1985) (Collection de l'École Francaise de Rome 98; 1987), 393–413. Also Patterson, "Survey Article: The City of Rome," 204–7, and Wallace-Hadrill, *Augustan Rome*, 26–28, 31–32, 47–62.

94. Wallace-Hadrill, *Houses and Society*, 29.

95. This corresponds to the philosophy of the period that the city grows "out of" houses: Aristotle, *Pol.* 1 1253b 3; Arius Didymus, "Concerning House-hold Management" 2.147, 7 (Wachsmuth-Hense), trans. Balch, "House-hold Codes," 41.

96. Wallace-Hadrill, *Houses and Society*, 8–9; Laurence, *Roman Pompeii*, 125–29.

97. Laurence, *Roman Pompeii*, 127; cf. 131–32.

98. Roy Bowen Ward, personal letter of March 18, 1996, observing that the traditional view has been challenged by Bauman, *Women and Politics in An-cient Rome*. Cf. Ward's "The Public Priestesses of Pompeii," in *The Early Church in Its Context*, SuppNT (Leiden: E. J. Brill, forthcoming).

99. This is a second radical contrast with the Mithras cult (see n. 85), where women were not allowed; cf. Bakker, *Living and Working with the Gods*, 116. Richard L. Gordon, "Authority, Salvation, and Mystery in the Mys-teries of Mithras," in *Image and Mystery in the Roman World: Three Papers Given in Memory of Jocelyn Toynbee*, ed. P. Zanker, S. Walker, and R. Gor-don (Gloucester: Alan Sutton, 1989), 45–80 with plates 1–11, at pp.

70–71: some devotees of Mithras referred to women as "hyenas" (Porphyry, *De abstin.* 4.16.3, ed. and trans. M. Patillon and A. P. Segonds [Budé; Paris: Les Belles Lettres, 1995], 3:26 with n. 231). Cf. Gordon, "Reality, Evocation and Boundary in the Mysteries of Mithras," *Journal of Mithraic Studies* 3 (1980): 19–99, at pp. 42ff., 57–59, 65; and J. Toynbee, "Still More about Mithras," *Hibbert Journal* 54 (1955–56): 107–14.

100. *CIL* 10.810 and 811. Roy Bowen Ward delivered a paper, "Women in Pompeii," to the SNTS meeting in Edinburgh, Scotland, on August 3, 1994, introducing many of us to Eumachia and Julia Felix. See August Mau, "The Building of Eumachia," *Pompeii: Its Life and Art* (New Rochelle, NY: Caratzas Brothers, 1982; orig. English trans. 1899), chap. 15, pp. 110–18. Cf. Paul Zanker, "Pompeji: Stadtbilder als Spiegel von Gesellschaft und Herrschaftsreform," *Trierer Winckelmannsprogramm 1987* (Mainz: Von Zabern, 1987), 1–46, at pp. 29–31, and Zanker, *Pompeji*, 99–109 with figs. 45–50.

101. Walter O. Moeller, *The Wool Trade of Ancient Pompeii*, Studies of the Dutch Archaeological and Historical Society III (Leiden: E. J. Brill, 1976), 57–71. Cf. also Richardson, *Pompeii*, 194–98, and Laurence, *Roman Pompeii*, 28, and for placement of the inscriptions, p. 33.

102. Paavo Castrén, *Ordo Populusque Pompeianus: Polity and Society in Roman Pompeii*, Acta Instituti Romani Finlandiae 8 (Rome: Bardi, 1975), 165–66, 197–98.

103. *CIL* 10.813. The statue of 1.94 meters is pictured in *Women in the Classical World*, ed. Elaine Fantham et al. (New York: Oxford University Press, 1994), 335, and Zanker, *Pompeji*, 107. Also plate 46, fig. 1, in Frances Stahl Bernstein, "The Public Role of Pompeian Women," diss., University of Maryland, 1987, directed by Wilhelmina Jashemski; cf. further 97, 106–23, with plates 28–31 on the Eumachia family and building. Bernstein's appendix (210–64) lists names and bibliography for 245 women known from Pompeii. Roy Bowen Ward has a longer list that corrects some of the *CIL* numbers and place locations in Bernstein; he observes that Liisa Savunen of Helsinki will soon publish her dissertation on Pompeian women based on her epigraphical work.

104. La Rocca, de Vos, and de Vos, *Pompei*, 19; cf. 121–25 on her building, 272 on her tomb. Willem Jongman, *The Economy and Society of Pompeii*, Dutch Monographs on Ancient History and Archaeology 4 (Amsterdam: J. C. Gieben, 1988), 127, on clay amphorae of the type "L. Eumachii," which evidences her family in trade; plate 21 pictures Eumachia's tomb.

105. Cf. Antonia D'Ambrosio and Stefano De Caro, *Un impegno per Pompei: Fotopiano e documentaztione della necropoli di Porta Nocera* (Milan: Touring Club Italiano, 1983): Eumachia's tomb is designated 11 OS (ouest = west).

106. *CIL* 4.1136. For her house plan, see Jashemski, *Gardens of Pompeii*, 1:48, with figs. 81–85, and 2:86, with figs. 96–99. Christopher Parslow, "Documents Illustrating the Excavations of the Praedia of Julia Felix in Pompeii," *Rivista di Studi Pompeiani* 2 (1988): 37–48; Christopher Charles Parslow, *Rediscovering Antiquity: Karl Weber and the Excavation of*

Herculaneum, Pompeii, and Stabiae (Cambridge: Cambridge University Press, 1995), 107–22, 166–76. Also the exhibition catalog *Rediscovering Pompeii* (Rome: L'Erma di Bretschneider, 1990, 1993), 29, 31, calls her building a meeting place of the *pilicrepi,* football players of the time, "but not only respectable persons or those of high descent are to be found in the Julia Felix complex." The catalog cites a number of erotic inscriptions.

107. Cf. Wendy Cotter, "Women's Authority Roles in Paul's Churches: Countercultural or Conventional?" *NT* 36, no. 4 (1994): 350–72.

108. Wallace-Hadrill, *Houses and Society,* 10; cf. 36, 39.

109. Cf. Grant, *Eros in Pompeii,* 66ff., 85ff., and on pp. 156–57 a wall painting from the house of Caecilius Iucundus that includes the *cubicularius,* a slave whose task it was to serve in the bedroom (*cubiculum*), dutifully hovering in the background while a couple make love. The same painting is clearer in Jean Marcadé, *Roma Amor: Essay on Erotic Elements in Etruscan and Roman Art* (Geneva: Nagel, 1961), 15. On erotic art recently discovered at the Suburban Baths, see Luciana Jacobelli, *Le pitture erotiche delle Terme Suburbane di Pompei,* Ministero per i beni culturali ed ambientali, Soprintendenza archaeologica di Pompei, Monografie 10 (Rome: L'Erma di Bretschneider, 1995).

110. Bradley, *Slavery and Society,* 84–86.

111. Cicero, *Pis.* 67; Martial, *Epigrams* 10.66; Petronius, *Sat.* 34; Horace, *Sat.* 2.4.78–87, references cited by Foss, "Kitchens and Dining Rooms," 54–56.

112. Wallace-Hadrill, *Houses and Society,* 39, with figs. 3.3–4. Cf. Bradley, *Slavery and Society,* 84–86.

113. Two examples of the explicit erotic art discussed by Antonio Varone, *Erotica Pompeiana: Iscrizioni d'amore sui muri di Pompei,* Studia Archaeologica 71 (Roma: L'Erma di Bretschneider, 1994), figs. 16–17, are in this house on the walls of the slaves' quarters.

114. Wallace-Hadrill, *Houses and Society,* figs. 3.5–6. Cf. Franciscis, "La Villa Romana di Oplontis," 9–39, with plates 1–39. Plate 1 (p. 11) is a plan of the villa. Plates 17 and 19–23 are of a triclinium (room #14 in the plan); plates 38–39 show "rustic" zebra stripes of an "oriental internal garden" (area #32 in the plan). Also Bradley, *Slavery and Society,* 85.

115. Wallace-Hadrill, *Houses and Society,* 44, citing Pliny, *Ep.* 5.6.41; 2.17.9.

116. Both the Mithras cult and early Christianity involved significant percentages of slaves: White, *Building God's House,* 56n120, cites Vivienne J. Walters, *The Cult of Mithras in the Roman Provinces of Gaul,* EPRO 21 (Leiden: E. J. Brill, 1974), 32, who observes that Mithraic inscriptions there were dedicated by men with Greek *cognomina* spread by orientals, slaves, freedmen, and members of corporations. Liebeschuetz, "Expansion of Mithraism," 200–5, 212, observes something similar at Ostia. Cf. Gordon, "Mithraism and Roman Society," 92–121, at pp. 103–7 with n. 67.

117. Wallace-Hadrill, *Houses and Society,* 113 with fig. 5.15, citing Tacitus, *Dial.* 29.

118. See esp. White, *Building God's House,* 44, 47–59, 107, 166–67 (with nn. 86–90), 169 (with nn. 4–5), 171–73 (with nn. 112–14 and 133).

119. For measurements, see White, *Building God's House,* 48n90: typical dimensions of the sanctuary were 16.5 m. long, 8.5 m. wide. Gordon, "Mithraism and Roman Society," 100: "Every Mithraic cell was a small face-to-face organization."

120. J. P. Kane, "The Mithraic Cult Meal in Its Greek and Roman Environment," in *Mithraic Studies,* ed. John R. Hinnells (Rowman: Manchester University, 1975), 2.313–51, at pp. 326 and 350, citing W. S. Ferguson, "The Attic Orgeones," *HTR* (1944): 62–146.

121. White, *Building God's House,* 107: "It seems that assembly was regularly convened in the dining room of the house, which in some cases might open onto a peristyle or portico. Often the triclinium, or dining room, was the largest area in the house and the most suitable for a gathering of people." This may be compatible with Smith and Lampe, who suggest gatherings in the peristyle (see chap. 8, n. 27, below), and larger houses often had peristyles significantly more spacious than their dining rooms.

122. Pliny, *Ep.* 10.96.8, writes to Trajan that he tortured two slave women, "whom they call deacons (*ministrae*)."

123. Liebeschuetz, "Expansion of Mithraism," supported by Lewis M. Hopfe, "Archaeological Indications on the Origins of Roman Mithraism," in *Uncovering Ancient Stones: Essays in Memory of H. Neil Richardson* (Winona Lake, Ind.: Eisenbrauns, 1994), 147–56. See Gordon, "Mithraism and Roman Society," 111.

124. Liebeschuetz, "Expansion of Mithraism," 198–99.

125. Balch, *Let Wives Be Submissive,* 143–51, and idem, "Household Codes," 25–50.

126. Packer, in "Housing and Population in Imperial Ostia and Rome," 80–95, and in *Insulae of Imperial Ostia,* estimated that at Ostia approximately 8 percent of the population lived in a domus or "luxury apartment" in a favored location of an insula; 73 percent in smaller apartments; and approximately 19 percent with no regular housing at all. See discussion in Verner, *Household of God,* 56–59. On the rental market in Rome, see Brian Rapske, *The Book of Acts in Its First-Century Setting,* vol. 3: *Paul in Roman Custody,* ed. David W. J. Gill and Conrad Gempf (Grand Rapids: Wm. B. Eerdmans Publishing Co., 1994), 228–36. Parkin, *Demography and Roman Society,* 5, gives the consensus estimate of 750,000 to a million inhabitants of Rome during the early empire.

127. Juvenal, *Satires* 3.232–38.

128. See references in Parkin, *Demography and Roman Society,* 180n6. Detailed descriptions of the sanitary conditions of ancient cities are in Carney, *Shape of the Past,* 84–106; John G. Stambaugh, *The Ancient Roman City* (Baltimore: Johns Hopkins University Press, 1988), 123–41; Stark, "Antioch as the Social Situation for Matthew's Gospel," 189–210; and esp. Scobie, "Slums, Sanitation, and Mortality," 300–433.

129. See Parkin, *Demography and Roman Society,* esp. pp. 92–111. He estimates that 30 percent of a birth group died in the first year, 50 percent

by age ten. Of those who survived to age five, however, 30 percent would reach age sixty. Similar statistics in Carney, *Shape of the Past,* 88.

130. The expression *kat'oikon* used here is often understood as "from house to house," implying no regular pattern or venue, but should probably rather be understood as "at home" after the custom implied by the other references, and the use of the same Greek term in 1 Cor. 16:19 and Philemon 2. Cf. White, *Building God's House,* 188n7. On the evidence from Acts for the importance of the house church, see Blue, "Acts and the House Church," 119–89.

131. This time frame corresponds to the first period of architectural development posited by Krautheimer, *Early Christian and Byzantine Architecture,* 24–25; see also discussion in White, *Building God's House,* 19–20.

132. On the basis of an examination of size and available space in several houses of this period, Murphy-O'Connor concluded that a maximum of fifty people could have assembled in an average house, though more comfortably thirty or forty (*St. Paul's Corinth,* 153–61). This analysis, however, is based on limited and sometimes incomplete evidence, e.g., the example of the House of the Vettii at Pompeii does not consider use of the very large peristyle garden. Cf. chap. 8, "Community Meals in Pauline House Churches," below.

133. Discussion in Blue, "Acts and the Roman House Church," 167–71, and White, *Domus Ecclesiae,* 1.188–201, largely based on R. Krautheimer, *Corpus Basilicarum Christianarum Romae* (Vatican City: Pontifical Gregorian Institute, 1937–77), 1.117–36, 267–303.

134. See Jude 12, the first to call it by this name; Hippolytus, *Apostolic Tradition;* Charles P. Bobertz, "The Role of Patron in the *Cena Dominica* of Hippolytus' *Apostolic* Tradition," *JTS* 44 (1993): 170–84.

135. Literally, "house of the church," a term that has come to be used for the earliest forms of Christian worship space, probably first used by Adolf von Harnack (White, *Building God's House,* 154n36).

136. White, *Building God's House,* 108–9, 120–23; idem, *Domus Ecclesiae,* 1.140–48; Graydon F. Snyder, *Ante Pacem* (Macon, Ga.: Mercer University Press, 1985), 68–71. Along the same row of buildings were a mithraeum and a synagogue, both also in structures that were originally private, the synagogue more extensively renovated than the others.

137. For the next stage, extensive renovation of existing buildings into large halls, White coins the expression *aula ecclesiae,* "hall of the church," after the familiar *domus ecclesiae* and Harnack's *Saalkirche* (*Building God's House,* 22, 128, 155n49). His principal argument is that the common assumption of a transition from renovated private house to basilica in the Constantinian era is unfounded. Rather, the phase of the aula ecclesiae seems to have lasted at some locations into the fifth century (pp. 23–24). A late stage of the transition from house to church building is represented by Canon 58 of the Council of Laodicea: "Bishops and presbyters may no longer celebrate the offering in houses" (cited in Branick, *House Church in the Writings of Paul,* 133, and Klauck, *Hausgemeinde and Hauskirche im frühen Christentum,* 77). Here the transition is still being

resisted but is legislated. The canons may really be a collection of operative procedures in fourth-century Phrygia rather than the text of an actual council. A brief discussion is in Gryson, *Ministry of Women*, 53–54.

Notes to Chapter 2. Cultural Anthropology

1. For discussion of the use of the social sciences in the study of ancient societies and early Christianity in particular, see Carney, *Shape of the Past;* Saldarini, *Pharisees,* 12–34; Carolyn Osiek, *What Are They Saying about the Social Setting of the New Testament?* rev. ed. (Mahwah, N.J.: Paulist Press, 1992), 1–7; Susan R. Garrett, "Sociology (Early Christianity)," *Anchor Bible Dictionary* 6.89–99; John H. Elliott, *What Is Social-Science Criticism?* (Minneapolis: Fortress Press, 1993).

2. See esp. Gerhard E. Lenski, *Power and Privilege: A Theory of Social Stratification* (New York: McGraw-Hill Book Co., 1966). See also descriptions in Carney, *Shape of the Past;* Saldarini, *Pharisees,* 35–49; Richard L. Rohrbaugh, "The Pre-industrial City in Luke-Acts: Urban Social Relations," in *The Social World of Luke-Acts: Models for Interpretation,* ed. Jerome H. Neyrey (Peabody, Mass.: Hendrickson, 1991), 125–37.

3. Lenski, *Power and Privilege.*

4. Notably: Peristiany, *Honour and Shame: Mediterranean Family Structures;* Pitt-Rivers, *Fate of Shechem;* Paul Friedrich, "Sanity and the Myth of Honor: The Problem of Achilles," *Ethos* 5 (1977): 281–305; Gilmore, *Honor and Shame;* J. G. Peristiany and Julian Pitt-Rivers, eds., *Honor and Grace in Anthropology* (Cambridge: Cambridge University Press, 1992); Halvor Moxnes, "BTB Readers Guide: Honor and Shame," *Biblical Theology Bulletin* 23, no. 4 (1993): 167–76. Some question whether honor and shame, while unquestionably important cultural elements, should be seen as exact opposites. See, for example, the critique of Michael Herzfeld, "Honour and Shame: Problems in the Comparative Analysis of Moral Systems," *Man* (Royal Anthropological Institute) 15 (1980): 339–51; Unni Wikan, "Shame and Honour: A Contestable Pair," *Man* 19 (1984): 635–52; Gideon M. Kressel, "Shame and Gender," *Anthropological Quarterly* 65 (1992): 34–46 [35].

5. See esp. Peristiany, *Honour and Shame,* 21–77; Bruce J. Malina, *The New Testament World: Insights from Cultural Anthropology,* rev. ed. (Louisville, Ky.: Westminster/John Knox Press, 1993), 28–62; David D. Gilmore, *Manhood in the Making: Cultural Concepts of Masculinity* (New Haven, Conn.: Yale University Press, 1990), 30–55.

6. Carney, *Shape of the Past,* 90. See further Saller, *Personal Patronage.*

7. See Pitt-Rivers, *Fate of Shechem,* 94–112, esp. pp. 96–97. In the whole chapter, Pitt-Rivers examines the question why in the *Odyssey* Odysseus unmercifully slayed the suitors upon returning home, when they did not seem to be guilty of a crime deserving of death. His answer: They had violated the rules of hospitality by behaving as hosts in a house where they were no more than guests, but no one was sufficiently powerful to stop them.

8. As is still thought in the Middle East and traditional Mediterranean societies today. Women are thought to be unable to resist men's sexual advances, and must therefore be protected from them. Cf. Carol Delaney, "Seeds of Honor, Fields of Shame," in Gilmore, *Honor and Shame,* 35–48 [41].

9. Note Paul's use of the language of shame in 1 Corinthians in regard to gendered behavior: For men to wear long hair is to their dishonor (*atimia,* 11:14), while for women to speak in the public assembly is shameful (*aischron,* 14:35). The terminology of shame is not limited in this literature to matters of gender, however.

10. E.g., Maureen J. Giovannini, "Female Chastity Codes in the Circum-Mediterranean: Comparative Perspectives," in Gilmore, *Honor and Shame,* 61–74 [68].

11. E.g., Delaney, "Seeds of Honor," argues that this configuration results from the perceived nature of procreation that was also traditional in ancient times: the penis and male seed are active, lifegiving, and capable of self-perpetuation, while the vagina and womb are the receptacle or field that nourishes the seed but is not capable of self-perpetuation. (They of course know nothing of natural parthenogenesis.) Compare Clement of Alexandria, who, while speaking about restraint in drinking, remarks that nothing unbecoming is appropriate to man who is rational, much less to woman, for whom the mere realization of what she is brings shame (*Pedagogue* 2.2 [PG 8.430; ANF 2.246]).

12. See discussion in Stanley Brandes, "Reflections on Honor and Shame in the Mediterranean," in Gilmore, *Honor and Shame,* 121–34, esp. 122–23; Kressel, "Shame and Gender," 38–40.

13. E.g., Wikan, "Shame and Honour." One of the most trenchant criticisms of the honor-shame schema comes from Sally Cole, *Women of the Praia* (Princeton, N.J.: Princeton University Press, 1991), who claims "that the anthropological conceptualization of honor and shame mirrors the ideology of the family promulgated by the Roman Catholic church and the fascist states in power throughout the Mediterranean . . . at the time the first anthropologists of Mediterranean societies were writing" (p. 79). Yet even she acknowledges that in the Portuguese fishing village she studied, shame (*vergonha*), used with wide reference for both men and women, is used in the area of sexuality only for women (p. 83).

14. A modern example of this is the Portuguese fishing village in which Cole (*Women of the Praia,* 45) reports that the women of the poorer, landless fishing people (*pescadores*) had considerably more social freedom, economic power, and personal pride than the women of the more affluent, landed farmers (*lavradores*), who were more often confined to their houses and were not allowed to contribute economically to the family.

15. As reiterated by Sheryl B. Ortner at the opening of her famous essay, "Is Female to Male as Nature Is to Culture?" in *Woman, Culture, and Society,* ed. Michelle Zimbalist Rosaldo and Louise Lamphere (Stanford, Calif.: Stanford University Press, 1974), 67–87 [68–71].

16. Martin K. Whyte, *Status of Women in Preindustrial Societies* (Ann Arbor: Books on Demand, 1978), 178–80.

17. For surveys: Dale F. Eickelman, *The Middle East: An Anthropological Approach,* 2d ed. (Englewood Cliffs, N.J.: Prentice-Hall, 1989), 151–78; K. C. Hanson, "BTB Readers Guide: Kinship," *Biblical Theology Bulletin* 24, no. 4 (1994): 183–94.

18. One of the authors of the present volume, visiting an Arab family in the Middle East, witnessed a sixteen-year-old boy sit unashamedly—and rather awkwardly—on his mother's lap for a family photo. The mother-son relationship in ancient Greece is explored from a psychoanalytic perspective by Philip Slater, *The Glory of Hera: Greek Mythology and the Greek Family* (Boston: Beacon Press, 1968). Cf. Peristiany, *Honour and Shame: Mediterranean Family Structures,* 13–15.

19. See John J. Pilch, "'Beat His Ribs While He Is Young' (Sir. 30:12): A Window on the Mediterranean World," *Biblical Theology Bulletin* 23, no. 3 (1993): 101–13.

20. For a brief and substantive summary of space as social boundary, see Stephen C. Barton, "Paul's Sense of Place: An Anthropological Approach to Community Formation in Corinth," *NTS* 32 (1986): 225–46 [226–28].

21. See further Yvon Thébert, "'Private' and 'Public' Spaces: The Components of the Domus," in *A History of Private Life from Pagan Rome to Byzantium,* ed. Paul Veyne (Cambridge, Mass.: Harvard University Press, 1987), 353–81.

22. Philo, *Special Laws* 3.169. Trans. LCL 7.581.

23. For a broad political analysis of this division, see Jean Bethke Elshtain, *Public Man, Private Woman: Women in Social and Political Thought* (Princeton, N.J.: Princeton University Press, 1981).

24. Jerome H. Neyrey, "Ceremonies in Luke-Acts: The Case of Meals and Table Fellowship," in *The Social World of Luke-Acts: Models for Interpretation,* ed. Jerome H. Neyrey (Peabody, Mass.: Hendrickson, 1991), 361–87 [368].

25. Smith and Taussig, *Many Tables,* 22.

26. Wallace-Hadrill, "The Social Structure of the Roman House," 50–51. The author alludes to Vitruvius's remarks about the differences in housing, and to Cornelius Nepos, *On Illustrious Men* (c. 99–24 B.C.E.), *Preface* 6–8, who, in the context of explaining to Romans the differences between Greek and Roman society, describes the *matrona* of the household as moving about in the middle of male company.

27. Of interest for this question in the context of the romanization of Corinth are Thompson, "Hairstyles, Head-coverings, and St. Paul," 99–115; David W. J. Gill, "The Importance of Roman Portraiture for Head-Coverings in 1 Corinthians 11:2–16," *Tyndale Bulletin* 41 (1990): 245–60. Both show that even the traditional Roman portraiture usually depicts women veiled, but that increasingly, the veil is omitted. Yet when a feminine figure is portrayed as the ideal of womanhood and virtue, the veil often reappears, as is shown in the coin portrait attributed to Livia in Thompson, p. 107.

28. The often-cited contradiction is Cicero, *Against Verres* 2.66, in which an abusive Roman governor, Verres, and his assistant, Rubrius, demand the exhibition of the beautiful unmarried daughter of Philodamus, a leading citizen of Lampsacus in the province of Asia, at whose home they are dining.

The host tells them it is against Greek custom for women to be present at men's banquets, and refuses. A nasty brawl ensues, in which all the members of the household rally to defend the daughter, and the whole town's outrage necessitates a hasty exit for the Roman contingent. This example must be treated with caution, however, as Cicero is deliberately portraying Verres as a scoundrel whose intention is clearly seduction, and there is nothing in the story that would lead us to assume that expecting a nubile daughter to be present at a political banquet and drinking bout was a Roman custom either.

29. "Roman domestic architecture is obsessionally concerned with distinctions of social rank," even "within the social space of the house" (Wallace Hadrill, "Social Structure of the Roman House," 52). Architecture is the replication of social worldview.

Notes to Chapter 3. Social World

1. In cross-cultural and diachronic perspective, for example: Jeremy Boissevain, *Friends of Friends: Networks, Manipulators and Coalitions* (New York: St. Martin's Press, 1974); Eisenstadt and Roniger, *Patrons, Clients and Friends;* John K. Campbell, *Honour, Family, and Patronage: A Study of Institutions and Moral Values in a Greek Mountain Community* (Oxford: Clarendon Press, 1964); Ernest Gellner and John Waterbury, eds., *Patrons and Clients in Mediterranean Societies* (London: Gerald Duckworth & Co., 1977). On patronage in the ancient Mediterranean: Saller, *Personal Patronage;* Andrew Wallace-Hadrill, *Patronage in Ancient Society* (London: Routledge, 1989); G.E.M. de Ste. Croix, "Suffragium: From Vote to Patronage," *British Journal of Sociology* 5 (1954): 33–48. For a shorter treatment: Garnsey and Saller, *Roman Empire,* 148–59; Peter White, "*Amicitia* and the Profession of Poetry in Early Imperial Rome," *Journal of Roman Studies* 68 (1978): 74–92. With particular relevance to the New Testament and early Christianity: Frederick W. Danker, *Benefactor: Epigraphic Study of a Graeco-Roman and New Testament Semantic Field* (St. Louis: Clayton, 1982); Bruce J. Malina, "Patron and Client: The Analogy behind Synoptic Theology," *Forum* 4, no. 1 (1988): 2–32; John E. Stambaugh and David L. Balch, *The New Testament in Its Social Environment,* ed. Wayne A. Meeks, Library of Early Christianity (Philadelphia: Westminster Press, 1986), 63–64, 70–72.

2. Carney, *Shape of the Past,* 171, 215; Eisenstadt and Roniger, *Patrons, Clients and Friends,* 204–19; Malina, "Patron and Client," 3–5; Saller, *Personal Patronage,* 1. Carney reveals a bit of prejudice in calling patronage "a rudimentary and primitive type of human relationship" that "perverts the legal process, due process, the operation of the market, bureaucratic ethics and what have you." Yet he acknowledges that its presence "even in highly industrialized WASP technostructures is proof of the vitality of this form of relationship" (p. 171).

3. Garnsey and Saller, *Roman Empire,* 149–50.

4. Saller, *Personal Patronage,* 8.

5. Ibid., 10–11.

6. Inventory no. 125891, in the Terme Museum, Rome; Antonio Giuliano, ed., *Museo Nazionale Romano: Le Sculture* (Rome: De Luca, 1981), 1.2, #2.4, p. 86: Ulpiae Domnine patrone nostre Ulp. Eutycius, Ulp. Geminus, Ulp. Exuperantus, Ulp. Basilius, alumni cum coiuges suas. Some of the names, esp. Domnina and Exuperantius, were common later among Christians.

7. Saller, *Personal Patronage,* 11. The bibliography is extensive, including: L. A. W. H. Adkins, "'Friendship' and 'Self-Sufficiency' in Homer and Aristotle," *Classical Quarterly* 13 (1963): 30–45; P. A. Brunt, "'Amicitia' in the Late Roman Republic," *Proceedings of the Cambridge Philosophical Society* 11 (1965): 1–20; Ludovac Dugas, *L'amitié antique d'après les moeurs populaires et les théories des philosophes,* 2d ed. (Paris: Félix Alcan, 1914); J. C. Fraisse, *Philia: La notion d'Amitié dans la philosophie antique* (Paris: J. Vrin, 1974); H. Hutter, *Politics as Friendship* (Waterloo, Ont.: Wilfred Laurier, 1978); A. W. Price, *Love and Friendship in Plato and Aristotle* (Oxford: Clarendon Press, 1989); J. M. Rist, "Epicurus on Friendship," *Classical Philology* 75 (1980): 121–29.

8. Saller, *Personal Patronage,* 11–12.

9. Documented by Karen Jo Torjesen, *When Women Were Priests: Women's Leadership in the Early Church and the Scandal of Their Subordination in the Rise of Christianity* (New York: HarperCollins, 1993), 89–109.

10. *Corpus inscriptionum latinarum* 10.810, 813 = *Inscriptiones Latinae Selectae* 3785, 6368; texts and discussion in Lefkowitz and Fant, *Women's Life,* 159–60; also Gill, "Acts and the Urban Elite," 115–16. See further discussion above, pp. 27–28, 233n100.

11. Lefkowitz and Fant, *Women's Life,* 160; Gill, "Acts and the Urban Elite," 116.

12. See M. T. Boatwright, "Plancia Magna of Perge: Women's Roles and Status in Roman Asia Minor," in *Women's History and Ancient History,* ed. S. Pomeroy (Chapel Hill: University of North Carolina Press, 1991), 249–72. Other examples of public and association patronage by women are given in: MacMullen, "Women in Public," 208–18 [212–14]; Fant and Lefkowitz, *Women's Life,* 158–61; Paul Trebilco, *Jewish Communities in Asia Minor,* SNTSMS 69 (Cambridge: Cambridge University Press, 1991), 113–26.

13. *Corpus inscriptionum iudaicarum* 2.738. On women's prominence in the synagogue, see Brooten, *Women Leaders.*

14. Brooten, "Iael *Prostates* in the Jewish Donative Inscription from Aphrodisias," 149–62. Though the name can also be male, Brooten argues persuasively that in this case it is female.

15. *Corpus inscriptionum latinarum* 6.21975.

16. For instance, Bernadette Brooten, in *Women Leaders in the Ancient Synagogue,* has shown the lack of evidence for this interpretation with regard to women in synagogue leadership.

17. MacMullen, "Women in Public," 215. This is an immensely important insight in the whole discussion of women's actual public role and has a direct bearing on the interpretation of women's leadership activities in Jewish and Christian communities.

18. Discussion in Saller, *Personal Patronage,* 15–22; description of the *salutatio* in Garnsey and Saller, *Roman Empire,* 122.

19. See Bauman, *Women and Politics in Ancient Rome;* Suzanne Dixon, "A Family Business: Women's Role in Patronage and Politics at Rome 80–44 B.C.,"

Classica et Mediaevalia 34 (1983): 91–112; Ramsay MacMullen, "Women's Power in the Principate," *Klio* 68 (1986): 434–43.

20. See Dixon, *Roman Mother* (London: Routledge, 1988), esp. 168–209.
21. E.g., Paul and Phoebe (Rom. 16:1–2); Philemon and Paul (Philemon 8); Luke and Theophilus (Luke 1:1–4).
22. Citations range from Plato (*Meno* 73A) to Philo (*Special Laws* 3.169, 171–77; *In Flac.* 2.89).
23. Discussion of the facts and the common modern confusion are in Peskowitz, " 'Family/ies' in Antiquity," 9–36 [26–28]. See further discussion above, pp. 43–45.
24. For general discussions of ancient Mediterranean gender constructions, see John Winkler, *The Constraints of Desire: The Anthropology of Sex and Gender in Ancient Greece* (New York: Routledge, 1990); Prudence Allen, *The Concept of Woman: The Aristotelian Revolution, 750 B.C.–A.D. 1250* (Grand Rapids: Eerdmans, 1996); and K. Aspegren, *The Male Woman*, 11–98.
25. Aristotle, *Politics* 1.5 (1259a35–1260b20, passim). Translations conveniently collected in Lefkowitz and Fant, *Women's Life*, 38–41.
26. On Socrates: Aristotle, *Politics* 1260a20; Plato, *Meno* 73A–B; O'Brien Wicker, "Mulierum Virtutes," 106–34 [113n25].
27. Esp. Plato, *Republic* 454D–457B; idem, *Laws* 6.780e. Plato has long confused scholars of ancient attitudes toward women with his seemingly liberated and egalitarian ideas in some passages, and traditional gender-biased ideas in others. One interpretation is that his ideas on gender equality were reserved for utopia, while the more traditional ones are what he really thought: Dorothea Wender, "Plato, Misogynist, Paedophile, and Feminist," *Arethusa* 6 (1973): 75–90. On female weakness, see *New Docs* 4.30; 1 Peter 3:7. In the fifth century, the Christian theologian Theodoret of Cyrrhus, a scholar of the classics and classical philosophy, took the egalitarian position of arguing that differences of sex are in the body, not in the soul, and therefore women have the same religious responsibilities as men (*Cure for Greek Maladies* 5.56–57).
28. Wicker, "Mulierum Virtutes," 109. Earlier examples are listed in Wicker's n. 11.
29. Plutarch, *On the Bravery of Women* 242F.
30. Ibid. Plutarch's lost treatise *A Woman, Too, Should Be Educated* may have carried his own thinking further, but the surviving fragments do not tell us much (LCL 15.242–49). A colleague tells of living with a contemporary Palestinian family and watching the mother scold her husband for talking about her among his friends.
31. E.g., women's sexual shame: 249D, 251B, 253E (of a corpse); women shaming men: 248B, 262B–C.
32. Plutarch, *Advice to the Married* 142E.
33. Philo, *Questions on Exodus* 1.8; idem, *Questions on Genesis* 2.49, passim.
34. Tosefta Berakot 7.18; pBerakot 9.2; cf. bMenahot 436. Attributed to Socrates and Thales by Diogenes Laertius, *Lives of Philosophers* 1.33; to Plato by Lactantius, *Institutes* 3.19; to Marius by Plutarch, *Marius* 46.1; Wayne A. Meeks, "The Image of the Androgyne: Some Uses of a Symbol in Earliest Christianity," *HR* 13 (1974): 167–80 [168].

35. Philo, *On the Contemplative Life* 60–62. See discussion in Stowers, *A Rereading of Romans*, 49–52, 94–97, 336n25; Leland J. White, "Does the Bible Speak about Gays or Same-Sex Orientation? A Test Case in Biblical Ethics: Part I," *BTB* 25:1 (1995): 14–23. On the meaning of *andreia*, see Elizabeth Castelli, "Virginity and Its Meaning in Early Christianity," *Journal of Feminist Studies in Religion* 2 (1986): 61–88.

36. Musonius Rufus, "On Sexual Indulgence," frag. 12; Lutz, *Musonius Rufus*, 87–89.

37. Martial, *Epigrams* 8.12.

38. "There are hardly any other men who have over their children a power such as we have" (Gaius, *Institutes* 1.55); quoted in Saller, *Patriarchy, Property and Death*, 114. For discussion of patria potestas, besides pp. 114–32, passim of this book, see W. K. Lacey, "Patria Potestas," in *The Family in Ancient Rome: New Perspectives*, ed. Beryl Rawson (Ithaca, N.Y.: Cornell University Press, 1986), 121–44.

39. See Lacey, *Family in Classical Greece*, 21–25, for the general lines of the Greek system. How Greek law and custom functioned in the Greek East during the Roman imperial period can only be conjectured.

40. Full discussion of *tutela* is in Gardner, *Women in Roman Law and Society* (Bloomington, Ind.: Indiana University Press, 1991), 5–29.

41. See Garnsey and Saller, *Roman Empire*, 130–31, for further discussion some of the nonacceptance of this freedom in later European adaptations of Roman law.

42. Pomeroy, *Goddesses, Whores, Wives, and Slaves*, 126–27.

43. Text in translation in Lefkowitz and Fant, *Women's Life in Greece and Rome*, 124–25. The petition by Aurelia Thaisus, "also called Lolliane," is dated to 263 C.E.

44. Some sources of collected information are the following: MacMullen, *Roman Social Relations*, 179n86; idem, "Women in Public," 208–18; Trebilco, *Jewish Communities in Asia Minor*, 113–26; R. A Kearsely, "Asiarchs, Archiereis, and the *Archiereiai* of Asia," *Greek, Roman and Byzantine Studies* 27 (1986): 183–92; idem, "Women in Public Life in the Roman East," 124–37; idem, "Women in Public Life," 6.3; M. T. Boatwright, "Plancia Magna of Perge," in *Women's History and Ancient History*, ed. S. Pomeroy (Chapel Hill: University of North Carolina Press, 1991), 249–72. General discussion is in L. Cracco Ruggini, "Women in Roman Patriarchal Society," *Klio* 71 (1989): 604–19.

45. One survey of brick stamps found that most factory owners were from the senatorial class; one-third of the sample were women (Päivi Setälä, *Private Domini in Roman Brick Stamps of the Empire*, Annales Academiae Scientiarum Fennicae, Dissertationes Humanarum Letterarum 10 [Helsinki: Suomalainen Tiedeakatemia, 1977]).

46. Concrete evidence in addition to the New Testament house churches is difficult to find, but two literary examples can be cited from the aristocracy at Rome: Ummidia Quadratilla, who ran her own household in a pleasure-loving way until the ripe age of seventy-nine, to the displeasure of Pliny the Younger (*Letters* 7.24); and Matidia, great-aunt of Marcus Aure-

lius (Cornelius Fronto 1.30; 2.94–97). These references are from Richard Saller. For examples from the papyri, see Horsley, *New Docs* 2.25–32.

47. Pliny, *Natural History* 35.147, lists six by name and famous works.

48. The two most famous are Hipparchia and Hypatia. About the first, Cynic wife of Crates, Diogenes Laertius has a few remarks and says there are many more stories about her—but declines to tell them (*Diog. Laer.* 6.96–98). The mathematician and neoplatonist Hypatia was killed by a Christian mob in Alexandria in 415 C.E. (Socrates, *Church History* 7.15). Material on sixty-five women philosophers in antiquity is collected by Gilles Ménage, *The History of Women Philosophers,* trans. Beatrice H. Zedler (Lanham/New York/London: University Press of America, 1984, from Latin original, Paris, 1690).

49. Afrania (PW 3 [1899]: 1589), and Maesia (Valerius Maximus 8.3.1 and PW 14, no. 1 [1928]: 282), about whom Valerius Maximus made an exception to his general dislike of women speaking in public, since she was possessed of an *animus virilis* (a virile soul).

50. Tacitus, *Ann.* 15.32.3 (this passage actually indicates high-status women, too); Suetonius *Dom.* 4.1; Martial, *De spec* 6; Statius, *Silvae* l.6.51–56; Dio Cassius, *Roman History* 66.25.1; 67.8.4; 76.16.1. These references are from unpublished material by Thomas Sienkewicz, NEH Seminar, Rome, 1991.

51. Susan Treggiari, "Jobs for Women," *American Journal of Ancient History* 1, no. 2 (1976): 76–104; Natalie B. Kampen, *Image and Status: Roman Working Women in Ostia* (Berlin: Gebr. Mann Verlag, 1981).

52. Bauman, *Women and Politics in Ancient Rome.*

53. E.g., Philo, *Special Laws* 3.169–77. Philo simply repeats common male elite attitudes: K. J. Dover, "Classical Greek Attitudes to Sexual Behavior," *Arethusa* 6 (1973): 59–73. See discussion of Vitruvius's differences between the Greek and Roman house, above, chapter 1. This is to contrast only Greek and Roman customs, however. Other local cultures sometimes granted much more independence to women in marriage and in law, e.g., the evidence for Egypt, where, it is argued, women lost economic freedom under Greek influence (S. R. Llewelyn, "Paul's Advice on Marriage and the Changing Understanding of Marriage in Antiquity," *New Docs* 6.1, p. 7 n.9); also Deborah Hobson, "The Role of Women in the Economic Life of Roman Egypt: A Case Study of First Century Tebtunis," *Echos du monde classique/Classical Views* (University of Calgary) 28, n.s. 3:3 (1984): 373–90.

54. Discussion and further refs. in Corley, *Private Women,* 24–52.

55. See discussion above, pp. 8–10.

56. Cornelius Nepos, *On Illustrious Men,* preface, 6–7, author's translation. See also Lacey, *Family in Classical Greece,* 159.

57. Cicero, *Against Verres* 2.1.26.65–68. See chap. 2, n. 26, above.

58. Dio Cassius, *Roman History* 48.44.3; 55.2.4, 8.2; 57.12.5.

59. Athenaeus, *Deipnosophists* 14.644D; Lucian, *Symposium* 8–9; and perhaps Petronius, *Satyricon* 67–69.

60. Plutarch, *Convivial Questions* 612F–613A, 8–9; idem, *Banquet of the Seven Sages* 150B–155E.

61. Corley, *Private Women,* 25.

62. See discussion in Garnsey and Saller, *Roman Empire,* 132–36.

63. On Greek and Egyptian marriage law and custom, see Lacey, *Family in Classical Greece,* esp. 100–118; *New Docs* 6.1 (pp. 1–18).

64. Translations of legal texts given in Lefkowitz and Fant, *Women's Life in Greece and Rome,* 112–14, and more generally on Roman marriage, pp. 111–17. Discussion in Gardner, *Women in Roman Law and Society,* 31–80; Garnsey and Saller, *Roman Empire,* 130–32; J. A. Crook, *Law and Life of Rome, 90 B.C.–A.D. 212* (Ithaca, N.Y.: Cornell University Press, 1967), 98–104.

65. See Saller, *Patriarchy, Property and Death,* 76–78.

66. Discussion in Saller, *Patriarchy, Property and Death,* 207–11, 221. Full discussion of the legal aspects of dowry in Gardner, *Women in Roman Law and Society,* 97–116.

67. *Justinianic Code* 5.4.3.

68. E.g., ten examples of funerary commemorations to *patrona et conjux* (patron and wife) in CIL 6 (city of Rome) alone: 14014, 14462, 15106, 15548, 16445, 21657, 23915, 25504, 28815, 35973. Discussion in P. R. C. Weaver, "Children of Freedmen (and Freedwomen)," in *Marriage, Divorce, and Children in Ancient Rome,* ed. Beryl Rawson (Oxford: Clarendon Press, 1991), 166–90, esp. 180. Commemorators would hardly have made a point of calling attention to the relationship if social pressure had been greatly opposed to it. In the early third century, sanctioning such marriages was one of the issues held against Roman Bishop Callistus by his opponent, Hippolytus (*Against Heresies* 9.12).

69. Dixon, *Roman Family,* 53–55.

70. Lacey, *Family in Classical Greece,* 106, 162, 284n38, 294n27.

71. Keith Hopkins, "The Age of Roman Girls at Marriage," *Population Studies* 18 (1965): 309–27; Brent Shaw, "The Age of Roman Girls at Marriage: Some Reconsiderations," *Journal of Roman Studies* 77 (1987): 30–46; Saller, *Patriarchy, Property and Death,* 25–41. The epigraphical evidence is circumstantial but probably fairly accurate: It is based on the age at which commemoration of deceased girls is done by husbands rather than parents. The only factor that might skew the data would be deceased young divorcés, not yet remarried.

72. On the legal aspects of divorce, see Gardner, *Women in Roman Law and Society,* 81–93.

73. M. Lightman and W. Zeisel, "*Univira:* An Example of Continuity and Change in Roman Society," *Church History* 46 (1977): 19–32; Suzanne Dixon, *Roman Family,* 83–90.

74. W. J. Harrington, "Jesus' Attitude towards Divorce," *Irish Theological Quarterly* 37 (1970): 199–209; P. Hoffman, "Jesus' Saying about Divorce and Its Interpretation in the New Testament Tradition," *Concilium* 5, no. 6 (May 1970): 51–66; J. Fitzmyer, "The Matthean Divorce Texts and Some New Palestinian Evidence," *Theological Studies* 37 (1976): 197–226; B. Vawter, "Divorce and the New Testament," *Catholic Biblical Quarterly* 39 (1977): 528–42; Raymond F. Collins, *Divorce in the New Testament* (Collegeville: Liturgical Press, 1992).

75. Frags. 3, 4 of Lutz, *Musonius Rufus,* 39–49; also in A. C. van Geytenbeek, *Musonius Rufus and Greek Diatribe* (Assen: Van Gorcum, 1962).

76. Musonius, frag. 12 (Lutz edition).

77. Ibid., 13A, 13B, 14. Furthermore, Musonius opines that children ought

not to be abandoned in order to limit the family, but that many children are a blessing (15). His vision of life so resembled the later-developing Christian ethos that Origen (*Against Celsus* 3.66) considered the opinion of some that Musonius, along with Socrates, Heracles, and Odysseus, was one of the pre-Christian saints (Lutz, *Musonius Rufus,* 3).

78. Plutarch, *Amatorius* 769.
79. Musonius, frag. XIIIA, "What Is the Chief End of Marriage?" in Lutz, *Musonius Rufus,* 88–89.
80. Hopkins, *Death and Renewal,* chap. 1. Cf. Otto Kiefer, *Sexual Life in Ancient Rome* (New York: Barnes & Noble, 1951), chap. 2: "The Romans and Cruelty," pp. 68–74, on education.
81. Menander 573, trans. Allinson in LCL.
82. Seneca, *Ep.* 33.7, trans. Gummere in LCL, cited by Wiedemann, *Adults and Children,* 28–29.
83. Eyben, *Restless Youth* 9, 256–57.
84. Ibid., 181–202.
85. John Boswell, *The Kindness of Strangers: The Abandonment of Children in Western Europe from Late Antiquity to the Renaissance* (New York: Pantheon Books, 1988).
86. Polybius 36.17.5–8, trans. Paton in LCL.
87. See Parkin, *Demography and Roman Society,* and Reinhartz, "Philo on Infanticide," 42–58.
88. Juvenal 6.593ff., trans. Ramsay in LCL.
89. Soranus, *Gynecology* 1.4, trans. Temkin, 7. On the contemporary debate about abortion, prohibited by the Hippocratic Oath, and contraception, see *Gyn.* 1.60–65 in Temkin, pp. 62–68.
90. Pliny the Younger, *Letters* 10.65–66. Cf. Westermann, *Slave Systems,* 6, 28, 86, 136.
91. Rousselle, *Porneia,* 50.
92. See Cicero, *Laws* 3.19, and Dionysius Halicarnassus, *Ant. Rom.* 2.15, who see this paternal choice as ancient, legitimate, and legal.
93. Diodorus Siculus 40.3.8; Tacitus, *Histories* 5.5.
94. See Philo, *Special Laws* 3.114–15; Josephus, *Against Apion* 1.60.
95. E.g., Barnabas 19, early second century C.E.
96. Wiedemann, *Adults and Children,* 36–37.
97. See Müller, *In der Mitte der Gemeinde,* 30n51; 108n99; 395n30.
98. Soranus, *Gyn.* II.15, 42.
99. Pliny the Elder, *Nat. Hist.* 7.2–3, cited by Rousselle, *Porneia,* 51–54.
100. Wallace-Hadrill, *Houses and Society,* 194, 209.
101. Tacitus, *Dialogue on Orators* 29, cited ibid., 223, 227.
102. Plutarch, *Tiberius Gracchus* 1.
103. Rawson, *Family in Ancient Rome,* 8.
104. Wiedemann, *Adults and Children,* 15.
105. Ibid., 153.
106. Ibid., 158–59.
107. Cicero, *Pro Caelio,* 12,28; 17,41; 31, 75–77; for some restrictions, see Cicero, ibid., 18,42, cited by Eyben, *Restless Youth,* 15; cf. 75–80, 207, 232.

108. Gielen, *Tradition und Theologie neutestamentlicher Haustafelethik,* 152–53; Pöhlmann, *Der Verlorene Sohn und das Haus,* 98–102.
109. Pisani, *Plutarco, L'educazione.*
110. Philo, *De Congressu* 11, 141–42, trans. Colson and Whitaker in LCL.
111. Cf. Rousselle, *Porneia,* 40ff., for Greek doctors' advice.
112. Eyben, *Restless Youth* 142.
113. Frags. 128–33 from Stobaeus 3.18.27, 31–32; 4.32.15; 52.43; in LCL, vol. 15, 242–49.
114. Rousselle, *Porneia* 61.
115. Ibid., 11.
116. Philo, "Preliminary Studies," 15, "For grammar teaches us to study literature in the poets and historians." Introductory studies include "grammar, geometry, astronomy, rhetoric, music, and all the other branches of intellectual study" (ibid. 11; cf. 15–19, 74–77, 140–57 [esp. 148], 180 and Plutarch 22F). When Plutarch suggests, "let us begin with the gods" (23A), Philo would have agreed, only making the subject of study singular.
117. See Wilhelm Bousset, *Jüdisch-Christlicher Schulbetrieb in Alexandria und Rom: Literarische Untersuchungen zu Philo und Clemens von Alexandria, Justin und Irenäus* (Hildesheim: Georg Olms, 1975, originally published 1915) and Alan Mendelson, *Secular Education in Philo of Alexandria* (Monographs of the Hebrew Union College 7; Cincinnati: Hebrew Union College, 1982).
118. Philo, "Preliminary Studies," 64–70, discusses listening to lectures in similar terms.
119. Aristotle, *Pol.* 1 1253b 21–23.
120. Plato, *Gorgias* 483B.
121. Plato, *Laws* 11.915A. See Westermann, *Slave Systems,* index s.v. "Paramone" on paramone manumission (indentured service), in which the duties extracted from the person involved were limited, so that the condition was not complete slavery.
122. Aristotle, *Pol.* 1.1253b 6–7, trans. Rackham in Loeb.
123. Ibid., line 33 and 1254a 16.
124. Ibid., line 24; cf. 1260a 13.
125. Seneca, *Ep.* 47.12, trans. Gummere in Loeb.
126. Bradley, *Slavery and Society at Rome* 137; cf. 138–42 on the real world of slaves reflected in Artemidorus's "Dream Book."
127. Juvenal, *Satires* 6.219–223.
128. Ibid., 16
129. Ibid., 24; cf. 65, 130.
130. See Bartchy, *Mallon Chresai,* 45–50.
131. Josephus, *Ant.* 12.156.
132. 1 Macc. 3:41; 2 Macc. 8:10–11, 34–35.
133. Josephus, *War* 3.305, 336, 539–41; 4.394.
134. Westermann, *Slave Systems,* 86n14. Cf. Bradley, *Slavery and Society,* chap. 3, here p. 40.
135. Cf. Pliny, *Letters* 10.65–66.
136. Westermann *Slave Systems,* 70, 128.
137. Ibid., 87n51.

138. Patterson, *Slavery and Social Death,* 354.
139. Keith Hopkins, *Conquerors and Slaves: Sociological Studies in Roman History* (Cambridge: Cambridge University Press, 1978), 99–102.
140. Westermann, *Slave Systems,* 23, 97, 104. See Lloyd A. Thompson, *Romans and Blacks* (Oklahoma City: Oklahoma University Press, 1989).
141. Martin, *Slavery as Salvation,* chap. 1.
142. Ibid., 9–10.
143. See Wallace-Hadrill, *Houses and Society,* chap. 6.
144. Bradley, *Slavery and Society,* 61–63, citing S. M. Treggiari, "Jobs in the Household of Livia," *Papers of the British School at Rome* 43 (1975): 48–77.
145. J. Andreau, *Les Affaires de Monsieur Jucundus,* Collection de l'Ecole Francaise de Rome 19 (1974). Caroline E. Dexter, "The Casa di L. Cicilio Giocondo in Pompeii," Ph.D. diss., Duke University, Durham, N.C., 1974; Lionel Casson, *Ancient Trade and Society* (Detroit: Wayne State University Press, 1984), 104–110; Martin, *Slavery as Salvation,* 18–19; Bradley, *Slavery and Society,* 76.
146. Bradley, *Slavery and Society,* 87; cf. 96–97.
147. Cf. Plutarch, *Solon* 1.3; Anthologia Lyrica Graeca, ed. Diehl, frags. 3, 23–25.
148. Westermann, *Slave Systems,* 30.
149. Cato, *De agricultura;* Varro, *De re rustica* 1.17.5; cf. Columella, *De re rustica* 1.8.19, from the first century C.E.
150. Livy 38: 24, 2–5; 39: 9:5; for relations of Scipio Africanus the Elder with a young slave girl, see Valerius Maximus 7.6.1, cited by Westermann, *Slave Systems,* 74, nn. 112, 113. Cf. Bradley, *Slavery and Society,* 21–28, 138.
151. Plutarch, *Cato Elder* 24.
152. Ibid., 21, 2.
153. Quintus Cicero, *De petitione consulatus* 8.
154. Plutarch, *Crassus* 5.2. Cf. Grant, *Eros in Pompeii,* 66ff., 85ff.
155. Westermann, *Slave Systems,* 109, 113–14.
156. Varro, *De re rustica* 1.17.5, trans. Hooper and Ash in LCL.
157. Columella, *De re rustica* 1.8.5, trans. Ash in LCL.
158. Bradley, *Slaves and Masters,* 53.
159. Ibid., 55.
160. Theodosianus, *Codex* 2.25.1.
161. Bradley, *Slavery and Society,* chap. 7, e.g., pp. 144, 147, 150–53, 157–58, an effective critique of the claim that Christianity changed slaves' social status and experience; he comments on the social setting of key New Testament texts. Cf. chap. 7, n. 23.
162. Ibid., 49.
163. Theodosianus, *Codex* 5.9.1.
164. Westerman, *Slave Systems,* 105. Cf. Bradley, *Slavery and Society,* 28–29.
165. Bradley, *Slavery and Society,* 4–5, citing Ulpian, *Dig.* 21.1.8.
166. Ibid., 165–71, for the Sassia's repeated tortures of her three slaves in order to fabricate evidence.
167. Ibid., 44.
168. E.g., Seneca, *De ira* 3.19.2; 32.1.

169. Juvenal, *Sat.* 14.23–24.
170. Mihail Rostovtzeff, revised by P. M. Fraser, *The Social and Economic History of the Roman Empire,* 2d ed. (Oxford: Clarendon Press, 1957), opposite p. 62, plate IX, fig 2.
171. Cato, *De agricultura* 56; Columella, *De re rustica* 1.6.3.
172. Diodorus, 34–35.2.10; cf. Strabo, *Geography* 6.2.6.
173. Ibid., 34–35.2.18.
174. *Script. Hist. Aug., Hadrian* 18, 9.
175. Bradley, *Slaves and Society,* 118–21. 126–30.
176. E.g., in Lucian, *The Runaway Slaves.*
177. Columella, *De re rustica,* 1.7.6–7, trans. Ash in LCL.
178. Bradley, *Slaves and Masters,* 28n26 and 35n54 with additional texts.
179. Tacitus, *Hist.* 1.3, trans. Wellesley in LCL.
180. Bradley, *Slavery and Society,* 162–65.
181. Livy, 41.9.11.
182. Ibid., 45.15.5.
183. Cato, *Agr.* 143.2; Horace, *Iamb.* 2.65f.; idem, *Serm.* 2.6.65ff.; Cicero, *Leg.* 2.27, cited by Bakker, *Living and Working with the Gods,* 9–10, 42; Orr, "Roman Domestic Religion," 1557–91. Bömer and Herz, *Religion in Rom,* 6, note that classical studies, including Westermann, ignore slaves' religion; cf. 32–56 on slaves and the *Lares.*
184. Bakker, *Living and Working with the Gods,* 32–33, on the Domus del Ninfeo, and 34, on the Domus on Via del Tempio Rotondo.
185. Ibid., 37, 40–41, 179–81, all dated from the second to the fifth century C.E. Private religion in the North African domus was also almost always in or near the courtyard: ibid., 41, citing Thébert, "Private Life and Domestic Architecture in Roman Africa," 363–64, who, however, does not catalogue the evidence. This observation is in tension with White's suggestion, *Building God's House in the Roman World,* 17, 19, 40–41, 47, that Christian worship occurred primarily in the triclinium.
186. Cicero, *De Deorum Natura* 2.68; Columella, *De re rustica* 11.1.19; Pliny the Elder, *Nat. Hist.* 19.50.
187. Bakker, *Living and Working with the Gods,* 42, with nn. 100 and 104, citing Columella, *De re rustica* 11.1.19. Bömer and Herz, *Religion in Rom,* 32–50, 57–78, 203–4.
188. Bömer and Herz, *Religion in Rom,* 46–47, 52, 54–56.
189. Suetonius, *Caligula* 5.
190. Bömer and Herz, *Religion in Rom,* 29, 31.
191. Cicero, *Pis.* 8–9; Sallust, *Cat.* 24.4; 46.3; 51.1; 56.5. Cf. Bömer and Herz, *Religion in Rom,* 35, for bibliography; these authors (39–40) place Pliny's exchange with Christians within this history of collegia (Pliny, *Ep.* 10.33–34, 92, 96–97). The organization of Christians was identical with that of forbidden *collegia* or *hetaeriae,* so the authors find it highly likely that slaves belonged to the forbidden collegium.
192. Ibid., 40–42.
193. Cf. Tacitus, *Ann.* 1.73.1ff., on the trial of Falasius and Rubrius.
194. Bömer and Herz, *Religion in Rom,* 54.
195. Lacey, *Family in Classical Greece,* 15.

196. Plutarch, *Advice to Bride and Groom* 19.
197. At Athens, illegitimate children of citizens seem to have been excluded (Lacey, *Family in Classical Greece,* 112). For initiation of new slaves into the family cult, see ibid., 31.
198. For the general shape of Greek and Roman wedding celebrations, see "Marriage Ceremonies," *OCD* 3d ed., 927–28; for more detail on the Roman wedding ceremony, Daniel P. Harmon, "The Family Festivals of Rome," *ANRW* 2, 2.16.2 (1978): 1592–1603 [1598–1600].
199. T. E. V. Pearce, "The Role of the Wife as *Custos,"* *Eranos* 72 (1974): 16–33.
200. Harmon, "Family Festivals," 1596.
201. Some of the texts are: Cicero, *To Atticus* 11.9.3; Suetonius, *Nero* 6.1; Terence, *The Self-Tormentor* 626–30; Plautus, *Amphitryon* 501; Quintillian, *Oratorical Institution* 4.2.42; Augustine, *City of God* 4.11.
202. Harmon, "Family Festivals," 1597.
203. Among preserved evidence: the Street of the Tombs at Pompeii; Isola Sacra near Ostia; many ancient burial chambers in Malta.
204. On Roman funerals in general, see Harmon, "Family Festivals," 1600–1603. On the practice of the *refrigerium,* see: H. Leclerq, "Refrigerium," *DACL* 14B.2179–2190; André Parrot, *Le "Refrigerium" dans l'audelà* (Paris: P. Geuthner, 1937); Theodor Klauser, "Das altchristliche Totenmahl nach dem heutigen Stande der Forschung," *Theologie und Glaube* 20 (1928): 599–608. Charles A. Kennedy ("The Cult of the Dead in Corinth," in *Love and Death in the Ancient Near East: Essays in Honor of Marvin H. Pope,* ed. John H. Marks and Robert M. Good [Guilford, Conn.: Four Quarters, 1987], 227–36) argues that the *refrigerium* of family and friends is the real issue for Paul in the discussion of meal problems in 1 Corinthians 8 and 10.
205. Most of the surviving exemplars are Christian and Jewish, only because these burial contexts have been better preserved. Glasses with pagan themes are also known, and some were found in Christian burial sites. The custom seems to have been widespread, as similar vessels and other shapes not intended for drinking are known from all over Europe. Some were undoubtedly used for purposes other than funerary, then were buried with the deceased, but some seem to have been made explicitly for funerary banquets, since they depict the deceased by portrait and name with a wish for life. Others were probably made for the celebration of funerary or "agape" meals in the churches at the anniversary of a saint's death, a practice that was very popular in the fourth century. Cf. Anton Kisa, *Das Glas in Altertume* (Leipzig: Hiersemann, 1908), 3.834–900; J. Leclerq, "Fond de Coupes," *DACL* 5 (1923): 1819–59; Charles R. Morey, *The Gold-Glass Collection of the Vatican Library* (Vatican City: Bilioteca Apostolica Vaticana, 1959); Franca Zanchi Roppo, *Vetri paleocristiani a figure d'oro conservati in Italia* (Bologna: Patron, 1969).
206. Orr, "Roman Domestic Religion," 1557–91 [1560–62].
207. Ibid., 1563–69; *OCD* 578–79. On *lares, penates,* and *genius:* Harmon, "Family Festivals," 1593–95.
208. Orr, "Roman Domestic Religion," 1562–63; "Penates, di," *OCD* 1135.
209. Veyne, *History of Private Life,* 197.

210. See the satirical portrayal of the presentation of *Lares* and *Genius* for sacrifice at the banquet of Trimalchio (*Satyricon* 60), and a sample of dedicatory inscriptions to various *genii* and *lares* in Jane F. Gardner and Thomas Wiedemann, eds., *The Roman Household: A Sourcebook* (London/New York: Routledge, 1991), 31–34.

211. Horace, *Ep.* 2.2.188; cf. 2.1.144; 1.7.94, where the speaker swears by the interlocutor's *genius* and *penates*. Orr, "Roman Domestic Religion," 1569–75; "Genius," *OCD* 630.

212. Further discussion and illustrations in Orr, "Roman Domestic Religion," 1575–90; Bakker, *Living and Working with the Gods*.

213. In Foss's study, 126 were located in garden or peristyle, 94 in kitchens, 67 in atria, and 3 in the dining area ("Kitchens and Dining Rooms," 164). Cf. our text below at chap. 8, nn.40–41.

214. For general discussion of the house, see Wallace-Hadrill, *Houses and Society,* 109–11, 125–27. Originally a splendid domus owned by a family, the house had deteriorated under different ownership and was divided up into shops below and apartments above.

215. Further discussion in Orr, "Roman Domestic Religion," 1585–86, with further bibliography. Orr does exactly what most discussions of the subject do: they present the evidence, give both interpretations, say that there were Christians in the area, and give no conclusions. An exception is the official guidebook to Herculaneum by Amedeo Maiuri (*Herculaneum,* 7th English ed. [Roma: Istituto Poligrafico dello Stato, 1977]), which treats the object removed from the wall as "the Cross" (capitalized), "one of the most precious testimonies of the earliest history of the Church" (p. 47). On the contrary, Lampe rightly discounts the Christian import of the wall remnant (*Städtrömischen Christen,* 3). For further discussion of Christianity in Pompeii: Paul Berry, *The Christian Inscription at Pompeii* (Lewiston/Queenston/Lampeter: Edwin Mellen, 1995.

Part 2:
Early Christian Families and House Churches

Notes to Chapter 4.
Social Location of Early Christians

1. See the critique of earlier attempts that began with modern assumptions of the middle class or Marxist theory in Finley, *Ancient Economy,* 49–50; also Cardascia, "L'apparition dans le droit des classes d'honestiores' et d'humiliores,'" 333.

2. Finley, *Ancient Economy,* 45; Cardascia, "L'apparition," 332. Further discussion in Garnsey and Saller, *Roman Empire,* 112–18.

3. Garnsey, *Social Status,* 279–80; Garnsey and Saller, *Roman Empire,* 115–16.

4. Wallace-Hadrill, "Social Structure of the Roman House"; cf. discussion in Garnsey and Saller, *Roman Empire,* 118–23.

5. E.g., Macmullen, *Roman Social Relations,* 105–20 with nn. 49–105 on pp. 192–202; also A. N. Sherwin-White, *Racial Prejudice in Imperial Rome* (Cambridge: Cambridge University Press, 1967), 84–86.

6. Finley, *Ancient Economy,* 46–47.

7. Examples of impoverished senatorial families: Suetonius, *Octavian* 41; idem, *Nero* 10; idem, *Vespasian* 17; Tacitus, *Annales* 2.37–38. These and other refs. in Dill, *Roman Society from Nero to Marcus Aurelius,* 71–72.

8. This is probably why the Roman citizen Attalus, one of the martyrs of Lugdunum, met his death with the beasts in the amphitheater along with other noncitizens, even though some of the group who were citizens had their sentence to the beasts mitigated in favor of beheading (*The Martyrs of Lyons,* 44, 47, 50–51 in Eusebius, *Ecclesiastical History* 5.1.44–5).

9. Crucifixion, originally only for slaves, was extended to *humiliores* and later replaced by *furca* (execution on a forked wooden frame) by Constantine. By the end of the third century, crucifixion and condemnation to the beasts were commonly used for *humiliores* accused of offenses involving magic and sacrilege. Burning was usually reserved for slaves and *humiliores* accused of sacrilege, magic, arson, desertion, and plotting against their masters (Garnsey, *Social Status,* 111–52).

10. Suetonius, *Tiberius* 51; idem, *Gaius* 27 (refs. in Cardascia, "L'apparition," 472–73); Josephus, *Jewish War* 2.308 (ref. in Garnsey, *Social Status,* 127); *Acts of Perpetua and Felicitas* 1. Further discussion of the Christian evidence is in Timothy D. Barnes, *Tertullian: A Historical and Literary Study* (Oxford: Clarendon Press, 1971), 147–48; A. N. Sherwin-White, *The Letters of Pliny: A Historical and Social Commentary* (Oxford: Clarendon Press, 1966), 698.

11. Cardascia, "L'apparition," 467–71; Justinian, *Digest* 48.5.39.8; 13.8.2.

12. Garnsey, *Social Status,* 277–81.

13. Cicero, *De off.* 1.150–51.

14. On *collegia* generally, see Jean-Paul Waltzing, *Etude historique sur les corporations professionelles chez les Romains,* 4 vols. (Louvain: F. Hayez, 1895–1900); "Collegia," *DACL* 3.2.2107–2140; Sherwin-White, *Letters of Pliny,* 608–10; Garnsey and Saller, *Roman Empire,* 156–59.

15. Suetonius, *Augustus* 32.1.

16. Ramsay Macmullen, *Enemies of the Roman Order* (Cambridge, Mass.: Harvard University Press, 1966), 173–84, 199.

17. Tertullian, *Apology* 38, 39.1–7. At the end of the last century, the theory was propounded by the great Roman archaeologist of early Christianity, Giovanni Battista de Rossi, and rejected by Waltzing. For more recent discussion, see E. A. Judge, *The Social Pattern of the Christian Groups in the First Century* (London: Tyndale, 1960), 40–48; Robert L. Wilken, "Collegia, Philosophical Schools, and Theology," in *Early Church History: The Roman Empire as the Setting of Primitive Christianity,* ed. Stephen Benko and John J. O'Rourke (London: Lowe & Brydone, 1972), 268–91; Robert Wilken, *The Christians as the Romans Saw Them* (New Haven, Conn.: Yale University Press, 1984) 32–47; Harry O. Maier, *The Social Setting of the Ministry as Reflected in the Writings of Hermas, Clement and Ignatius,* Dissertations SR

1 (Ontario: Wilfrid Laurier University Press, 1991), 22–23 (but without ascribing a connection with Christian groups). Cf. chap. 3, n. 191 above.

18. Adolf Deissmann, *Light from the Ancient East,* 4th ed. (Grand Rapids: Wm. B. Eerdmans Publishing Co., 1965; 1st English ed., 1911, from 3d German ed. of 1909).

19. Discussion in Malherbe, *Social Aspects of Early Christianity,* 29–36; Meeks, *First Urban Christians,* 51–53.

20. Including two ex-consuls, Titus Flavius Clemens and Manlius Acilius Glabrio, along with Clemens's wife, Flavia Domitilla (also niece of Domitian), executed (the two men) or exiled (the woman) by Domitian at the end of the first century for atheism and judaizing (Dio Cassius 67.14; Suetonius, *Domitian* 10, 15, 17). For Eusebius over two centuries later, Domitilla was a Christian (*Ecclesiastical History* 3.18.4). By his day, the connection of one of the major Christian catacombs of Rome with the name of Domitilla was well known. The origins of the burial place are probably with a family vault of the Domitius family in the late first century; "christianizing" could easily have been perceived by outsiders that early as "judaizing"; yet the evidence is circumstantial. This and other possible cases are discussed in Osiek, *Rich and Poor,* 92–96; Lampe, *Die stadtrömischen Christen,* 164–72.

21. Eusebius, *Ecclesiastical History* 5.21.1; cf. Lampe, *Die stadtrömischen Christen,* 94–103.

22. E.g., Matt. 9:10 and par.; 11:19; 15:1–2; Luke 7:37; 15:1.

23. As an example, Gerd Theissen's interpretation of the trouble with the Lord's Supper in 1 Cor. 11:17–34 as status abuses has been widely accepted (*Social Setting,* 121–74).

24. David W. J. Gill ("Acts and the Urban Elites," 105–18) has not made the case to the contrary.

25. Theissen, *Social Setting,* 69–119. For earlier discussions of Christian social status in general, see: John G. Gager, *Kingdom and Community: The Social World of Early Christianity* (Englewood Cliffs, N.J.: Prentice-Hall, 1975), 93–113; Frederick W. Norris et al., "The Social Status of Early Christianity," *Gospel in Context* 2 (1979): 4–29; more recently, Meeks, *First Urban Christians,* 51–72.

26. Theissen, *Social Setting,* 73.

27. Discussed at length by Theissen, *Social Setting,* 75–83; also by Meeks, *First Urban Christians,* 58; Bartchy, "Slavery" (New Testament), p. 67.

28. Norris, "Social Status," 9.

29. For discussion of the integrity of Romans with chap. 16, see Fitzmyer, *Romans,* 56–62.

30. Suggested by Judge, *Pattern of Social Groups,* 37; also discussed by Meeks, *First Urban Christians,* 57–58.

31. Theissen, *Social Setting,* 92–94.

32. Jewett, "Tenement Churches and Communal Meals," 23–43.

33. Kearsley, "Women in Public Life"; Brooten, "Iael *prostates*"; Horsley, *New Documents,* 4:122 (pp. 241–44); Fitzmyer, *Romans,* 731, with further refs., and bibliography, pp. 732–33; Theissen (*Social Setting,* 88–89) inexplicably

discusses Phoebe's title of minister or deacon (*diakonos*), but not of patron (*prostatis*). For a full and competent study of the language of *diakonia* in early Christianity within its Hellenistic setting, see Collins, *Diakonia*.

34. Theisson, *Social Setting*, 95.

35. Meeks, *First Urban Christians*, 73. For full discussion of the social level of early Christians, see pp. 51–73.

36. See Osiek, *Rich and Poor*, esp. 15–38.

37. Justin, *Apology* 2.10.8; Tatian, *Oration against the Greeks* 32. See discussion in Osiek, *Rich and Poor*, 97. Tatian uses the conventional contrast of rich and poor (*ploutountes* and *penetes*). In Greek terminology, a *plousios* is one who can live properly on one's own income; a *penes* one who could not, and could be subject to compulsion and exploitation; a *ptochos* a pauper entirely without resources (Finley, *Ancient Economy*, 41, based on Aristophanes, *Plutus* 552–54).

38. Minucius Felix, *Octavius* 8.3–4; 12.7; 16.5; 31.6; 36.3–7.

39. One of the places of Christian activity according to Celsus is the *gynaikonitis*, literally, women's quarters, and therefore where women worked at spinning and weaving, but there is some indication that the term had by this time come to mean a wool-workers' shop, regardless of the sex of the workers: W. den Boer, "Gynaeconitis, a Centre of Christian Propaganda," *Vigiliae Christianae* 4 (1950): 61–64.

40. Origen, *Against Celsus* 1.62; 3.18, 44, 50, 55, 74. The best translation is by Henry Chadwick, *Origen contra Celsum* (Cambridge: Cambridge University Press, 1953). Further discussion is in Osiek, *Rich and Poor*, 98–101.

41. Libanius, *Oration* 16.47.

42. Theodoret, *Cure for Greek Maladies* 5.60–69.

43. Tertullian, *Apology* 1.7; 37.4.

44. See discussion in A.H.M. Jones, "The Social Background of the Struggle between Paganism and Christianity," in *The Conflict between Paganism and Christianity in the Fourth Century*, ed. Arnaldo Momigliano (Oxford: Clarendon Press, 1963), 17–37.

Notes to Chapter 5.
Gender Roles, Marriage, and Celibacy

1. Cf. J. Jensen, "Does *Porneia* Mean Fornication? A Critique of Bruce Malina," *NovT* 20 (1978): 161–84.

2. Zaas, "Catalogues and Context" 628 (from a 1982 dissertation at the University of Chicago). Zaas successfully corrects the consensus represented, e.g., by Hans Conzelmann, *1 Corinthians*, Hermeneia (Philadelphia: Fortress Press, 1975), 101: "The recognition of the fact that we have here a traditional form forbids an assessment in terms of the contemporary scene, as if, for example, we had to do with a realistic description of conditions in Corinth." Also Betz, *Galatians*, 283: "Also typical of the phenomena of evil is that they occur without order or system. When Paul makes use of the form of the 'lists of vices' he puts together a random collection of terms, describing the ordinary occurrences of evil among men."

3. Zaas, "Catalogues and Context," 627 (his italics).

4. See the insightful discussion in Countryman, *Dirt Greed and Sex,* 104–23. He notes that the three vices of "*porneia,* impurity, and license" also occur in the lists of Gal. 5:19–21 and 2 Cor. 12:20–21, arguing that the list is stereotypical, so that Paul's real concern is idolatry. However, in 1 Corinthians Paul is discussing an actual case of a son having sex with his father's wife (5:1), whether Corinthian Christian males should continue using prostitutes (6:15–18), and whether a Christian couple already married should have sex (7:2–5), so that in this specific epistolary setting, *porneia* is quite fleshly and cannot be reduced simply to a symbol of idolatry.

5. See Stowers, *Rereading of Romans,* chap. 2. Following the discussion of sexual morality in 1 Corinthians 5—7, Paul discusses food offered to idols in chaps. 8–10, related topics.

6. Cf. Mitchell, *Paul and the Rhetoric of Reconciliation,* 235: "Still under the overarching category of *porneia,* Paul gives advice on specific cases of marriage and sexual behavior about which the Corinthians have written him."

7. Contrast Deming, *Paul on Marriage and Celibacy,* 135, 220.

8. John J. Collins, *Between Athens and Jerusalem: Jewish Identity in the Hellenistic Diaspora* (New York: Crossroad, 1983), chap. 4: "The Common Ethic," p. 142. Earlier see Wendland, "Die Therapeuten und die Philonische Schrift vom Beschaulichen Leben," 711–12.

9. Philo, *Hypothetica,* 7.1–9, Josephus, *Against Apion* 2.190–219, and Pseudo-Phocylides. P. W. van der Horst, *The Sentences of Pseudo-Phocylides with Introduction and Commentary* (Leiden: E. J. Brill, 1978), 82, dates this text within the reigns of Augustus and Tiberius (30 B.C.E.–C.E. 37) or earlier.

10. Ibid., 143–44, and the rest of the chapter. On some Roman doctors' rejection of abortion, cf. Soranus, *Gynecology* 1.19.60–65 as well as the earlier Hippocratic Oath. John M. Riddle, *Contraception and Abortion from the Ancient World to the Renaissance* (Cambridge, Mass.: Harvard University Press, 1992).

11. Cf., e.g., Sirach 38:1–15.

12. For some parallels and bibliography see Owsei Temkin, *Hippocrates in a World of Pagans and Christians* (Baltimore: Johns Hopkins University Press, 1991); F. Kundlien, "Cynicism in Medicine," *Bulletin of the History of Medicine* 48 (1974): 305–19; idem, "Heilkunde," *RAC* 14 (1988): 223–49; Gary B. Ferngren and Darrel W. Amundsen, "Virtue and Health/Medicine in Pre-Christian Antiquity," in *Virtue and Health: Explorations in the Character of Medicine,* ed. Earl E. Shelp (Boston: D. Reidel, 1985), 3–22. G. B. Ferngren and D. W. Amundsen, "Medicine and Christianity in the Roman Empire: Compatibilities and Tensions," *ANRW* 2.37.3 (1996): 2957–80.

13. Ann Ellis Hanson and Monica H. Green, "Soranus of Ephesus, Methodicorum Princeps," *ANRW* II.37.2 (1994): 968–1075, at p. 975.

14. Ibid., 993.

15. Rousselle, *Porneia,* 21–22.

16. Soranus, *Gynecology* 1.40.

17. For a discussion of connections between Greek medicine and philosophy, see the preface to Celsus, *De Medicina,* trans. Spencer (LCL, 1935), a work

from the early first century C.E. On Plutarch, cf. Scarborough, *Roman Medicine,* 59, 62, 103, 138–39. And cf. "The Relation of Ancient Philosophy to Medicine" and "The Distinctive Hellenism of Greek Medicine" in *Ancient Medicine: Selected Papers of Ludwig Edelstein,* ed. Owsei Temkin and C. Lilian Temkin (Baltimore: Johns Hopkins Press, 1967), 349–97.

18. Oribasius, *Collectiones medicae* 7.37, line 1 in *Oeuvres d'Oribase,* trans. Bussemaker and Daremberg, vol. 1, p. 536. Oribasius (c. C.E. 320–400) was the personal physician of Julian, for whom he made a collection of excerpts from earlier medical doctors, in this case from Galen of Pergamum, "On Intercourse" (*peri aphrodision*) (c. C.E. 129–199); in the excerpt Galen cites Epicurus. Cited by Rousselle, *Porneia,* 9. Cf. Barry Baldwin, "The Career of Oribasius," *Acta Classica* 18 (1975): 85–97. For the debate about Epicurus's opinion of sex and marriage, see Fred E. Brenk, review of A. A. Long and D. N. Sedley, *The Hellenistic Philosophers* (1987), 2 vols., in *Biblica* 71 (1990): 137–41 at 139, and Nussbaum, *Therapy of Desire,* 149–54.

19. Epicurus, *Diog. Laert.* 10.118. Cited by Nussbaum, *Therapy of Desire,* 150–51 with n. 22. See also Robert D. Brown, *Lucretius on Love and Sex* (Leiden: E. J. Brill, 1987), 113–27.

20. Celsus, *De Medicina* I.1.4, trans. Scarborough, *Roman Medicine* 61. Cf. Philippe Mudry, "Celse. Rapport Bibliographique," *ANRW* II.37.1 (1993): 787–99.

21. Celsus, *De Med.* I.2.1, trans. W. G. Spencer, *Celsus De Medicina* (LCL, 1935).

22. Rufus of Ephesus, "On Intercourse," an excerpt in Oribasius, *Collectiones medicae* VI.38; Daremberg, *Oeuvres d'Oribase,* vol. 1, p. 541, lines 2–3. Cf. *Oeuvres de Rufus d'Éphese, Texte collationné,* traduit par C. Daremberg and C. Émile Ruelle (Paris: L'Imprimerie Nationale, 1879). Rufus was a physician under Trajan (C.E. 98–117); he probably studied in Alexandria and practiced in Ephesus. Cf. Alexander Sideras, "Rufus von Ephesus und sein Werk im Rahmen der antiken Medizin," *ANRW* II.37.2 (1994): 1077–1253.

23. The date given by Rousselle, *Porneia,* 12. The interest in virginity is, then, not "new" in the third century C.E. (contrast Deming, *Paul on Marriage and Celibacy,* 105).

24. *Soranus' Gynecology,* trans. Temkin, 23. Soranus was born in Ephesus, studied in Alexandria, and then practiced in Rome under Trajan (98–117) and Hadrian (117–138). Temkin (38) contrasts modern and ancient Roman attitudes toward medicine: "The educated layman was much more likely to form his own judgment about medical matters, to . . . treat himself or his family. In the case of Celsus, we even have a layman who compiled a classical medical text with such expertness that it is hard for us to believe that the author was not a medical practitioner. In short then, the most likely answer to the question of Soranus' reading public would be that the *Gynecology* was intended for physicians, midwives, *and* laymen" (Temkin's emphasis) Cf. Ann Ellis Hanson and Monica H. Green, "Soranus of Ephesus: Methodicorum princips," *ANRW* II.37.2 (1994): 968–1075, and G.E.R. Lloyd, *Science, Folklore and Ideology: Studies in the Life Sciences in Ancient Greece* (Cambridge: Cambridge University Press, 1983), 168–200.

25. Philo (cf. n. 33 below), writing early in the first century C.E., and the doctors engaged in these medical debates summarized by Soranus, late in the same century, use "virgin" to refer to permanent sexual abstinence, which is then a possible meaning of the term in 1 Cor. 7:25, 28, 34, 36, 37, 38.

26. The same root word for "harmful" was used centuries earlier by Epicurus (*Diog. Laert.* 10.118).

27. Cf. the same term in 1 Cor. 4:10, etc., five times in the Corinthian correspondence.

28. Temkin, *Soranus' Gynecology* 1.7.30–32 at pp. 27–30. Ioannes Ilberg, *Sorani, Gynaeciorum Libri IV . . .*, Corpus Medicorum Graecorum IV (Leipzig: Teubner, 1927), 20–21. Galen's opinion is that, "for those with faultless constitutions it is not necessary to refrain completely from sex relations," *A Translation of Galen's Hygiene (De Sanitate Tuenda),* by Robert Montraville Green (Springfield, Conn.: Charles C. Thomas, 1951), 253 (from chap. 7), similar to Celsus's opinion a century and a half earlier; cf. pp. 133–34, 244, 273–75.

29. See, e.g., Hippocrates, "On Generation" 1, in Iain M. Lonie, *The Hippocratic Treatises "On Generation," "On the Nature of the Child," "Diseases IV":* *A Commentary,* Ars Medica II.7 (Berlin: Walter de Gruyter, 1981), 1. Robert Joly, *Hippocrate XI: De la Génération, De la Nature de l'Enfant, Des Maladies IV, Du Foetus de huit Mois,* Budé (Paris: Société d'Édition "Les Belles Lettres," 1970), 44.

30. T. C. Allbutt, *Greek Medicine in Rome* (London: Macmillan & Co., Ltd., 1921), 321. For fourth-century B.C.E. theories see the treatise on "Seed," in *Hippocratic Writings,* ed. G.E.R. Lloyd (New York: Penguin, 1950, 1983), 317–23. For dates of the three main theories concerning origin of sperm, compare the third-century B.C.E. physician in *Herophilus: The Art of Medicine in Early Alexandria, Edition, translation and essays,* by Heinrich von Staden (Cambridge: Cambridge University Press, 1989), 288–92.

31. Galen, "Concerning Sperm," an extract in Oribasius, *Collectiones medicae* XXII.2, in Daremberg, *Oeuvres d'Oribase,* vol. 3, pp. 40–52, here 3.40,13. Galen is quoted by Rousselle, *Porneia,* 14–15.

32. Translated in Rousselle, *Porneia,* 14–15, from Daremberg, *Oeuvres d'Oribase,* vol. 3, pp. 46, 1–47, 14.

33. Philo, *On the Contemplative Life* 68 (trans. Colson in LCL); cf. 6, 11–12, 65, 90.

34. Ibid., 11–13, 18–19.

35. FGrH 618, F6; also in van der Horst, *Chaeremon,* frgs. 10–11.

36. Josephus, *Against Apion* I.288ff.

37. Wendland, "Die Therapeuten," 703–4, 754–56, and Van der Horst, *Chaeremon,* 9 and 56.

38. *The Testament of Job, Greek text and English translation,* ed. Robert A. Kraft et al., Texts and Translations 5 (Missoula, Mont.: Scholars Press, 1974). For persuasive arguments against a late Christian (Montanist) origin of the *Testament of Job* and a suggestion about the date of chaps. 44–53, see Van der Horst, "Images of women in the Testament of Job," 108–9, 116, a version of which is also in his *Essays on the Jewish World of Early Christianity,* NTOA

(Göttingen: Vandenhoeck & Ruprecht, 1990), 94–110. See also his "Con-flicting Images of Women in Ancient Judaism," 73–95, esp. 89–91. Also Kraemer, *Her Share of the Blessings*, 109, 123, and Rebecca Lesses, "The Daughters of Job," in Schüssler Fiorenza, *Searching the Scriptures*, 2.139–49.

39. Van der Horst, "Images of women in the Testament of Job," 105n33, notes an interpolation of MS. V at 48.1, where it is said of Hemera: "and imme-diately she was outside of her own flesh." The reference to "angelic lan-guage" has a close parallel in 1 Cor. 13:1.

40. Cf. Col. 3:2, "Set your minds on things that are above, not on things that are on earth (*ges*)," in relation to the vice list in 3:5, baptism in 2:11, and the discipline in 2:23.

41. Cf. Gal. 6:14; 1 Cor. 7:31; Titus 2:12. The parallel between *Testament of Job* 50.2 and Gal. 6:14 helps explain Paul's sexual asceticism: "May I never boast of anything except the cross of our Lord Jesus Christ, by which the world (*kosmos*) has been crucified to me, and I to the world." Both Gal. 6:14 and 1 Cor. 7:31 make it highly improbable that Paul would write a chapter as some Stoics did shoring up the Greco-Roman cities of this "world" by marriage.

42. Digest 48.9.5 in Corpus Juris Civilis XI.

43. Countryman, *Dirt Greed and Sex*, 199, with n. 6. Cf. D. Martin, *Corinthian Body*, 174–79, published after our chapter was written.

44. Adela Yarbro Collins, "The Function of 'Excommunication' in Paul," *HTR* 73 (1980): 251–63, at p. 259.

45. Countryman, *Dirt Greed and Sex*, 201. Antoinette Wire, "1 Corinthians," in Schüssler Fiorenza, *Searching the Scriptures*, 2.153–95, at 167, specu-lates that the court case involved a sexual issue.

46. Cf. Countryman, *Dirt Greed and Sex*, 117–20.

47. Aristotle, *History of Animals* IX.1 608a 32–608b 18, trans. Balme in LCL. Cited by Maryanne Cline Horowitz, "Aristotle and Woman," *Journal of the History of Biology* 9, no. 2 (1976): 183–213, at p. 210.

48. Holt N. Parker, "Love's Body Anatomized: The Ancient Erotic Handbooks and the Rhetoric of Sexuality," in *Pornography and Representation in Greece and Rome*, ed. Amy Richlin (New York: Oxford University Press, 1992), 90–107, at pp. 98–99.

49. Mitchell, *Paul and the Rhetoric of Reconciliation*, 234; cf. 119–120 on the verb *kollasthai*, "to glue together."

50. F. C. Babbitt, *Plutarch's Moralia* (LCL; 1971) 2.297.

51. In the legends of Rome's founding, a free woman's reduction to slavery means that she is sexually available to her new owner, a threat to her male relatives' political status; see the clear exposition by Sandra R. Joshel, "The Body Female and the Body Politic: Livy's Lucretia and Verginia," in Rich-lin, *Pornography and Representation in Greece and Rome*, 112–30.

52. Cf. Laurence, *Roman Pompeii*, chap. 5: "Deviant Behavior," esp. p. 71, and Renate Kirchhoff, *Die Sünde gegen den eigenen Leib: Studien zu porne und porneia in 1 Kor 6,12–20 und dem sozio-kulturellen Kontext der paulinischen Adressaten* (Göttingen: Vandenhoeck & Ruprecht, 1994), 67, 196.

53. Lutz, *Musonius Rufus*, 86, 14; 86, 30–88, 1.

54. Rousselle, *Porneia,* 64; cf. 4.

55. Cf. Plato, *Republic,* VIII.558D–559C.

56. Counryman, *Dirt Greed and Sex,* 204.

57. Hans Conzelmann, *1 Corinthians,* Hermeneia (Philadelphia: Fortress Press, 1975), 115. On this whole topic, see D. Martin, *Corinthian Body,* chap. 8, published after our chapter was written.

58. 2 Macc. 4:38; 10:35; 14:45; 3 Macc. 4:2, cited by Michael Barré, "To Marry or to Burn: *Purousthai* in 1 Cor. 7:9," *CBQ* 36 (1974): 193–202, at p. 195.

59. As in Isa. 1:25; Jer. 9:7; Zech. 13:9; cf. the noun in Rev. 18:9, 18.

60. Musonius, frag. 13A, trans. Lutz.

61. Paul Veyne, ed., *A History of Private Life,* (Cambridge, Mass.: Harvard University Press, 1987), 36–37, 42–45. But see the review article by Averil Cameron in *JRS* 76 (1986): 266–71, and the negative evaluation by B. Rawson, "From 'Daily Life' to 'Demography,'" in *Women in Antiquity: New Assessments,* ed. R. Hawley and B. Levick (New York: Routledge & Kegan Paul, 1995), 2–3.

62. Ward, "Women in Roman Baths," esp. 131–34, and Georg Schöllgen, "Balnea Mixta: Entwicklungen der spätantiken Bademoral im Spiegel der Textüberlieferung der Syrischen Didaskalie," in *Panchaia: Festschrift für Klaus Thraede,* ed. Manfred Wacht, JAC Ergänzungsband 22 (Münster: Aschendorf, 1995), 182–94, esp. 193n86 on the chronology.

63. Cf. the outrage of (some) Jews in 1 Macc. 1:13 and 2 Macc. 4:9, 12, 14 and the acceptance of the practice by the Christian Hermas, *Vis.* 1.1.2.

64. Corley, *Private Women, Public Meals,* 8n28, observes that classical scholars of the past two centuries found the notion of sex with minors aged nine to twelve so abhorrent that they rejected their sources as impossible. Cf. Treggiari, "Roman Social History," 160–61. However, "females of non-elite families in Rome and Italy of the first two or three centuries of the Christian era probably married in their late teens," according to Rawson, "From 'Daily Life' to 'Demography,'" 9.

65. Klauck, *Gemeinde zwischen Haus und Stadt,* 95–123.

66. See Balch, "1 Cor. 7:32–35 and Stoic Debates about Marriage, Anxiety, and Distraction," 429–39, objected to by Deming, *Paul on Marriage and Celibacy,* 7–8, 197. Deming observes that *amerimnos* (1 Cor. 7:32) does not refer to psychological "anxiety," but to lack of concern about or attention to outward routine. However, to exclude all psychological nuances from this term is mistaken. Cf., e.g., Luke 21:34 where Jesus exhorts his disciples, "be on guard so that your hearts are not weighed down with . . . the worries [anxieties] of this life," an injunction compatible with his warnings about other feelings during the eschatological crisis (21:9, 17, 23, 26).

67. Deming, *Paul on Marriage and Celibacy,* 176–77, points out a remarkable Stoic parallel in Arius Didymus (*Stobaeus* 1.86.1–16, trans. Wachsmuth-Hense).

68. Gordon D. Fee, *The First Epistle to the Corinthians* (Grand Rapids: Wm. B. Eerdmans Publishing Co., 1987), 699–711, and now esp. Philip B. Payner, "Fuldensis, Sigla for Variants in Vaticanus, and 1 Cor. 14.34–35," *NTS* 41,

no. 2 (1995): 240–62, including the new observation that the best Greek manuscript of the NT, the Vaticanus (B), has a sign (the bar-umlaut) at these verses indicating a textual problem.

69. Cf. the repeated use of the same verb/participle demanding "submission" in deutero-Pauline literature: Col. 3:18; Eph. 5:21–22; Titus 2:5, 9; 1 Peter 2:18; 3:1, 5; cf. 5:5; and in the "apostolic fathers," see *1 Clem.* 1.3, *Didache* 4.11, *Barnabas* 19.7, as well as Plutarch, *Advice to Bride and Groom* 142E. The same verbal form occurs in the following texts, but surprisingly, without demanding submission in the household: *1 Clem.* 20.1; 34.5; 37.2; 38.1; 57.1–2; Ignatius, *Eph.* 2.2; 5.3; idem, *Mag.* 2.1; 13.2; idem, *Tral.* 2.1–2; 13.2; idem, *Letter to Polycarp* 2.1; 6.1; Polycarp, *Phil.* 2.1; Hermas, *Man.* 12.4.2; 12.5.1; Hermas, *Sim.* 9.22.3; *Letter to Diognetus* 10.2. Most surprisingly, the household code does *not* occur in Ignatius, *Letter to Polycarp* 4 or 13 or Polycarp, *Phil.* 4.

70. Wire, *Corinthian Women Prophets*. Cf. the review by Margaret M. Mitchell in *RSR* 10, no. 4 (1993): 308–11, the comments by Schottroff, *Lydia's Impatient Sisters*, 184n7; 203n78, and Jouette Bassler, "1 Corinthians," in *The Women's Bible Commentary*, ed. Carol A. Newsom and Sharon H. Ringe (Louisville, Ky.: Westminster/John Knox Press, 1992), 327–28.

71. Klauck, *Gemeinde zwischen Haus und Stadt,* 59–69, at p. 68. On this couple's high social status, see Stowers, *A Rereading of Romans,* 75–76.

72. Schüssler Fiorenza, *In Memory of Her,* 169–75.

73. Nils A. Dahl, "Euodia and Syntyche and Paul's Letter to the Philippians," in *The Social World of the First Christians: Essays in Honor of Wayne A. Meeks,* ed. L. Michael White and O. Larry Yarbrough (Minneapolis: Fortress Press, 1995), 3–15, at pp. 14, 10.

74. Balch, "Household Codes," 25–50, and Mary Rose D'Angelo, "Colossians," in Schüssler Fiorenza, *Searching the Scriptures,* 2.313–24.

75. Aristotle, *Pol.* I 1253b 7–8, 12–14, trans. Rackham in LCL. For a contrast of Aristotle and Xenophon, see Sarah B. Pomeroy, *Xenophon Oeconomicus: A Social and Historical Commentary* (Oxford: Clarendon Press, 1994, 1995), 34, 66.

76. E.g., Aristotle, *Pol.* I 1254a 22–24, and *Nic. Eth.* 8 1160b 23ff.

77. Dio Cassius, *Roman History* 50.28.3, cited by Balch, *Let Wives Be Submissive,* 71. Also Stowers, "Rome and the Moral Politics of the Augustan Revolution," in *A Rereading of Romans,* 52–56, citing Zanker, *Power of Images,* whose interpretation is praised by Andrew Wallace-Hadrill, "Rome's Cultural Revolution," *JRS* 79 (1989): 157–64. Cf. Cahill, "Sex and Gender Ethics as NT Social Ethics."

78. Balch translates Arius Didymus's epitome in "Household Codes," 41–44.

79. E. Elizabeth Johnson, "Colossians," in Newsome and Ringe, *Women's Bible Commentary,* 347.

80. See Joshel and Kirchhoff in nn. 51, 52 above.

81. Eduard Schweizer, "soma," *TDNT* 7 (1971): 1024–94, at pp. 1038–39, citing Seneca, *Ep.* 92.30; 95.52, who also says the state is the body of the emperor (Nero): *De Clementia* I.5.1; cf. Plutarch, *De Solone* 18; *Pomp.* 51; cf. Philo, *Abr.* 74. J. Paul Sampley, "Ephesians," in *The Deutero-Pauline*

Letters: Ephesians, Colossians, 2 Thessalonians, 1–2 Timothy, Titus, ed. Gerhard Krodel, Proclamation Commentaries (Minneapolis: Fortress Press, 1993), 1–23, at pp. 8–10.

82. Dionysius Halicarnassus, *Ant. Rom.* 6.86, trans. Cary in LCL; cf. Livy 2.32.

83. Ibid., 6.87.1.

84. Johnson, "Ephesians," 340–41.

85. Joanna Dewey, "1–2 Timothy and Titus," in Newsom and Ringe, *Women's Bible Commentary,* 353–61, and Linda M. Maloney, "The Pastoral Epistles," in Schüssler Fiorenza, *Searching the Scriptures,* 2.361–80.

86. Are the creation stories (Genesis 1—3) the reference to the "law" made by the interpolator in 1 Cor. 14:34? Dependent on Greek sources, the Hellenistic Jews Philo, *Hypothetica* 7.3, and Josephus, *Against Apion* 2.199, write the same: "the woman, says the law, is in all things inferior to the man. Let her accordingly be submissive."

87. Sheila E. McGinn, "The Acts of Thecla," in Schüssler Fiorenza, *Searching the Scriptures,* 2.800–28.

88. Ibid., 803n11.

89. Maloney, "Pastoral Epistles," 2.368.

90. Cf. Theissen, *Social Reality,* 165, 189–96.

91. Dionysius, *Ant. Rom.* 3.13.4. Dionysius completed his *Roman Antiquities* in the first decade B.C.E. Compare Livy, 1.23–26.

92. Dionysius, *Ant. Rom.* 3.16.2–3, 5.

93. Ibid., 3.18–20.

94. Ibid., 3.21.6, trans. Cary in LCL.

95. Epictetus, *Diss.* 3.22.76; cf. 3.22.47, 67–82.

96. Epictetus, *Diss.* 3.22.72, trans. Oldfather in LCL.

97. As translated and interpreted by Hans-Josef Klauck, "Brotherly Love in Plutarch and in 4 Maccabees," in *Greeks, Romans and Christians: Essays in Honor of Abraham J. Malherbe,* ed. David L. Balch, Everett Ferguson, and Wayne Meeks (Minneapolis: Fortress Press, 1990), 144–56, at pp. 151–52, who dates it c. 100 C.E.

98. Paul Hoffmann, "QR und der Menschensohn: Eine Vorläufige Skizze," in *The Four Gospels 1992: Festschrift Frans Neirynck,* ed. F. van Segbroeck et al. (Louvain: Leuven University Press, 1992), 1.421–56, pointing to parallels between Luke 11:49–51, 13:34–35, and Josephus, *War* 6.285–315, 458, an argument accepted by James M. Robinson, "Foreword," in John J. Rousseau and Rami Arav, *Jesus and His World: An Archaeological and Cultural Dictionary* (Minneapolis: Fortress Press, 1995), 18, n. 59. See Kristen, *Familie.* An older work is Schroeder, *Eltern und Kinder in der Verkündigung Jesu.*

99. Luise Schottroff, "The Sayings Source Q," in Schüssler-Fiorenza, *Searching the Scriptures,* 2:512.

100. Schottroff, *Lydia's Impatient Sisters,* 152–73. Cf. Seim, *Double Message,* 208–12, and Kristen, *Familie,* 141–48, 154.

101. Kristen, *Familie,* 202, 317–22, argues that this saying belongs to Q1, which, according to his hypothesis, was an early sapiential stratum, not

to Q2, a later apocalyptic stratum of the document. However, the early wisdom stratum was not Cynic (29). For critique of this methodology of dividing the hypothetical document Q further into two, three, or four more hypothetical strata, the earliest of which is noneschatological or nonapocalyptic, see Dieter Zeller, "Redaktionsprozesse und wechselnder 'Sitz im Leben' beim Q-Material," in *Logia: The Sayings of Jesus,* ed. J. Delobel, BETL 59 (Louvain: Leuven University Press, 1982), 395–409; Dieter Zeller, "Eine weisheitliche Grundschrift in der Logienquelle?" in *The Four Gospels: Festschrift Frans Neirynck,* ed. F. Van Segbroeck et al. (Louvain: Leuven University Press, 1992), 1.389–402. Werner H. Kelber, "Jesus and Tradition: Words in Time, Words in Space," *Semeia* 65 (1994): 139–67. Arland D. Jacobson, *The First Gospel: An Introduction to Q* (Sonoma, Calif.: Polebridge, 1992), observes that both wisdom and deuteronomic themes can be distinguished in Q, but denies that these can be divided into chronologically different strata.

102. Kristen, *Familie,* 126, 133–34, 150–51, argues that Q1 is antifamily: Q 14:26 means that one cannot be a disciple and have intact family relationships.

103. David Catchpole, "Jesus and the Community of Israel—The Inaugural Discourse in Q," *BJRL* 68 (1986): 296–316.

104. See esp. Barton, *Discipleship,* chap. 3, to which our discussion is indebted.

105. Barton, *Discipleship,* 80, and Raymond E. Brown, *Mary in the New Testament* (Philadelphia: Fortress Press, 1978), 61–64.

106. Barton, *Discipleship* 69, 80–81, 90, 99, 104, and E. S. Malbron, *Narrative Space and Mythic Meaning in Mark* (San Francisco: Harper & Row, 1986).

107. R. Pesch, *Das Markusevangelium,* Herders Theologischer Kommentar zum NT (Freiburg: Herder, 1976–77), 2.128–30, argues that these materials were associated in a pre-Marcan source, an idea opposed by Best, "Mark 10:13–16," 119–34, 209–14. See Kristen, *Familie,* 153–70.

108. Schüssler Fiorenza, *In Memory of Her,* 147, 150. Cf. Kristen, *Familie,* 161.

109. Barton, *Discipleship,* 112. Compare the Q passage discussed above (Matt. 10:35–36//Luke 12:52–53).

110. Mary Ann Tolbert, "Mark," in Newson and Ringe, *Women's Bible Commentary,* 263–74, at p. 263, and Joanna Dewey, "The Gospel of Mark," in Schüssler Fiorenza, *Searching the Scriptures,* 2:470–509. Among other factors, Eumachia's huge edifice and Julia Felix's enormous house in Pompeii are convincing evidence that Roman cities and houses in this same decade had influential women leaders; cf. chap. 1.

111. Corley, *Private Women, Public Meals,* 28–29 (citing an exception: Plutarch, *Banquet of the Seven Sages* 150B, 154B, 155E), 31, 34, 43–44, 53–54, 60–61, 70–71.

112. See Jan Fredrik Kindstrand, *Anacharsis: The Legend and the Apophthegmata* (Uppsala: Almquist & Wiksell, 1981), 44–48; Anne M. McGuire,

"The Epistles of Anacharsis," in *The Cynic Epistles,* ed. Abraham J. Malherbe, SBLSBS 12 (Missoula, Mont.: Scholars Press, 1977), 6–9, 35–51.

113. Plutarch, *Dinner of the Seven Sages* 148B–E, trans. Babbitt in LCL.

114. David E. Aune, "Septem Sapientium Convivium (Moralia 146B–164D)," in *Plutarch's Ethical Writings and Early Christian Literature,* ed. Hans Dieter Betz, Studia ad Corpus Hellenisticum Novi Testamenti 4 (Leiden: E. J. Brill, 1978), 51–105, at p. 98.

115. Juvenal, *Sat.* 6.434–56. Lucian imagines "Dialogues of the Courtesans" (280–325), including one with a lesbian (289–92). Similarly, Athenaeus's book 13 "Concerning Women," the only one with a title, gives dialogues of prostitutes at symposia, for example those of Lamia, Mania, and Gnathaena, collected by the comic poet Machon, "Bright Sayings" (577d–583d), and of Leontion (585def), a source cited by Ronald F. Hock, "Introduction," *The Chreia in Ancient Rhetoric,* vol. 1, *The Progymnasmata,* by R. F. Hock and Edward N. O'Neill, SBLTT 27, Graeco-Roman Religion Series 9 (Atlanta: Scholars Press, 1986), 44.

116. Cf. Corley, *Private Women, Public Meals,* 102, 104, 107, 125, 133, 145–47, 152, 156, 166, 168, 176, 178, 181–84 , and for typical symposium scenes, see J. Ward-Perkins and A. Claridge, *Pompeii A.D. 79: Treasures from the National Archaeological Museum, Naples, with contributions from the Pompeii Antiquarium and the Museum of Fine Arts, Boston* (Boston: Museum of Fine Arts, 1978), 198–99, nos. 244–47. In no. 245 a couple reclines on the left-hand couch, both nude from the waist up.

117. David Rhoads and Donald Michie, *Mark as Story: An Introduction to the Narrative of a Gospel* (Philadelphia: Fortress Press, 1982), 96–100.

118. L. E. Keck, "Ethos and Ethics in the New Testament," in *Essays in Morality and Ethics,* ed. J. Gaffney (New York: Paulist Press, 1980), 29–49, at 38–40, and Wayne A. Meeks, *The Moral World of the First Christians* (Philadelphia: Westminster Press, 1986), 141.

119. Barton, *Discipleship,* 125, 155, with n. 113, 162–63. In this section we are indebted to Barton.

120. Ulrich Luz, *Das Evangelium nach Matthäus (Mt 8—17)* (Zurich: Benziger, 1990), 2. 78–79, 154. Contrast his essay, "The Disciples in the Gospel according to Matthew," with Georg Strecker, "The Concept of History in Matthew," both in *The Interpretation of Matthew,* ed. Graham Stanton (Philadelphia: Fortress Press, 1983), 98–128 and 67–84 respectively.

121. Barton, *Discipleship,* 168.

122. Lucian, *Peregrinus,* 12–13.

123. Barton, *Discipleship,* 13, 69, 176–77, 191, 222.

124. With a parallel in 5:17, "do not think that I have come" is redactional, Matthean.

125. Barton, *Discipleship,* 177–78, 222, and Carter, *Households,* 208–13.

126. Carter, *Households,* 17–22, who depends on L. Hartman, "Some Unorthodox Thoughts on the 'Household-Code Form,'" in *The Social World of Formative Christianity and Judaism: Essays in Tribute to Howard Clark Kee,* ed. J.

Neusner et al. (Philadelphia: Fortress Press, 1988), 219–32. Barton writes that Matthew addresses "discipleship issues of a broadly household-related nature" (*Discipleship,* 96), a better characterization than in Hartman, who names the content of chapters like these a "household code" or in Carter, who identifies them with Greco-Roman treatises on "household management." All Greco-Roman "household codes" and treatises "on household management" emphasize the subordination of some social groups to others, which Matthew 19—20 does not, so the latter does not belong to the genre.

127. Carter's use of Turner is inspired by Dennis Duling, "Matthew and Marginality," in *SBL 1993 Seminar Papers* (Atlanta: Scholars Press, 1993), 642–71. The Matthean narrative constructs permanent liminality for these Syrian churches, but historically, the early–second-century bishop Ignatius attempted to return these churches to an emphasis on Roman hierarchical values.

128. Ceslas Sqicq, "isos," *Theological Lexicon of the New Testament* (Peabody, Mass.: Hendrickson, 1994), 2.223–32, at pp. 228–29.

129. Carter, *Households,* 213.

130. Ibid., 206, citing Victor Turner, *The Ritual Process* (Ithaca, N.Y.: Cornell University Press, 1969, 1977), 112, 133.

131. Wainwright, *Towards a Feminist Critical Reading of the Gospel according to Matthew,* 339–52. Wainwright, "The Gospel of Matthew," in Schüssler Fiorenza, *Searching the Scriptures* 2:635–77, at p. 644 recommends Crosby, *House of Disciples,* because he suggests that "the 'house' was the primary metaphor in the Matthean Gospel, the center of the economic, political, religious, and ecclesial life depicted in the narrative." Crosby (pp. 104–6) suggests that *collegia* and *koina* were nonpatriarchal models for the house churches envisioned by Matthew.

132. Dionysius, *Ant. Rom.* 2.25.7.

133. Carter, *Households,* 71; Barton, *Discipleship,* 195.

134. Cf. a contemporary Cynic who writes "equal rights laws for children" (pseudo-Heraclitus 9.1) in *Cynic Epistles,* ed. J. Abraham Malherbe, SBLSBS 12 (Missoula, Mont.: Scholars Press, 1977), 210. Cf. H. W. Attridge, *First-Century Cynicism in the Epistles of Heraclitus,* HTS 29 (Missoula, Mont.: Scholars Press, 1976), 83, who translates: "you are writing laws granting equal civic rights to freedmen and equal social status to their offspring."

135. Müller, *In der Mitte der Gemeinde,* 77.

136. Philo, *Therapeutae* 13: "they abandon their property."

137. See Josephus, *Jewish War* 2.122.

138. Frags. 10.6 and 11, describing some Egyptian priests; Van der Horst, *Chaeremon,* 16–17, 22–23.

139. Epictetus, *Diss.* 3.22.37, 67–76, 81; pseud.-Diogenes 38.5; 47 and pseudo-Socrates 6.5–9 in Malherbe, *Cynic Epistles,* 162, 178, 234–37.

140. Cf. Crosby, *House of Disciples,* 263.

141. E.g., 9:10; cf. the function of houses in Seneca, *Ep.* 21.6; Tacitus, *Dial.* 6; Cicero, *Att.* 1.16, 18; 2.22, references cited by Carter, *Households,* 136n4.

142. The parable refers to *ergatoi* ("workers"), not *douloi* ("slaves"). Beavis, "Ancient Slavery," 37–54, at p. 37, includes it among slave parables. Carter overlooks the earlier debate about the unity of this section cited in n. 107 above and in Crosby, *House of Disciples,* 119–25, 263. On "workers," see Matt. 9:37//Luke 10:2, 7b; again, workers/slaves are models for church leaders, missionaries. Kristen, *Familie,* 20, 77, 99–103, 126, 154.

143. Carter, *Households,* 172.

144. Cf. Carter, *Households,* 191, who contrasts Matthew with Ephesians.

145. Cf. J. Ramsey Michaels, *1 Peter,* Word Biblical Commentary 49 (Waco, Tex.: Word, 1988), 135, 141.

146. Wainwright, "Gospel of Matthew," 2:642, and idem, *Towards a Feminist Critical Reading of the Gospel according to Matthew,* esp. 325–52, where she discusses women in Matthean house churches. But see Corley, *Private Women, Public Meals,* 147–52, 157, 166, 184.

147. Amy-Jill Levine, "Matthew," in Newsom and Ringe, *Women's Bible Commentary,* 253.

148. Levine (ibid., p. 256) chooses the former (noting the parallels in 4:11; 25:44); both Wainwright (pp. 648–49) and Corley (pp. 170–76, with persuasive arguments interpreting 8:15, 25:44, and 27:55) choose the latter.

149. Schottroff, *Lydia's Impatient Sisters,* 79–90.

150. Corley, *Private Women, Public Meals,* 166.

151. Ibid., 159–60.

152. John S. Kloppenborg, *Q Parallels: Synopsis, Critical Notes, and Concordance* (Sonoma, Calif.: Polebridge, 1988), 168–71, includes "wife" in Q's list, but Dieter Zeller, *Kommentar zur Logienquelle,* Stuttgarter Kleiner Kommentar, NT 21 (Stuttgart: Katholisches Bibelwerk, 1984), 50, 74, 85–88, omits "wife." Kristen, *Familie,* 125–27 is ambivalent.

153. See Braun, *Feasting.*

154. Seim, *Double Message,* 113–16, 200–7, 252, 256–57.

155. Ibid., 71, 198, 116–18, 185, 220, 237–39, 247–48, 259.

156. Turid Karlsen Seim, "The Gospel of Luke," in Schüssler Fiorenza, *Searching the Scriptures,* 2:728–62, at p. 755, and her *Double Message,* 185–248.

157. Seim, *Double Message,* 128, 131.

158. For the following see Seim, *Double Message* 95, 229–47, 258.

159. On the widow of Nain and the importunate widow in Luke's special material, see Gerd Petzke, *Das Sondergut des Evangeliums nach Lukas,* Zürcher Werkkommentare zur Bibel (Zurich: Theologischer Verlag, 1990), 90–102, 158–61, 230, 246, 253–54.

160. Richter Reimer, *Women in the Acts of the Apostles,* 31–69.

161. This is not the point of the parable, but her action would be realistic for Luke's audience.

162. Pöhlmann, *Der verlorene Sohn und das Haus.* Cf. also Wendy J. Cotter, "Children Sitting in the Agora: Q (Luke) 7:31–35," *Forum* 5, no. 2 (1989): 63–82.

163. See above, chap. 3, n. 108.

164. Seim, *Double Message,* 14–15, lists seven, or expanding the definition, ten pairs plus thirteen man-woman parallels in Luke-Acts.

165. Heinz Schürmann, *Das Lukasevangelium: Kommentar zu Kap. 1,1–9,50,* 4th ed. (Freiburg: Herder, 1990), 448, suggests that 8:2–3 forms the general conclusion to a Palestinian source of stories about women which included 7:11–17 and 7:36–50, a fascinating hypothesis; but 8:1–3 is rather Lukan redaction. On these verses, see Robert J. Karris, "Women and Discipleship in Luke," *CBQ* 56, no. 1 (1994): 5–10.

166. Seim, *Double Message,* 80.

167. Elisabeth Schüssler Fiorenza, "Biblische Grundlegung," in *Feministische Theologie: Perspektiven zur Orientierung,* ed. M. Kassel (Stuttgart: Kreuz 1988), 13–44.

168. Cf. 4:39; 10:40; 12:37; 17:8; 22:26–27; Acts 6:1, cited by Seim, *Double Message,* 58–62, 72, 74, 81, 83, 85, 99–100, 108–12, 252. Cf. Collins, *Diakonia,* 245, who concludes that "in the gospels [in contrast to Paul and Acts], the words under discussion mainly designate menial attendance." Collins's great book is weakest on the Gospels, which need further study.

169. Seim, *Double Message,* 97–108; Corley, *Private Women, Public Meals,* 133–44.

170. Cf. Plutarch's story cited n. 113 above.

171. Seim, *Double Message,* 79, 81, 88.

172. See Braun, *Feasting,* 27–28.

173. Seim, *Double Message,* 147–63, esp. 150, 154.

174. The final sentence in Seim's insightful book.

175. The relationship between Jesus and the beloved disciple is normative for all other disciple relationships in John, and may mirror the Greco-Roman fixation of teachers on favorites: see Sjef van Tilborg, *Imaginative Love in John,* Biblical Interpretation Series 2 (Leiden: E. J. Brill, 1993), with cautions raised by Mark Kiley (*CBQ* 57 [1995]: 196–97).

176. John does not seem to know a tradition of virginal conception, though 6:42 is meant ironically to contrast the opponents' assurance of their knowledge of Jesus' origins with his true heavenly origins of which they are ignorant. Luke's two references to Jesus as son of Joseph (Luke 3:23; 4:22) are both tongue in cheek, following the account of virginal conception in chap. 1. Cf. Ernst Haenchen, *A Commentary on the Gospel of John,* Hermeneia (Philadelphia: Fortress Press, 1984), 1.292; Raymond E. Brown, *The Gospel according to John,* Anchor Bible 29 (New York: Doubleday, 1966), 1.82–83; 270–71.

177. John 6:35–40, 50–51; 4:10–14; cf. Sirach 24:19–22, 30–34. For a full study of the wisdom theme in John, see Martin Scott, *Sophia and the Johannine Jesus,* JSNTSup 71 (Sheffield: Sheffield Academic Press, 1992).

178. It is unlikely from the context that Jesus' directive to Mary Magdalene to tell "my brothers" is intended only for Jesus' family, though this could be the case.

179. Raymond E. Brown, "Roles of Women in the Fourth Gospel," in *The Community of the Beloved Disciple* (New York: Paulist Press, 1979),

183–98; Sandra M. Schneiders, "Women in the Fourth Gospel and the Role of Women in the Contemporary Church," *Biblical Theology Bulletin* 12 (1982): 35–40; Gail R. O'Day, "John," in Newsom and Ringe, *Women's Bible Commentary*, 293–304; Adele Reinhartz, "The Gospel of John," in Schüssler Fiorenza, *Searching the Scriptures* 2:561–600 [572–73, 592–93].

180. Rev. 2:20–23. The frequent translation of *kline* in v. 22 as "sickbed" (RSV) and related terms is not justified by anything in the text. On the contrary, the association with adultery in the same verse suggests a sexual context, and the Greek term is strongly associated with both dining and sexual activity. Cf. Tina Pippin, *Death and Desire: The Rhetoric of Gender in the Apocalypse of John,* Literary Currents in Biblical Interpretation (Louisville, Ky.: Westminster/John Knox Press, 1992).

181. Polycarp, *Philippians* 4.2–3.

182. *1 Clement* 1.3.

183. *2 Clement* 12.2–6; related sayings in Clement of Alexandria, *Miscellanies* 3.13 (92–93) as from the *Gospel of the Egyptians; Gospel of Thomas* 22; *Gospel of Peter* 38; *Gospel of Phillip* 140. See discussion in *New Testament Apocrypha*, rev. ed., ed. Wilhelm Schneemelcher (Louisville, Ky.: Westminster/John Knox Press, 1991), 1:212–13.

184. *Gospel of Thomas* 37.

185. The authenticity of the scene is often cast in doubt because of the many literary connotations of a beautiful woman being spied on in her bath. One author has compiled a list from Graeco-Roman literature of nine scenes in which a mortal man surprises a bathing goddess, eighteen references to washing of goddess statues and pictures, nine erotic scenes connected with bathing, and three biblical scenes with similar themes (Martin Leutzsch, *Die Wahrnehmung sozialer Wirklichkeit im 'Hirten des Hermas'* [Göttingen: Vandenhoeck & Ruprecht, 1989], 31–39).

186. *Visions* 1.1–2.

187. *Visions* 2.2.3; 2.3.1.

188. *Visions* 1.2; 3.2–3,10–13.

189. *Visions* 1.4.3. See Steve Young, "Being a Man: The Pursuit of Manliness in *The Shepherd of Hermas*," *Journal of Early Christian Studies* 2:3 (1994): 237–55.

190. *Visions* 3.12.2.

191. *Visions* 3.8.4. She is girt (as an athlete) and *andrizomene*. Kirsopp Lake's translation, "looks like a man," (*Apostolic Fathers*, LCL [Cambridge, Mass.: Harvard University Press, 1955], 2.47) should more accurately be rendered "acts like a man."

192. *Similitude* 9.2.5. The language of *andreia* is also used once of the Son of God (*Similitude* 5.6.6).

193. *Similitude* 9.11.; 10.3.

194. It has been suggested that in the developing Christian tradition, Peter's family became exemplary disciples to counteract the family divisiveness of the Synoptic tradition. Peter's paralyzed virgin daughter in the *Acts of Peter* remains paralyzed for the good of her soul, and his wife is portrayed as

exemplary martyr with Peter cheering her on (Clement, *Miscellanies* 7.11.63–64; also quoted in Eusebius, *Ecclesiastical History* 3.30.2): Pheme Perkins, *Peter: Apostle for the Whole Church* (Columbia: University of South Carolina Press, 1994), 42–43, 144.

195. E.g., *2 Clement* 14 on female imagery for church, probably based on Ephesians 5; *Didache* 4.9–11 on children and slaves; Ignatius, *Trall.* 2–3 on submission to the bishop; Ignatius, *Pol.* 5 and Polycarp, *Phil.* 4.2 on the relationship of husband and wife; *Barn.* 19.7 on slaves; *Herm. Mandate* 4 on marriage.

196. *Herm. Mandate* 4.1,4.

197. *Diognetus* 5.6–7.

198. *Acts of Perpetua and Felicitas* 2. Quite mysteriously, there is no mention of her husband in the text, though he must be alive, or she would be called a widow.

199. Athenagorus, *Plea for Christians* 33.1–2, 4.

200. Justin, *Apology* 1.15, 29. It has been argued that Justin does not forbid a second marriage, but forbids bigamy, because he has just quoted with approval Matt. 5:32, which forbids marriage to a divorcée. But bigamy was also forbidden by Greek and Roman law, so it is unlikely that he was making this a special point. See *Writings of Saint Justin Martyr,* trans. Thomas B. Falls, Fathers of the Church (New York: Christian Heritage, 1948), 48n5.

201. Minucius Felix, *Octavius* 31.5.

202. *Herm. Mandate* 4.4.

203. Clement, *Miscellanies* 3.15.96. See Jean-Paul Broudéhoux, *Mariage et famille chez Clément d'Alexandrie,* Théologie Historique 2 (Paris: Beauchesne, 1970).

204. Clement, *Miscellanies* 3.12.82, 88, 90; cf. Justin, *Apology* 1.15.

205. Clement, *Miscellanies* 3.12.79, 88.

206. Ibid., 2.23.137–141; 3.6.53; 7.70. Deming, *Paul on Marriage,* 101–4, situates Clement's arguments within the Stoic-Cynic debate on the same question, the Cynics more often responding in the negative for ascetic and philosophical reasons, the Stoics more often positively, with the conviction that the duties and intimacies of marriage can successfully be combined with the pursuit of philosophy.

207. Clement, *Miscellanies* 3.7.57.

208. Clement, *Pedagogue* 2.10.83.

209. Ibid., 2.92.

210. Clement, *Miscellanies* 3.10.68.

211. Ibid., *Miscellanies* 3.6.53.

212. Brown, *Body and Society,* 137–38. Brown suggests more: that Clement may have represented the upper-status lay population of his church over against lower-status persons who could rise in ecclesiastical status through celibacy.

213. Clement, *Miscellanies* 3.1–3, 26; idem, *Excerpt from Theodotus* 67.2–3.

214. Michael A. Williams, "Gnostic Kinship Imagery and Social Reality," paper presented at the Social History of Early Christianity Group, Soci-

ety of Biblical Literature, 1988; material in revised form in chap. 7 of *Rethinking Gnosticism* (Princeton, N.J.: Princeton University Press, 1996).

215. See above, chap. 3, n. 73.

216. Tertullian, *To His Wife* 1.2, 3; cf. idem, *Exhortation to Chastity* 5–6. Some of these texts are conveniently collected in David G. Hunter, ed., *Marriage in the Early Church,* Sources of Christian Thought (Minneapolis: Augsburg, 1992).

217. 1 Tim. 3:2, 12; 5:14.

218. Tertullian, *Exhortation to Chastity* 1.

219. See above, Roman family religion, pp. 82–87.

220. Tertullian, *To His Wife* 2.4, 6.

221. Hippolytus, *Refutation of All Heresies* 9.7.

222. This ascetic virginity or celibacy is to be distinguished from the tradition of clerical celibacy, which was developing more slowly and along different lines; see Roger Gryson, *Les origines du célibat ecclésiastique du premier au septième siècle,* Recherches et synthèses de sciences religieuses, section d'histoire 2 (Gembloux: Duclos, 1970).

223. For instance, *1 Clement* 30.3; 35.2; 62.2; *2 Clement* 15.1; *Barnabas* 2.2; Polycarp, *Phil.* 11.1; 12.2; also *hagneia* (innocence) in 5.2 (but 4.2 uses *enkrateia* of married women); *Hermas Mandate* 1; 6.1.1 and *Hermas Similitude* 9.15.2 (though Hermas also uses *enkrateia* in its general sense, e.g., *Mandate* 8, and he is called *ho enkrateis,* the self-controlled one, though he is married, *Vis.* 1.2); later, however, he is told to cease sexual relations with his wife ("she will henceforth be to you as a sister," *Vis.* 2.2.3; cf. 2.3.1) because of his prophetic task.

224. E.g., Justin, *Apology* 1.15, 29; Minucius Felix, *Octavius* 31.5.

225. Ignatius, *Smyrnaeans* 13.1. This peculiar title seems to indicate that "widows" could be a generic term for groups of celibate women. The comment may be illumined by Tertullian's objection that he knows of a twenty-year-old virgin who was enrolled in the order of widows (*On the Veiling of Virgins* 9). These two texts should warn us that not every mention of widows as a group in early Christian texts need be literal.

226. Justin, *Apology* 1.15, 29.

227. Minucius Felix, *Octavius* 31.5.

228. Cyprian, *On the Dress of Virgins* 22–23.

229. Esp. Jerome, *Epistle* 22 to Eustochium; Virginia Burrus, *Chastity as Autonomy: Women in the Stories of the Apocryphal Acts* (Lewiston, N.Y.: Edwin Mellen Press, 1987). In general, Brown, *Body and Society;* Elizabeth A. Clark, *Ascetic Piety and Women's Faith* (Lewiston, N.Y.: Edwin Mellen Press, 1986); Richard Horsley, "Spiritual Marriage with Sophia," *Vigiliae Christianae* 33 (1979): 30–54; Jo Ann McNamara, "Sexual Equality and the Cult of Virginity in Early Christian Thought," *Feminist Studies* 3.3–4 (1976): 146–58; Rosemary Rader, *Breaking Boundaries: Male/Female Friendship in Early Christian Communities* (New York: Paulist Press, 1983).

230. Cyprian, *On the Dress of Virgins* 2–4, 6–7, 15–19, 22.

231. Tertullian, *Exhortation to Chastity* 1; Cyprian, *On the Dress of Virgins* 21; cf. Athanasius, *Letter* 48.2; Ambrose, *On Virginity* 1.60; Jerome, *Letters* 22.15; 48.3; 66.2; 120.19; Jerome, *Against Jovinian* 1.3; Augustine, *On Holy Virginity* 45.

232. For example, the early–fifth-century monastic historian Palladius speaks not only of heroic monastic men, but of *gynaikōn andreiōn* (masculine women) who were granted by God trials equal to those of men, so that no one could claim women could not practice heroic virtue (*Lausiac History* 41.1). See Elizabeth A. Clark, "Ideology, History, and the Construction of 'Woman' in Late Ancient Christianity," *Journal of Early Christian Studies* 2, no. 2 (1994): 154–84; Kerstin Aspegren, *The Male Woman: A Feminine Ideal in the Early Church*, Uppsala Women's Studies, Women in Religion 4, ed. René Kieffer (Uppsala: Almqvist & Wiksell, 1990).

233. The most famous is *Gospel of Thomas* 114: When Simon Peter declares that Mary (Magdalen) should leave their company because women cannot inherit divine life, Jesus declares that he will lead her and make her male, "for every female who makes herself male will enter the kingdom of heaven."

234. E.g., Hippolytus, *Refutation of All Heresies* 8.13; Epiphanius, *Panarion* 2–3.

235. Alfred C. Rush, "Death as Spiritual Marriage: Individual and Ecclesial Eschatology," *Vigiliae Christianae* 26, no. 2 (1972): 81–101. The *Symposium* of the late–third-century Methodius of Olympus, a sustained dinner conversation among a group of consecrated virgins, is full of bridal imagery and provides a good example of the kind of spirituality already being developed.

236. Bibliography includes H. Achelis, *Virginae subintroductae: Ein Beitrag zum VII Kapitel des 1 Kor.* (Leipzig, 1902); Pierre de Labriolle, "Le Mariage spirituel dans l'antiquité chrétienne," *Revue Historique* 46 (1921): 204–25; Henry Chadwick, "All Things to All Men," *New Testament Studies* 1 (1955): 261–75; Elizabeth A. Clark, "John Chrysostom and the Subintroductae," *Church History* 36, no. 2 (1977): 171–85 (also in Clark, *Ascetic Piety and Women's Faith*).

237. *Hermas Vis.* 2.2.3. She is later referred to as his "sister" (*Vis.* 2.3.1).

238. Tertullian, *Exhortation to Chastity* 12.2; idem, *On Monogamy* 16.3.

239. Jerome, *Epistle* 22.14; for further references, see Clark, "John Chrysostom and the Subintroductae."

Notes to Chapter 6. Education and Learning

1. See Yarbrough, "Parents and Children," 126–41.

2. Related to his view that Paul and the Corinthians are discussing exclusively Cynic-Stoic views of marriage, Will Deming, *Paul on Marriage and Celibacy*, 188 with n. 314, 216, must argue that Paul purposely avoids mentioning childbearing, although vv. 4, 14, and 34 show it was a concern for the Corinthians. Contrast Yarbrough, "Parents and Children," 130.

3. Yarbrough, "Parents and Children," 132.

4. Ibid., 132, 138.
5. Philo is translated by Colson and Whitaker in LCL, Plutarch by Babbitt in LCL.
6. These two are closely related by Greeven, "Propheten, Lehrer, Vorsteher," 1–43, at p. 2. Boring, *Continuing Voice,* 117–19, cites earlier, contrasting opinions on p. 110. Alexander, "Paul and the Hellenistic Schools," 60–83, at p. 78, n. 34, citing Lucian, *Peregr.* 11. Schlarb, *Die Gesunde Lehre,* 134.
7. Philo, "Preliminary Studies" 113, 132 for prophecy, and 12, 24, 35–36, 114, 112, 113, 122, 127 for teaching.
8. Lucian, *Peregrinus* 11.
9. Plutarch, "How to Study Poetry" 29C for the "seer" and 18AB, 31EF, 32E, 35F, 39A for the teacher.
10. Cf. Testament of Job 46–52, the hymns of Hemera, Kassia, and Amaltheias-keras to God, in *The Testament of Job according to the SV Text,* ed. and trans. Robert A. Kraft, SBLTT 5 (Missoula, Mont.: Scholars Press, 1974), 78–85; Wire, *Corinthian Women Prophets,* whose "selected texts from the Early Empire" include Montanist women (nos. 38–44, 74–75, 78–80, pp. 252–53, 262–65).
11. *Manthano* is usually translated "learn," but it means "experience" in Phil. 4:9; Gal. 3:2; and 1 Cor. 14:31. Greeven, "Propheten, Lehrer, Vorsteher," 10–11.
12. Plutarch, "On Listening to Lectures" 44CDE.
13. Plutarch, "How to Study Poetry" 23A; further cf. 20D, 26B, 41AB, 42A: "In making his examination (*krisin*) of the lecture . . . " And for "testing" (*dokimazo*), see Plutarch, "How to Study Poetry," 18F.
14. Boring, *Continuing Voice,* 99–101.
15. Ibid., 108.
16. 1QpHab 2.2–3, cited by Boring, *Continuing Voice,* 44, 139.
17. Lucian, *Peregrinus* 11, trans. Harmon in LCL.
18. Philo, "Preliminary Studies" 133, trans. Colson and Whitaker in LCL.
19. Plutarch, "How to Read Poetry" 29C. Cf. 1 Cor. 14:24–25 and Mark 6:17–18.
20. See further Boring, *Continuing Voice,* 206–11, 250–52.
21. Ibid., 194–206.
22. Ibid., 221–22.
23. Ibid., 218–19. John Koenig, *Charismata* (1978) 66, 128, 134, notes the giftlike quality of suffering.
24. Boring, "Continuing Voice," 236–42, 254, 258, 261.
25. Ibid., 159–60 on Apollo, Montanus, and the Revelation of John.
26. See Eugene M. Boring, *Sayings of the Risen Jesus: Christian Prophecy in the Synoptic Tradition* (Cambridge: Cambridge University Press, 1982). That Christian prophets played a creative role in the sayings attributed to Jesus and that post-Easter prophets claimed to speak for the risen Lord is disputed. See David Aune, *Prophecy in Early Christianity and the Ancient Mediterranean World* (Grand Rapids: Wm. B. Eerdmans Publishing Co., 1983).
27. K. H. Rengstorf, "didaskō," *TDNT* 2 (1964): 135–65, at p. 158, mistakenly describes teachers as "non-pneumatics."
28. Paul lists teaching before leading (1 Cor. 12:28), which was to change.

29. Cf. Balch, "The Canon," 183–205. After the invention of the printing press, human beings began general silent reading, but Plutarch gave both his tractates on education titles involving "hearing." The English translation is "How the young man should study poetry," but the Greek is, "How the young must hear (*akouein*) poetry." When they read a text, they typically heard it, since they read it aloud. The second tractate is "On listening to lectures," but in Greek simply, "On hearing." See also Paul Achtemeier, "OMNE VERBUM SONAT: The New Testament and the Oral Environment of Late Western Antiquity," *JBL* 109 (1990): 3–27. M. Slusser, "Reading Silently in Antiquity," *JBL* 111, no. 3 (1992): 499. F. D. Gilliard, "More Silent Reading in Antiquity: NON OMNE VERBUM SONABAT," *JBL* 112, no. 4 (1993): 689–96.
30. Schrage, "Lehre," 234.
31. Greeven, "Propheten, Lehrer, Vorsteher," 19.
32. Ibid., 20, and Schrage, "Lehre," 236.
33. Schlarb, *Gesunde Lehre,* 136.
34. Rengstorf, "didaskō," 141n33: "teach" is used absolutely in the Gospels, as a technical term without an object, so this text is exceptional.
35. Greeven, "Propheten, Lehrer, Vorsteher," 25.
36. Schrage, "Lehre," 243, 245. Schlarb, *Gesunde Lehre,* 134–37.
37. Schlarb, *Gesunde Lehre,* 135.
38. See Paul Blomenkamp, "Erziehung," *RAC* 6 (1966): 502–59. Horst-Theodor Johann, ed., *Erziehung und Bildung in der heidnischen und christlichen Antike,* WdF 377 (Darmstadt: Wissenschaftliche Buchgesellschaft, 1976). Alexander, "Schools, Hellenistic," 1005–11, and her "Paul and the Hellenistic Schools," 60–83. John T. Townsend, "Education, Greco-Roman Period," *Anchor Bible Dictionary* 2 (1992): 312–17.
39. Philo, "Preliminary Studies" 48–49; cf. 57, 105, 133.
40. Plutarch, "How to Study Poetry" 28D.
41. Plutarch, "On Listening to Lectures" 41AB.
42. Philo, "Preliminary Studies" 107, 175–76.
43. Plutarch, "How to Study Poetry" 28D, 33D, 35D, 46D.
44. Philo, "Preliminary Studies" 57; cf. 6, 160, 171.
45. Schrage, "Lehre," 247.
46. Schlarb, *Gesunde Lehre,* 139.
47. Ibid., 327n47. The following sketch depends on pp. 344–47. See also Yann Redalié, *Paul aprés Paul: Le temps, le salut, le morale selon les épitres a Timothé et a Tite,* Le Monde de la Bible 31 (Geneva: Labor et Fides, 1994).
48. "Acts of Paul and Thecla," in *New Testament Apocrypha,* ed. Edgar Hennecke and Wilhelm Schneemelcher (Philadelphia: Westminster Press, 1964), 2.322–90, e.g., 3.5 (p. 354), 3.11–12 (p. 356), 3.26 (p. 360), 3.34 (p. 362), 3.41 (p. 364).
49. Plutarch, "On Listening to Lectures" 48D.
50. *Didache* 2.2; 5.2; par. *Barnabas* 20.1–2; 19.5; Justin, *Apology* 1.27, 29; also *Letter to Diognetus* 5.6; Minucius Felix, *Octavius* 30.2; Athenagoras, *Plea for Christians* 35.6; Tertullian, *Apology* 7.1; 9.6–8; idem, *Against the Nations* 1.15; *Apocalypse of Peter* 26; Clement of Alexandria, *Pedagogue* 2.96.1.

Among Jewish writers: Philo, *On the Special Laws* 3.108–15; idem, *On the Virtues* 131–32; Josephus, *Against Apion* 2.202; Pseudo-Phocylides 184–85. Justin advances a rather bizarre reason: Most abandoned children are raised as slaves for prostitution; a father who abandons a child might therefore, years later, commit incest unknowingly! Clement of Alexandria repeats the same idea when arguing the downside of promiscuity, not of abandonment of babies (*Pedagogue* 3.3.21). Justin's second reason strikes us as more sane: some abandoned children are not adopted, but die; then a Christian would be guilty of murder.

51. Ross S. Kraemer, "Jewish Mothers and Daughters in the Greco-Roman World" in Cohen, *Jewish Family in Antiquity*, 108n51, cites one exception in a Jewish tax register from Arsinoe in Egypt, 73 C.E. (*Corpus Papyrorum Judaicarum* 421).

52. *Presbyterous,* which could mean "presbyters," but that meaning is unlikely in this household context.

53. *1 Clement* 21.6, 8. V 8 is quoted in Clement of Alexandria, *Miscellanies* 4.108.4.

54. *Didache* 4.9 par. *Barnabas* 19.7.

55. *Hermas, Visions* 1.1.1; 1.9; 1.3.1–2; 2.2.2–3; 2.3.1; 3.1.6; *Hermas, Mandate* 2.7; 12.3.6; *Hermas, Similitude* 5.3.9; 7.6. Because these family references are ubiquitous in the text, Martin Dibelius and others have argued that they do not refer to a real family but are a literary fiction for a church of which Hermas is the leader (Dibelius, *Der Hirt des Hermas*, De Apostolischen Väter 4 [Tübingen: Mohr (Siebeck), 1923], 445–46). A more balanced position is that there is a real family with problems, but that their situation echoes that of the church, and at some points merges into it.

56. E.g., *Hermas, Visions* 1.1.8; 3.9.4–6; *Hermas, Mandate* 10.1.4; *Hermas, Similitude* 4.5; 8.9.1. Cf. Osiek, *Rich and Poor,* esp. pp. 39–57.

57. Clement of Alexandria, *Pedagogue* 1.21.2. See Broudéhoux, *Mariage et Famille,* 157–66.

58. Clement of Alexandria, *Pedagogue* 1.75.1, partially quoting Sirach 7:23–24.

59. Ibid., 8.70.

60. This is not to say that no one else questioned these practices in antiquity: see, e.g., Cicero, *Pro Cluentio* 2.32; Ovid, *Amores* 2.13–14; Juvenal, *Satires* 6.592–600.

61. Emiel Eyben, "Roman Notes on the Course of Life," *Ancient Society* 4 (1973): 213–38; Moses I. Finley, "The Elderly in Classical Antiquity," *Greece and Rome* 28 (1981): 156–71.

62. *Hermas, Similitude* 1.8; *Hermas, Visions* 3.9.2–6; *Hermas, Mandate* 2.4; 8.10; Osiek, *Rich and Poor,* passim.

63. Countryman, *The Rich Christian in the Church of the Early Empire;* Bobertz, "The Role of Patron in the *Cena Dominica* of Hippolytus' Apostolic Tradition," 170–84.

64. R. A. Campbell, "*Kai malista oikeion*—A New Look at 1 Timothy 5:8," *NTS* 41 (1995): 157–60, argues that v. 8 refers not only to one's own relatives in general, but especially to one's *Christian* relatives.

65. Justin, *Apology* 1.67; Tertullian, *Apology* 39.5–6.

66. Letter of Bishop Cornelius of Rome to Fabius of Antioch, quoted in Eusebius, *Ecclesiastical History* 6.43.11.
67. Texts in Thesleff, *Pythagorean Texts;* Discussion in Pomeroy, *Goddesses, Whores, Wives, and Slaves,* 133–36, 242.
68. Balch, "Neopythagorean Moralists," 398, 401. Theano was the name of Pythagoras's wife or daughter, but this is probably a pseudonym.
69. Ibid., 399. The name of Plato's mother: either this is another pseudonym, or another woman by the same name.
70. Cf. Clement of Alexandria, *Pedagogue* 2.104–27 passim; see Balch, "Neophythagorean Moralists," 399–401; Cynthia L. Thompson, "Women's 'Cosmetics': The Social Power of Clichés," paper presented to Society of Biblical Literature Annual Meeting, Women in the Biblical World Section, 1988; idem, "Hairstyles, Head-Coverings, and St. Paul," 99–115.
71. Stobaeus, *Anthologium* 4.28.10, quoted in Pomeroy, *Goddesses, Whores, Wives, and Slaves,* 136, from Thesleff, *Pythagorean Texts,* 145.
72. If 2 Timothy is from the same author, the normative tradition is ascribed also to the women of Timothy's family in the person of grandmother Lois and mother Eunice (2 Tim. 1:5).
73. A contemporary study is Lila Abu-Lughod, *Veiled Sentiments: Honor and Poetry in a Bedouin Society* (Berkeley: University of California Press, 1986).
74. The overall portrait of the opponents in the Pastorals includes asceticism regarding food and sex and a spiritualized idea of resurrection. Some kind of gnostic or proto-gnostic group is usually suspected, though the doctrinally orthodox profile of the *Acts of Paul and Thecla* would also fit. For discussion, see Martin Dibelius and Hans Conzelmann, *The Pastoral Epistles,* Hermeneia (Philadelphia: Fortress Press, 1972), 64–67; MacDonald, *The Legend and the Apostle,* 54–77.
75. MacDonald, *The Legend and the Apostle,* 78–96.
76. This is undoubtedly a reference to the Clement who is by tradition responsible for what is known as the *First Letter of Clement,* a treatise addressed to the church of Corinth in the midst of a leadership crisis, probably in the late first century. Whether the reference in *Hermas* is authentic or literary is more debatable, and depends on the dating assigned to both documents.
77. Clement, *Miscellanies* 3.6.52; Vitruvius, *De architectura* 6.7; see discussion above, pp. 8–10, 27, 34.
78. Cyprian, *On the Dress of Virgins* 24.
79. On the ordained deaconesses of the early church, see J. G. Davies, "Deacons, Deaconesses and the Minor Orders in the Patristic Period," *JEH* 14 (1963): 1–15; Peter Hünermann, "Conclusions Regarding the Female Diaconate," *Theological Studies* 36, no. 2 (June 1975): 325–33; Roger Gryson, *The Ministry of Women in the Early Church* (Collegeville, Minn.: Liturgical Press, 1976); Lucy Blyskal, "The Question of Ordaining Deaconesses in the Church," *New Theology Review* 8, no. 2 (1995): 59–69. The authoritative study is Aimé Georges Martimort, *Deaconesses: An Historical Study* (San Francisco: St. Ignatius, 1986).
80. *Didascalia* 16.3 in Connolly edition (R. H. Connolly, *Didascalia Apostolorum* [Oxford: Clarendon Press, 1929]); 3.12.1–4 with parallels in the

fourth-century *Apostolic Constitutions* (*Didascalia et Constitutiones Apostolorum*, ed. F. X. Funk [Paderborn: Schoeningh, 1905]), 208–11.

81. *Apostolic Constitutions* 2.26.6 (Funk, *Didascalia*, 105). The disciplinary regulation is cast, as are the surrounding ones, in trinitarian images: just as no one can believe in Christ except through the Holy Spirit, so no woman should approach a deacon, who is a type of Christ, except accompanied by a deaconess, who is a type of the Holy Spirit!

82. "The Life of St. Pelagia the Harlot," in *The Desert Fathers*, ed. Helen Waddell (Ann Arbor: University of Michigan Press, 1960), 177–88 [182–86]). Also available in Kraemer, *Maenads, Martyrs*, 316–24. Pelagia goes off to become the saintly monk Pelagius, and, as is typical in these stories of ascetic women, is discovered to be a woman only after her death.

83. *Testamentum Domini* 1.40. Text in Syriac and modern Latin translation: *Testamentum Domini Nostri Jesu Christi*, ed. Ignatius E. Rahmani (Hildesheim: Georg Olms, 1968); English translation, Grant Sperry White, *The Testamentum Domini: A Text for Students* (Bramcote, Nottingham: Grove, 1991). Discussion in Gryson, *Ministry of Women*, 64–69. The widows of the *Testamentum Domini* preside to the left of the bishop at eucharistic celebrations and are clearly among the higher clergy. For a further study on widows in the earlier centuries, see Bonnie B. Thurston, *The Widows: A Women's Ministry in the Early Church* (Minneapolis: Fortress Press, 1989).

84. Egeria 23.2–3: John Wilkinson, *Egeria's Travels to the Holy Land*, rev. ed. (Jerusalem: Ariel; Warminster, England: Aris and Phillips, 1981), 121–22.

85. Jerome, *Letter* 127.5, 8, to Principia.

86. Jerome, *Letter* 108.20, to Eustochium.

87. John Chrysostom, *Life of Olympias*, 10, 12.

88. Available in translation in Kraemer, *Maenads, Martyrs*, 280–88; Wilhelm Schneemelcher, ed., *New Testament Apocrypha* (Louisville, Ky.: Westminster/John Knox Press, 1992), 2.239–46.

89. For instance, Steven Davies, *Revolt of the Widows: The Social World of the Apocryphal Acts* (Carbondale, Southern Illinois University Press, 1980); MacDonald, *Legend and the Apostle*, 34–40.

Notes to Chapter 7. Slaves

1. M. I. Finley, *Ancient Slavery and Modern Ideology* (New York: Viking Press, 1980), 17 (his emphasis and masculine pronouns), quoted by Harrill, *Manumission of Slaves in Early Christianity*, 92.

2. D. J. Kyrtatas, "Christianity and the familia Caesaris," in *The Social Structure of the Early Christian Communities* (New York: Verso, 1987), 75–86, and Martin, *Slavery as Salvation*, 1–49.

3. Weiser, *Knechtsgleichnisse*, 22–25.

4. Brian J. Dodd, "Christ's Slave, People Pleasers and Galatians 1.10," *NTS* 42, no. 1 (1996): 90–104.

5. On the pseudonymity of Colossians, the most contested of these epistles, see Petr Pokorny, *Colossians: A Commentary* (Peabody, Mass.: Hendrickson, 1991).

6. Winter, "Paul's Letter to Philemon," 1–15, preceded by her "Methodological Observations on a New Interpretation of Paul's Letter to Philemon," 203–12.

7. Harrill, *Manumission of Slaves,* 3.

8. Collins, *Diakonia,* 150–51.

9. Lucian, *Cont.* 1, cited by Collins, *Diakonia,* 91.

10. *Testament of Abraham* 9.24, cited by Collins, *Diakonia,* 99.

11. Ibid., 139–45.

12. Ibid., 222.

13. Lampe, "Keine 'Sklavenflucht' des Onesimus," 135–37, supported by B. M. Rapske, "The Prisoner Paul in the Eyes of Onesimus," *NTS* 37 (1991): 187–203, and Bartchy, "Philemon, Epistle to," 305–10.

14. Justinian, *Digest* 21.1.17.4.

15. Bartchy, "Slavery (Greco-Roman)," 66, 71, following G. Alföldy, "Die Freilassung von Sklaven und die Struktur der Sklaverei in der römischen Kaiserzeit," *Rivista Storica dell' Antichità* 2 (1972): 97–129, who is opposed by T. Wiedemann, "The Regularity of Manumission at Rome," *Classical Quarterly* 35 (1981): 162–75.

16. See Ronald F. Hock, "A Support for His Old Age: Paul's Plea on Behalf of Onesimus," in *The Social World of the First Christians: Essays in Honor of Wayne A. Meeks,* ed. L. Michael White and O. Larry Yarbrough (Minneapolis: Fortress Press, 1995), 67–81, at p. 77.

17. See John T. Fitzgerald, "Philippians, Epistle," *ABD* 5 (1992): 318–26, at pp. 322–23, although Fitzgerald favors Rome.

18. Theissen, *Social Reality,* 164–65, 189, 190–96, compares Phil. 2:7–8, 1 Cor. 7:22–23, Gal. 3:28, and other texts.

19. For a recent interpretation, see Stowers, *Rereading of Romans,* 219–22. Alternatively, Weiser, *Knechtsgleichnisse,* 44, suggests deutero-Isaiah as the source.

20. See the social/psychological description of the experience by Bradley, *Slavery and Society,* 44–49.

21. Compare the Greco-Roman pattern of humiliation and exaltation discussed by Balch, "Rich and Poor, Proud and Humble in Luke-Acts," 214–33.

22. Betz, *Galatians,* 181.

23. Ibid., 189–90. Cf. the denial of this by Bradley, *Slavery and Society,* 145–53. Bradley's criticisms are crucially important, but his critique homogenizes all of early Christianity. Colossians begins the philosophical acculturation of Christianity to Greco-Roman slavery; Augustine (*The City of God* 19.15) justified it, claiming that slavery was God's punishment for Adam's sin. Colossians and Augustine are not identical.

24. For one sketch of assumptions behind this conflict, see Bruce Chilton, *A Feast of Meanings: Eucharistic Theologies from Jesus through Johannine Circles,* SuppNT 72 (Leiden: E. J. Brill, 1994), chaps. 3, 5.

25. For leadership in Pauline communities, see 1 Thess. 5:12 and Margaret Y. MacDonald, *The Pauline Churches: A Socio-historical Study of Institutionalization in the Pauline and Deutero-Pauline Writings,* SNTSMS 60 (Cambridge: Cambridge University Press, 1988).

26. Cf. the discussion by S. Scott Bartchy, *Mallon Chresai* (SBLDS 11; Missoula: Scholars Press, 1973), 23, 26. Harrill, *Manumission of Slaves,* 76.

27. Balch, "Background of 1 Cor. VII," 351–64, argues that these Lukan sayings are closely related to the conflict in 1 Corinthians. This is accepted by S. Scott Bartchy, *1 Corinthians 7:21,* 146–48, modified by Seim, *Double Message,* 180, 189, 215, 226, and rejected by Deming, *Paul on Marriage and Celibacy,* 7, 11, 23, 27, although see 168n244. Cf. also Schlarb, *Die Gesunde Lehre,* 133.

28. Schottroff, *Lydia's Impatient Sisters,* 121–35.

29. Bartchy, *1 Corinthians 7:21,* 134.

30. Luther developed his theology of God's call to a certain social status, although his exegesis of 1 Cor. 7:21 is that Paul encourages slaves to "use freedom." Cf. Harrill, *Manumission of Slaves,* 79–80.

31. Cf. Rom. 2:25–29. This means that Paul "spiritualized" particular commandments like circumcision. E. R. Goodenough, *Introduction to Philo,* 2d ed. (Oxford: Basil Blackwell Publisher, 1962), 79, cites Philo, *Migration of Abraham* 89–90, and relates this method of interpretation to Paul. Paul also stressed "story" more than commandments, *haggadah* more than *halachah;* see James A. Sanders, "Torah and Paul," in *God's Christ and His People: Studies in Honour of Nils Alstrup Dahl,* ed. Jacob Jervell and Wayne A. Meeks (Oslo: Universitetsforlaget, 1977), 132–40, at p. 138, now in James A. Sanders, *From Sacred Story to Sacred Text* (Philadelphia: Fortress Press, 1987), 107–232, at pp. 111, 121.

32. Acts 16:1–3, Paul circumcising Timothy, is not historical.

33. Against Bartchy, *1 Corinthians, 7:21,* 139–43, 151, who concludes that "for Paul religious and social-legal statuses are neither hindrances nor advantages with respect to 'living according to God's calling'" (139–40). Similarly, Deming, *Paul on Marriage and Celibacy,* 158: "undue concern for changing the circumstances of one's life disregards the efficacy of God's call, and thereby represents a form of slavery in itself." Both are repeating an old German Lutheran slogan. Contrast Schottroff, *Lydia's Impatient Sisters,* 121–35.

34. Harrill, *Manumission of Slaves,* 74. Harrill (p. 121) observes that if Paul opposed manumission, not opposed by Roman conservatives such as Cicero, his position would be unparalleled.

35. Strabo, *Geography* 14.1.38, cited by Harrill, *Manumission of Slaves,* 88.

36. Appian, *Bella Civilia* 1.69, cited in Harrill, *Manumission of Slaves,* 89.

37. Plutarch, *Life of Marius* 42.2, cited in Harrill, *Manumission of Slaves,* 89. Quoting Bradley, Harrill also cites Appian, *Bella Civilia* 1.26, 58, and 65.

38. Harrill, *Manumission of Slaves,* 8; cf. 118 and the grammatical analysis at pp. 108–17.

39. Ibid., 118.

40. Ibid., 123. This would be Stoic: see A. Bodson, *La morale sociale des derniers Stoiciens* (Paris: Société d'Edition "Les Belles lettres," 1967), 41–44.

41. Schweizer, "Traditional Ethical Patterns," 379–413.

42. J. Paul Sampley, "Ephesians," in *The Deutero-Pauline Letters: Ephesians, Colossians, 2 Thessalonians, 1–2 Timothy, Titus,* Proclamation Commentaries (Minneapolis: Fortress Press, 1993), 7.

43. Eduard Schweizer, "sōma," *TDNT* 7 (1971): 1024–94, at pp. 1038–39, citing many sources including the Roman Stoic Seneca, *Ep.* 92.30; 95.52, who also says the state is the body of the emperor (Nero): *De Clementia* I.5.1; cf. Plutarch, *Solon* 18; Plutarch, *Pomp.* 51; cf. Philo, *Abr.* 74. But see the subtle suggestions of T. K. Seim, "A Superior Minority? The Problem of Men's Headship in Ephesians 5," in *Mighty Minorities? Minorities in Early Christianity—Positions and Strategies: Essays in Honour of Jacob Jervell on his Seventieth Birthday,* ed. D. Hellholm, H. Moxnes, and T. K. Seim (Oslo: Scandinavian University Press, 1955), 167–81.

44. See chap. 1 above.

45. Cf. David L. Balch, "Hellenization/Acculturation in 1 Peter," in *Perspectives on 1 Peter,* ed. Charles H. Talbert (Macon, Ga.: Mercer University Press, 1986), 79–101, p. 97, citing J. J. Thierry, "Note sur 'TA ELACHISTA TON ZOON' au chapitre XX de la 1a Clementis," *VC* 14 (1960): 235–44, discussing Dio Chrysostom 40.32–41 and 48.16.

46. Schweizer, "Traditional Ethical Patterns," 206, with the following examples. Cf. Bradley, *Slavery and Society,* 146–53.

47. The superscript of this section (1 Clem. 19.1 and 20.1) focuses the ethic on subordination, but strikingly, neither wives nor children are exhorted to be submissive; slaves are not mentioned. All are to be submissive, not one social class to another, so that 1 Clement 20–21 is unlike the deutero-Pauline codes.

48. See Balch, "Household Codes," 46–47.

49. Bradley, *Slavery and Society,* 150.

50. Philo, *Spec. leg.* 2.67–68; 3.137; *Testament of Joseph* 10:1–3; 11:1–2.

51. E.g., in the Neopythagorean Callicratidas 107–9-11 (Thesleff, *Pythagorean Texts*).

52. Weiser, *Knechtsgleichnisse,* 45.

53. Slaves carry on a dialogue with the master of the house in the parable of the tares (Matt. 13:24–30). Some appear in the parable of the wicked tenants (Mark 12:1–11//Matt. 21:33–44//Luke 20:9–18), others in the parable of the great supper (Matt. 22:1–10, 11–13//Luke 14:16–24). Weiser, *Knechtsgleichnisse,* 45. Crossan, *In Parables,* 96–120: "The Servant Parables." Scott, *Hear Then the Parable,* part 3: "Masters and Slaves," esp. 208n10, criticizing Weiser for including only parables that use the word *doulos:* "the actual terms used are irrelevant. It could be king as well as master; a servant, a slave, or steward. What is important is the invocation of the patron-client model." Beavis, "Ancient Slavery," 37.

54. See Beavis, "Ancient Slavery," 48n66, for a master's more typical response.

55. A. N. Sherwin-White, "Galilean Narrative," 136; Weiser, *Knechtsgleichnisse,* 100.

56. Beavis, "Ancient Slavery," 41.

57. Scott, *Hear Then the Parable,* 212–13, argues that this parable is not authentic, for it has nothing distinctive of Jesus' parables. He has overlooked the startling reversal in who serves the meal. Crossan, *In Parables,* 99, concludes that "the basic story, the debris of a parable of Jesus, is still quite visible."

58. Weiser, *Knechtsgleichnisse*, 151.

59. Ibid., 194, points out close parallels to the Ahikar story from the fifth century B.C.E. On vicious punishment of slaves, an object of Roman amusement, see Beavis, "Ancient Slavery," 42–43. Scott, *Hear Then the Parable*, 208–12, argues for the parable's authenticity.

60. Weiser, *Knechtsgleichnisse*, 177.

61. Beavis, "Ancient Slavery," 42, 53–54. Cf. Nelson, *Leadership and Discipleship*, 47–48, 241–42.

62. The parable refers to *ergatoi* ("workers"), not *douloi* ("slaves"); therefore, Weiser omits it. Crossan, Scott, and Beavis include it. Cf. Schürmann, " . . . und Lehrer," 137–38, 140, 152.

63. Cf. Scott, *Hear Then the Parable*, 281–98, at p. 297: "the householder makes all equal (*isoys*). . . . It is not wages or hierarchy that counts but the call to go into the vineyard. . . . The parable's strategy is not unlike Paul's argument that with God there is no distinction, that justification (making right) is through gift (Rom. 3:22–24)." Paradoxically, the parable about slaves concerns leadership.

64. Beavis, "Ancient Slavery," 50, citing Crossan, *In Parables*, 110.

65. Beavis, "Ancient Slavery," 47–48, 51.

66. Weiser, *Knechtsgleichnisse*, 260–61, cites C. H. Dodd and Joachim Jeremias. For Israel and/or Israel's leaders as slaves of God in the Hebrew Bible and early Judaism, see the texts he assembles on pp. 22–25, 30–41. Also K. H. Rengstorf, "Doulos," *TDNT* 2 (1964): 266–69, 273–79. Alternatively, see Martin, *Slavery as Salvation*, chap. 3: "The Enslaved Leader as Rhetorical Topos."

67. Weiser, *Knechtsgleichnisse*, 271.

68. For a very different interpretation of this parable than the usual one, see Richard L. Rohrbaugh, "A Peasant Reading of the Parable of the Talents/Pounds: A Text of Terror?" *BTB* 23 (1993): 32–39.

69. See Nelson, *Leadership and Discipleship*, 149–54, on this verb. He interprets the Lukan text to critique ordinary patterns of ruling, in which the client is confirmed in an inferior position.

70. Cf. Phil. 2:7. Robert W. Funk with Mahlon H. Smith, *The Gospel of Mark: Red Letter Edition* (Sonoma, Calif.: Polebridge, 1991), 148–50, 168, classifies Mark 9:35 and 10:43 as gray. "The sayings in Mark 10:42–44 and their parallels probably vaguely reflect something Jesus might have said: those who aspire to greatness must become servants, and those who want to be 'number one' must become slaves. Yet these sayings are so intimately bound up with the leadership struggles that ensued in the Christian communities that it is impossible to untangle them" (p. 168, note). However, Crossan, *In Parables*, 99, disagrees (cf. n. 57, above).

71. R. Bultmann, *The History of the Synoptic Tradition* (New York: Harper & Row, 1963), 147. Cf. the biblical and rabbinic texts in Weiser.

72. Ibid., 330, 332.

73. Troels Engberg-Pedersen, "Stoicism in Philippians," in *Paul in His Hellenistic Context*, ed. Troels Engberg-Pedersen (Minneapolis: Fortress Press, 1955), 256–90, at pp. 275, 287 (Arius Didymus in H. von Arnim, SVF 2.528).

74. Stowers, *A Rereading of Romans,* 219–22, citing Abraham J. Malherbe, "Antisthenes and Odysseus, and Paul at War," *HTR* 76 (1983): 143–73.

75. Weiser, *Knechtsgleichnisse,* 44. For references to this discussion of deutero-Isaiah, see Collins, *Diakonia,* 52, 54–56, 251.

76. Philo, "Preliminary Studies" 107, 175–76.

77. Plutarch, *Mor.* 28D, 33D, 35D, 46D.

78. Weiser, *Knechtsgleichnisse,* 137–38, considers the core of this parable authentic, although the word "authority" is Markan redaction. Robert W. Funk et al., *The Parables of Jesus: Red Letter Edition, A Report of the Jesus Seminar* (Sonoma, Calif.: Polebridge, 1988), 62, color the "returning master" gray, noting that "it may be a distant echo of a Jesus parable." Scott agrees (cf. n. 57); Crossan's evaluation of its authenticity is more positive (cf. nn. 57 and 70, above); see also chap. 8, n. 63.

79. Beavis, "Ancient Slavery," 53.

80. Compare Bartchy, "Slavery (Greco-Roman)," 68, on Matt. 18:27, 33, where forgiveness removes grounds for enslaving people for debt.

81. Dale B. Martin, "Slavery and the Ancient Jewish Family," in *The Jewish Family in Antiquity,* ed. Cohen (BJS 289; Atlanta: Scholars Press, 1993), 113–29.

82. See discussion above of the terminology of friendship in the clientage system in chapter 1. Much has been written about the Graeco-Roman theme of friendship, and about its applicability to this passage, but few have seen the connection with patron-client terminology. Cf. esp. Wisd. Sol. 7:27.

83. Use of the term *metaphor* for these images in 1 Peter does not imply a stand on whether they refer to the recipients' social and political status as well as theological self-perception: see Elliott, *A Home for the Homeless.* For an opposite view, see Reinhard Feldmeier, *Die Christen als Fremde: Die Metapher der Freunde in der Antiken Welt, im Urchristentum und im 1. Petrusbrief,* WUNT 64 (Tübingen: J.C.B. Mohr [Paul Siebeck], 1992). Whether or not the terminology corresponds to actual social status, it is used in the letter also with theological intent.

84. See Balch, "Household Codes," 33–34; idem, *Let Wives Be Submissive,* 96–97, 125–27.

85. Cf. Harrill, "Ignatius, *Ad Polycarp.* 4.3," 107–42; idem, *Manumission of Slaves.*

86. The use of community funds for the ransom of captives was an established custom that originally in Israelite context meant ransom from enslavement, but continued in some changed forms in early Christianity: Osiek, "Ransom of Captives," 365–86.

87. Pliny the Younger, *Letters* 10.96.8.

88. Justin, *Apology* 2.12.4. Such charges of secret atrocities were rampant in the rumor mills of the second century; see Minucius Felix, *Octavius* 9.

89. Athenagoras, *Plea for Christians* 35.3.

90. Hippolytus, *Apostolic Tradition* 15.4–5.

91. Aristides, *Apology* 15.

92. Tertullian, *Apology* 39.6.

93. Clement of Alexandria, *Pedagogue* 3.4.26; 5.32; 6.34; 7.38; 9.48; 11.58, 74; 12.84, 94.

94. S[ervus sum] Felicis arc(hi)diac(oni): tene me ne fugiam: Horsley, New Documents, 1.91 (pp. 140–41).

Notes to Chapter 8.
Family Life, Meals, and Hospitality

1. Wallace-Hadrill, Houses and Society, 29.
2. Smith, Communal Meals, popularly summarized in Smith and Taussig, Many Tables, 21–69.
3. Lampe, "The Eucharist," 39–40, based on his "Das korinthische Herrenmahl," 183–213.
4. Smith, Communal Meals, Appendix A.3, and Carl Roebuck, Corinth XIV: The Asklepieion and Lerna (Princeton, N.J.: American School of Classical Studies at Athens, 1951), 51–57, with Plan C.
5. Smith, Communal Meals, 87–90; trans. of Oxyrhynchus papyrus by Smith. Cf. J. F. Gilliam, "Invitations to the Kline of Sarapis," Collectanea Papyrologica: Texts Published in Honor of H. C. Youtie, ed. A. E. Hanson, Papyrologische Texte und Abhandlungen 19 (Bonn: Rudolf Habelt, 1976), 1.315–24.
6. Smith, Communal Meals, 6, 26. Laurence, Roman Pompeii, 127–31.
7. Smith, Communal Meals, 52–56, 73, 95–96, 147–48, 170–73, 176.
8. Plutarch, Table-Talk I.2, 615C–619A, trans. Clement and Hoffleit in LCL.
9. Cf. 1 Cor. 11:34.
10. F. Ullrich, Entstehung und Entwicklung der Literaturgattung des Symposion (Würzburg: Stürtz, 1908–1909) 2.14–56, on Lucian's satire of Plato's symposium; cited by Braun, Feasting, 140n22.
11. Smith, Communal Meals, 153.
12. Foss, "Kitchens and Dining Rooms," 49, observes that Roman men and women commonly dined together; his n. 225 refers to Valerius Maximus 2.1.2; Isidorus, Origines 20.11.9. On whether women sat or reclined, see chap. 3 above and Osiek, "Family in Early Christianity," nn. 46–50.
13. Smith, Communal Meals, 7, 42, 71, and Lampe, "Das korinthische Herrenmahl," 198n44, who cites A. Mau, "Comissatio," PW 4/1 (1900): 610–19, at pp. 618–19.
14. See Wendland, "Die Therapeuten," 693–772. He demonstrates that the group is Jewish, not Christian.
15. Cf. Wendland, "Die Therapeuten," 704, for an outline.
16. This has a parallel among Essenes, some of whom do not marry.
17. Collins, Diakonia, 163, suggests rather that "Philo is adverting to the Greek ideal . . . that slaves render a gathering unholy (Dieuchidas, FHG 4.389; Athenaeus 263a) and thus impervious to divine presences." On the "young," compare Luke 22:26 and Acts 5:6, 10, perhaps an established group in the church.
18. Wallace-Hadrill, Houses and Society, 39; cf. p. 36. Foss, "Kitchens and Dining Rooms," 5, 40, 165, 168, 173, describes the areas where the slaves worked.
19. Foss, "Kitchens and Dining Rooms," 139, 173. See figure 8, above.
20. Ibid., 168.
21. Ibid., 176.

22. Laurence, *Roman Pompeii*, 125–29. Cf. Gerd Theissen, "Social Integration and Sacramental Activity: An Analysis of 1 Cor. 11:17–34," in his *Social Setting*, 145–74, at p. 155n20; Lampe, "The Eucharist," 39–40, and "Das korinthische Herrenmahl," 192.

23. Lampe, "Eucharist," 37, and idem, "Das korinthische Herrenmahl," 187. See also A. Mau, "Cena," PW 3, no. 2 (1899): 1895–97; also Mau, "Convivium," PW 4, no. 1 (1900): 1201–8; and Mau, "Comissatio," PW 4, no. 1 (1900): 610–19. A. Hug, "Symposion," PW 11 4/1 (1931): 1266–70.

24. Lampe, "Das korinthische Herrenmahl," 196.

25. Lampe, "Eucharist," 42.

26. Murphy-O'Connor, *St. Paul's Corinth*, 156.

27. Smith, *Communal Meals*, 183n8, and Lampe, "Das korinthische Herrenmahl," 197n43, citing W. H. Gross, "Triclinium," *KP* 5 (1975): 955.

28. Wallace-Hadrill, *Houses and Society*, 67–89.

29. Foss, "Kitchens and Dining Rooms," 145.

30. Ibid., 144n122.

31. See the plan in La Rocca et al., *Pompei*, 176, and Jashemski, *Gardens of Pompeii*, 2.29. The central peristyle is the largest and has huge side rooms. From the entrance, one sees through the atrium into the first peristyle, from which one descends ten steps to the second. There is a wall between the second and third peristyles, but it has six arched windows and two doors "which afforded a magnificent view into the southern peristyle" (Jashemski, 2.31). There is also a second atrium between the middle peristyle and a side entrance that was reserved for slaves (La Rocca, 177). Between Augustus and Claudius, the house was owned by the family Popidii, indigenous to Pompeii, not an imperial or historically important family (La Rocca, 176–77).

32. Foss, "Kitchens and Dining Rooms," 86, says that the functions of rooms were flexible, that many *oeci* could also serve diners with a simple change of furniture (p. 98), and that large banquets could be held concurrently in a house's dining halls (176). The Casa dell'Efebo had an outdoor dining area in the garden (fig. 5.89). Foss notes (p. 115) that slaves and children sat on benches. Cicero entertained two thousand at the Saturnalia (*Att.* 13.52.1–2; Foss, p. 99).

33. Ibid., 144n122. See the plan in La Rocca, *Pompei*, 184; Jashemski, *Gardens of Pompeii*, 1.92; 2.47–48; and Clarke, *Houses of Roman Italy*, 170, 188, with figs. 2, 6, who measures the axial view from the vestibule to the rear wall of the excedra/peristyle as 141 feet or 43.5 meters. A kitchen garden ("R" in Clarke and La Rocca, "b" in Jashemski) is nine steps down, west of the peristyle. This house has a beautiful private sauna (*terme*) in its southwestern corner, and two lararia, one in the front atrium, another at the rear of the large peristyle. Another example of a house with two large peristylia is the House of the Faun; see Clarke, *Houses of Roman Italy*, fig. 22.

34. See the plan in La Rocca, *Pompei*, 250; McKay, *Houses, Villas*, 44–45; Jashemski, *Gardens of Pompeii*, 2.78.

35. See Jashemski, *Gardens of Pompeii*, 1.236; 2.61.

36. La Rocca, *Pompei*, 235, and Jashemski, *Gardens of Pompeii*, 1.240, who observes that the House of the Hebrew (1.11.14), thought to be the gathering place of the Jewish community at Pompeii, was nearby.

37. See the plan of the house in La Rocca, *Pompei*, 253; Jashemski, *Gardens of Pompeii*, 2.86; and in Christopher Charles Parslow, *Rediscovering Antiquity: Karl Weber and the Excavations of Herculaneum, Pompeii, and Stabiae* (Cambridge: Cambridge University Press, 1955), 109. Besides the large peristyle, the house has atria at both entrances with a commercial termopolium and kitchen beside entrance number 7.

38. Jashemski, *Gardens of Pompeii*, 2.88.

39. Cf. further Branick, *House Church*, and Klauck, *Gemeinde zwischen Haus und Stadt*.

40. Bakker, *Living and Working with the Gods*, 11, with n. 31. When Germanicus died in 19 C.E., Romans threw their statuetes of the Lares Familiares into the streets, expressing their anger and frustration that the gods could not prevent his death, an expression of their loss of faith in the future, which depended on the emperor and his successor (Suetonius, *Caligula* 5).

41. Ibid., 40. Cf. chap. 1, n. 121 and chap. 3, n. 185.

42. Ibid., 37, 41.

43. Contrast Branick, *House Church*, 110–11. Pliny, *Ep.* 10.96, discovers that Christians were accustomed to gather "on a fixed day before daylight and sing by turns (antiphonally) a hymn to Christ as a god" and to gather later for a second meeting at which they "take food, but ordinary and harmless food."

44. Smith, *Communal Banquets*, 215–20, and Lampe, "Das korinthische Herrenmahl," 188–89.

45. Braun, *Feasting*, 28.

46. Ibid., 33n39, citing Stobaeus, *Flor.* 3.10.45, and M. Billerbeck, *Der Kyniker Demetrius: Ein Beitrag zur Geschichte der frühkaiserzeitlichen Popularphilosophie*, Philosophia Antiqua 36 (Leiden: E. J. Brill, 1979), 25n48.

47. Braun, *Feasting*, 65, 133, 144, 162–64. Braun employs the second-century C.E. rhetorician Hermogenes, but Vernon Robbins, "The Beelzebul Controversy and the Great Banquet: Rhetorical Elaboration from 'The Parts,'" (typescript) argues that Theon is more relevant.

48. Braun, *Feasting*, 170.

49. Ibid., 136–44.

50. Ibid., 121.

51. Ibid., 61, 140.

52. Ibid., 62, 72, 74, 84, 94. The quotation is from Dionysius Halicarnassus, *Ant. Rom.* 8.71.3. Cicero, *Att.* 1.16.11, too, writes of the "filth and dregs of the city" (both cited by Braun, *Feasting*, 84, 86). Wallace-Hadrill has shown, however, that rich and poor often lived in the same spaces, that the conception of rich occupying the center of the city while the nonelite lived in outlying sectors (Braun, *Feasting*, 87) is mistaken.

53. Richard Rohrbaugh, "The Pre-industrial City in Luke-Acts: Urban Social Relations," in *The Social World of Luke-Acts: Models for Interpretation*, ed. J. H. Neyrey (Peabody, Mass.: Hendrickson, 1991), 125–49, at p. 145.

54. Bobertz, "*Cena Dominica* of Hippolytus' Apostolic Tradition," 170–84.

55. Braun, *Feasting*, 113. That this is "against the entire system" (p. 115) overstates the social choices involved. Braun has after all provided good analogies from Lucian. Plutarch's brother (*Table-Talk* 1.2, 615C–619A) provides

another argument against the reigning values with parallels to Jesus' parable of the great supper. Luke voices protests also seen in Lucian and Plutarch.

56. Nelson, *Leadership and Discipleship*, 2.

57. Ibid., 51–74.

58. Heinz Schürmann, "Jesu Abschiedsrede Lk 22, 21–38," in *III. Teil einer quellenkritischen Untersuchung des lukanischen Abendmahlsberichtes Lk 22,7–38,* NTAbh 20/5 (Münster: Aschendorff, 1957), 64–65, 92.

59. The chart is modified from Nelson, *Leadership and Discipleship,* 133 (cf. 147–55), and assumes that David J. Lull, "The Servant-Benefactor as a Model of Greatness (Luke 22:24–20)," *NovT* 28 (1986): 289–305, is incorrect that kings/benefactors are positive models.

60. Nelson, *Leadership and Discipleship,* 134, 155.

61. Ibid., 154.

62. *Diakoneo* does not appear in John 13, but *doulos* ("slave," John 13:16) does. And "slave" does not occur in Luke 22:24–20, although it does in Mark 10:44.

63. Cf. Nelson, *Leadership and Discipleship,* 47, 165–66, 241. Cf. chap. 7, nn. 57, 61.

64. Robert J. Karris, "The Theme of Food," in *Luke, Artist and Theologian: Luke's Passion Account as Literature* (Mahwah, N.J.: Paulist Press, 1985), 47–78, at p. 68, and David L. Tiede, *Luke* (Minneapolis: Augsburg, 1988), 384–85.

65. This reads Luke 12, 14, and 22 together. Lucian's Cynic parodies of other symposia do provide parallels (e.g., *Sat.* 18; cf. n. 10, above). Does Lucian's *Saturnalia* go beyond Luke? It is, of course, possible that Luke is not the most radical writer in the culture (pace Rohrbaugh and Braun).

66. Corley, *Private Women, Public Meals,* 22, 102.

67. Ibid., 147–51, 184.

68. Lampe,"Family' in Church and Society of New Testament Times," 8–12; Donald Wayne Riddle, "Early Christian Hospitality: A Factor in the Gospel Transmission," *JBL* 57 (1938): 141–54.

69. D'Arms, "The Roman *Convivium* and the Idea of Equality," 308–20, shows that however much the rhetoric of equality was part of the social customs of dining, the reality mirrored the inequalities of the culture. See also Theissen, *Social Setting,* 145–74. For a sensitive methodological portrayal of the footwashing, see Sandra M. Schneiders, "The Foot Washing (John 13:1–20): An Experiment in Hermeneutics," *CBQ* 43, no. 1 (1981): 76–92.

70. Surveys and proposals in Malherbe, *Social Aspects,* 92–112; Raymond E. Brown, *The Epistles of John,* Anchor Bible 30 (Garden City, N.Y.: Doubleday, 1982), 728–39. Both in their own proposals rightly focus more on the hospitality issue than the theological one.

71. See also 1 John 2:23; 4:2.

72. Even so, the RSV and NRSV translation of 3 John 9—10 is questionable. The same verb, *epidechomai,* is translated as "acknowledge my authority" on the part of the Presbyter in v. 9 and "welcome" on the part of others in v. 10. Simply "receive," "welcome," or "acknowledge" suffices for both, even if there is some issue of authority involved. See comment by Malherbe, *Social Aspects,* 106.

73. *Hermas, Similitude* 9.27.2; *Hermas, Mandate* 8.10 also combines the exercise of hospitality with help toward the needy.

74. Compare Ignatius, *Smyrnaeans* 13; Ignatius, *Polycarp* 8.2; Tertullian, *To His Wife* 2.4. Other names are cited by Ignatius at the same time, but as individuals, not heads of households: Alce (also greeted in Ignatius, *Polycarp* 8.3), Daphnos, and Euteknos. Tavia may be the wife of a nonbeliever named Epitropos, which may also be not a proper name but a title of public office (procurator or administrator); *Polycarp* 8.2 greets the wife of Epitropos (but not Epitropos himself) with her household and children. This would be very strange if the husband were also Christian, but not at all strange if the Christian wife was hostess for Ignatius. For the same identity but a different conclusion (Tavia is the widow of Epitropos), see William R. Schoedel, *Ignatius of Antioch*, Hermeneia (Philadelphia: Fortress Press, 1985), 280n14.

75. Ignatius, *Smyrnaeans* 1–4. The deviant theology seems to take the same drift as that spoken against in the Johannine letters: 1 John 4:2; 2 John 7.

76. *Didache* 11.3–6. Chap. 12 later seems to take a softer approach: Three days are permissible, and it is even possible for an itinerant to settle down in a local place, provided he can work according to his ability.

77. *Didache* 11.7–12. One senses in the text an inability either to approve or to disapprove of this practice completely. Exactly what it means has never been adequately explained, but it probably has something to do with bridal imagery and symbolic marital union, perhaps by utilizing Eph. 5:26–32 or an equivalent (cf. *2 Clement* 14). The gnostic *Gospel of Philip*, for instance, has a sacrament of the bridal chamber which probably was a ritual of mystical union with a heavenly counterpart. Willy Rordorf and André Tuilier, *La Doctrine des douze Apôtres (Didachè)*, Sources Chrétiennes 248 (Paris: Cerf, 1978), 186–88, understand the phrase to mean "the mystery of the church in the world," and reconstruct it as the mystical relationship of celibate prophets with the church. Jean-Paul Audet, *La Didachè: Instructions des Apôtres* (Paris: Gabalda, 1958), 451–53, argues for an interpretation relative to apocalyptic imagery rather than marital, but he is in the minority.

78. Murphy-O'Connor estimates fifty maximum, based on study of some of the archaeological evidence (*St. Paul's Corinth*, 153–58), but his calculations do not include, in the case of the House of the Vettii at Pompeii, the very large peristyle. See discussion above, pp. 201–203.

79. Ignatius, *Smyrnaeans* 8.1.

80. Justin, *Apology* 1.65–67.

81. *Didache* 9.

82. This provenance is not absolutely certain, and the text, reconstructed from many sources, bears resemblances to some Eastern church orders. A brief history of the text is in Bobertz, "*Cena Dominica* of Hippolytus' *Apostolic Tradition*," 170–71n1–2. The chapter numbers of Hippolytus's *Apostolic Tradition* used here are those of the critical edition of Bernard Botte, *La Tradition Apostolique de saint Hippolyte*, Sources Chrétiennes 11 (Paris: Cerf, 1984). Those of the other critical edition, by Gregory Dix (*The Apostolic Tradition of St. Hippolytus*, 2d ed. by H. Chadwick [London: SPCK], 1968), are slightly different.

83. Justin, *Apology* 1.66.
84. Bobertz, "The Role of Patron," 182.
85. Hippolytus, *Apostolic Tradition,* chap. 10.
86. "Blemishes on your love-feasts" (RSV, NRSV). For discussion, see Jerome H. Neyrey, *2 Peter, Jude,* Anchor Bible 37C (New York: Doubleday, 1993), 75.
87. Ignatius, *Smyrnaeans* 8.2.
88. Thomas M. Finn, "Agape (Love Feast)," *Encyclopedia of Early Christianity,* ed. Everett Ferguson et al., Garland Reference Library of the Humanities 846 (New York: Garland, 1990), 16–17.
89. Tertullian, *Apology* 39.16–19.
90. Clement of Alexandria, *Pedagogue* 2.1.4–20.
91. Charles A. Bobertz, "Cyprian of Carthage as Patron: A Social Historical Study of the Role of Bishop in the Ancient Christian Community of North Africa," Ph.D. diss., Yale University, New Haven, Conn., 1988; Countryman, *Rich Christian in the Church.*
92. Hippolytus, *Apostolic Tradition* 41. Among books for private reading were certainly the scriptures, including by this time not only the Hebrew scriptures but the Gospels and at least the Pauline letters, and probably other readings not used in church but judged suitable for private reading, like the *Shepherd of Hermas* and what are now called the Apocryphal Gospels and Acts. Still worth consulting, though written with denominational polemic, is Adolf Harnack, *Bible Reading in the Early Church* (New York: Putnam, 1912); most recently, Harry Y. Gamble, *Books and Readers in the Early Church* (New Haven, Conn.: Yale University Press, 1995).
93. Asterius of Amaseia (fourth century), *Homily* 1, quoted in Eunice Dauterman Maguire et al., *Art and Holy Powers in the Early Christian House,* Illinois Byzantine Studies 2 (Urbana/Chicago: University of Illinois Press, 1989), 31; see also Harnack, *Bible Reading,* 86, 101.

Glossary

amicitia (Latin)—Friendship, but in Roman culture, a term that embraces not only relationships between peers but also the more elusive unequal relationships of patronage.

andreia (Greek)—Courageous behavior, generally thought to be limited to males.

arete (Greek)—The highest quality of human characteristics; virtue.

atrium (Latin)—A room at the front of the Italian house with open roof at the center, originally for the smoke from the hearth to escape, later for the collection of rainwater.

diakonos (Greek)—In pre-Christian language, a servant, steward, or representative; in Christian terminology by the third century, a lesser church official, assistant and official representative of the bishop.

domus (Latin)—A house or household.

domus ecclesiae (Latin)—The second stage of church development after private house church meetings, whereby private houses were remodeled for exclusive use of Christian communities by enlarging assembly areas and other architectural adjustments.

ekklesia (Greek)—Assembly of free citizens; for Christians beginning with Paul, the assembly of the baptized; church.

enkrateia (Greek; also transliterated *egkrateia*)—Self-restraint, moderation; in later Christian usage, celibacy or continence.

episkopos (Greek)—Overseer, superintendent; at an early stage of Christian development, synonymous with presbyter; later, the single bishop in charge of a community.

familia (Latin)—All persons descended from, or under the legal control of, a senior male authority; a house and all its dependents and property.

genius (Latin)—A protecting divine spirit of a person or place.

hetaira (Greek)—An educated, refined courtesan for male companionship.

honestiores (Latin)—A quasi-legal term for those with social and legal privilege due to birth status; complement of *humiliores*.

honor—Social sensitivity to one's worth as it is publicly recognized by appropriate persons.

humiliores (Latin)—Those lacking social and legal privilege; complement of *honestiores*.

impluvium (Latin)—In an Italian house, opening in the central roof of the atrium, originally to allow smoke to escape from the central hearth, later to allow rainwater to fall into the *compluvium* below, where it was collected.

insula (Latin)—Literally, island, but used in an urban context to mean a large, multi-unit housing complex; also in modern classical archaeology, a city block of an ancient Roman city.

lararium (Latin)—The household shrine of the family's tutelary divinities.

lares (Latin)—Roman tutelary deities of cities, associations, and households.

libertus/ae (Latin)—Man or woman, formerly a slave, now freed.

manus (Latin)—Literally, a human hand; legal term for legal power of husband over wife; Roman marriage could be *cum manu,* with transfer of power from father to husband, or increasingly in imperial times, *sine manu,* without transfer of control.

materfamilias (Latin)—Matron or mistress of a household.

oecus (Latin, from Greek *oikos,* but with different meaning)—Hall or formal room in a private house, especially for entertainment.

oikos, oikia (Greek)—House, household with property and persons; roughly equivalent to Latin *domus* or *familia.*

ordo (Latin)—As used here, one of the two identifiable privileged social ranks in Roman society, senatorial and equestrian.

paterfamilias (Latin)—Male head of household and family.

patronus/ae (Latin)—Patron, protector; a slave's former owner, to whom certain obligations are due.

penates (Latin)—Tutelary divinities of a storeroom, cupboard, or house; usually mentioned along with *lares.*

peristyle (from Greek, *peristylos,* surrounded by columns)—An open area of a house or public building surrounded by a colonnaded portico.

presbyteros (Greek)—Elder, member of a council of elders; in later Christian use, member of the bishop's council, presbyter, eventually the role that became that of priest.

refrigerium (Latin, literally, cooling refreshment)—A ritual meal for the dead held at the burial place in ancient Near East, Greece, and Rome, usually including a libation or food offering by which the deceased participate.

shame—Proper sensitivity to honor; the absence of honor and incentive to restore it.

stibadium (Greek)—Originally, an informal or outdoor dining arrangement; later, a circular dining couch popular by the second and third centuries C.E.; by the fourth century, the preferred replacement of the triclinium.

subintroducta (Latin, equivalent of Greek *syneisakta*)—In Christian practice, a woman brought into a man's house as "sister-wife," to share living arrangements without conjugal union.

sui juris (Latin)—Legal term for one who is legally independent of paternal (*patriapotestas*) or marital (*manus*) control.

thermopolium (Latin)—A shop that sells hot drinks and other food and drink.

triclinium (Latin)—Squared three-sided dining couch for formal dining, the most common form until gradually replaced by the stibadium.

tutela (Latin)—Legal guardianship of a minor or woman.

univira (Latin)—Wife of one husband; a romantic ideal of marital fidelity in Latin literature.

Bibliography

Alexander, Loveday C. A. "Paul and the Hellenistic Schools: The Evidence of Galen." In *Paul in His Hellenistic Context,* ed. Troels Engberg Pedersen, 60–83. Minneapolis: Fortress Press, 1995.

———."Schools, Hellenistic." *ABD* 5 (1992): 1005–11.

Aspegren, Kerstin. *The Male Woman: A Feminine Ideal in the Early Church.* Uppsala Women's Studies; Women in Religion 4, ed. Rene Kieffer. Uppsala: Almqvist & Wiksell, 1990.

Bakker, Jan T. *Living and Working with the Gods: Studies of Evidence for Private Religion and Its Material Environment in the City of Ostia (100–500 A.D.).* Dutch Monographs on Ancient History and Archaeology 12. Amsterdam: J. C. Gieben, 1994.

Balch, David L. "Backgrounds of 1 Cor. 7: Sayings of the Lord in Q; Moses as an Ascetic *Theios Aner* in 2 Cor. 3." *NTS* 18 (1972): 351–64.

———. "The Canon: Adaptable and Stable, Oral and Written. Critical Questions for Kelber and Reisner." *Forum* 7, nos. 3–4 (1993): 183–205.

———. "1 Cor. 7:32–35 and Stoic Debates about Marriage, Anxiety, and Distraction." *JBL* 102 (1983): 429–39.

———. "Household Codes." In *Greco-Roman Literature and the New Testament,* ed. David E. Aune, 25–50. SBLSBS 21. Atlanta: Scholars Press, 1988.

———. *Let Wives Be Submissive: The Domestic Code in 1 Peter.* SBLMS 26. Chico, Calif.: Scholars Press, 1981.

———. "Neopythagorean Moralists and the New Testament Household Codes." *Aufstieg und Niedergang der römischen Welt* 2.26.1 (1992): 380–411.

———. "Philodemus, 'On Wealth,' and 'On Household Management': Naturally Wealthy Epicureans against poor Cynics." In *Philodemus and the New Testament World,* ed. John T. Fitzgerald. SuppNT. Leiden: E. J. Brill, forthcoming.

———. "Rich and Poor, Proud and Humble in Luke-Acts." In *The Social World of the First Christians: Essays in Honor of Wayne A. Meeks,* ed. L. Michael White and O. Larry Yarbrough, 214–233. Minneapolis: Fortress Press, 1995.

Bartchy, S. Scott. *Mallon Chrēsai: First Century Slavery and 1 Corinthians 7:21.* SBLDS 11. Missoula, Mont.: Scholars Press, 1973.

————. "Philemon, Epistle to." *ABD* 5 (1992): 305–10.

————. "Slavery (Greco-Roman)." *ABD* 6 (1992): 65–73.

Barton, Stephen C. *Discipleship and Family Ties in Mark and Matthew.* SNTSMS 80. Cambridge: Cambridge University Press, 1994.

Bauman, Richard A. *Women and Politics in Ancient Rome.* London: Routledge, 1992.

Beavis, Mary Ann. "Ancient Slavery as an Interpretive Context for the New Testament Servant Parables with Special Reference to the Unjust Steward (Luke 16:1–8)." *JBL* 111 (1992): 37–54.

Best, Ernest. "Mark 10:13–16: The Child as Model Recipient." In *Biblical Studies: Essays in Honour of William Barclay,* ed. J. R. McKay and J. F. Miller, 119–34, 209–18. London: Collins, 1976.

Betz, Hans Dieter. *Galatians.* Hermeneia. Philadelphia: Fortress Press, 1979.

Blue, Bradley. "Acts and the House Church." In *The Book of Acts in Its First Century Setting,* Vol. 2: *Graeco-Roman Setting,* ed. David W. J. Gill and Conrad Gempf, 119–89. Grand Rapids: Wm. B. Eerdmans Publishing Co., 1994.

Bobertz, Charles A. "The Role of Patron in the *Cena Dominica* of Hippolytus' *Apostolic Tradition." JTS* 44 (1993): 170–84.

Bömer, Franz, and Peter Herz. *Untersuchungen über die Religion der Sklaven in Griechenland und Rom.* Erster Teil: *Die Wichtigsten Kulte und Religionen in Rom und im Lateinischen Westen,* 2d ed. Forschungen zur Antiken Sklaverei 14.3. Stuttgart: Franz Steiner, 1981.

Boring, M. Eugene. *The Continuing Voice of Jesus: Christian Prophecy and the Gospel Tradition.* Louisville, Ky.: Westminster/John Knox Press, 1991.

Bradley, K. R. *Slavery and Society at Rome.* Cambridge, London, New York: Cambridge University Press, 1994.

————. *Slaves and Masters in the Roman Empire: A Study in Social Control.* Collection Latomus 185. Brussels: Revue d'études latines, 1984.

Branick, Vincent. *The House Church in the Writings of Paul.* Wilmington, Del.: Michael Glazier, 1989.

Braun, Willi. *Feasting and Social Rhetoric in Luke 14.* SNTSMS 85. Cambridge: Cambridge University Press, 1995.

Brooten, Bernadette J. "Iael *prostates* in the Jewish Donative Inscription from Aphrodisias." In *The Future of Early Christianity: Essays in Honor of Helmut Koester,* ed. Birger A. Pearson, 149–62. Minneapolis: Fortress Press, 1991.

————. *Women Leaders in the Ancient Synagogue: Inscriptional Evidence and Background Issues.* BJS 36. Chico, Calif.: Scholars Press, 1982.

Broudéhoux, Jean-Paul. *Mariage et famille chez Clément d'Aléxandrie.* Théologie Historique 2. Paris: Beauchesne, 1970.

Brown, Peter. *The Body and Society: Men, Women, and Sexual Renunciation in Early Christianity.* Lectures on the History of Religions 13. New York: Columbia University Press, 1988.

Bussemaker, U. C., and Ch. Daremberg, trans. *Oeuvres d'Oribase, Texte Grec . . . traduit . . . en Francais.* 5 vols. Paris: L'Imprimerie Nationale, 1851–1858.

Cahill, Lisa Sowle. "Sex and Gender Ethics as NT Social Ethics." In *The Bible in Ethics,* ed. J. Rogerson. Sheffield: Sheffield Academic Press, 1996, 272–95.

Cardascia, G. "L'apparition dans le droit des classes d'honestiores' et d'humiliores.'" *Revue historique de droit français et étranger* 28 (1950): 305–37, 461–85.

Carney, T. F. *The Shape of the Past: Models and Antiquity.* Lawrence, Kans.: Coronado, 1975.

Carter, Warren. *Households and Discipleship: A Study of Matthew 19–20.* JSNTSup 103. Sheffield: JSOT Press, 1994.

Clarke, John. *The Houses of Roman Italy 100 B.C.–A.D. 250.* Berkeley: University of California Press, 1991.

Cohen, Shaye J. D., ed. *The Jewish Family in Antiquity.* BJS 289. Atlanta: Scholars Press, 1993.

Collins, John N. *Diakonia: Re-interpreting the Ancient Sources.* New York: Oxford University Press, 1990.

Corley, Kathleen E. *Private Women, Public Meals: Social Conflict in the Synoptic Tradition.* Peabody, Mass.: Hendrickson, 1993.

Countryman, L. William. *Dirt Greed and Sex: Sexual Ethics in the New Testament and their Implications for Today.* Philadelphia: Fortress Press, 1988, 1990.

———. *The Rich Christian in the Church of the Early Empire: Contradictions and Accommodations.* Texts and Studies in Religion. New York/Toronto: Edwin Mellen, 1980.

Crosby, Michael H. *House of Disciples: Church, Economics, and Justice in Matthew.* Maryknoll, N.Y.: Orbis Books, 1988.

Crossan, John Dominic. *In Parables.* New York: Harper & Row, 1973.

Dahl, Nils A. "Euodia and Syntyche and Paul's Letter to the Philippians." In *The Social World of the First Christians: Essays in Honor of Wayne A. Meeks,* ed. L. Michael White and O. Larry Yarbrough, 3–15. Minneapolis: Fortress Press, 1995.

D'Arms, John. "The Roman *Convivium* and the Idea of Equality." In *Sympotica: A Symposium on the Symposium,* ed. Oswyn Murray, 308–20. Oxford: Clarendon Press, 1990.

Deiss, Joseph Jay. *Herculaneum: Italy's Buried Treasure.* 2d ed. Malibu, Calif.: J. Paul Getty Museum, 1989.

Deming, Will. *Paul on Marriage and Celibacy: The Hellenistic Background of 1 Corinthians 7.* SNTSMS 83. Cambridge: Cambridge Unversity Press, 1995.

Dill, Samuel. *Roman Society from Nero to Marcus Aurelius.* Cleveland: World Publishing Co., 1904; repr. Meridian, 1962.

Dixon, Suzanne. *The Roman Family.* Baltimore: Johns Hopkins University Press, 1992.

————. *The Roman Mother*. London: Routledge, 1988.

Downey, Glanville. *Ancient Antioch*. Princeton, N.J.: Princeton University Press, 1963.

Dwyer, Eugene. "The Pompeian Atrium House in Theory and in Practice." In *Roman Art in the Private Sphere,* ed. Elaine K. Gazda, 25–48. Ann Arbor: University of Michigan Press, 1991.

Eisenstadt, S. N., and L. Roniger. *Patrons, Clients and Friends: Interpersonal Relations and the Structure of Trust in Society.* Cambridge: Cambridge University Press, 1984.

Elliott, John H. *A Home for the Homeless: A Sociological Exegesis of 1 Peter, Its Situation and Strategy*. Rev. ed. Minneapolis: Fortress Press, 1991.

Eyben, Emiel. *Restless Youth in Ancient Rome*. London/New York: Routledge, 1993.

Finley, M. I. *The Ancient Economy*. 2d ed. Berkeley: University of California Press, 1985.

Fitzmyer, Joseph A. *Romans*. AB 33. New York: Doubleday, 1992.

Foss, Pedar William. "Kitchens and Dining Rooms at Pompeii: The Spatial and Social Relationship of Cooking to Eating in the Roman Household." Dissertation, University of Michigan, Ann Arbor, Mich., 1994.

Franciscis, Alfonso de. "La Villa Romana di Oplontis." In *Neue Forschungen in Pompeii und den anderen vom Vesuvausbruch 79 n. Chr. verschütteten Städten,* ed. B. Andreae and H. Kyrieleis, 9–39 with plates 1–39. Deutsches Archäologisches Institut. Recklinghausen: Aurel Bongers, 1975.

Gardner, Jane. *Women in Roman Law and Society*. Bloomington, Ind.: Indiana University Press, 1991.

Garnsey, Peter. *Social Status and Legal Privilege in the Roman Empire*. Oxford: Clarendon Press, 1970.

Garnsey, Peter, and Richard Saller. *The Roman Empire: Economy, Society and Culture*. Berkeley: University of California Press, 1987.

Gazda, Elaine K. "Introduction." In *Roman Art in the Private Sphere*. Ann Arbor: University of Michigan, 1991.

Gielen, Marlis. *Tradition und Theologie neutestamentlicher Haustafelethik: Ein Beitrag zur Frage einer christlichen Auseinandersetzung mit gesellschaftlichen Normen*. BBB 75. Frankfurt: Anton Hain, 1990.

Gill, David W. J. "Acts and the Urban Elite." In *The Book of Acts in Its First Century Setting*. Vol. 2: *Graeco-Roman Setting*, ed. David W. J. Gill and Conrad Gempf, 105–18. Grand Rapids: Wm. B. Eerdmans Publishing Co., 1994.

Gilmore, David D., ed. *Honor and Shame and the Unity of the Mediterranean*. American Anthropological Association Special Publication 22. Washington, D.C.: American Anthropological Association, 1987.

Gordon, R. L. "Mithraism and Roman Society: Social factors in the Explanation of Religious Change in the Roman Empire." *Religion: A Journal of Religion and Religions* 2, no. 2 (1972): 92–121.

Grant, Michael. *Eros in Pompeii: The Secret Rooms of the National Museum of Naples*. New York: William Morrow & Co., 1975.

Greeven, H. "Propheten, Lehrer, Vorsteer bei Paulus." *ZNW* 44 (1952–53): 1–43.

Gryson, Roger. *The Ministry of Women in the Early Church*. Collegeville, Minn.: Liturgical Press, 1976.

Hallett, Judith. *Fathers and Daughters in Roman Society: Women and the Elite Family*. Princeton, N.J.: Princeton University Press, 1984.

Harrill, J. Albert. "Ignatius, *Ad Polycarp* 4.3 and the Corporate Manumission of Christian Slaves." *Journal of Early Christian Studies* 1, no. 2 (1993): 107–42.

———. *The Manumission of Slaves in Early Christianity*. HUT 32. Tübingen: J.C.B. Mohr (Paul Siebeck), 1995.

Hawley, R., and B. Levick, eds. *Women in Antiquity: New Assessments*. New York: Routledge, 1995.

Hermansen, Gustav. "Domus and Insula in the City of Rome." *Classica et Mediaevalia: Dissertationes* (1973): 333–41.

Hopkins, Keith. *Death and Renewal*. Cambridge: Cambridge University Press, 1983.

Horsley, G. H. R. *New Documents Illustrating Early Christianity*. 7 vols. Sydney: Ancient History Documentary Research Center, Macquarie University, 1981–1994.

Jashemski, Wilhelmina F. *The Gardens of Pompeii*. 2 vols. New Rochelle, N.Y.: Aristide D. Caratzas, 1979 and 1993.

Jewett, Robert. "Tenement Churches and Communal Meals in the Early Church: The Implications of a Form-Critical Analysis of 2 Thessalonians 3:10." *BR* 38 (1993): 23–43.

Judge, E. A. *The Social Pattern of Christian Groups in the First Century*. London: Tyndale, 1960.

Kearseley, R. A. "Women in Public Life." In *New Documents Illustrating Early Christianity*, vol. 6, ed. S. R. Llewelyn and R. A. Kearsley, 24–27. Sydney: Macquarie University, 1992.

———. "Women in Public Life in the Roman East: Junia Theodora, Claudia Metrodora and Phoebe, Benefactress of Paul." *Ancient Society: Resources for Teachers* 15 (1985): 124–37.

Klauck, Hans-Josef. *Gemeinde zwischen Haus und Stadt: Kirche bei Paulus*. Freiburg: Herder, 1992.

———. *Hausgemeinde und Hauskirche im frühen Christentum*. Stuttgart: Katholisches Bibelwerk, 1981.

Koloski-Ostrow, A. *The Sarno Bath Complex*. Ministero per i beni culturali ed ambientali soprintendenza archaeologica di Pompei, Monografie 4. Rome: L'Erma di Bretschneider, 1990.

Kraemer, Ross Shepard. *Her Share of the Blessings: Women's Religions among Pagans, Jews, and Christians in the Greco-Roman World*. Oxford: Oxford University Press, 1992.

————, ed. *Maenads, Martyrs, Matrons, Monastics: A Sourcebook on Women's Religions in the Greco-Roman World*. Philadelphia: Fortress Press, 1988.

Krautheimer, Richard. *Early Christian and Byzantine Architecture*. 3d ed. New York: Penguin, 1977.

Kristen, Peter. *Familie, Kreuz und Leben: Nachfolge Jesu nach Q und dem Markusevangelium*. Marburger Theologische Studien 42. Marburg: N. G. Elwert, 1995.

Lacey, W. K. *The Family in Classical Greece*. Ithaca, N.Y.: Cornell University Press, 1968.

Lampe, Peter. "The Eucharist: Identifying with Christ on the Cross." *Int* 48, no. 1 (1994): 36–49.

————. "'Family' in Church and Society of New Testament Times." *Affirmation* (Union Theological Seminary in Virginia) 5, no. 1 (1992): 1–20.

————. "Keine 'Sklavenflucht' des Onesimus." ZNW 76 (1985): 135–37.

————. "Das korinthische Herrenmahl im Schnittpunkt hellenistisch-römischer Mahlpraxis und paulinischer Theologia Crucis (1 Kor 11,17–34)," ZNW 82, nos. 3–4 (1991): 183–213.

————. *Die städtrömischen Christen in den ersten beiden Jahrhunderten*. WUNT 2.18. Tübingen: J.C.B. Mohr (Paul Siebeck), 1987; 2d ed., 1989.

La Rocca, Eugenio, Mariette de Vos, and Arnold de Vos. *Pompei*. Rev. ed. Guide Archeologiche Mondadori. Milan: Arnoldo Mondadori, 1994.

Laurence, Ray. *Roman Pompeii: Space and Society*. New York: Routledge, 1994.

Lefkowitz, Mary R., and Maureen B. Fant. *Women's Life in Greece and Rome: A Sourcebook in Translation*. 2d ed. Baltimore: Johns Hopkins University Press, 1992.

Liebeschuetz, Wolf. "The Expansion of Mithraism among Religious Cults of the Second Century." In *Studies in Mithraism*, ed. J. R. Hinnells, 195–216. Rome: Bretschneider, 1994.

Lutz, Cora E., ed. *Musonius Rufus "The Roman Socrates."* Yale Classical Studies 10. London: Oxford University Press, and New Haven, Conn.: Yale University Press, 1947.

MacDonald, Dennis Ronald. *The Legend and the Apostle: The Battle for Paul in Story and Canon*. Philadelphia: Westminster Press, 1983.

MacMullen, Ramsay. *Roman Social Relations, 50 B.C. to A.D. 284*. New Haven, Conn.: Yale University Press, 1974.

————. "Women in Public in the Roman Empire." *Historia* 29 (1980): 208–18.

Malherbe, J. Abraham. *Social Aspects of Early Christianity*. 2d ed. Philadelphia: Fortress Press, 1983.

Martin, Clarice J. "The *Haustafeln* (Household Codes) in African American Biblical Interpretation: 'Free Slaves' and 'Subordinate Women.'" *Stony the Road We Trod: African American Biblical Interpretation*, ed. Cain H. Felder, 206–31. Minneapolis: Fortress Press, 1991.

Martin, Dale B. "The Construction of the Ancient Family: Methodological Considerations," *JRS* 86 (1996): 40–60.

———. *The Corinthian Body.* New Haven: Yale University, 1995.

———. *Slavery as Salvation: The Metaphor of Slavery in Pauline Christianity.* New Haven, Conn.: Yale University Press, 1990.

McKay, A. G. *Houses, Villas and Palaces of the Roman World.* Ithaca, N.Y.: Cornell University Press, 1975.

Meeks, Wayne A. *The First Urban Christians: The Social World of the Apostle Paul.* New Haven, Conn.: Yale University Press, 1983.

Meiggs, Russell. *Roman Ostia.* 2d ed. Oxford: Clarendon Press, 1973.

Mendelson, Alan. *Secular Education in Philo of Alexandria.* Monographs of the Hebrew Union College 7. Cincinnati: Hebrew Union College, 1982.

Mitchell, Margaret M. *Paul and the Rhetoric of Reconciliation: An Exegetical Investigation of the Language and Composition of 1 Corinthians.* HUT 28. Tübingen: J.C.B. Mohr (Paul Siebeck), 1991.

Müller, Peter. *In der Mitte der Gemeinde: Kinder im Neuen Testament.* Neukirchen-Vluyn: Neukirchener, 1992.

Murphy-O'Connor, Jerome. *St. Paul's Corinth: Texts and Archaeology.* Wilmington, Del.: Michael Glazier, 1983.

Nelson, Peter K. *Leadership and Discipleship: A Study of Luke 22:24–30.* SBLDS 138. Atlanta: Scholars Press, 1994.

Newsom, Carol A., and Sharon H. Ringe, eds. *The Women's Bible Commentary.* Louisville, Ky.: Westminster/John Knox Press, and London: SPCK, 1992.

Nussbaum, Martha C. *The Therapy of Desire: Theory and Practice in Hellenistic Ethics.* Princeton, N.J.: Princeton University Press, 1994.

Orr, David G. "Roman Domestic Religion: The Evidence of the Household Shrines." *ANRW* 2.16.2 (1978): 1557–91.

Osiek, Carolyn. "The Family in Early Christianity: 'Family Values' Revisited." *CBQ* 58, no. 1 (1996): 1–24.

———. "The Ransom of Captives: Evolution of a Tradition." *HTR* 74, no. 4 (1981): 365–86.

———. *Rich and Poor in the Shepherd of Hermas.* CBQMS 15. Washington, D.C.: Catholic Biblical Association, 1983.

———. "The Widow as Altar: The Rise and Fall of a Symbol." *Second Century* 3, no. 3 (1983): 159–69.

Overbeck, Johannes A. *Pompeii.* Rome: L'Erma di Bretschneider, 1968; orig. pub., 1884.

Packer, James E. "Housing and Population in Imperial Ostia and Rome." *JRS* 57 (1967): 80–95.

———. *The Insulae of Imperial Ostia.* Memoirs of the American Academy of Rome 31, 1971.

————. "Middle and Lower Class Housing in Pompeii and Herculaneum: A Preliminary Survey." In *Neue Forshungen in Pompeii und den anderen vom Vesuvausbruch 79 n. Chr. verschütteten Städten,* ed. B. Andreae and H. Kyrieleis, 133–46. Recklinghausten: Aurel Bongers, 1975.

Parkin, Tim G. *Demography and Roman Society.* Baltimore: Johns Hopkins University Press, 1992.

Patterson, John R. "Survey Article: The City of Rome, from Republic to Empire," *JRS* 82 (1992): 186–215.

Patterson, Orlando. *Slavery and Social Death: A Comparative Analysis.* Cambridge, Mass.: Harvard University Press, 1982.

Peristiany, J. G., ed. *Honour and Shame: Mediterranean Family Structures.* Cambridge: Cambridge University Press, 1976.

————. *Honour and Shame: The Values of Mediterranean Society.* Chicago: University of Chicago Press, 1966.

Peskowitz, Miriam. " 'Family/ies' in Antiquity: Evidence from Tannaitic Literature and Roman Galilean Architecture." *The Jewish Family in Antiquity,* ed. Shaye J. D. Cohen, 9–36. BJS 289. Atlanta: Scholars Press, 1993.

Pisani, Giuliano. *Plutarco, L'educazione.* Pordenone: Edizioni Biblioteca dell'Immagine, 1994.

Pitt-Rivers, Julian A. *The Fate of Shechem or The Politics of Sex: Essays in the Anthropology of the Mediterranean.* Cambridge: Cambridge University Press, 1977.

Pöhlmann, Wolfgang. *Der Verlorene Sohn und das Haus: Studien zu Lukas 15:11–32 im Horizont der antiken Lehre von Haus, Erziehung und Ackerbau.* WUNT 68. Tübingen: J.C.B. Mohr (Paul Siebeck), 1993.

Pomeroy, Sarah B. *Goddesses, Whores, Wives, and Slaves: Women in Classical Antiquity.* New York: Schocken Books, 1976.

Rawson, Beryl. "From 'Daily Life' to 'Demography.'" In *Women in Antiquity: New Assessments,* ed. R. Hawley and B. Levick, 1–20. New York: Routledge, 1995.

————, ed. *The Family in Ancient Rome: New Perspectives.* Ithaca, N.Y.: Cornell University Press, 1986.

————, ed. *Marriage, Divorce, and Children in Ancient Rome.* Oxford: Clarendon Press, 1991.

Reimer, Ivoni Ritchter. *Women in the Acts of the Apostles: A Feminist Liberation Perspective.* Minneapolis: Fortress Press, 1995.

Reinhartz, Adele. "Philo on Infanticide." *Studia Philonica Annual* 4; ed. David T. Runia (1992): 42–58.

Richardson, Lawrence, Jr. *Pompeii: An Architectural History.* Baltimore: Johns Hopkins University Press, 1988.

Rousselle, Aline. *Porneia: On Desire and the Body in Antiquity.* Oxford: Basil Blackwell Publisher, 1988.

Saldarini, Anthony J. *Pharisees, Scribes and Sadducees in Palestinian Society: A Sociological Approach.* Wilmington, Del.: Michael Glazier, 1988.

Saller, Richard. *Patriarchy, Property and Death in the Roman Family.* Cambridge: Cambridge University Press, 1994.

———. *Personal Patronage under the Early Empire.* Cambridge: Cambridge University Press, 1982.

Scarborough, John. *Roman Medicine.* Ithaca, N.Y.: Cornell University Press, 1969.

Schlarb, Engberg. *Die Gesunde Lehre: Häresie und Wahrheit im Spiegel der Pastoralbriefe.* Marburger Theologische Studien 28. Marburg: N. G. Elwert, 1990.

Schottroff, Luise. *Lydia's Impatient Sisters: A Feminist History of Early Christianity.* Louisville, Ky.: Westminster John Knox Press, 1995.

Schrage, Wolfgang. "Einige Beobachtungen zur Lehre im Neuen Testament." *EvT* 42 (1982): 233–51.

Schroeder, Hans-Hartmut. *Eltern und Kinder in der Verkündigung Jesu: Eine Hermeneutische und Exegetische Untersuchung.* TF 53. Hamburg: Herbert Reich, 1972.

Schürmann, Heinz. "'. . . und Lehrer': Die geistliche Eigenart des Lehrdienstes und sein Verhältnis zu anderen geistlichen Diensten im neutestamentlichen Zeitalter." In *Orientierungen am Neuen Testament: Exegetische Gesprächsbeiträge,* 116–56. Düsseldorf: Patmos, 1978.

Schüssler Fiorenza, Elisabeth. *In Memory of Her: A Feminist Theological Reconstruction of Christian Origins.* New York: Crossroad, 1983, 1994.

———, ed. *Searching the Scriptures.* Vol. 2: *A Feminist Commentary.* New York: Crossroad, 1994.

Schweizer, Eduard. "Traditional Ethical Patterns in Pauline and Post-Pauline Letters." In *Text and Interpretation: Studies in the New Testament presented to Matthew Black,* ed. E. Best and R. McL. Wilson, 195–209. Cambridge: Cambridge University Press, 1979.

Scobie, A. "Slums, Sanitation, and Mortality in the Roman World." *Klio* 68 (1986): 300–433.

Scott, Bernard Brandon. *Hear Then the Parable: A Commentary on the Parables of Jesus.* Minneapolis: Fortress Press, 1989.

Seim, Turid Karlsen. *The Double Message: Patterns of Gender in Luke and Acts.* Nashville: Abingdon Press, 1994.

Sherwin-White, A. N. "The Galilean Narrative and the Greco-Roman World." In *Roman Society and Roman Law in the New Testament,* 120–43. Oxford: Clarendon Press, 1963.

Smith, Dennis Edwin. "Social Obligation in the Context of Communal Meals: A Study of the Christian Meal in 1 Corinthians in Comparison with Graeco-Roman Meals." Th.D. dissertation, Harvard University, Cambridge, Mass., 1980.

Smith, Dennis Edwin, and Hal E. Taussig. *Many Tables: The Eucharist in the New Testament and Liturgy Today,* 21–69. Philadelphia: Trinity Press International, 1990.

Stark, Rodney. "Antioch as the Social Situation for Matthew's Gospel." In *Social History of the Matthean Community: Cross-Disciplinary Approaches,* ed. David L. Balch, 189–210. Minneapolis: Fortress Press, 1991.

Stowers, Stanley K. *A Rereading of Romans: Justice, Jews, and Gentiles.* New Haven, Conn.: Yale University Press, 1994.

Temkin, Owsei, trans. *Soranus' Gynecology.* Baltimore: Johns Hopkins Press, 1956.

Thébert, Yvon. "Private Life and Domestic Architecture in Roman Africa." In *A History of Private Life,* ed. Paul Veyne. Vol. 1: *From Pagan Rome to Byzantium,* 315–408. Cambridge, Mass.: Harvard University Press, 1987.

Theissen, Gerd. *Social Reality and the Early Christians: Theology, Ethics, and the World of the New Testament.* Minneapolis: Fortress Press, 1992.

————. *The Social Setting of Pauline Christianity.* Philadelphia: Fortress Press, 1982.

Thesleff, Holger. *The Pythagorean Texts of the Hellenistic Period.* Acta Academiae Aboensis. Ser. A. Humaniora 30.1. Åbo, Finland: Åbo Akademi University Press, 1965.

Thompson, Cynthia L. "Hairstyles, Head-Coverings, and St. Paul: Portraits from Roman Corinth," *BA* 51, no. 2 (1988): 99–115.

Trebilco, Paul. *Jewish Communities in Asia Minor.* SNTSMS 69. Cambridge: Cambridge University Press, 1991.

Treggiari, Susan. "Roman Social History: Recent Interpretations," *Social History* 8 (1975): 149–64.

Van der Horst, Pieter Willem. *Chaeremon: Egyptian Priest and Stoic Philosopher, The Fragments collected and translated with explanatory notes.* EPRO. Leiden: E. J. Brill, 1984.

————. "Conflicting Images of Women in Ancient Judaism." In *Hellenism-Judaism-Christianity: Essays on Their Interpretation,* 73–95. Kampen: Kok Pharos, 1994.

————. "Images of Women in the Testament of Job." In *Studies on the Testament of Job,* ed. M. A. Knibb and P. W. van der Horst, 93–116. Cambridge: Cambridge University Press, 1989.

Verner, David C. *The Household of God: The Social World of the Pastoral Epistles.* SBLDS 71. Chico, Calif.: Scholars Press, 1983.

Wainwright, Elaine Mary. "The Gospel of Matthew." In *Searching the Scriptures,* ed. Elisabeth Schüssler Fiorenza. Vol. 2: *A Feminist Commentary,* 635–77. New York: Crossroad, 1994.

————. *Towards a Feminist Critical Reading of the Gospel according to Matthew.* BZNW 60. Berlin: Walter de Gruyter, 1991.

Wallace-Hadrill, Andrew. *Augustan Rome.* Classical World Series. London: Bristol Classical Press, 1993.

————. "Houses and Households: Sampling Pompeii and Herculaneum." In *Marriage, Divorce, and Children in Ancient Rome,* ed. Beryl Rawson, 191–227. Oxford: Oxford University Press, 1991.

———. *Houses and Society in Pompeii and Herculaneum.* Princeton, N.J.: Princeton University Press, 1994.

———. "Public honour and private shame: The urban texture of Pompeii." In *Urban Society in Roman Italy,* ed. Tim Cornell and Kathryn Lomas, 39–62. New York: St. Martin's Press, 1955.

———. "The Social Structure of the Roman House." *Papers of the British School at Rome* 56 (1988): 43–97.

Ward, Roy Bowen. "Women in Roman Baths." HTS 85, no. 2 (1992): 125–47.

Weiser, Alfons. *Die Knechtsgleichnisse der Synoptischen Evangelien.* SANT 29. Munich: Kösel, 1971.

Wendland, Paul. "Die Therapeuten und die philonische Schrift vom beschaulichen Leben." *Jahrbücher für classische Philologie,* Supplement 22 (1886): 693– 772.

Westermann, William L. *Slave Systems of Greek and Roman Antiquity.* Memoirs of the American Philosophical Society 40. Philadelphia: American Philosophical Society, 1955.

White, L. Michael. *Building God's House in the Roman World: Architectural Adaptation among Pagans, Jews, and Christians.* Baltimore: Johns Hopkins University Press, 1990.

———. "Domus Ecclesiae-Domus Dei: Adaptation and Development in the Setting for Early Christian Assembly," Ph.D. diss., Yale University, 1982; Ann Arbor: University Microfilms, 1983.

Wicker, Kathleen O'Brien. "Mulierum Virtutes (Moralia 242E–263C)." In *Plutarch's Ethical Writings and Early Christian Literature,* ed. Hans D. Betz, 106–34. SCHNT 4. Leiden: E. J. Brill, 1978.

Wiedemann, Thomas. *Adults and Children in the Roman Empire.* London: Routledge, 1989.

Winter, Sara C. "Methodological Observations on a New Interpretation of Paul's Letter to Philemon." *Union Seminary Quarterly Review* 39 (1984): 203–12.

———. "Paul's Letter to Philemon." NTS 33 (1987): 1–15.

Wire, Antoinette. *The Corinthian Women Prophets: A Reconstruction through Paul's Rhetoric.* Minneapolis: Fortress Press, 1990.

Yarbrough, O. Larry. "Parents and Children in the Letters of Paul." In *The Social World of the First Christians: Essays in Honor of Wayne A. Meeks,* ed. L. Michael White and O. Larry Yarbrough, 126–41. Minneapolis: Fortress Press, 1995.

Zaas, Peter S. "Catalogues and Context: 1 Corinthians 5 and 6." NTS 34 (1988): 622–29.

Zanker, Paul. *Pompeji: Stadtbild und Wohngeschmack.* Kulturgeschichte der antiken Welt 61. Mainz: Philipp von Zabern, 1995.

———. *The Power of Images in the Age of Augustus.* Ann Arbor: University of Michigan Press, 1988.

Index of Subjects

Index of Modern Authors

Index of Ancient Authors

Index of Scripture and Ancient Texts